D0984274

WOMAN

ON THE

AMERICAN FRONTIER

BY WILLIAM W. FOWLER

Source Book Press

WOMAN

ON THE

AMERICAN FRONTIER.

A Valuable and Authentic History

OF THE

HEROISM, ADVENTURES, PRIVATIONS, CAPTIVITIES,
TRIALS, AND NOBLE LIVES AND DEATHS OF THE
"PIONEER MOTHERS OF THE REPUBLIC."

By WILLIAM W. FOWLER.

———

ILLUSTRATED WITH NUMEROUS ENGRAVINGS.

———

HARTFORD:
S. S. SCRANTON & COMPANY.
1879.

PREFACE.

The history of our race is the record mainly of men's achievments, in war, in statecraft and diplomacy. If mention is made of woman it is of queens and intriguing beauties who ruled and schemed for power and riches, and often worked mischief and ruin by their wiles.

The story of woman's work in great migrations has been told only in lines and passages where it ought instead to fill volumes. Here and there incidents and anecdotes scattered through a thousand tomes give us glimpses of the wife, the mother, or the daughter as a heroine or as an angel of kindness and goodness, but most of her story is a blank which never will be filled up. And yet it is precisely in her position as a pioneer and colonizer that her influence is the most potent and her life story most interesting.

The glory of a nation consists in its migrations and the colonies it plants as well as in its wars of conquest. The warrior who wins a battle deserves a laurel no more rightfully than the pioneer who leads his race into the wilderness and builds there a new empire.

The movement which has carried our people from the Atlantic to the Pacific Ocean and in the short space of two centuries and a half has founded the greatest republic which the world ever saw, has already taken its place in history as one of the grandest achievments of humanity since the world began. It is a moral as well as a physical triumph, and forms an epoch in the advance of civilization. In this grand achievement, in this triumph of physical and moral endurance, woman must be allowed her share of the honor.

It would be a truism, if we were to say that our Republic would not have been founded without her aid. We need not enlarge on the necessary position which she fills in human society every where. We are to speak of her now as a soldier and laborer, a heroine and

(3)

comforter in a peculiar set of dangers and difficulties such as are met with in our American wilderness. The crossing of a stormy ocean, the reclamation of the soil from nature, the fighting with savage men are mere generalities wherein some vague idea may be gained of true pioneer life. But it is only by following woman in her wanderings and standing beside her in the forest or in the cabin and by marking in detail the thousand trials and perils which surround her in such a position that we can obtain the true picture of the heroine in so many unmentioned battles.

The recorded sum total of an observation like this would be a noble history of human effort. It would show us the latent causes from which have come extraordinary effects. It would teach us how much this republic owes to its pioneer mothers, and would fill us with gratitude and self-congratulation—gratitude for their inestimable services to our country and to mankind, self-congratulation in that we are the lawful inheritors of their work, and as Americans are partakers in their glory.

In the preparation of this work particular pains have been taken to avoid what was trite and hackneyed, and at the same time preserve historic truth and accuracy. Use has been made to a limited extent of the ancient border books, selecting the most note-worthy incidents which never grow old because they illustrate a heroism, that like "renown and grace cannot die." Thanks are due to Mrs. Ellet, from whose interesting book entitled "Women of the Revolution," a few passages have been culled. The stories of Mrs. VanAlstine, of Mrs. Slocum, Mrs. McCalla, and Dicey Langston, and of Deborah Samson, are condensed from her accounts of those heroines.

A large portion of the work is, however, composed of incidents which will be new to the reader. The eye-witnesses of scenes which have been lately enacted upon the border have furnished the writer with materials for many of the most thrilling stories of frontier life, and which it has been his aim to spread before the reader in this work.

ILLUSTRATIONS.

CONTENTS.

(7)

CHAPTER III.

CHAPTER IV.

CHAPTER V.

CHAPTER VI.

CHAPTER VII.

CHAPTER VIII.

CHAPTER IX.

CHAPTER X.

CHAPTER XI.

CHAPTER XII.

CHAPTER XIII.

CHAPTER XIV.

16 CONTENTS.

CHAPTER I.

WOMAN AS A PIONEER.

EVERY battle has its unnamed heroes. The common soldier enters the stormed fortress and, falling in the breach which his valor has made, sleeps in a nameless grave. The subaltern whose surname is scarcely heard beyond the roll-call on parade, bears the colors of his company where the fight is hottest. And the corporal who heads his file in the final charge, is forgotten in the " earthquake shout" of the victory which he has helped to win. The victory may be due as much, or more, to the patriot courage of him who is content to do his duty in the rank and file, as to the dashing colonel who heads the regiment, or even to the general who plans the campaign: and yet unobserved, unknown, and unrewarded the former passes into oblivion while the leader's name is on every tongue, and perhaps goes down in history as that of one who deserved well of his country.

Our comparison is a familiar one. There are other battles and armies besides those where thousands of disciplined men move over the ground to the sounds of the drum and fife. Life itself is a battle, and no grander army has ever been set in motion since the world began than that which for more than two centuries and a half has been moving across our continent from the Atlantic to the Pacific, fighting its way through countless hardships and dangers, bearing the

2   (17)

banner of civilization, and building a new republic in
the wilderness.

In this army WOMAN HAS BEEN TOO OFTEN THE
UNNAMED HEROINE.

Let us not forget her now. Her patience, her courage, her fortitude, her tact, her presence of mind in
trying hours; these are the shining virtues which we
have to record. Woman *as a pioneer* standing beside her rougher, stronger companion—man; first on
the voyage across a stormy ocean, from England to
America; then at Plymouth, and Jamestown, and all
the settlements first planted by Europeans on our
coast; then through the trackless wilderness, onward
across the continent, till every river has been forded,
and every chain of mountains has been scaled, the
Peaceful Ocean has been reached, and fifty thousand
cities, towns, and hamlets all over the land have been
formed from those aggregations of household life
where woman's work has been wrought out to its
fullness.

Among all the characteristics of woman there is
none more marked than the self-devotion which she
displays in what she believes is a righteous cause, or
where for her loved ones she sacrifices herself. In
India we see her wrapped in flames and burned to
ashes with the corpse of her husband. Under the
Moslem her highest condition is a life-long incarcera-
tion. She patiently places her shoulders under the
burden which the aboriginal lord of the American
forest lays upon them. Calmly and in silence she
submits to the onerous duties imposed upon her by
social and religious laws. Throughout the whole
heathen world she remained, in the words of an

elegant French writer, "anonymous, indifferent to herself, and leaving no trace of her passage upon earth."

The benign spirit of Christianity has lifted woman from the position she held under other religious systems and elevated her to a higher sphere. She is brought forward as a teacher; she displays a martyr's courage in the presence of pestilence, or ascends the deck of the mission-ship to take her part in "perils among the heathen." She endures the hardships and faces the dangers of colonial life with a new sense of her responsibility as a wife and mother. In all these capacities, whether teaching, ministering to the sick, or carrying the Gospel to the heathen, she shows the same self-devotion as in "the brave days of old;" it is this quality which peculiarly fits her to be the pioneer's companion in the new world, and by her works in that capacity she must be judged.

If all true greatness should be estimated by the good it performs, it is peculiarly desirable that woman's claims to distinction should thus be estimated and awarded. In America her presence has been acknowledged, and her aid faithfully rendered from the beginning. In the era of colonial life; in the cruel wars with the aborigines; in the struggle of the Revolution; in the western march of the army of exploration and settlement, a grateful people must now recognize her services.

There is a beautiful tradition, that the first foot which pressed the snow-clad rock of Plymouth was that of Mary Chilton, a fair young maiden, and that the last survivor of those heroic pioneers was Mary Allerton, who lived to see the planting of twelve out

of the thirteen colonies, which formed the nucleus of
these United States.

In the *Mayflower*, nineteen wives accompanied their
husbands to a waste land and uninhabited, save by
the wily and vengeful savage. On the unfloored hut,
she who had been nurtured amid the rich carpets and
curtains of the mother-land, rocked her new-born babe,
and complained not. She, who in the home of her
youth had arranged the gorgeous shades of embroidery, or, perchance, had compounded the rich venison
pasty, as her share in the housekeeping, now pounded
the coarse Indian corn for her children's bread, and
bade them ask God's blessing, ere they took their
scanty portion. When the snows sifted through the
miserable roof-tree upon her little ones, she gathered
them closer to her bosom; she taught them the Bible,
and the catechism, and the holy hymn, though the
war-whoop of the Indian rang through the wild.
Amid the untold hardships of colonial life she infused
new strength into her husband by her firmness, and
solaced his weary hours by her love. She was to him,

> "———— an undergoing spirit, to bear up
> Against whate'er ensued."

The names of these nineteen pioneer-matrons should
be engraved in letters of gold on the pillars of American history.

The Wives of the Pilgrims.

Mrs. Catharine Carver.	Mrs. Elizabeth Hopkins.
Mrs. Dorothy Bradford.	Mrs. ———— Tilley.
Mrs. Elizabeth Winslow.	Mrs. ———— Tilley.
Mrs. Mary Brewster.	Mrs. ———— Tinker.
Mrs. Mary Allerton.	Mrs. ———— Ridgdale.

Mrs. Rose Standish.　　　　Mrs. —— Eaton.
Mrs. —— Martin.　　　　　Mrs. —— Chilton.
Mrs. —— Mullins.　　　　 Mrs. —— Fuller.
Mrs. Susanna White.　　　 Mrs. Helen Billington.
　　　　　Mrs. Lucretia Brewster.

Nor should the names of the daughters of these heroic women be forgotten, who, with their mothers and fathers shared the perils of that winter's voyage, and bore, with their parents, the toils, and hardships, and changes of the infant colony.

The Daughters of the Pilgrim Mothers.

Elizabeth Carver.　　　　 Sarah Allerton.
Remember Allerton.　　　　Constance Hopkins.
Mary Allerton.　　　　　　Mary Chilton.
　　　　　Priscilla Mullins.

The voyage of the *Mayflower;* the landing upon a desolate coast in the dead of winter; the building of those ten small houses, with oiled paper for windows; the suffering of that first winter and spring, in which woman bore her whole share; these were the first steps in the grand movement which has carried the Anglo-Saxon race across the American continent. The next steps were the penetration of the wilderness westward from the sea, by the emigrant pioneers and their wives. Fighting their way through dense forests, building cabins, block-houses, and churches in the clearings which they had made; warred against by cruel savages; woman was ever present to guard, to comfort, to work. The annals of colonial history teem with her deeds of love and heroism, and what are those recorded instances to those which had no chronicler? She loaded the flint-lock in the block-house while it was surrounded by yelling savages; she exposed herself to the scalping-knife to save her babe; in her forest-home she worked and watched, far from the loved ones in Old England; and by discharging a thousand duties in the household and the field, did her share in a silent way towards building up the young Republic of the West.

Sometimes she ranged herself in battle beside her husband or brother, and fought with the steadiness and bravery of a veteran. But her heroism never shone so brightly as in undergoing danger in defense of her children.

In the early days of the settlement of Royalton, Vermont, a sudden attack was made upon it by the Indians. Mrs. Hendee, the wife of one of the settlers, was working alone in the field, her husband being absent on military duty, when the Indians entered her house and capturing her children carried them across the White river, at that place a hundred yards wide and quite deep for fording, and placed them under keepers who had some other persons, thirty or forty in number, in charge.

Returning from the field Mrs. Hendee discovered the fate of her children. Her first outburst of grief was heart-rending to behold, but this was only transient; she ceased her lamentations, and like the lioness who has been robbed of her litter, she bounded on the trail of her plunderers. Resolutely dashing into the river, she stemmed the current, planting her feet firmly on the bottom and pushed across. With pallid face, flashing eyes, and lips compressed, maternal love dominating every fear, she strode into the Indian camp, regardless of the tomahawks menacingly flourished round her head, boldly demanded the release of her little ones, and persevered in her alternate upbraidings and supplications, till her request was granted. She then carried her children back through the river and landed them in safety on the other bank.

Not content with what she had done, like a patriot as she was, she immediately returned, begged for the release of the children of others, again was rewarded with success, and brought two or three more away; again returned, and again succeeded, till she had rescued the whole fifteen of her neighbors' children who had been thus snatched away from their distracted parents. On her last visit to the camp of the enemy, the Indians were so struck with her conduct that one of them declared that so brave a squaw deserved to be carried across the river, and offered to take her on his back and carry her over. She, in the same spirit, accepted the offer, mounted the back of the gallant savage, was carried to the opposite bank, where she collected her rescued troop of children, and hastened away to restore them to their overjoyed parents.

During the memorable Wyoming massacre, Mrs. Mary Gould, wife of James Gould, with the other women remaining in the village of Wyoming, sought safety in the fort. In the haste and confusion attending this act, she left her boy, about four years old, behind. Obeying the instincts of a mother, and turning a deaf ear to the admonitions of friends, she started off on a perilous search for the missing one. It was dark; she was alone; and the foe was lurking around; but the agonies of death could not exceed her agonies of suspense; so she hastened on. She traversed the fields which, but a few hours before,

"Were trampled by the hurrying crowd,"

where—

"—— fiery hearts and armed hands,
Encountered in the battle cloud,"

and where unarmed hands were now resting on cold and motionless hearts. After a search of between one and two hours, she found her child on the bank of the river, sporting with a little band of playmates. Clasping her treasure in her arms, she hurried back and reached the fort in safety.

During the struggles of the Revolution, the privations sustained, and the efforts made, by women, were neither few nor of short duration. Many of them are delineated in the present volume. Yet innumerable instances of faithful toil, and patient endurance, must have been covered with oblivion. In how many a lone home, from which the father was long sundered by a soldier's destiny, did the mother labor to perform to their little ones both his duties and her own, having no witness of the extent of her heavy burdens and sleepless anxieties, save the Hearer of prayer.

A good and hoary-headed man, who had passed the limits of fourscore, once said to me, "My father was in the army during the whole eight years of the Revolutionary War, at first as a common soldier, afterwards as an officer. My mother had the sole charge of us four little ones. Our house was a poor one, and far from neighbors. I have a keen remembrance of the terrible cold of some of those winters. The snow lay so deep and long, that it was difficult to cut or draw fuel from the woods, or to get our corn to the mill, when we had any. My mother was the possessor of a coffee-mill. In that she ground wheat, and made coarse bread, which we ate, and were thankful. It was not always we could be allowed as much, even of this, as our keen appetites craved. Many is the time that we have gone to bed, with only a drink of water for our supper, in which a little molasses had been mingled. We patiently received it, for we knew our mother did as well for us as she could; and we hoped to have something better in the morning. She was never heard to repine; and young as we were, we tried to make her loving spirit and heavenly trust, our example.

"When my father was permitted to come home, his stay was short, and he had not much to leave us, for the pay of those who achieved our liberties was slight, and irregularly given. Yet when he went, my mother ever bade him farewell with a cheerful face, and told him not to be anxious about his children, for she would watch over them night and day, and God would take care of the families of those who went forth to defend the righteous cause of their country. Sometimes we wondered that she did not mention the cold weather, or our short meals, or her hard work, that we little ones might be clothed, and fed, and taught. But she would not weaken his hands, or sadden his heart, for she said a soldier's life was harder than all. We saw that she never complained, but always kept in her heart a sweet hope, like a well of water. Every night ere we slept, and every morning when we arose, we lifted our little hands for God's blessing on our absent father, and our endangered country.

" How deeply the prayers from such solitary homes and faithful hearts were mingled with the infant liberties of our dear native land, we may not know until we enter where we see no more 'through a glass darkly, but face to face.'

" Incidents repeatedly occurred during this contest of eight years, between the feeble colonies and the strong mother-land, of a courage that ancient Sparta would have applauded.

" In a thinly settled part of Virginia, the quiet of the Sabbath eve was once broken by the loud, hurried roll of the drum.   Volunteers were invoked to go forth and prevent the British troops, under the pitiless Tarleton, from forcing their way through an important mountain pass.   In an old fort resided a family, all of whose elder sons were absent with our army, which at the north opposed the foe.   The father lay enfeebled and sick.   By his bedside the mother called their three sons, of the ages of thirteen, fifteen, and seventeen.

" ' Go forth, children,' said she, " to the defence of your native clime.   Go, each and all of you; I spare not my youngest, my fair-haired boy, the light of my declining years.

" ' Go forth, my sons!   Repel the foot of the invader, or see my face no more.' "

In order to get a proper estimate of the greatness of the part which woman has acted in the mighty onward-moving drama of civilization on this continent, we must remember too her peculiar physical constitution.   Her highly strung nervous organization and her softness of fiber make labor more severe and suffering keener.   It is an instinct with her to tremble at dan-

A VIRGINIA MATRON ENCOURAGING THE PATRIOTISM OF HER SONS AT THE DEATH-BED OF THEIR FATHER.   Page 26.

ger; her training from girlhood unfits her to cope with the difficulties of outdoor life. "Men," says the poet, "must work, and women must weep." But the pioneer women must both work and weep. The toils and hardships of frontier life write early wrinkles upon her brow and bow her delicate frame with care. We do not expect to subject our little ones to the toils or dangers that belong to adults. Labor is pain to the soft fibers and unknit limbs of childhood, and to the impressible minds of the young, danger conveys a thousand fears not felt by the firmer natures of older persons. Hence it is that all mankind admire youthful heroism. The story of Casabianca on the deck of the burning ship, or of the little wounded drummer, borne on the shoulders of a musketeer and still beating the *rappel*—while the bullets are flying around him—thrill the heart of man because these were great and heroic deeds performed by striplings. It is the bravery and firmness of the weak that challenges the highest admiration. This is woman's case: and when we see her matching her strength and courage against those of man in the same cause, with equal results, what can we do but applaud?

A European traveler lately visited the Territory of Montana—abandoning the beaten trail, in company only with an Indian guide, for he was a bold and fearless explorer. He struck across the mountains, traveling for two days without seeing the sign of a human being. Just at dusk, on the evening of the second day, he drew rein on the summit of one of those lofty hills which form the spurs of the Rocky Mountains. The solitude was awful. As far as the eye could see stretched an unbroken succession of mountain peaks, bare of forest—a wilderness of rocks with stunted trees at their base, and deep ravines where no streams were running.   In all this desolate scene there was no sign of a living thing.   While they were tethering their horses and preparing for the night, the sharp eyes of the Indian guide caught sight of a gleam of light at the bottom of a deep gorge beneath them.

Descending the declivity, they reached a cabin rudely built of dead wood, which seemed to have been brought down by the spring rains from the hill-sides to the west.   Knocking at the door, it was opened by a woman, holding in her arms a child of six months. The woman appeared to be fifty years of age, but she was in reality only thirty.   Casting a searching look upon the traveler and his companion, she asked them to enter.

The cabin was divided into two apartments, a kitchen, which also served for a store-room, dining-room, and sitting-room; the other was the chamber, or rather bunk-room, where the family slept.   Five children came tumbling out from this latter apartment as the traveler entered, and greeted him with a stare of childlike curiosity.   The woman asked them to be seated on blocks of wood, which served for chairs, and soon threw off her reserve and told them her story, while they awaited the return of her husband from the nearest village, some thirty miles distant, whither he had gone the day before to dispose of the gold-dust which he had "panned out" from a gulch near by. He was a miner.   Four years before he had come with his family from the East, and pushing on in advance of the main movement of emigration in the territory, had discovered a rich gold placer in this lonely gorge. While he had been working in this placer, his wife had with her own hands turned up the soil in the valley below and raised all the corn and potatoes required for the support of the family; she had done the housework, and had made all the clothes for the family. Once when her husband was sick, she had ridden thirty miles for medicine. It was a dreary ride, she said, for the road, or rather trail, was very rough, and her husband was in a burning fever. She left him in charge of her oldest child, a girl of eleven years, but she was a bright, helpful little creature, able to wait upon the sick man and feed the other children during the two days' absence of her mother.

Next summer they were to build a house lower down the valley and would be joined by three other families of their kindred from the East. "Have you never been attacked by the Indians?" inquired the traveler.

"Only three times," she replied. "Once three prowling red-skins came to the door, in the night, and asked for food. My husband handed them a loaf of bread through the window, but they refused to go away and lurked in the bushes all night; they were stragglers from a war-party, and wanted more scalps. I saw them in the moonlight, armed with rifles and tomahawks, and frightfully painted. They kindled a fire a hundred yards below our cabin and stayed there all night, as if they were watching for us to come out, but early in the morning they disappeared, and we saw them no more.

"Another time, a large war-party of Indians encamped a mile below us, and a dozen of them came up and surrounded the house. Then we thought we were lost: they amused themselves aiming at marks in the logs, or at the chimney and windows; we could hear their bullets rattle against the rafters, and you can see the holes they made in the doors. One big brave took a large stone and was about to dash it against the door, when my husband pointed his rifle at him through the window, and he turned and ran away. We should have all been killed and scalped if a company of soldiers had not come up the valley that day with an exploring party and driven the red-skins away.

" One afternoon as my husband was at work in the diggings, two red-skins came up to him and wounded him with arrows, but he caught up his rifle and soon made an end of them.

"When we first came there was no end of bears and wolves, and we could hear them howling all night long. Winter nights the wolves would come and drum on the door with their paws and whine as if they wanted to eat up the children. Husband shot ten and I shot six, and after that we were troubled no more with them.

" We have no schools here, as you see," continued she; " but I have taught my three oldest children to read since we came here, and every Sunday we have family prayers. Husband reads a verse in the Bible, and then I and the children read a verse in turn, till we finish a whole chapter. Then I make the children, all but baby, repeat a verse over and over till they have it by heart; the Scripture promises do comfort us all, even the littlest one who can only lisp them.

" Sometimes on Sunday morning I take all the children to the top of that hill yonder and look at the sun as it comes up over the mountains, and I think of the old folks at home and all our friends in the East. The hardest thing to bear is the solitude. We are awful lonesome. Once, for eighteen months, I never saw the face of a white person except those of my husband and children. It makes me laugh and cry too when I see a strange face. But I am too busy to think much about it daytimes. I must wash, and boil, and bake, or look after the cows which wander off in search of pasture; or go into the valley and hoe the corn and potatoes, or cut the wood; for husband makes his ten or fifteen dollars a day panning out dust up the mountain, and I know that whenever I want him I have only to blow the horn and he will come down to me. So I tend to business here and let him get gold. In five or six years we shall have a nice house farther down and shall want for nothing. We shall have a saw-mill next spring started on the run below, and folks are going to join us from the States."

The woman who told this story of dangers and hardships amid the Rocky Mountains was of a slight, frail figure. She had evidently been once possessed of more than ordinary attractions; but the cares of maternity and the toils of frontier life had bowed her delicate frame and engraved premature wrinkles upon her face: she was old before her time, but her spirit was as dauntless and her will to do and dare for her loved ones was as firm as that of any of the heroines whom history has made so famous. She had been reared in luxury in one of the towns of central New

York, and till she was eighteen years old had never known what toil and trouble were.

Her husband was a true type of the American explorer and possessed in his wife a fit companion; and when he determined to push his fortune among the Western wilds she accompanied him cheerfully; already they had accumulated five thousand dollars, which was safely deposited in the bank; they were rearing a band of sturdy little pioneers; they had planted an outpost in a region teeming with mineral wealth, and around them is now growing up a thriving village of which this heroic couple are soon to be the patriarchs. All honor to the names of Mr. and Mrs. James Manning, the pioneers of Montana.

The traveler and his guide, declining the hospitality which this brave matron tendered them, soon returned to their camp on the hill-top; but the Englishman made notes of the pioneer woman's story, and pondered over it, for he saw in it an epitome of frontier life.

If a tourist were to pass to-day beyond the Mississippi River, and journey over the wagon-roads which lead Westward towards the Rocky Mountains, he would see moving towards the setting sun innumerable caravans of emigrants' canvas-covered wagons, bound for the frontier. In each of these wagons is a man, one or two women with children, agricultural tools, and household gear. At night the horses or oxen are tethered or turned loose on the prairie; a fire is kindled with buffalo chips, or such fuel as can be had, and supper is prepared. A bed of prairie grass suffices for the man, while the women and children rest in the covered wagon. When the morning dawns they resume their Westward journey. Weeks, months, sometimes, roll by before the wagon reaches its destination; but it reaches it at last. Then begin the struggle, and pains, the labors, and dangers of border life, in all of which woman bears her part. While the primeval forest falls before the stroke of the man-pioneer, his companion does the duty of both man and woman at home. The hearthstone is laid, and the rude cabin rises. The virgin soil is vexed by the ploughshare driven by the man; the garden and house, the dairy and barns are tended by the woman, who clasps her babe while she milks, and fodders, and weeds. Danger comes when the man is away; the woman must meet it alone. Famine comes, and the woman must eke out the slender store, scrimping and pinching for the little ones; sickness comes, and the woman must nurse and watch alone, and without the sympathy of any of her sex. Fifty miles from a doctor or a friend, except her weary and perhaps morose husband, she must keep strong under labor, and be patient under suffering, till death. And thus the household, the hamlet, the village, the town, the city, the state, rise out of her "homely toils, and destiny obscure." Truly she is one of the founders of the Republic.

3

CHAPTER II.

THE American Frontier has for more than two
centuries been a vague and variable term. In
1620–21 it was a line of forest which bounded the
infant colony at Plymouth, a few scattered settlements
on the James River, in Virginia, and the stockade on
Manhattan Island, where Holland had established a
trading-post destined to become one day the great
commercial city of the continent.

Seventy years later, in 1690, the frontier-line had
become greatly extended. In New England it was
the forest which still hemmed in the coast and river
settlements: far to the north stretched the wilderness
covering that tract of country which now comprises
the states of Maine, New Hampshire, and Vermont.
In New York the frontier was just beyond the posts
on the Hudson River; and in Virginia life outside of
the oldest settlements was strictly *"life on the border."*
The James, the Rappahannock, and the Potomac Rivers made the Virginia frontier a series of long lines
approaching to a parallel. But the European settlements were still sparse, as compared with the area of
uninhabited country. The villages, hamlets, and single
homesteads were like little islands in a wild green
waste; mere specks in a vast expanse of wilderness.
Every line beyond musket-shot was a frontier-line.

(34)

Every settlement, small or large, was surrounded by a dark circle, outside of which lurked starvation, fear, and danger. The sea and the great rivers were perilous avenues of escape for those who dwelt thereby, but the interior settlements were almost completely isolated and girt around as if with a wall built by hostile forces to forbid access or egress.

The grand exodus of European emigrants from their native land to these shores, had vastly diminished by the year 1690, but the westward movement from the sea and the rivers in America still went forward with scarcely diminished impetus: and as the pioneers advanced and established their outposts farther and farther to the west, woman was, as she had been from the landing, their companion on the march, their ally in the presence of danger, and their efficient co-worker in establishing homes in the wilderness.

The heroic enterprises recorded in the history of man have generally been remarkable in proportion to their apparent original weakness. This is true in an eminent degree of the settlement of European colonies on the western continent. The sway which woman's influence exercised in these colonial enterprises is all the more wonderful when we contemplate them from this point of view. Three feeble bands of men and women;—the first at Jamestown, Virginia, in 1609–1612; the second at Plymouth, in 1620; the third on the Island of Manhattan, in 1624;—these were the dim nuclei from which radiated those long lines of light which stretch to-day across a continent and strike the Pacific ocean. This is a simile borrowed from astronomy. To adopt the language of the naturalist, those three little colonies were the puny germs which bore within themselves a vital force vastly more potent and wonderful than that which dwells in the heart of the gourd seed, and the acorn whose nascent swelling energies will lift huge boulders and split the living rock asunder: vastly more potent because it was not the blind motions of nature merely, but a force at once physical, moral, and intellectual.

These feeble bands of men and women took foothold and held themselves firmly like a hard-pressed garrison waiting for re-enforcements. Re-enforcements came, and then they went out from their works, and setting their faces westward moved slowly forward. The vanguard were men with pikes and musketoons and axes; the rearguard were women who kept watch and ward over the household treasures. Sometimes in trying hours the rearguard ranged itself and fought in the front ranks, falling back to its old position when the crisis was past.

In order to appreciate the actual value of woman as a component part of that mighty impulse which set in motion, and still impels the pioneers of our country, we must remember that she is really the cohesive power which cements society together; that when the outward pressure is greatest, the cohesive power is strongest; that in times of sore trial woman's native traits of character are intensified; that she has greater tact, quicker perceptions, more enduring patience, and greater capacity for suffering than man; that motherly, and wifely, and sisterly love are strongest and brightest when trials, labors, and dangers impend over the loved ones.

We must bear in mind too, that woman and man were possessed of the same convictions and impulses in their heroic enterprise—the sense of duty, the spirit of liberty, the desire to worship God after their own ideas of truth, the desire to possess, though in a wilderness, homes where no one could intrude or call them vassals; and deep down below all this, the instincts, the gifts, and motive power of the most energetic race the world has ever seen—the Anglo-Saxon; thus we come to see how in each band of pioneers and in each household were centered that solid and constant moving force which made each man a hero and each woman a heroine in the struggle with hostile nature, with savage man more cruel than the storm or the wild beasts, with solitude which makes a desert in the soul; with famine, with pestilence, that "wasteth at noon-day,"—a struggle which has finally been victorious over all antagonisms, and has made us what we are in this centennial year of our existence as an independent republic.

Another powerful influence exercised by woman as a pioneer was the influence of religion. The whole nature certainly of the Puritan woman was transfused with a deep, glowing, unwavering religious faith. We picture those wives, mothers, and daughters of the New England pioneers as the saints described by the poet,

"Their eyes are homes of silent prayer."

How the prayers of these good and honorable women were answered events have proved.

Hardly had the Plymouth Colony landed before they were called upon to battle with their first foes—the cold, the wind, and the storms on the bleak New England coast. Famine came next, and finally pestilence. The blast from the sea shook their frail cabins; the

frost sealed the earth, and the snow drifted on the pillow of the sick and dying.   Five kernels of corn a day
were doled out to such as were in health, by those
appointed to this duty.   Woman's heart was full then,
but it kept strong though it swelled to bursting.

Within five months from the landing on the Rock,
forty-six men, women, and children, or nearly one-half
of the *Mayflower's* passengers had perished of disease
and hardships, and the survivors saw the vessel that
brought them sail away to the land of their birth.   To
the surviving women of that devoted Pilgrim band
this departure of the *Mayflower* must have added a
new pang to the grief that was already rending their
hearts after the loss of so many dear ones during that
fearful winter.   As the vessel dropped down Plymouth
harbor, they watched it with tearful eyes, and when
they could see it no more, they turned calmly back to
their heroic labors.

Mrs. Bradford, Rose Standish, and their companions
were the original types of women on our American
frontier.   Nobly, too, were they seconded by the matrons and daughters in the other infant colonies.   Who
can read the letters of Margaret Winthrop, of the
Massachusetts Colony, without recognizing the loving,
devoted woman sharing with her noble husband the
toils and privations of the wilderness, in order that
God's promise might be justified and an empire built
on this Western Continent.

In her we have a noble type of the Puritan woman
of the seventeenth century, representing, as she did,
a numerous class of her sex in the same condition.
Reared in luxury, and surrounded by the allurements
of the superior social circle in which she moved in her

native England, she nevertheless preferred a life of
self-denial with her husband on the bleak shores where
the Puritans were struggling for existence. She had
fully prepared her mind for the heroic undertaking.
She did not overlook the trials, discouragements, and
difficulties of the course she was about to take. For
years she had been habituated to look forward to it as
one of the eventualities of her life. She was now
beyond the age of romance, and cherished no golden
dreams of earthly happiness to be realized in that far-
off western clime.

Two traits are most prominent in her letters: her
religious faith, and her love for and trust in her husband. She placed a high estimate on the wisdom, the
energy, and the talents of her husband, and felt that he
could best serve God and man by helping to lay broad
and deep the foundations of a new State, and to secure
the present and future prosperity, both temporal and
spiritual, of the colony. With admiration and esteem
she blended the ardent but balanced fondness of the
loving wife and the sedate matron. In no less degree
do her letters show the power and attractiveness of
genuine religion. The sanctity of conjugal affection
tallies with and is hallowed by the Spirit of Grace.
The sense of duty is harmoniously mingled with the
impulses of the heart. That religion was the domi-
nant principle of thought and action with Margaret
Winthrop, no one can doubt who reflects how severely it was tested in the trying enterprise of her
life. A sincere, deep, and healthful piety formed in
her a spring of energy to great and noble actions.

There are glimpses in the correspondence between
her and her husband of a kind of prophetic vision,

that the planting of that colony was the laying of one of the foundation-stones of a great empire. May we not suppose that by the contemplation of such a vision she was buoyed up and soothed amid the many trials and privations, perils and uncertainties that surrounded her in that rugged colonial life.

The influence of Puritanism to inspire with unconquerable principle, to infuse public spirit, to purify the character from frivolity and feebleness, to lift the soul to an all-enduring heroism and to exalt it to a lofty standard of Christian excellence, is grandly illustrated by the life of Margaret Winthrop, one of the pioneer-matrons of the Massachusetts colony.

The narrations which we set forth in this book must of course be largely concerning families and individuals. The outposts of the advancing army of settlement were most exposed to the dangers and hardships of frontier life. Every town or village, as soon as it was settled, became a garrison against attack and a mutual Benefit-Aid-Society, leagued together against every enemy that threatened the infant settlement; it was also a place of refuge for the bolder pioneers who had pushed farther out into the forest.

But as time rolled on many of these more adventurous settlers found themselves isolated from the villages and stockades. Every hostile influence they had to meet alone and unaided. Cold and storm, fire and flood, hunger and sickness, savage man and savage beast, these were the foes with which they had to contend. The battle was going on all the time while the pioneer and his wife were subjugating the forest, breaking the soil, and gaining shelter and food for themselves and their children.

It is easy to see what were the added pains, privations, and hardships of such a situation to the mind and heart of woman, craving, as she does, companionship and sympathy from her own sex. It is a consoling reflection to us who are reaping the fruits of her self-sacrifice that the very multiplicity of her toils and cares gave her less time for brooding over her hard and lonely lot, and that she found in her religious faith and hope a constant fountain of comfort and joy.

One of the greatest hardships endured by the first settlers in New England was the rigorous and changeable climate, which bore most severely, of course, on the weaker sex. This makes the fortitude of Mrs. Shute all the more admirable. Her story is only one of innumerable instances in early colonial life where wives were the preservers of their husbands.

In the spring of 1676, James Shute, with his wife and two small children, set out from Dorchester for the purpose of settling themselves on a tract of land in the southern part of what is now New Hampshire, but which then was an unbroken forest. The tract where they purposed making their home was a meadow on a small affluent of the Connecticut.

Taking their household goods and farming tools in an ox-cart drawn by four oxen and driving two cows before them, they reached their destination after a toilsome journey of ten days. The summer was spent in building their cabin, and outhouses, planting and tending the crop of Indian corn which was to be their winter's food, and in cutting the coarse meadow-grass for hay.

Late in October they found themselves destitute of many articles which even in those days of primitive

housewifery and husbandry, were considered of prime
necessity. Accordingly, the husband started on foot
for a small trading-post on the Connecticut River,
about ten miles distant, at which point he expected to
find some trading shallop or skiff to take him to Springfield, thirty-eight miles further south. The weather
was fine and at nightfall Shute had reached the river,
and before sunrise the next morning was floating down
the stream on an Indian trader's skiff.

Within two days he made his purchases, and hiring a
skiff rowed slowly up the river against the sluggish
current on his return. In twelve hours he reached
the trading-post. It was now late in the evening.
The sky had been lowering all day, and by dusk it began to snow. Disregarding the admonitions of the
traders, he left his goods under their care and struck
out boldly through the forest over the trail by which
he came, trusting to be able to find his way, as the
moon had risen, and the clouds seemed to be breaking.
The trail lay along the stream on which his farm was
situated, and four hours at an easy gait would, he
thought, bring him home.

The snow when he started from the river was already
nearly a foot deep, and before he had proceeded a mile
on his way the storm redoubled in violence, and the
snow fell faster and faster. At midnight he had only
made five miles, and the snow was two feet deep.
After trying in vain to kindle a fire by the aid of flint
and steel, he prayed fervently to God, and resuming
his journey struggled slowly on through the storm.
It had been agreed between his wife and himself that
on the evening of this day on which he told her he
should return, he would kindle a fire on a knoll about

two miles from his cabin as a beacon to assure his wife of his safety and announce his approach.

Suddenly he saw a glare in the sky.

During his absence his wife had tended the cattle, milked the cows, cut the firewood, and fed the children. When night came she barricaded the door, and saying a prayer, folded her little ones in her arms and lay down to rest. Three suns had risen and set since she saw her husband with gun on his shoulder disappear through the clearing into the dense undergrowth which fringed the bank of the stream, and when the appointed evening came, she seated herself at the narrow window, or, more properly, opening in the logs of which the cabin was built, and watched for the beacon which her husband was to kindle. She looked through the falling snow but could see no light. Little drifts sifted through the chinks in the roof upon the bed where her children lay asleep; the night grew darker, and now and then the howling of the wolves could be heard from the woods to the north.

Seven o'clock struck—eight—nine—by the old Dutch clock which ticked in the corner. Then her woman's instinct told her that her husband must have started and been overtaken by the storm. If she could reach the knoll and kindle the fire it would light him on his way. She quickly collected a small bundle of dry wood in her apron and taking flint, steel, and tinder, started for the knoll. In an hour, after a toilsome march, floundering through the snow, she reached the spot. A large pile of dry wood had already been collected by her husband and was ready for lighting, and in a few moments the heroic woman was warming her shivering limbs before a fire which blazed far up through the crackling branches and lighted the forest around it.

For more than two hours the devoted woman watched beside the fire, straining her eyes into the gloom and catching every sound. Wading through the snow she brought branches and logs to replenish the flames. At last her patience was rewarded : she heard a cry, to which she responded. It was the voice of her husband which she heard, shouting. In a few moments he came up staggering through the drifts, and fell exhausted before the fire. The snow soon ceased to fall, and after resting till morning, the rescued pioneer and his brave wife returned in safety to their cabin.

Mrs. Frank Noble, in 1664, proved herself worthy of her surname. She and her husband, with four small children, had established themselves in a log-cabin eight miles from a settlement in New Hampshire, and now known as the town of Dover.

Their crops having turned out poorly that autumn, they were constrained to put themselves on short allowance, owing to the depth of the snow and the distance from the settlement. As long as Mr. Noble was well, he was able to procure game and kept their larder tolerably well stocked. But in mid-winter, being naturally of a delicate habit of body, he sickened, and in two weeks, in spite of the nursing and tireless care of his devoted wife, he died. The snow was six feet deep, and only a peck of musty corn and a bushel of potatoes were left as their winter supply. The fuel also was short, and most of the time Mrs. Noble could only keep herself and her children warm by huddling in the bed-clothes on bundles of straw, in the loft which served

LOST IN A SNOW-STORM.

them for a sleeping room. Below lay the corpse of Mr. Noble, frozen stiff. Famine and death stared them in the face. Two weeks passed and the supply of provisions was half gone. The heroic woman had tried to eke out her slender store, but the cries of her children were so piteous with hunger that while she denied herself, she gave her own portion to her babes, lulled them to sleep, and then sent up her petitions to Him who keeps the widow and the fatherless. She prayed, we may suppose, from her heart, for deliverance from her sore straits for food, for warmth, for the spring to come and the snow to melt, so that she might lay away the remains of her husband beneath the sod of the little clearing.

Every morning when she awoke, she looked out from the window of the loft. Nothing was to be seen but the white surface of the snow stretching away into the forest. One day the sun shone down warmly on the snow and melted its surface, and the next morning there was a crust which would bear her weight. She stepped out upon it and looked around her. She would then have walked eight miles to the settlement but she was worn out with anxiety and watching, and was weak from want of food. As she gazed wistfully toward the east, her ears caught the sound of a crashing among the boughs of the forest. She looked toward the spot from which it came and saw a dark object floundering in the snow. Looking more closely she saw it was a moose, with its horns entangled in the branches of a hemlock and buried to its flanks in the snow.

Hastening back to the cabin she seized her husband's gun, and loading it with buckshot, hurried out and killed the monstrous brute. Skilled in wood-craft, like most pioneer women, she skinned the animal and cutting it up bore the pieces to the cabin. Her first thought then was of her children, and after she had given them a hearty meal of the tender moose-flesh she partook of it herself, and then, re-freshed and strengthened, she took the axe and cut a fresh supply of fuel. During the day a party came out from the settlement and supplied the wants of the stricken household. The body of the dead husband was borne to the settlement and laid in the graveyard beneath the snow.

Nothing daunted by this terrible experience, this heroic woman kept her frontier cabin and, with friendly aid from the settlers, continued to till her farm. In ten years, when her oldest boy had become a man, he and his brothers tilled two hundred acres of meadow land, most of it redeemed from the wilderness by the skill, strength, and industry of their noble mother.

The spring season must have been to the early settlers, particularly to the women, even more trying than the winter. In the latter season, except after extraordinary falls of snow, transit from place to place was made by means of sledges over the snow or on ox-carts over the frozen ground. Traveling could also be done across or up and down rivers on the ice, and as bridges were rare in those days the crossing of rivers on the ice was much to be preferred to fording them in other seasons of the year. Fuel too was more easily obtained in the winter than in the spring, and as roads were generally little more than passage-ways or cow-paths through the meadows or the woods, the depth of the mud was often such as to form a barrier to the locomotion of the heavy vehicles of the period or even to prevent travel on horseback or on foot.

Other dangers and hardships in the spring of the year were the freshets and floods to which the river dwellers were exposed. Woman, be it remembered, is naturally as alien to water as a mountain-fowl, which flies over a stream for fear of wetting its feet. We can imagine the discomfort to which a family of women and children were exposed who lived, for example, on the banks of the Connecticut in the olden time. In some seasons families were, as they now are, driven to the upper stories of their houses by the overflow of the river. But it should be remembered that the houses of those days were not the firm, well-built structures of modern times. Sometimes the settler found himself and family floating slowly down stream, cabin and all, borne along by the freshet caused by a sudden thaw: as long as his cabin held together, the family had always hopes of grounding as the flood subsided and saving their lives though with much loss of property, besides the discomfort if not positive danger to which they had been exposed.

But sometimes the flood was so sudden and violent that the cabin would be submerged or break to pieces, and float away, drowning some or all of the family. It might be supposed that the married portion of the pioneers would select other sites than on the borders of a large river subject every year to overflow, but the richness of the alluvial soil on the banks of the Connecticut was so tempting that other considerations were overlooked, and to no part of New England was the tide of emigration turned so strongly as to the Connecticut Valley.

In the year 1643, an adventurous family of eight persons embarked on a shallop from Hartford (to which place they had come shortly before from Watertown, Mass.), and sailing or rowing up the river made a landing on a beautiful meadow near the modern town of Hatfield.

The family consisted of Peter Nash and Hannah his wife, David, their son, a youth of seventeen, Deborah and Mehitabel, their two daughters, aged respectively nineteen and fourteen, Mrs. Elizabeth Nash, the mother of Peter, aged sixty-four, and Mr. and Mrs. Jacob Nash. They found the land all ready for ploughing, and after building a spacious cabin and barns, they had nothing to do but to plant and harvest their crops and stock their farm with cattle which they brought from Springfield, driving them up along the river. For four years everything went on prosperously. They harvested large crops, added to their barns, and had a great increase in stock. Although the wolves and wild cats had made an occasional foray in their stock and poultry yard and the spring freshets had made inroads into their finest meadow, their general course had been only one of prosperity.

Their house and barns were built upon a tongue of land where the river made a bend, and were on higher ground than the surrounding meadow, which every spring was submerged by the freshets. Year after year the force of the waters had washed an angle into this tongue of land and threatened some time to break through and leave the houses and barns of the pioneers upon an island. But the inroads of the waters were gradual, and the Nashes flattered themselves that it would be at least two generations before the river would break through.

Mrs. Peter Nash and her daughter were women of almost masculine courage and firmness. They all handled axe and gun as skilfully as the men of the household; they could row a boat, ride horseback, swim, and drag a seine for shad; and Mehitabel, the younger daughter, though only fourteen years old, was already a woman of more than ordinary size and strength. These three women accompanied the men on their hunting and fishing excursions and assisted them in hoeing corn, in felling trees, and dragging home fuel and timber.

The winter of 1647–8 was memorable for the amount of snow that fell, and the spring for its lateness. The sun made some impression on the snow in March, but it was not till early in April that a decided change came in the temperature. One morning the wind shifted to the southwest, the sun was as hot as in June; before night it came on to rain, and, before the following night, nearly the whole vast body of snow had been dissolved into water which had swelled all the streams to an unprecedented height. The streams poured down into the great river, which rose with fearful rapidity, converting all the alluvial meadows into a vast lake.

All this took place so suddenly that the Nash family had scarcely a warning till they found themselves in the midst of perils. When the rain ceased, on the evening of the second day, the water had flooded the surrounding meadows and risen high up into the first story of their house. The force of the current had already torn a channel across the tongue of land on

4

which the house stood and had washed away the barns and live-stock. One of their two boats had been floated off but had struck broadside against a clump of bushes and was kept in its place by the force of the current. The other boat had been fastened by a short rope to a stout sapling, but this latter boat was ten feet under water, held down by the rope.

The water had now risen to the upper story, and the family were driven to the roof. If the house would stand they might yet be saved. It was firmly built but it shook with the force and weight of the waters. If either of the boats could be secured they might reach dry land by rowing out of the current and over the meadows where the water was stiller The oars of the submerged boat had been floated away, but in the other boat they could be seen from the roof of the house lying safely on the bottom.

It was decided that Jacob Nash should swim out and row the boat up to the house. He was a strong swimmer, and though the water was icy cold it was thought the swift current would soon enable him to reach the skiff which lay only a few rods below the house. Accordingly, he struck boldly out, and in a moment had reached the boat, when he suddenly threw up his hands and sank, the current whirling him out of sight in an instant, amid the shrieks of his young wife, who was then a nursing mother and holding her babe in her arms as her husband went down. Mrs. Nash, the elder, gazed for a moment speechless at the spot where her son had sunk, and then fell upon her knees, the whole family following her example, and prayed fervently to Almighty God for deliverance from their awful danger. Then rising from her kneeling posture, she bade her other son make one more trial to reach the boat.

Peter Nash and his son Daniel then plunged into the water, reached the boat, and took the oars, but the force of the current was such that they could make, by rowing, but little headway against it. The two daughters then leaped into the flood, and in a few strokes reached and entered the boat. By their united force it was brought up and safely moored to the chimney of the cabin. In two trips the family were conveyed to the hillside. Then the brave girls returned and brought away a boat-load of household gear. Not content with that they rowed to the submerged boat, and diving down, cut the rope, baled out the water, and in company with their mother, father, and brother, brought away all the moveables in the upper stories of the house. Their courage appeared to have been rewarded in another way, since the house stood through the flood, and in ten days they were assisting to tear down the house and build another on a hill where the floods never came.

As soldiers fall in battle, so in the struggles and hardships of border life, the delicate frame of woman often succumbs, leaving the partner of her toils to mourn her loss and meet the onset of life alone. Such a loss necessarily implies more than when it occurs in the comfortable homes of refined life, since it removes at once a loving wife, a companion in solitude, and an efficient co-worker in the severe tasks incident to life in frontier settlements. Sometimes the husband's career is broken off when he loses his wife under such circumstances, and he gives up both hope and effort.

About sixty years since, and while the rich prairies of Indiana began to be viewed as the promised land of the adventurous pioneer, among the emigrants who were attracted thither by the golden dreams of happiness and fortune, was a Mr. H., a young man from an eastern city, who came accompanied by his newly married wife, a dark-eyed girl of nineteen. Leaving his bride at one of the westernmost frontier-settlements, he pushed on in search of a favorable location for their new home. Near the present town of LaFayette he found a tract which pleased his eye and promised abundant harvests, and after his wife had been brought to view it and expressed her satisfaction and delight at the happy choice he had made, the site was selected and the house was built.

They moved into their prairie-home in the first flush of summer. Their cabin was built upon a knoll and faced the south. Sitting at the door at eventide they contemplated a prospect of unrivaled beauty. The sun-bright soil remained still in its primeval greatness and magnificence, unchecked by human hands, covered with flowers, protected and watched by the eye of the sun. The days were glorious; the sky of the brightest blue, the sun of the purest gold, and the air full of vitality, but calm; and there, in that brilliant light, stretched itself far, far out into the infinite, as far as the eye could discern, an ocean-like extent, the waves of which were sunflowers, asters, and gentians, nodding and beckoning in the wind, as if inviting millions of beings to the festival set out on the rich table of the earth. Mrs. H. was an impressible woman with poetic tastes, and a strong admiration for the beautiful in nature; and as she gazed upon the glorious expanse her whole face lighted up and glowed with pleasure. Here she thought was the paradise of which she had long dreamed.

As the summer advanced a plenteous harvest promised to reward the labors of her husband. Nature was bounteous and smiling in all her aspects, and the young wife toiled faithfully and patiently to make her rough house a pleasant home for her husband. She had been reared like him amid the luxuries of an eastern city, and her hands had never been trained to work. But the influences of nature around her, and the almost idolatrous love which she cherished for her husband, cheered and sweetened the homely toils of her prairie life.

Eight months sped happily and prosperously away; the winter had been mild, and open, and spring had come with its temperate breezes, telling of another summer of brightness and beauty.

Soon after the middle of April in that year, commenced an extraordinary series of storms. They occurred daily, and sometimes twice a day, accompanied by the most vivid lightning, and awful peals of thunder; the rain poured down in a deluge until it seemed as if another flood was coming to purify the earth. For more than sixty days those terrible scenes recurred, and blighted the whole face of the country for miles around the lonely cabin. The prairies, saturated with moisture, refused any longer to drink up the showers. Every hollow and even the slightest depression became a stagnant pool, and when the rains ceased and the sun came out with the heat of the summer solstice, it engendered pestilence, which rose from the green plain that smiled beneath him, and stalked resistless among the dwellers throughout that vast expanse.

Of all the widely isolated and remote cabins which sent their smoke curling into the dank morning air of the region thereabouts, there was not one in which disease was not already raging with fearful malignity. Doctors or hired nurses there were none; each stricken household was forced to battle single-handed with the destroyer who dealt his blows stealthily, suddenly, and alas! too often, effectually.   The news of the dreadful visitation soon reached the family of Mr. H—— and for a period they were in a fearful suspense.   They were surrounded by the same malarial influences that had made such havoc among their neighbors, and why should they escape?   They were living directly over a noisome cess-pool; their cellar was filled with water which could not be drained away, nor would the saturated earth drink it up.   Centuries of vegetable accumulations forming the rich mould in which the cellar was dug, gave out their emanations to the water, and the fiery rays of the sun made the mixture a decoction whose steams were laden with death.

There was no escape unless they abandoned their house, and this they were reluctant to do, hoping that the disease would pass by them.   But this was a vain hope; in a few days Mr. H. was prostrated by the fever. Mrs. H. had preserved her courage and energy till now, but her impressible nature began to yield before the onset of this new danger.   Her life had been sunny and care-free from a child; her new home had till recently been the realization of her dreams of happiness; but the loss of her husband would destroy at once every fair prospect for the future.   All that a loving wife could do as a nurse or watcher or doctress, was done by her, but long before her husband had turned the sharp corner between death and life, Mrs. H. was attacked and both lay helpless, dependent upon the care of their only hired man. Neighbors whose hearts had been made tender and sympathetic by their own bereavements, came from their far-off cabins and for several weeks watched beside their bedside. The attack of the wife commenced with a fever which continued till after the birth of her child. For three days longer she lingered in pain, sinking slowly till the last great change came, and Mr. H., now convalescent, saw her eyes closed for ever.

The first time he left the house was to follow the remains of his wife and child to their last resting place, beneath an arbor of boughs which her own hands had tended. We cannot describe the grief of that bereaved husband. His very appearance was that of one who had emerged from the tomb. Sickness had blanched his dark face to a ghastly hue, and drawn great furrows in his cheeks, which were immovable, and as if chiseled in granite. During his sickness he had seen little of her before she was stricken down, for his mind was clouded. When the light of reason dawned he was faintly conscious that she lay near him suffering, first from the fever, and then from woman's greatest pain and trial, but that he was unable to soothe and comfort her; and finally that her last hours were hours of intense agony, which he could not alleviate. He was as one in a trance; a confused consciousness of his terrible loss slowly took possession of him. When at length his weakened intellect comprehended the truth with all its sad surrounding, a great cloud of desolation settled down over his whole life.

That cloud, sad to say, never lifted. As he stood by the open grave, he lifted the lid, gazed long and intently on that sweet pale face, bent and kissed the marble brow, and as the· mother and child were lowered into the grave, he turned away a broken-hearted man.

CHAPTER III.

EARLY PIONEERS—WOMAN'S ADVENTURES AND HEROISM.

FOR nearly one hundred years after the settlement of Plymouth, the whole of the territory now known as the State of Maine was, with the exception of a few settlements on the coast and rivers, a howling wilderness. From the sea to Canada extended a vast forest, intersected with rapid streams and dotted with numerous lakes. While the larger number of settlers were disinclined to attempt to penetrate this trackless waste, some few hardy pioneers dared to advance far into the unknown land, tempted by the abundance of fish in the streams and lakes or by the variety of game which was to be found in the forests. It was the land for hunters rather than for tillers of the soil, and most of its early explorers were men who were skillful marksmen, and versed in forest lore. But occasionally women joined these predatory expeditions against the denizens of the woods and waters.

In the history of American settlements too little credit has been given to the hunter. He is often the first to penetrate the wilderness; he notes the general features of the country as he passes on his swift course; he ascertains the fertility of the soil and the capabilities of different regions; he *reconnoiters* the Indian tribes, and learns their habits and how they are affected towards the white man. When he returns to the settlements he makes his report concerning the region which he has explored, and by means of the knowledge thus obtained the permanent settlers were and are enabled to push forward and establish themselves in the wilderness. In the glory and usefulness of these discoveries woman not unfrequently shared. Some of the most interesting narratives are those in which she was the companion and coadjutor of the hunter in his explorations of the trackless mazes of our American forests.

In the year 1672 a small party of hunters arrived at the mouth of the Kennebec in two canoes. The larger one of the canoes was paddled up stream by three men, the other was propelled swiftly forward by a man and a woman. Both were dressed in hunters' costume; the woman in a close-fitting tunic of deer-skin reaching to the knees, with leggins to match, and the man in hunting-shirt and trowsers of the same material. Edward Pentry, for this was the name of the man, was a stalwart Cornishman who had spent ten years in hunting and exploring the American wilderness. Mrs. Pentry, his wife, was of French extraction, and had passed most of her life in the settlements in Canada, where she had met her adventurous husband on one of his hunting expeditions. She was of manly stature and strength, and like her husband, was a splendid shot and skillful fisher. Both were passionately fond of forest life, and perfectly fearless of its dangers, whether from savage man or beast.

It was their purpose to explore thoroughly the region watered by the upper Kennebec, and to establish a trading-post which would serve as the headquarters of fur-traders, and ultimately open the country for settlement. Their outfit was extremely simple: guns, traps, axes, fishing-gear, powder, and bullets, &c., with an assorted cargo of such trinkets and other articles as the Indians desired in return for peltry.

In three weeks they reached the head-waters of the Kennebec, at Moosehead Lake. There they built a large cabin, divided into two compartments, one of which was occupied by three of the men, the other by Mr. and Mrs. Pentry. All of the party were versed in the Indian dialect of the region, and as Mrs. Pentry could speak French, no trouble was anticipated from the Indians, who in that part of the country were generally friendly to the French.

The labors of the men in felling trees and shaping logs for the cabin, as well as in framing the structure, were shared in by Mrs. Pentry, who in addition did all the necessary cooking and other culinary offices. They decided to explore the surrounding country for the purpose of discovering the lay of the land and the haunts of game. No signs of any Indians had yet been seen, and it was thought best that the four men should start, each in a different direction, and having explored the neighboring region return to the cabin at night, Mrs. Pentry meanwhile being left alone—a situation which she did not in the least dread. Accordingly, early in the morning, after eating a hunter's breakfast of salt pork, fried fish, and parched corn, the quartette selected their several routes, and started, taking good care to mark their trail as they went, that they could the more readily find the way back.

It was agreed that they should return by sunset, which would give them twelve good hours for exploration, as it was the month of July, and the days were long. After their departure Mrs. P. put things to rights about the house, and barring the door against intruders, whether biped or quadruped, took her gun and fishing-tackle and went out for a little sport in the woods.

The cabin stood on the border of Moosehead Lake. Unloosing the canoes, she embarked in one, and towing the other behind her, rowed across a part of the lake which jutted in shore to the southwest; she soon reached a dense piece of woods which skirted the lake, and there mooring her canoe, watched for the deer which came down to that place to drink. A fat buck before long made his appearance, and as he bent down his head to quaff the water, a brace of buck-shot planted behind his left foreleg laid him low, and his carcase was speedily deposited in the canoe.

The sun was now well up, and as Mrs. P. had provided for the wants of the party by her lucky shot, and no more deer made their appearance, she lay down in the bottom of the boat, and soon fell fast asleep. Hunters and soldiers should be light sleepers, as was Mrs. Pentry upon this occasion.

How long she slept she never exactly knew, but she was awakened by a splash; lifting her head above the edge of the boat, she saw nothing but a muddy spot on the water some thirty feet away, near the shore. This was a suspicious sign. Looking more closely, she saw a slight motion beneath the lily-pads, which covered closely, like a broad green carpet, the surface of the lake. Her hand was on her gun, and as she leveled the barrel towards the turbid spot, she saw a head suddenly lifted, and at the same moment a huge Indian sprang from the water and struggled up through the dense undergrowth that lined the edge of the lake.

It was a sudden impulse rather than a thought, which made Mrs. P. level the gun at his broad back and pull the trigger. The Indian leaped into the air, and fell back in the water dead, with half a dozen buck-shot through his heart. At the same moment she felt a strong grasp on her shoulder, and heard a deep guttural "ugh!" Turning her head she saw the malignant face of another Indian standing waist-deep in the water, with one hand on the boat which he was dragging towards the shore.

A swift side-blow from the gun-barrel, and he tumbled into the water; before he could recover, the brave woman had snatched the paddle, and sent the canoe spinning out into the lake. Then dropping the paddle and seizing her gun she dashed in a heavy charge of powder, dropped a dozen buck-shot down the muzzle, rammed in some dry grass, primed the pan, and leveled it again at the savage, who having recovered from the blow, was floundering towards the shore, turning and shaking his tomahawk at her, meanwhile, with a ferocious grin. Again the report of her gun awakened the forest echoes, and before the

THE HUNTRESS OF THE LAKE SURPRISED BY INDIANS.   Page 60.

echoes had died away, the savage's corpse was floating on the water.

She dared not immediately approach the shore, fearing that other savages might be lying in ambush; but after closely scrutinizing the bushes, she saw no signs of others, besides the two whom she had shot. She then cut long strips of raw hide from the dead buck, and towing the bodies of the Indians far out into the lake sunk them with the stones that served to anchor the canoes. Returning to the shore, she took their guns which lay upon the shelving bank, and rapidly paddled the canoe homeward.

It was now high noon. She reached the cabin, entered, and sat down to rest. She supposed that the savages she had just killed were stragglers from a war-party who had lagged behind their comrades, and attracted by the sound made by her gun when she shot the buck, had come to see what it was. The thought that a larger body might be in the vicinity, and that they would capture and perhaps kill her beloved husband and his companions, was a torture to her. She sat a few moments to collect her thoughts and resolve what course to pursue.

Her resolution was soon taken. She could not sit longer there, while her husband and friends were exposed to danger or death. Again she entered the canoe and paddled across the arm of the lake to the spot where the waters were still stained with the blood of the Indians. Hastily effacing this bloody trace, she moored the canoes and followed the trail of the savages for four miles to the northwest. There she found in a ravine the embers of a fire, where, from appearances as many as twenty redskins had spent the pre-

ceding night. Their trail led to the northwest, and
by certain signs known to hunters, she inferred that
they had started at day-break and were now far on
their way northward.

When her four male associates selected their respective routes in the morning, her husband had,
she now remembered, selected one which led directly
in the trail of the Indian war-party, and by good cal-
culation he would have been about six miles in their
rear. Not being joined by the two savages whose
bodies lay at the bottom of the lake, what was more
likely than that they would send back a detachment
to look after the safety of their missing comrades ?

The first thing to be done was to strike her husband's trail and then follow it till she overtook him or
met him returning. Swiftly, and yet cautiously, she
struck out into the forest in a direction at right angles
with the Indian camp. Being clad in trowsers of deer
skin and a short tunic and moccasins of the same material, she made her way through the woods as easily
as a man, and fortunately in a few moments discovered
a trail which she concluded was that of her husband.
Her opinion was soon verified by finding a piece of
leather which she recognized as part of his accoutre-
ments. For two hours she strode swiftly on through
the forest, treading literally in her husband's tracks.

The sun was now three hours above the western
horizon; so taking her seat upon a fallen tree, she
waited, expecting to see him soon returning on his
trail, when she heard faintly in the distance the report
of a gun; a moment after, another and still another
report followed in quick succession. Guided by the
sound she hurried through the tangled thicket from

which she soon emerged into a grove of tall pine trees, and in the distance saw two Indians with their backs turned toward her and shielding themselves from some one in front by standing behind large trees. Without being seen by them she stole up and sheltered herself in a similar manner, while her eye ranged the forest in search of her husband who she feared was under the fire of the red-skins.

At length she descried the object of their hostility behind the trunk of a fallen tree. It was clearly a white man who crouched there, and he seemed to be wounded. She immediately took aim at the nearest Indian and sent two bullets through his lungs. The other Indian at the same instant had fired at the white man and then sprang forward to finish him with his tomahawk. Mrs. Pentry flew to the rescue and just as the savage lifted his arm to brain his foe, she drove her hunting knife to the haft into his spine.

Her husband lay prostrate before her and senseless with loss of blood from a bullet-wound in the right shoulder. Staunching the flow of blood with styptics which she gathered among the forest shrubs, she brought water and the wounded man soon revived. After a slow and weary march she brought him back to the cabin, carrying him part of the way upon her shoulders. Under her careful nursing he at length recovered his strength though he always carried the bullet in his shoulder. It appears he had met three Indians who told him they were in search of their two missing companions. One of them afterwards treacherously shot him from behind through the shoulder, and in return Pentry sent a ball through his heart. Then becoming weak from loss of blood he could only point his gun-barrel at the remaining Indians, and this was his situation when his wife came up and saved his life.

After receiving such an admonition it is natural to suppose the whole party were content to remain near their forest home for a season, extending their rambles only far enough to enable them to procure game and fish for their table; and this was not far, for the lake was alive with fish; and wild turkeys, deer, and other game could be shot sometimes even from the cabin door.

The party were also deterred by this experience from attempting to drive any trade with the Indians until the following spring, when they expected to be joined by a large party of hunters.

The summer soon passed away, and the cold nights of September and October admonished our hardy pioneers that they must prepare for a rigorous winter. Mrs. Pentry made winter clothing for the men and for herself out of the skins of animals which they had shot, and snow-shoes from the sinews of deer stretched on a frame composed of strips of hard wood. She also felled trees for fuel and lined the walls of the cabin with deer and bear skins; she was the most skilful mechanic of the party, and having fitted runners of hickory to one of the boats she rigged a sail of soft skins sewed together, and once in November, after the river was frozen, and when the wind blew strongly from the northwest, the whole party undertook to reach the mouth of the river by sailing down in their boat upon the ice. A boat of this kind, when the ice is smooth and the wind strong, will make fifteen miles an hour.

They were interrupted frequently in their course by the falls and rapids, making portages necessary; nevertheless in three days and two nights they reached the mouth of the river.

Here they bartered their peltry for powder, bullets, and various other articles' most needed by frontiersmen, and catching a southeast wind started on their return. In a few hours they had made seventy miles, and at night, as the sky threatened snow, they prepared a shelter in a hollow in the bank of the river. Before morning a snow-storm had covered the river-ice and blocked their passage. For three days, the snow fell continuously. They were therefore forced to abandon all hopes of reaching their cabin at the head-waters of the Kennebec. The hollow or cave in the bank where they were sheltered they covered with saplings and branches cut from the bluff, and banked up the snow round it. Their supply of food was soon exhausted, but by cutting holes in the ice they caught fish for their subsistence.

The depth of the snow prevented them from going far from their place of shelter, and the nights were bitter cold. The ice on the river was two feet in thickness; and one day, in cutting through it to fish, their only axe was broken. No worse calamity could have befallen them, since they were now unable to cut fuel or to procure fish. Mr. Pentry, who was still suffering from the effects of his wound, contracted a cold which settled in his lame shoulder, and he was obliged to stay in doors, carefully nursed and tended by his devoted wife. The privations endured by these unfortunates are scarcely to be paralleled. Short of food, ill-supplied with clothing, and exposed to the howling sever-

5

ity of the climate, the escape of any one of the number appears almost a miracle.

A number of bear-skins, removed from the boat to
the cave, served them for bedding. Some days, when
there was nothing to eat and no means of making a
fire, they passed the whole time huddled up in the
skins. Daily they became weaker and less capable of
exertion. Wading through the snow up to the waist,
they were able now and then to shoot enough small
game to barely keep them alive.

After the lapse of a fortnight there came a thaw,
succeeded by a cold rain, which froze as it fell. The
snow became crusted over, to the depth of two inches,
with ice that was strong enough to bear their weight.
They extricated their ice-boat and prepared for departure. One of the party had gone out that morning on
the crust, hoping to secure some larger game to stock
their larder before starting; the rest awaited his
return for two hours, and then, fearing some casualty
had happened to him, followed his trail for half a mile
from the river and found him engaged in a desperate
struggle with a large black she-bear which he had
wounded.

The ferocious animal immediately left its prey and
rushed at Mrs. Pentry with open mouth, seizing her
left arm in its jaws, crunched it, and then, rising on its
hind legs, gave her a terrible hug. The rest of the
party dared not fire, for fear of hitting the woman.
Twice she drove her hunting knife into the beast's
vitals and it fell on the crust, breaking through into
the snow beneath, where the two rolled over in a
death-struggle. The heroic woman at length arose
victorious, and the carcase of the bear was dragged

forth, skinned, and cut up. A fire was speedily kindled, Mrs. Pentry's wounds were dressed, and after refreshing themselves with a hearty meal of bearsteak, the remainder of the meat was packed in the boat.

The party then embarked, and by the aid of a stiff easterly breeze, were enabled, in three days, to reach their cabin on the head-waters of the Kennebec. The explorations made along the Kennebec by Mrs. Pentry and her companions attracted thither an adventurous class of settlers, and ultimately led to the important settlements on the line of that river.

The remainder of Mrs. Pentry's life was spent mainly on the northern frontier. She literally lived and died in the woods, reaching the advanced age of ninety-six years, and seeing three generations of her descendants grow up around her. Possessing the strength and courage of a man, she had also all a woman's kindness, and appears to have been an estimable person in all the relations of life—a good wife and mother, a warm friend, and a generous neighbor. In fact, she was a representative woman of the times in which she lived.

The toils of a severer nature, such as properly belong to man, often fall upon woman from the necessities of life in remote and isolated settlements; she is seen plying strange vocations and undertaking tasks that bear hardly on the soft and gentle sex. Sometimes a hunter and trapper; and again a mariner; now we see her performing the rugged work of a farm, and again a fighter, stoutly defending her home. The fact that habit and necessity accustom her, in frontier life, to those employments which in older and more conventional communities are deemed unfitting

and ungraceful for woman to engage in, makes it none
the less striking and admirable, because in doing so
she serves a great and useful purpose; she is thereby
doing her part in forming new communities in the
places that are uninhabited and waste.

Vermont was largely settled by the soldiers who
had served in the army of the Revolution. The settlers, both men and women, were hardy and intrepid,
and seem to have been peculiarly adapted to subjugate
that rugged region in our New England wilderness.
The women were especially noted for the strength
and courage with which they shared the labors of the
men and encountered the hardships and dangers of
frontier life.

When sickness or death visited the men of the
family, the mothers, wives, or widows filled their places
in the woods, or on the farm, or among the cattle.
Often, side by side with the men, women could be
seen emulating their husbands in the severe task of
felling timber and making a clearing in the forest.

In the words of Daniel P. Thompson, author of
" The Green Mountain Boys ":—

" The women of the Green Mountains deserve as
much credit for their various displays of courage,
endurance, and patriotism, in the early settlement of
their State, as was ever awarded to their sex for similar exhibitions in any part of the world. In the
controversy with New York and New Hampshire,
which took the form of war in many instances; in
the predatory Indian incursions, and in the War of
the Revolution, they often displayed a capacity for
labor and endurance, a spirit and firmness in the hour
of danger, a resolution and hardihood in defending

their families and their threatened land against all enemies, whether domestic or foreign, that would have done honor to the dames of Sparta."

The first man who commenced a settlement in the town of Salisbury, Vermont, on the Otter Creek, was Amos Storey, who, in making an opening in the heart of the wilderness on the right of land to which the first settler was entitled, was killed by the fall of a tree. His widow, who had been left in Connecticut, immediately resolved to push into the wilderness with her ten small children, to take his place and preserve and clear up his farm. This bold resolution she carried out to the letter, in spite of every difficulty, hardship, and danger, which for years constantly beset her in her solitary location in the woods. Acre after acre of the dense and dark forest melted away before her axe, which she handled with the dexterity of the most experienced chopper. The logs and bushes were piled and burnt by her own strong and untiring hand; crops were raised, by which, with the fruits of her fishing and unerring rifle, she supported herself and her hardy brood of children. As a place of refuge from the assaults of Indians or dangerous wild beasts, she dug out an underground room, into which, through a small entrance made to open under an overhanging thicket on the bank of the stream, she nightly retreated with her children.

Frequently during the dreary winter nights she was kept awake by the howling of the wolves, and sometimes, looking through the chinks in the logs, she could see them loping in circles around the cabin, whining and snuffing the air as if they yearned for human blood. They were gaunt, fierce-looking crea-

tures, and in the winter-time their hunger made them
so bold that they would come up to the door and
scratch against it. The barking of her mastiff would
soon drive the cowardly beasts away but only a few
rods, to the edge of the clearing where, sitting on
their haunches, they frequently watched the house
all night, galloping away into the woods when day
broke.

Here she continued to reside, thus living, thus
laboring, unassisted, till, by her own hand and the
help which her boys soon began to afford her, she
cleared up a valuable farm and placed herself in
independent circumstances.

Miss Hannah Fox tells the following thrilling story
of an adventure that befel her while engaged in felling trees in her mother's woods in Rhode Island, in
the early colonial days.

We were making fine progress with our clearing
and getting ready to build a house in the spring. My
brother and I worked early and late, often going without our dinner, when the bread and meat which we
brought with us was frozen so hard that our teeth
could make no impression upon it, without taking too
much of our time. My brother plied his axe on the
largest trees, while I worked at the smaller ones or
trimmed the boughs from the trunks of such as had
been felled.

The last day of our chopping was colder than ever.
The ground was covered by a deep snow which had
crusted over hard enough to bear our weight, which
was a great convenience in moving from spot to spot
in the forest, as well as in walking to and from our
cabin, which was a mile away. My brother had gone

to the nearest settlement that day, leaving me to do my work alone.

As a storm was threatening, I toiled as long as I could see, and after twilight felled a sizeable tree which in its descent lodged against another. Not liking to leave the job half finished, I mounted the almost prostrate trunk to cut away a limb and let it down. The bole of the tree was forked about twenty feet from the ground, and one of the divisions of the fork would have to be cut asunder. A few blows of my axe and the tree began to settle, but as I was about to descend, the fork split and the first joints of my left-hand fingers slid into the crack so that for the moment I could not extricate them. The pressure was not severe, and as I believed I could soon relieve myself by cutting away the remaining portion, I felt no alarm. But at the first blow of the axe which I held in my right hand, the trunk changed its position, rolling over and closing the split, with the whole force of its tough oaken fibers crushing my fingers like pipe-stems; at the same time my body was dislodged from the trunk and I slid slowly down till I hung suspended with the points of my feet just brushing the snow. The air was freezing and every moment growing colder; no prospect of any relief that night; the nearest house a mile away; no friends to feel alarmed at my absence, for my mother would suppose that I was safe with my brother, while the latter would suppose I was by this time at home.

The first thought was of my mother. "It will kill her to know that I died in this death-trap so near home, almost within hearing of her voice! There must be some escape! but how?" My axe had fallen below me and my feet could almost touch it. It was impossible to imagine how I could cut myself loose unless I could reach it. My only hope of life rested on that keen blade which lay glittering on the snow.

Within reach of my hand was a dead bush which towered some eight feet above me, and by a great exertion of strength I managed to break it. Holding it between my teeth I stripped it of its twigs, leaving two projecting a few inches at the lower end to form a hook. With this I managed to draw towards me the head of the axe until my fingers touched it, when it slipped from the hook and fell again upon the snow, breaking through the crust and burying itself so that only the upper end of the helve could be seen.

Up to that moment the recollection of my mother and the first excitement engendered by hope had almost made me unconscious of the excruciating pain in my crushed fingers, and the sharp thrills that shot through my nerves, as my body swung and twisted in my efforts to reach the axe. But now, as the axe fell beyond my reach, the reaction came, hope fled, and I shuddered with the thought that I must die there alone like some wild thing caught in a snare. I thought of my widowed mother, my brother, the home which we had toiled to make comfortable and happy. I prayed earnestly to God for forgiveness of my sins, and then calmly resigned myself to death, which I now believed to be inevitable. For a time, which I afterwards found to be only five minutes, but which then seemed to me like hours, I hung motionless. The pain had ceased, for the intense cold blunted my sense of feeling. A numbness stole over me, and I seemed to be falling into a trance, from which I was roused by a sound of bells borne to me as if from a great distance. Hope again awoke, and I screamed loud and long; the woods echoed my cries, but no voice replied. The bells grew fainter and fainter, and at last died away. But the sound of my voice had broken the spell which cold and despair were fast throwing over me. A hundred devices ran swiftly through my mind, and each device was dismissed as impracticable. The helve of the axe caught my eye, and in an instant by an association of ideas it flashed across me that in the pocket of my dress there was a small knife—another sharp instrument by which I could extricate myself. With some difficulty I contrived to open the blade, and then withdrawing the knife from my pocket and griping it as one who clings to the last hope of life, I strove to cut away the wood that held my fingers in its terrible vise. In vain! the wood was like iron. The motion of my arm and body brought back the pain which the cold had lulled, and I feared that I should faint.

After a moment's pause I adopted a last expedient. Nerving myself to the dreadful necessity, I disjointed my fingers and fell exhausted to the ground. My life was saved, but my left hand was a bleeding stump. The intensity of the cold stopped the flow of blood. I tore off a piece of my dress, bound up my fingers, and started for home. My complete exhaustion and the bitter cold made that the longest mile I had ever traveled. By nine o'clock that evening I had managed to drag myself, more dead than alive, to my mother's door, but it was more than a week before I could again leave the house.

The difficulties encountered by the first emigrant-bands from Massachusetts, on their journey to Connecticut, may be understood best when we consider the face of the country between Massachusetts Bay and Hartford. It was a succession of ridges and deep valleys with swamps and rapid streams, and covered with forests and thickets where bears, wolves, and catamounts prowled. The journey, which occupies now but a few hours, then generally required two weeks to perform. The early settlers, men, women, and children, pursued their toilsome march over this rough country, picking their way through morasses, wading through rivers and streams, and climbing mountains; driving their cattle, sheep, and swine before them. Some came on horseback; the older and feebler in ox-carts, but most of them traveled on foot. At night aged and delicate women slept under trees in the forest, with no covering but the foliage and the cope of heaven.

The winter was near at hand, and the nights were already cold and frosty. Many of the women had been delicately reared, and yet were obliged to travel on foot for the whole distance, reaching their destination in a condition of exhaustion that ill prepared them for the hardships of the ensuing winter. Some were nursing mothers, who sheltered themselves and their babes in rude huts where the wind, rain, and snow drove in through yawning fissures which there were no means to close. Others were aged women, who in sore distress sent up their prayers and rolled their quavering hymns to the wintry skies, their only canopy. The story of these hapless families is told in the simple but effective language of the old historian.

" On the 15th of October [1632] about sixty men, women, and children, with their houses, cattle, and swine, commenced their journey from Massachusetts, through the wilderness, to Connecticut River. After a tedious and difficult journey through swamps and rivers, over mountains and rough grounds, which were passed with great difficulty and fatigue, they arrived safely at their respective destinations. They were so long on their journey, and so much time and pains were spent in passing the river, and in getting over their cattle, that after all their exertions, winter came upon them before they were prepared. This was an occasion of great distress and damage to the plantation. The same autumn several other parties came from the east— including a large number of women and children—by different routes, and settled on the banks of the Connecticut river.

"The winter set in this year much sooner than usual, and the weather was stormy and severe. By the 15th of November, the Connecticut river was frozen over, and the snow was so deep, and the season so tempestuous, that a considerable number of the cattle which had been driven on from the Massachusetts, could not be brought across the river. The people had so little time to prepare their huts and houses, and to erect sheds and shelter for their cattle, that the sufferings of man and beast were extreme. Indeed the hardships and distresses of the first planters of Connecticut scarcely admit of a description. To carry much provision or furniture through a pathless wilderness was impracticable. Their principal provisions and household furniture were therefore put on several small vessels, which, by reason of delays and the tempestuousness of the season, were cast away. Several vessels were wrecked on the coast of New Eng-

land, by the violence of the storms. Two shallops
laden with goods from Boston to Connecticut, were
cast away in October, on Brown's Island, near the
Gurnet's Nose; and the men with every thing on
board were lost. A vessel with six of the Connecticut people on board, which sailed from the river for
Boston, early in November, was, about the middle of
the month, cast away in Manamet Bay. The men
and women got on shore, and after wandering ten
days in deep snow and a severe season, without meeting any human being, arrived, nearly spent with cold
and fatigue, at New Plymouth.

" By the last of November, or beginning of December, provisions generally failed in the settlements on
the river, and famine and death looked the inhabitants
sternly in the face. Some of them driven by hunger
attempted their way, in that severe season, through
the wilderness, from Connecticut to Massachusetts.
Of thirteen, in one company, who made this attempt,
one in passing the river fell through the ice and was
drowned. The other twelve were ten days on their
journey, and would all have perished, had it not been
for the assistance of the Indians.

" Indeed, such was the distress in general, that by
the 3d and 4th of December, a considerable part of
the new settlers were obliged to abandon their habitations. Seventy persons, men, women, and children,
were compelled, in the extremity of winter, to go
down to the mouth of the river to meet their provisions, as the only expedient to preserve their lives.
Not meeting with the vessels which they expected,
they all went on board the Rebecca, a vessel of about
sixty tons. This, two days before, was frozen in, twenty
miles up the river; but by the falling of a small rain,

and the influence of the tide, the ice became so broken and was so far removed, that she made a shift to get out. She ran, however, upon the bar, and the people were forced to unlade her to get off. She was released, and in five days reached Boston. Had it not been for these providential circumstances, the people must have perished with famine.

" The people who kept their stations on the river suffered in an extreme degree. After all the help they were able to obtain, by hunting, and from the Indians, they were obliged to subsist on acorns, malt, and grains.

" Numbers of the cattle which could not be got over the river before winter, lived through without anything but what they found in the woods and meadows. They wintered as well, or better than those which were brought over, and for which all the provision was made and pains taken of which the owners were capable. However, a great number of cattle perished. The Dorchester or Windsor people, lost in this* way alone about two hundred pounds sterling. Their other losses were very considerable."

It is difficult to describe, or even to conceive, the apprehensions or distresses of a people in the circumstances of our venerable ancestors, during this doleful winter. All the horrors of a dreary wilderness spread themselves around them. They were compassed with numerous fierce and cruel tribes of wild and savage men, who could have swallowed up parents and children at pleasure, in their feeble and distressed condition. They had neither bread for themselves nor children; neither habitation nor clothing convenient for them. Whatever emergency might happen, they were cut off, both by land and water, from any succor or retreat. What self-denial, firmness, and magnanimity are necessary for such enterprises! How distressing, in the beginning, was the condition of those now fair and opulent towns on Connecticut River!

Under the most favorable circumstances, the lives of the pioneer-women must have been one long ordeal of hardship and suffering. The fertile valleys were the scenes of the bloodiest Indian raids, while the remote and sterile hill country, if it escaped the attention of the hostile savage, was liable to be visited by other ills. Famine in such regions was always imminent, and the remoteness and isolation of those frontier-cabins often made relief impossible. A failure in the little crop of corn, which the thin soil of the hillside scantily furnished, and the family were driven to the front for game and to the streams for fish, to supply their wants. Then came the winter, and the cabin was often blockaded with snow for weeks. The fuel and food consumed, nothing seemed left to the doomed household but to struggle on for a season, and then lie down and die. Fortunately the last sad catastrophe was of rare occurrence, owing to the extraordinary resolution and hardihood of the settlers.

It is a striking fact that in all the records, chronicles, and letters of the early settlers that have come down to us, there are scarcely to be found any complaining word from woman. She simply stated her sufferings, the dangers she encountered, the hardships she endured, and that was all. No querulous or peevish complaints, no moanings over her hard lot. She bore her pains and sorrows and privations in silence, looking forward to her reward, and knowing that she was making homes in the wilderness, and that future generations would rise up and call her blessed.

CHAPTER IV.

THE BLOCK-HOUSE, AND ON THE INDIAN TRAIL.

THE axe and the gun, the one to conquer the forces of wild nature, the other to battle against savage man and beast—these were the twin weapons that the pioneer always kept beside him, whether on the march or during a halt. In defensive warfare the axe was scarcely less potent than the gun, for with its keen edge the great logs were hewed which formed the block-house, and the tall saplings shaped, which were driven into the earth to make the stockade. We know too that woman could handle the gun and ply the axe when required so to do.

In one of our historical galleries there was exhibited not long since a painting representing a party of Indians attacking a block-house in a New England settlement. The house is a structure framed, and built of enormous logs, hexagonal in shape, the upper stories over-hanging those beneath, and pierced with loop-holes. There is a thick parapet on the roof, behind which are collected the children of the settlement guarded by women, old and young, some of whom are firing over the parapet at the yelling fiends who have just emerged from their forest-ambush. A glimpse of the interior of the block-house shows us women engaged in casting bullets and loading fire-arms which they are handing to the men. In the background a brave girl is returning swiftly to the garrison, with buckets of water which she has drawn from the spring, a few rods away from the house. A crouching savage has leveled his gun at her, and she evidently knows the danger she is in, but moves steadily forward without spilling a drop of her precious burden.

The block-house is surrounded by the primeval forest, which is alive with savages. Some are shaking at the defenders of the block-house fresh scalps, evidently just torn from the heads of men and women who have been overtaken and tomahawked before they could reach their forest-citadel: others have fired the stack of corn. A large fire has been kindled in the woods and a score of savages are wrapping dry grass around the ends of long poles, with which to fire the wooden walls of the block-house.

Thirty or forty men women and children in a wooden fort, a hundred miles, perhaps, from any settlement, and surrounded by five times their number of Pequots or Wampanoags thirsting for their blood! This is indeed a faithful picture of one of the frequent episodes of colonial life in New England!

Every new settlement was brought face to face with such dangers as we have described. The red-man and the white man were next door neighbors. The smokes of the wigwam and the cabin mingled as they rose to the sky. From the first there was more or less antagonism. Life among the white settlers was a kind of picket-service in which woman shared.

At times, as for example in the wars with the Pequots and King Philip, there was safety nowhere. Men went armed to the field, to meeting, and to bring home their brides from their father's house where they

had married them. Women with muskets at their
side lulled their babes to sleep. Like the tiger of the
jungles, the savage lay in ambush for the women and
children: he knew he could strike the infant colony
best by thus desolating the homes.

The captivities of Mrs. Williams and her children,
of Mrs. Shute, of Mrs. Johnson, of Mrs. Howe, and of
many other matrons, as well as of unmarried women,
are well-conned incidents of New England colonial
history. The story of Mrs. Dustin's exploit and escape reads like a romance. "At night," to use the
concise language of Mr. Bancroft, "while the household slumbers, the captives, each with a tomahawk,
strike vigorously, and fleetly, and with division of labor,—and of the twelve sleepers, ten lie dead; of one
squaw the wound was not mortal; one child was
spared from design. The love of glory next asserted
its power; and the gun and tomahawk of the mur-
derer of her infant, and a bag heaped full of scalps
were choicely kept as trophies of the heroine. The
streams are the guides which God has set for the stranger in the wilderness: in a bark canoe the three
descend the Merrimac to the English settlement,
astonishing their friends by their escape and filling
the land with wonder at their successful daring."

The details of Mrs. Rowlandson's sufferings after her
capture at Lancaster, Mass., in 1676, are almost too
painful to dwell upon. When the Indians began their
march the day after the destruction of that place,
Mrs. Rowlandson carried her infant till her strength
failed and she fell. Toward night it began to snow;
and gathering a few sticks, she made a fire. Sitting
beside it on the snow, she held her child in her arms,

6

through the long and dismal night. For three or four days she had no sustenance but water; nor did her child share any better for nine days. During this time it was constantly in her arms or lap. At the end of that period, the frost of death crept into its eyes, and she was forced to relinquish it to be disposed of by the unfeeling sextons of the forest.

She went through almost every suffering but death. She was beaten, kicked, turned out of doors, refused food, insulted in the grossest manner, and at times almost starved. Nothing but experience can enable us to conceive what must be the hunger of a person by whom the discovery of six acorns and two chestnuts was regarded as a rich prize. At times, in order to make her miserable, they announced to her the death of her husband and her children.

On various occasions they threatened to kill her. Occasionally, but for short intervals only, she was permitted to see her children, and suffered her own anguish over again in their miseries. She was obliged, while hardly able to walk, to carry a heavy burden, over hills, and through rivers, swamps, and marshes; and in the most inclement seasons. These evils were repeated daily; and, to crown them all, she was daily saluted with the most barbarous and insolent accounts of the burning and slaughter, the tortures and agonies, inflicted by them upon her countrymen. It is to be remembered that Mrs. Rowlandson was tenderly and delicately educated, and ill fitted to encounter such distresses; and yet she bore them all with a fortitude truly wonderful.

Instances too there were, where a single woman infused her own dauntless spirit into a whole garrison, and prevented them from abandoning their post. Mrs. Heard, "a widow of good estate, a mother of many children, and a daughter of Mr. Hull, a revered minister formerly settled in Piscataqua," having escaped from captivity among the Indians, about 1689, returned to one of the garrisons on the extreme frontier of New Hampshire. By her presence and courage this out-post was maintained for ten years and during the whole war, though frequently assaulted by savages. It is stated that if she had left the garrison and retired to Portsmouth, as she was solicited to do by her friends, the out-post would have been abandoned, greatly to the damage of the surrounding country.

Long after the New England colonies rested in comparative security from the attacks of the aboriginal tribes, the warfare was continued in the Middle, Southern, and Western States; and even at this hour, sitting in our peaceful homes we read in the journals of the day reports of Indian atrocities perpetrated against the families of the pioneers on our extreme western frontier.

Our whole history from the earliest times to the present, is full of instances of woman's noble achievements. East, west, north, south, wherever we wander, we tread the soil which has been wearily trodden by her feet as a pioneer, moistened by her tears as a captive, or by her blood as a martyr in the cause of civilization on this western continent.

The sorrows of maidens, wives, and mothers in the border wars of our colonial times, have furnished themes for the poet, the artist, and the novelist, but the reality of these scenes as described in the simple words of the local historians, often exceeds the most vivid dress in which imagination can clothe it.

One of the most deeply rooted traits of woman's nature is sympathy, and the outflow of that emotion into action is as natural as the emotion itself. When a woman witnesses the sufferings of others it is instinctive with her to try and relieve them, and to be thwarted in the exercise of this faculty is to her a positive pain.

We may judge from this of what her feelings must have been when she saw, as she often did, those who were dearest to her put to torture and death without being permitted to rescue them or even alleviate their agonies.

Such was the position in which Mrs. Waldron was placed, on the northern border, during the French and Indian war of the last century. She and her husband occupied a small block-house which they had built a few miles from Cherry Valley, New York, and here she was doomed to suffer all that a wife could, in witnessing the terrible fate of her husband and being at the same time powerless to rescue him.

"One fatal evening," to use the quaint words of our heroine, "I was all alone in the house, when I was of a sudden surprised with the fearful war-whoop and a tremendous attack upon the door and the palisades around. I flew to the upper window and seizing my husband's gun, which I had learned to use expertly, I leveled the barrel on the window-sill and took aim at the foremost savage. Knowing their cruelty and merciless disposition, and wishing to obtain some favor, I desisted from firing; but how vain and fruitless are the efforts of one woman against the united force of so many, and of such merciless monsters as I had here to deal with! One of them that could speak a little English, threatened me in return, 'that if I did not come out, they would burn me alive in the house.' My terror and distraction at hearing this is not to be expressed by words nor easily imagined by any person unless in the same condition. Distracted as I was in such deplorable circumstances, I chose to rely on the uncertainty of their protection, rather than meet with certain death in the house; and accordingly went out with my gun in my hand, scarcely knowing what I did. Immediately on my approach, they rushed on me like so many tigers, and instantly disarmed me. Having me thus in their power, the merciless villians bound me to a tree near the door.

"While our house and barns were burning, sad to relate, my husband just then came through the woods, and being spied by the barbarians, they gave chase and soon overtook him. Alas! for what a fate was he reserved! Digging a deep pit, they tied his arms to his side and put him into it and then rammed and beat the earth all around his body up to his neck, his head only appearing above ground. They then scalped him and kindled a slow fire near his head.

"I broke my bonds, and running to him kissed his poor bleeding face, and threw myself at the feet of his barbarous tormentors, begging them to spare his life. Deaf to all my tears and entreaties and to the piercing shrieks of my unfortunate husband, they dragged me away and bound me more firmly to the tree, smiting my face with the dripping scalp and laughing at my agonies.

Thank God! I then lost all consciousness of the dreadful scene; and when I regained my senses the monsters had fled after cutting off the head of the poor victim of their cruel rage."

When the British formed an unholy alliance with the Indians during the Revolutionary War and turned the tomahawk and scalping knife against their kinsmen, the beautiful valley of Wyoming became a dark and bloody battle-ground. The organization and disciplined valor of the white man, leagued with the cunning and ferocity of the red man, was a combination which met the patriots at every step in those then remote settlements, and spread rapine, fire, and murder over that lovely region.

The sufferings of the captive women, the dreadful scenes they witnessed, and the fortitude and courage they displayed, have been rescued from tradition and embodied in a permanent record by more than one historian. The names of Mrs. Bennet, Mrs. Myers, Mrs. Marcy, Mrs. Franklin, and a host of others, are inseparably associated with the household legends of the Wyoming Valley.

Miss Cook, after witnessing the barbarous murder and mutilation of a beautiful girl, whose rosy cheeks were gashed and whose silken tresses were torn from her head with the scalping knife, was threatened with instant death unless she would assist in dressing a bundle of fresh, reeking scalps cut from the heads of her friends and relatives. As she handled the gory trophies, expecting every moment that her own locks would be added to the ghastly heap, she saw something in each of those sad mementos that reminded her of those who were near and dear to her. At last she lifted one which she thought was her mother's; she gazed at the long tresses sprinkled with gray and called to mind how often she had combed and caressed them in happier hours: shuddering through her whole frame, the wretched girl burst into a passion of tears. The ruthless savage who stood guard over her with brandished tomahawk immediately forced her to resume and complete her horrible task.

In estimating the heroism of American women displayed in their conflicts with the aborigines, we must take into account her natural repugnance to repulsive and horrid spectacles. The North American savage streaked with war-paint, a bunch of reeking scalps at his girdle, his snaky eyes gleaming with malignity, was a direful sight for even a hardened frontiers-man; how much more, then, to his impressionable and delicate wife and daughter. The very appearance of the savage suggested thoughts of the tomahawk, the scalping knife, the butchered relations, the desolated homestead. Nothing can better illustrate the hardihood of these bold spirited women than the fact that they showed themselves not seldom superior to these feelings of dread and abhorrence, daring even in the midst of scenes of blood to denounce personally and to their face the treachery and cruelty of their foes.

* In the year 1763 a party of Shawnees visited the Block-House at Big Levels, Virginia, and after being hospitably entertained by the inhabitants, turned treacherously upon them and massacred every white man in the house. The women and children were carried away as captives, including Mrs. Glendenning, the late wife, and now the widow of one of the leading settlers. Notwithstanding the dreadful scenes

---

* DeHass.

through which she had passed, Mrs. Glendenning was not intimidated. Her husband and friends had been butchered before her eyes; but though possessed of keen sensibilities, her spirit was undaunted by the awful spectacle. Filled with indignation at the treachery and cruelty of the Indians, she loudly denounced them, and tauntingly told them that they lacked the hearts of great warriors who met their foes in fair and open conflict. The savages were astounded at her audacity; they tried to frighten her into silence by flapping the bloody scalp of her husband in her face and by flourishing their tomahawks above her head. The intrepid woman still continued to express her indignation and detestation. The savages, admiring her courage, refrained from inflicting any injury upon her. She soon after managed to effect her escape and returned to her desolate home, where she gave decent interment to the mangled remains of her husband. During all the trying scenes of the massacre and captivity Mrs. Glendenning proved herself worthy of being ranked with the bravest women of our Colonial history.

The region watered by the upper Ohio and its tributary streams was for fifty years the battle-ground where the French and their Indian allies, and afterwards the Indians alone, strove to drive back the Anglo-Saxon race as it moved westward. The country there was rich and beautiful, but what made its possession especially desirable was the fact that it was the strategic key to the great West. The French, understanding its importance, established their fortresses and trading-posts as bulwarks against the army of

English settlers advancing from the East, and also
instructed their savage allies in the art of war.

The Indian tribes in that region were warlike and
powerful, and for some years it seemed as if the
country would be effectually barred against the access
of the Eastern pioneer. But the same school that
reared and trained the daughters and grand-daughters
of the Pilgrims, and of the settlers of Jamestown,
and fitted them to cope with the perils and hardships
of the wilderness, and to battle with hostile aboriginal
tribes, also fitted their descendants for new struggles
on a wider field and against more desperate odds.
The courage and fortitude of men and women alike
rose to the occasion, and in those scenes of danger
and carnage, the presence of mind displayed by
women especially, have been frequent themes of
panegyric by the border annalists.

*The scene wherein Miss Elizabeth Zane, one of
these heroines, played so conspicuous a part, was at
Fort Henry, near the present city of Wheeling, Virginia, in the latter part of November, 1782. Of the
forty-two men who originally composed the garrisons,
nearly all had been drawn into an ambush and
slaughtered. The Indians, to the number of several
hundred, surrounded the garrison which numbered no
more than twelve men and boys.

A brisk fire upon the fort was kept up for six hours
by the savages, who at times rushed close up to the
palisades and received the reward of their temerity
from the rifles of the frontiersmen. In the afternoon
the stock of powder was nearly exhausted. There
was a keg in a house ten or twelve rods from the gate
of the fort, and the question arose, who shall attempt

* DeHass.

to seize this prize? Strange to say, every soldier proffered his services, and there was an ardent contention among them for the honor. In the weak state of the garrison, Colonel Shepard, the commander, deemed it advisable that only one person could be spared; and in the midst of the confusion, before any one could be designated, Elizabeth Zane interrupted the debate, saying that her life was not so important at that time as any one of the soldiers, and claiming the privilege of performing the contested services. The Colonel would not at first listen to her proposal, but she was so resolute, so persevering in her plea, and her argument was so powerful, that he finally suffered the gate to be opened, and she passed out. The Indians saw her before she reached her brother's house, where the keg was deposited; but for some cause unknown, they did not molest her until she reappeared with the article under her arm. Probably, divining the nature of her burden, they discharged a volley as she was running towards the gate, but the whizzing balls only gave agility to her feet, and herself and the prize were quickly safe within the gate.

The successful issue of this perilous enterprise infused new spirit into the garrison; re-enforcements soon reached them, the assailants were forced to beat a precipitate retreat, and Fort Henry and the whole frontier was saved, thanks to the heroism of Elizabeth Zane!

* The heroines of Bryant's Station deserve a place on the roll of honor, beside the name of the preserver of Fort Henry, since like her their courage preserved a garrison from destruction. We condense the story

---

* McClung's Sketches of Western Adventure.

A HEROIC EXPLOIT IN SUPPLYING WITH POWDER A BLOCK HOUSE BESIEGED BY INDIANS. Page 90.

from the several sources from which it has come down to us.

The station, consisting of about forty cabins ranged in parallel lines, stood upon a gentle rise on the southern banks of the Elkhorn, near Lexington, Kentucky. One morning in August, 1782, an army of six hundred Indians appeared before it as suddenly as if they had risen out of the earth. One hundred picked warriors made a feint on one side of the fort, trying to entice the men out from behind the stockade, while the remainder were concealed in ambush near the spring with which the garrison was supplied with water. The most experienced of the defenders understood the tactics of their wily foes, and shrewdly guessed that an ambuscade had been prepared in order to cut off the garrison from access to the spring. The water in the station was already exhausted, and unless a fresh supply could be obtained the most dreadful sufferings were apprehended. It was thought probable that the Indians in ambush would not unmask themselves until they saw indications that the party on the opposite side of the fort had succeeded in enticing the soldiers to an open engagement.

* Acting upon this impression, and yielding to the urgent necessity of the case, they summoned all the women, without exception, and explaining to them the circumstances in which they were placed, and the improbability that any injury would be done them, until the firing had been returned from the opposite side of the fort, they urged them to go in a body to the spring, and each to bring up a bucket full of water. Some, as was natural, had no relish for the undertaking; they observed they were not bullet-

---

* McClung's Sketches of Western Adventure.

proof, and asked why the men could not bring the water as well as themselves; adding that the Indians made no distinction between male and female scalps.

To this it was answered, that women were in the habit of bringing water every morning to the fort, and that if the Indians saw them engaged as usual, it would induce them to believe that their ambuscade was undiscovered, and that they would not unmask themselves for the sake of firing at a few women, when they hoped, by remaining concealed a few moments longer to obtain complete possession of the fort; that if men should go down to the spring, the Indians would immediately suspect that something was wrong, would despair of succeeding by ambuscade, and would instantly rush upon them, follow them into the fort, or shoot them down at the spring. The decision was soon made.

A few of the boldest declared their readiness to brave the danger, and the younger and more timid rallying in the rear of these veterans, they all marched down in a body to the spring, within point blank shot of more than five hundred Indian warriors! Some of the girls could not help betraying symptoms of terror, but the married women, in general, moved with a steadiness and composure which completely deceived the Indians. Not a shot was fired. The party were permitted to fill their buckets, one after another, without interruption, and although their steps became quicker and quicker, on their return, and when near the gate of the fort, degenerated into a rather un-military celerity, attended with some little crowding in passing the gate, yet only a small portion of the water was spilled. The brave water carriers were received with open arms and loud cheers by the garrison, who hailed them as their preservers, and the Indians shortly after retired, baffled and cursing themselves for being outwitted by the " white squaws."

The annals of the border-wars in the region of which we have been speaking abound in stories where women have been the victors in hand-to-hand fights with savages. In all these combats we may note the spirit that inspired those brave women with such wonderful strength and courage, transforming them from gentle matrons into brave soldiers. It was love for their children, their husbands, their kindred, or their homes rather than the selfish instinct of self-preservation which impelled Mrs. Porter, the two Mrs. Cooks, Mrs. Merrill, and Mrs. Bozarth to perform those feats of prowess and daring which will make their names live for ever in the thrilling story of border-warfare.

The scene where Mrs. Porter acted her amazing part was in Huntingdon county, Pennsylvania, and the time was during the terrible war instigated by the great Pontiac. While sitting by the window of her cabin, awaiting the return of her husband, who had gone to the mill, she caught sight of an Indian approaching the door. Taking her husband's sword from the wall where it hung, she planted herself behind the door; and when the Indian entered she struck with all her might, splitting his skull and stretching him a corpse upon the floor. Another savage entered and met the same fate. A third seeing the slaughter of his companions prudently retired.

Dropping the bloody weapon, she next seized the loaded gun which stood beside her and retreated to the upper story looking for an opportunity to shoot the savage from the port-holes. The Indian pursued her and as he set foot upon the upper floor received the contents of her gun full in the chest and fell dead in his tracks. Cautiously reconnoitering in all directions and seeing the field clear she fled swiftly toward the mill and meeting her husband, both rode to a neighboring block-house where they found refuge and aid. The next morning it was discovered that other Indians had burned their cabin, partly out of revenge and partly to conceal their discomfiture by a woman. The bones of the three savages found among the ashes were ghastly trophies of Mrs. Porter's extraordinary achievement.

In Nelson county, Kentucky, on a midsummer night, in 1787, just before the gray light of morning, John Merrill, attracted by the barking of his dog, went to the door of his cabin to reconnoiter. Scarcely had he left the threshold, when he received the fire of six or seven Indians, by which his arm and thigh were both broken. He managed to crawl inside the cabin and shouted to his wife to shut the door. Scarcely had she succeeded in doing so when the tomahawks of the enemy were hewing a breach into the apartment.

* Mrs. Merrill, with Amazonian courage and strength, grasped a large axe and killed, or badly wounded, four of the enemy in succession as they attempted to force their way into the cabin.

The Indians then ascended the roof and attempted to enter by way of the chimney, but here, again, they were met by the same determined enemy. Mrs. Merrill seized the only feather-bed which the cabin afforded, and hastily ripping it open, poured its contents upon the fire. A furious blaze and stifling smoke ascended the chimney, and quickly brought down two of the enemy, who lay for a few moments at the mercy of the lady. Seizing the axe, she despatched them, and was instantly summoned to the door, where the only remaining savage appeared, endeavoring to effect an entrance, while Mrs. Merrill was engaged at the chimney. He soon received a gash in the cheek which compelled him with a loud yell to relinquish his purpose, and return hastily to Chillicothe, where, from the report of a prisoner, he gave an exaggerated account of the fierceness, strength, and courage of the "Long knife squaw!"

The wives of Jesse and Hosea Cook, the "heroines of Innis station" (Kentucky), as they have been styled, are shining examples of a firmness of spirit which sorrow could not blench nor tears dim.

While the brothers Cook were peacefully engaged in the avocations of the farm beside their cabins, in April, 1792, little dreaming of the proximity of the savages, a sharp crack of rifles was heard and they both lay weltering in their blood. The elder fell dead, the younger was barely able to reach his cabin.

The two Mrs. Cooks with three children were instantly collected in the house and the door made fast. The thickness of the door resisted the hail of rifleballs which fell upon it, and the Indians tried in vain to cut through it with their tomahawks.

While the assault was being made on the outside of the cabin, within was heart-rending sorrow mingled with fearless determination and high resolve. The younger Cook while the door was being barred breathed his last in the arms of his wife, and the two Mrs. Cooks, thus sadly bereaved of their partners, were left the sole defenders of the cabin and the three children.

There was a rifle in the house but no balls could be found. In this extremity one of the women took a musket-ball and placing it between her teeth bit it into pieces. Her eyes streaming with tears, she loaded the rifle and took her position at an aperture from which she could watch the motions of the savages. She dried her tears and thought of vengeance on her husband's murderers and of saving the innocent babes which she was guarding.

After the failure of the Indians to break down the door, one of them seated himself upon a log, apprehending no danger from the "white squaws" who, he knew, were the only defenders of the cabin. A ball sped from the rifle in the hands of Mrs. Cook, and with a loud yell the savage bounded into the air and fell dead.

The Indians, infuriated at the death of their comrade, threatened, in broken English, the direst vengeance on the inmates of the cabin. A half dozen of the yelling fiends instantly climbed to the roof of the cabin and kindled a fire upon the dry boards around the chimney. As the flames began to take effect the destruction of the cabin and the doom of the unfortunate inmates seemed certain.

But the self-possession and intrepidity of the brave women were equal to the occasion. While one stood in the loft the other handed her water with which she extinguished the fire. Again and again the roof was fired, and as often extinguished. When the water was exhausted, the dauntless pair held the flames at bay by breaking eggs upon them. The Indians, at length fatigued by the obstinacy and valor of the brave defenders, threw the body of their comrade into the creek and precipitately fled.

The exploits of Mrs. Bozarth in defending her home and family against superior numbers, has scarcely been paralleled in ancient or modern history. Relying upon her firmness and courage, two or three families had gathered themselves for safety at her house, on the Pennsylvania border, in the spring of 1779. The forest swarmed with savages, who soon made their appearance near the stockade, severely wounding one of the only two men in the house. * The Indian who had shot him, springing over his prostrate body, engaged with the other white man in a struggle which ended in his discomfiture. A knife was wanting to dispatch the savage who lay writhing beneath his antagonist. Mrs. Bozarth seized an axe and with one blow clove the Indian's skull. Another entered and shot the white man dead. Mrs. Bozarth, with unflinching boldness, turned to this new foe and gave him several cuts with the axe, one of which laid bare his entrails. In response to his cries for help, his comrades, who had been killing some children out of doors, came rushing to his relief. The head of one of them was cut in twain by the axe of Mrs. Bozarth, and the others made a speedy retreat through the door. Rendered furious by the desperate resistance they had met, the Indians now besieged the house, and for several days they employed all their arts to enter and slay the weak garrison. But all their efforts were futile. Mrs. Bozarth and her wounded companion employed themselves so vigorously and vigilantly that the enemy were completely baffled. At length a party of white men arrived, put the Indians to flight, and relieved Mrs. Bozarth from her perilous situation.

---

* Doddridge's Notes.

7

CHAPTER V.

THE part that woman has taken in so many ways and under so many conditions, in securing the ultimate results represented by our present status as a nation, is given too small a place in the general estimate of those who pen the record of civilization on the North American continent. This is no doubt partly due to her own distaste for notoriety. While man stands as a front figure in the temple of fame, and celebrates his own deeds with pen and voice, she takes her place in the background, content and happy so long as her father, or husband, or son, is conspicuous in the glory to which she has largely contributed. Thus it is that in the march of grand events the historian of the Republic often passes by the woman's niche without dwelling upon its claims to our attention. But notwithstanding the self-chosen position of the weaker sex, their names and deeds are not all buried in oblivion. The filial, proud, and patriotic fondness of sons and daughters have preserved in their household traditions the memory of brave and good mothers; the antiquarian and the local historian, with loving zeal have wiped the dust from woman's urn, and traced anew the names and inscriptions which time has half effaced.

As we scan the pages of Woman's Record the roll

(98)

of honor lengthens, stretching far out like the line of Banquo's phantom-kings. Their names become impressed on our memory; their acts dilate, and their whole lives grow brighter the more closely we study them.

Among the many duties which from necessity or choice were assigned to woman in the remote and isolated settlements, was that of standing guard. She was *par excellence* the vigilant member of the household, a sentinel ever on the alert and ready to give alarm at the first note of danger. The pioneers were the pickets of the army of civilization: woman was a picket of pickets, a sentinel of sentinels, watchful of danger and the quickest to apprehend it. She was always a guardian, and not seldom the preserver of her home and of the settlement. Such duties as these, faithfully performed, contribute perhaps to the success of a campaign more even than great battles. As soon as the front line or picket-force of the pioneers was fairly established in the enemies' country, the work was more than half done, and the whole army— center, right, and left wings—could move forward with little danger, though labor, hard and continuous, was still required. In successive regions the same sentinel and picket duties were performed; in New England and on the Atlantic coast first; then in the interior districts, in the middle States; and already, a hundred years ago, the flying skirmish-line had crossed the great Appalachian range, and was fording the rivers of the western basin. On the march, on the halt, in the camp, that is, in the permanent settlement, woman was a sentinel keeping perpetual guard over the household treasures.

What materials for romance—for epic and tragic poetry—in the lives of those pioneer women! The lonely cabin in the depths of the forest; the father away; the mother rocking her babe to sleep; the howling of the wolves; the storm beating on the roof; the crafty savage lying in ambush; the war-whoop in the night; the attack and the repulse; or perchance the massacre and the cruel captivity; and all the thousand lights and shadows of border life!

During the French and Indian war, and while the northern border was being desolated by savage raids, a hardy settler named Mack, with his wife and two children, occupied a cabin and clearing in the forest a few miles south of Lake Pleasant, in Hamilton County, New York. For some months after the breaking out of the war no molestation was offered to Mr. Mack or his family, either owing to the sequestered situation in which they lived; or from the richer opportunities for plunder offered in the valleys some distance below the lonely and rock-encompassed forest where the Mack homestead lay. Encouraged by this immunity from attack, and placing unbounded confidence in the vigilance and courage of his wife, Mr. Mack, when summoned to accompany Sir William Johnson's forces on one of their military expeditions, obeyed the call and prepared to join his fellow-borderers. Mrs. Mack cheerfully and patriotically acquiesced in her husband's resolution, assuring him that during his absence she would protect their home and children or perish in the attempt.

The cabin was a fortress, such as befitted the exposed situation in which it lay, and was supplied by the provident husband before his departure with provisions and ammunition sufficient to stand a siege: it was furnished on each side with a loop-hole through which a gun could be fixed or a reconnoisance made in every direction.

Yielding to the dictates of prudence and desirous of redeeming the pledge which she had made to her husband, Mrs. Mack stayed within doors most of the time for some days after her husband had bade her farewell, keeping a vigilant look-out on every side for the prowling foe. No sound but the voices of nature disturbed the stillness of the forest. Everything around spoke of peace and repose. Lulled into security by these appearances and urged by the necessities of her out-door duties, she gradually relaxed her vigilance until she pursued the labors of the farm with as much regularity as she would have done if her husband had been at home.

One day while plucking ears of corn for roasting, she caught a glimpse of a moccasin and a brawny limb fringed with leggins, projecting behind a clump of bushes not twenty paces from her. Repressing the shriek which rose to her lips, she quietly and leisurely strolled back to the house with her basket of ears. Once she thought she heard the stealthy tread of the savage behind her and was about to break into a run; but a moment's reflection convinced her that her fears were groundless. She steadily pursued her course till she reached the cabin. With a vast weight of fear taken from her mind she now turned and cast a rapid glance towards the bushes where the foe lay in ambush; nothing was visible there, and having closed and barred the door she made a reconnoisance from each of the four loop-holes of her fortress, but saw nothing to alarm her.

It seemed to her probable that it was only a single prowling savage who was seeking an opportunity to plunder the cabin. Accordingly with a loaded gun by her side, she sat down before the loop-hole which commanded the spot where the savage lay concealed and watched for further developments. For two hours all was still and she began to imagine that he had left his hiding place, when she noticed a rustling in the bushes and soon after descried the savage crawling on his belly and disappearing in the cornfield. Night found her still watching, and as soon as her children had been lulled to sleep, she returned to her post and straining her eyes into the darkness, listened for the faintest sound that might give note of the approach of the enemy. It was near midnight when overcome with fatigue she leaned against the log wall and fell asleep with her gun in her hand.

She was conscious in her slumbers of some mesmeric power exerting an influence upon her, and awakening with a start saw for an instant by the faint light, a pair of snaky eyes looking directly into hers through the loop-hole. They were gone before she was fairly awake, and she tried to convince herself that she had been dreaming. Not a sound was audible, and after taking an observation from each of the loop-holes she became persuaded that the fierce eyes that seemed to have been watching her was the figment of a brain disturbed by anxiety and vigils.

Once more sleep overcame her and again she was awakened by a rattling sound followed by heavy breathing. The noise seemed to proceed from the chimney to which she had scarcely began to direct her attention, when a large body fell with a thud into the ashes of the fire-place, and a deep guttural "ugh" was uttered by an Indian who rose and peered around the room.

The first flickering light which follows the blackness of midnight, gave him a glimpse of the heroic matron who stood with her piece cocked and leveled directly at his breast. Brandishing his tomahawk he rushed towards her yelling so as to disconcert her aim. The brave woman with unshaken nerves pulled the trigger, and the savage fell back with a screech, dead upon the floor. Almost simultaneously with the report of the gun, a triumphant warwhoop was sounded outside the cabin, and peering through the aperture in the direction from which it proceeded she saw three savages rushing toward the door. Rapidly loading her piece she took her position at the loop-hole that commanded the entrance to the cabin, and taking aim, shot one savage dead, the ball passing completely through his body and wounding another who stood in range. The third made a precipitate retreat, leaving his wounded comrade who crawled into the cornfield and there died.

After the occurrence of these events we may well suppose that the life of Mrs. Mack was one of constant vigilance. For some days and nights she stood sentinel over her little ones, and then in her dread lest the Indians should return and take vengeance upon her and her children for the slaughter of their companions, she concluded the wisest course would be to take refuge in the nearest fort thirty miles distant. Accordingly the following week she made all her preparations and carrying her gun started for the fort with her children.

Before they had proceeded a mile on their course she had the misfortune to drop her powder-horn in a stream: this compelled her to return to the cabin for ammunition. Hiding her children in a dense copse and telling them to preserve silence during her absence, she hastened back, filled her powder-horn and returned rapidly upon her trail.

But what was her agony on discovering that her children were missing from the place where she left them! A brief scrutiny of the ground showed her the tracks of moccasins, and following them she soon ascertained that her children had been carried away by two Indians. Like the tigress robbed of her young, she followed the trail swiftly but cautiously and soon came up with the savages, whose speed had been retarded by the children. Stealing behind them she shot one of them and clubbing her gun rushed at the other with such fierceness that he turned and fled.

Pursuing her way to the fort she met her husband returning home from the war. The family then retraced their steps and reached their home, the scene of Mrs. Mack's heroic exploit.

It was during their captivities that women often learned the arts and practiced the perilous profession of a scout. Their Indian captors were sometimes the first to suffer from the knowledge which they themselves had taught their captive pupils. In this rugged school of Indian life was nurtured a brave girl of New England parentage, who acted a conspicuous part in protecting an infant settlement in Ohio.

* In the .year 1790, the block-house and stockade

above the mouth of the Hockhocking river in Ohio, was a refuge and rallying point for the hardy frontiersmen of that region. The valley of the Hockhocking was preëminent for the richness and luxuriance of nature's gifts, and had been from time immemorial the seat of powerful and warlike tribes of Indians, which still clung with desperate tenacity to a region which had been for so many years the chosen and beloved abode of the red man.

The little garrison, always on the alert, received intelligence early in the autumn that the Indian tribes were gathering in the north for the purpose of striking a final and fatal blow on this or some other important out-post. A council was immediately held by the garrison, and two scouts were dispatched up the Hockhocking, in order to ascertain the strength of the foe and the probable point of attack.

The scouts set out one balmy day in the Indian summer, and threading the dense growth of plum and hazel bushes which skirted the prairie, stealthily climbed the eastern declivity of Mount Pleasant, and cast their eyes over the extensive prairie-country which stretches from that point far to the north. Every movement that took place upon their field of vision was carefully noted day by day. The prairie was the *campus martius* where an army of braves had assembled, and were playing their rugged games and performing their warlike evolutions. Every day new accessions of warriors were hailed by those already assembled, with terrific war-whoops, which, striking the face of Mount Pleasant, were echoed and re-echoed till it seemed as if a myriad of yelling demons were celebrating the orgies of the infernal pit.

To the hardy scouts these well-known yells, so terrible to softer ears, were only martial music which woke a keener watchfulness and strung their iron nerves to a stronger tension. Though well aware of the ferocity of the savages, they were too well practiced in the crafty and subtle arts of their profession to allow themselves to be circumvented by their wily foes.

On several occasions small parties of warriors left the prairies and ascended the mount. At these times the scouts hid themselves in fissures of the rocks or beneath sere leaves by the side of some prostrate tree, leaving their hiding places when the unwelcome visitors had taken their departure. Their food was jerked beef and cold corn-bread, with which their knapsacks had been well stored. Fire they dared not kindle for the smoke would have brought a hundred savages on their trail. Their drink was the rain-water remaining in the excavations in the rocks. In a few days this water was exhausted, and a new supply had to be obtained, as their observations were still incomplete. McClelland, the elder of the two, accordingly set out alone in search of a spring or brook from which they could replenish their canteens. Cautiously descending the mount to the prairie, and skirting the hills on the north, keeping as much as possible within the hazel-thickets, he reached at length a fountain of cool limpid water near the banks of the Hockhocking river. Filling the canteens he rejoined his companion.

The daily duty of visiting the spring and obtaining a fresh supply, was after this performed alternately by the scouts. On one of these diurnal visits, after

White had filled his canteens, he sat watching the
limpid stream that came gurgling out of the bosom of
the earth. The light sound of footsteps caught his
practiced ear, and turning round he saw two squaws
within a few feet of him. The elder squaw at the
same moment spying White, started back and gave a
far-reaching war-whoop. He comprehended at once
his perilous situation. If the alarm should reach the
camp, he and his companion must inevitably perish.

A noiseless death inflicted upon the squaws, and in
such a manner as to leave no trace behind, was the
only sure course which the instinct of self-preservation
suggested. With men of his profession action follows
thought as the bolt follows the flash. Springing upon
his victims with the rapidity and power of a tiger, he
grasped the throat of each and sprang into the Hockhocking river. The head of the elder squaw he easily
thrust under the water, and kept it in that position;
but the younger woman powerfully resisted his efforts
to submerge her. During the brief struggle she addressed him to his amazement in the English language,
though in inarticulate sounds. Relaxing his hold she
informed him that she had been made a prisoner ten
years before, on Grave Creek Flats, that the Indians
in her presence had butchered her mother and two
sisters, and that an only brother had been captured
with her, but had succeeded on the second night in
making his escape, since which time she had never
heard of him.

During this narrative, White, unobserved by the
girl, had released his grip on the throat of the squaw,
whose corpse floated slowly down stream, and, directing the girl to follow him, he pushed for the Mount

with the greatest speed and energy. Scarcely had they proceeded two hundred yards from the spring before an Indian alarm-cry was heard some distance down the river. A party of warriors returning from a hunt had seen the body of the squaw as it floated past. White and the girl succeeded in reaching the Mount where they found McClelland fully awake to the danger they were in. From his eyrie he had seen parties of warriors strike off in every direction on hearing the shrill note of alarm first sounded by the squaw, and before White and the girl had joined him, twenty warriors had already gained the eastern acclivity of the Mount and were cautiously ascending, keeping their bodies under cover. The scouts soon caught glimpses of their swarthy faces as they glided from tree to tree and from rock to rock, until the hiding place of the luckless two was surrounded and all hope of escape was cut off.

The scouts calmly prepared to sell their lives as dearly as they could, but strongly advised the girl to return to the Indians and tell them that she had been captured by scouts. This she refused to do, saying that death among her own people was preferable to captivity such as she had been enduring. "Give me a rifle," she continued," and I will show you that I can fight as well as die! On this spot will I remain, and here my bones shall bleach with yours! Should either of you escape, you will carry the tidings of my fate to my remaining relatives."

All remonstrances with the brave girl proving useless, the two scouts prepared for a vigorous defense. The attack by the Indians commenced in front, where from the nature of the ground they were obliged to advance in single file, sheltering themselves as they best could, behind rocks and trees. Availing themselves of the slightest exposure of the warriors' bodies, the scouts made every shot tell upon them, and succeeded for a time in keeping them in check.

The Indians meanwhile made for an isolated rock on the southern hillside, and having reached it, opened fire upon the scouts at point blank range. The situation of the defenders was now almost hopeless; but the brave never despair. They calmly watched the movements of the warriors and calculated the few chances of escape which remained. McClelland saw a tall, swarthy figure preparing to spring from cover to a point from which their position would be completely commanded. He felt that much depended upon one lucky shot, and although but a single inch of the warrior's body was exposed, and at a distance of one hundred yards, yet he resolved to take the risk of a shot at this diminutive target. Coolly raising the rifle to his eye, and shading the sight with his hand, he threw a bead so accurately that he felt perfectly confident that his bullet would pierce the mark; but when the hammer fell, instead of striking fire, it crushed his flint into a hundred fragments. Rapidly, but with the utmost composure, he proceeded to adjust a new flint, casting meantime many a furtive glance towards the critical point. Before his task was completed he saw the warrior strain every muscle for the leap, and, with the agility of a deer, bound towards the rock; but instead of reaching it, he fell between and rolled fifty feet down hill. He had received a death-shot from some unseen hand, and the mournful

whoops of the savages gave token that they had lost
a favorite warrior.

The advantage thus gained was only momentary.
The Indians slowly advanced in front and on the flank,
and only the incessant fire of the scouts sufficed to
keep them in check.   A second savage attempted to
gain the eminence which commanded the position
where the scouts were posted, but just as he was
about to attain his object, McClelland saw him turn a
summerset, and, with a frightful yell, fall down the
hill, a corpse.   The mysterious agent had again inter-
posed in their behalf.   The sun was now disappearing
behind the western hills, and the savages, dismayed by
their losses, retired a short distance for the purpose of
devising some new mode of attack.   This respite was
most welcome to the scouts, whose nerves had been
kept in a state of severe tension for several hours.
Now for the first time they missed the girl and supposed that she had either fled to her old captors or had
been killed in the fight.   Their doubts were soon
dispelled by the appearance of the girl herself,
advancing toward them from among the rocks, with a
rifle in her hand.

During the heat of the fight she had seen a warrior
fall, who had advanced some fifty yards in front of the
main body; she at once resolved to possess herself of
his rifle, and crouching in the undergrowth, she crept
to the spot and succeeded in her enterprise, being all
the time exposed to the cross-fire of the defenders
and assailants; her practiced eye had early noticed
the fatal rock, and hers was the mysterious hand by
which the two warriors had fallen—the last being the
most wary, untiring, and bloodthirsty brave of the

Shawanese tribe. He it was who ten years before had scalped the family of the girl, and had led her into captivity. The clouds which had been gathering now shrouded the whole heavens, and, night coming on, the darkness was intense. It was feared that in the contemplated retreat they might lose their way or accidentally fall in with the enemy, which latter contingency was highly probable, if not almost inevitable. After consultation it was agreed that the girl, from her intimate knowledge of the localities, should lead the way, a few paces in advance.

Another advantage might be derived from this arrangement, for in case they should fall in with an outpost of savages, the girl's knowledge of the Indian tongue might enable them to deceive and elude the sentinel. The event proved the wisdom of the plan, for they had scarcely descended an hundred feet from their eyrie when a low "hush!" from the girl warned them of the presence of danger. The scouts threw themselves silently upon the earth, where by previous agreement they were to remain until another signal was given them by the girl, who glided away in the darkness. Her absence for more than a quarter of an hour had already begun to excite serious apprehensions for her safety, when she reappeared and told them that she had succeeded in removing two sentinels who were directly in their route, to a point one hundred feet distant.

The descent was noiselessly resumed, the scouts following their brave guide for half a mile in profound silence, when the barking of a small dog, almost at their feet, apprised them of a new danger. The click of the scout's rifle caught the ear of the girl, who quickly approached and warned them against making the least noise, as they were now in the midst of an Indian village, and their lives depended upon their implicitly following her instructions.

A moment afterwards the head of a squaw was seen at an opening in a wigwam, and she was heard to accost the girl, who replied in the Indian language, and without stopping pressed forward. At length she paused and assured the scouts that the village was cleared, and that they were now in safety. She had been well aware that every pass leading out through the prairies was guarded, and resolved to push boldly through the midst of the village as the safest route.

After three days rapid marching and great suffering from hunger, the trio succeeded in reaching the block-house in safety. The Indians finding that the scouts had escaped, and that their plan of attack was discovered, soon after withdrew to their homes; the girl, who by her courage, fortitude, and skill, thus preserved the little settlement from destruction, proved to be a sister of Neil Washburn, one of the most renowned scouts upon the frontier.

The situation of the earlier pioneers who settled on the outskirts of the Mississippi basin was one of peculiar peril. In their isolation and weakness, they were able to keep their position rather by incessant watchfulness, than by actual combat. How to extricate themselves from the snares and escape from the dangers that beset them, was the constant study of their lives. The knowledge and the arts of a scout were a part of the education, therefore, of the women as well as of the men.

Massy Herbeson and her husband were of those

bold pioneers who crossed the Alleghany Mountains and joined the picket-line, whose lives were spent in reconnoitering and watching the motions of the savage tribes which roamed over Western Pennsylvania.

* They lived near Reed's block-house, about twenty-five miles from Pittsburgh. Mr. Herbeson, being one of the spies, was from home ; two of the scouts had lodged with her that night, but had left her house about sunrise, in order to go to the block-house, and had left the door standing wide open. Shortly after the two scouts went away, a number of Indians came into the house, and drew her out of bed, by the feet.

The Indians then scrambled to secure the articles in the house. Whilst they were at this work, Mrs. Herbeson went out of the house, and hallooed to the people in the block-house. One of the Indians then ran up and stopped her mouth, another threatened her with his tomahawk, and a third seized the tomahawk as it was about to fall upon her head, and called her his squaw.

Hurried rapidly away by her captor, she remembered the lessons taught by her husband, the scout, and marked the trail as she went on. Now breaking a bush, now dropping a piece of her dress, and when she crossed a stream, slyly turning over a stone, she hoped thus to guide her husband in pursuit or enable herself to find her way back to the block-house. The vigilance of the Indians was relaxed by the nonchalance with which she bore her captivity, and in a few days she succeeded in effecting her escape and pursuing the trail which she had marked, reached home after a weary march of two days and nights, during which it rained incessantly.

---

*Massey Herbeson's Deposition.

These and countless other instances illustrate the watchfulness and courage of woman when exposed to dangers of such a description. In the west especially, the distances to be traversed, the sparseness of the population, and the perils to which settlers are exposed, render the profession of a scout a useful and necessary one, and woman's versatility of character enables her, when necessary, to practice the art.

The traveler of to-day, passing up the Mohawk Valley will be struck by its fertility, beauty, and above all by the air of quiet repose that broods over it.   One hundred years ago how different the scene !   It was then the battle-ground where the fierce Indian waged an incessant warfare with the frontier settlers.   Every rood of that fair valley was trodden by the wily and sanguinary foe.   The people who then inhabited that region were a mixture of adventurous New Englanders and of Dutch, with a preponderance of the latter, who were a brave, steadfast, hardy race; the women vieing with the men in deeds of heroism and devotion.

Womanly tact and presence of mind was often as serviceable amid those scenes of danger and carnage, as valor in combat; and when woman combined these traits of her sex with courage and firmness she became the "guardian angel" of the settlement.

Such preëminently was the title deserved by Mrs. Van Alstine, the "Patriot mother of the Mohawk Valley."

All the early part of her long life, (for she counted nearly a century of years before she died,) was passed on the New York frontier, during the most trying period of our colonial history.   Here, dwelling in the midst of alarms, she reared her fifteen children; here more than once she saved the lives of her husband and family, and by her ready wit, her daring courage, and her open-handed generosity shielded the settlement from harm.

Born near Canajoharie, about the year 1733, and married to Martin J. Van Alstine, at the age of eighteen, she settled with her husband in the valley of the Mohawk, where the newly wedded pair occupied the Van Alstine family mansion.

In the month of August, 1780, an army of Indians and Tories, led on by Brant, rushed into the Mohawk Valley, devastated several settlements, and killed many of the inhabitants; during the two following months, Sir John Johnson made a descent and finished the work which Brant had begun. The two almost completely destroyed the settlements throughout the valley. It was during those trying times that Mrs. Van Alstine performed a portion of her exploits.

During these three months, and while the hostile forces were making their headquarters at Johnstown, the neighborhood in which Mrs. Van Alstine lived enjoyed a remarkable immunity from attack, although in a state of continual alarm. Intelligence at length came that the enemy, having ravaged the surrounding country, was about to fall upon the little settlement, and the inhabitants, for the most part women and children, were almost beside themselves with terror.

Mrs. Van Alstine's coolness and intrepidity, in this critical hour, were quickly displayed. Calling her neighbors together, she tried to relieve their fears and urged them to remove with their effects to an island belonging to her husband, near the opposite side of the

river, believing that the savages would either not discover their place of refuge or would be in too great
haste to cross the river and attack them.

Her suggestion was speedily adopted, and in a few
hours the seven families in the neighborhood were removed to their asylum, together with a store of provisions and other articles essential to their comfort.
Mrs. Van Alstine was the last to cross and assisted to
place out of reach of the enemy, the boat in which
the passage had been made. An hour after they had
been all snugly bestowed in their bushy retreat, the
war-whoop was heard and the Indians made their appearance. Gazing from their hiding place the unfor-
nate women and children soon saw their loved homes
in flames, Van Alstine's house alone being spared, owing to the friendship borne the owner by Sir John
Johnson.

The voices and even the words of the Indian raid-
ers could be distinctly heard on the island, and as
Mrs. Van Alstine gazed at the mansion untouched by
the flames she rejoiced that she would now be able to
give shelter to the homeless families by whom she was
surrounded. In the following year the Van Alstine
mansion was pillaged by the Indians, and although
the house was completely stripped of furniture and
provisions and clothing, none of the family were killed
or carried away as prisoners.

The Indians came upon them by surprise, entered
the house without ceremony, and plundered and destroyed everything in their way. "Mrs. Van Alstine
saw her most valued articles, brought from Holland,
broken one after another, till the house was strewed
with fragments. As they passed a large mirror with-

DARING EXPLOIT OF MISS VAN ALSTINE.   Page 117.

out demolishing it, she hoped it might be saved; but presently two of the savages led in a colt from the stables and the glass being laid in the hall, compelled the animal to walk over it. The beds which they could not carry away they ripped open, shaking out the feathers and taking the ticks with them. They also took all the clothing. One young Indian, attracted by the brilliancy of a pair of inlaid buckles on the shoes of the aged grandmother seated in the corner, rudely snatched them from her feet, tore off the buckles, and flung the shoes in her face. Another took her shawl from her neck, threatening to kill her if resistance was offered."

The eldest daughter, seeing a young savage carrying off a basket containing a hat and cap her father had brought her from Philadelphia, and which she highly prized, followed him, snatched her basket, and after a struggle succeeded in pushing him down. She then fled to a pile of hemp and hid herself, throwing the basket into it as far as she could. The other Indians gathered round, and as the young girl rose clapped their hands, shouting "Brave girl," while he skulked away to escape their derision. During the struggle Mrs. Van Alstine had called to her daughter to give up the contest; but she insisted that her basket should not be taken.

Winter coming on, the family suffered severely from the want of bedding, woolen clothes, cooking utensils, and numerous other articles which had been taken from them. Mrs. Van Alstine's arduous and constant labors could do but little toward providing for so many destitute persons. Their neighbors were in no condition to help them; the roads were almost impassable besides being infested with the Indians, and all their best horses had been driven away.

This situation appealing continually to Mrs. Van Alstine as a wife and a mother, so wrought upon her as to induce her to propose to her husband to organize an expedition, and attempt to recover their property from the Indian forts eighteen or twenty miles distant, where it had been carried. But the plan seemed scarcely feasible at the time, and was therefore abandoned.

The cold soon became intense and their necessities more desperate than ever. Mrs. Van Alstine, incapable longer of witnessing the sufferings of those dependent upon her, boldly determined to go herself to the Indian country and bring back the property. Firm against all the entreaties of her husband and children who sought to move her from her purpose, she left home with a horse and sleigh accompanied by her son, a youth of sixteen.

Pushing on over wretched roads and through the deep snow she arrived at her destination at a time when the Indians were all absent on a hunting excursion, the women and children only being left at home. On entering the principal house where she supposed the most valuable articles were, she was met by an old squaw in charge of the place and asked what she wanted. "Food," she replied; the squaw sullenly commenced preparing a meal and in doing so brought out a number of utensils that Mrs. Van Alstine recognized as her own. While the squaw's back was turned she took possession of the articles and removed them to her sleigh. When the custodian of the plunder discovered that it was being reclaimed, she was about to interfere forcibly with the bold intruders and take the property into her possession. But Mrs. Van Alstine showed her a paper which she averred was an order signed by "Yankee Peter," a man of great influence among the savages, and succeeded in convincing the squaw that the property was removed by his authority.

She next proceeded to the stables and cut the halters of the horses belonging to her husband: the animals recognized their mistress with loud neighs and bounded homeward at full speed. The mother and son then drove rapidly back to their house. Reaching home late in the evening they passed a sleepless night, dreading an instant pursuit and a night attack from the infuriated savages.

The Indians came soon after daylight in full war-costume armed with rifles and tomahawks. Mrs. Van Alstine begged her husband not to show himself but to leave the matter in her hands. The Indians took their course to the stables when they were met by the daring woman alone and asked what they wanted. "Our horses," replied the marauder. "They are ours," she said boldly, "and we mean to keep them."

The chief approached in a threatening manner, and drawing her away pulled out the plug that fastened the door of the stable, but she immediately snatched it from his hand, and pushing him away resumed her position in front of the door. Presenting his rifle, he threatened her with instant death if she did not immediately move. Opening her neck-handkerchief she told him to shoot if he dared.

The Indians, cowed by her daring, or fearing punishment from their allies in case they killed her, after some hesitation retired from the premises. They afterwards related their adventure to one of the settlers, and said that were fifty such women as she in the settlement, the Indians never would have molested the inhabitants of the Mohawk Valley.

On many subsequent occasions Mrs. Van Alstine exhibited the. heroic qualities of her nature. Twice by her prudence, courage, and address, she saved the lives of her husband and family. Her influence in settling difficulties with the savages was acknowledged throughout the region, and but for her it may well be doubted whether the little settlement in which she lived would have been able to sustain itself, surrounded as it was by deadly foes.

Her influence was felt in another and higher way. She was a Christian woman, and her husband's house was opened for religious worship every Sunday when the weather would permit. She was able to persuade many of the Indians to attend, and as she had acquired their language she was wont to interpret to them the word of God and what was said by the minister. Many times their rude hearts were touched, and the tears rolled down their swarthy faces, while she dwelt on the wondrous story of our Redeemer's life and death, and explained how the white man and the red man alike could be saved by the grace of the Lord Jesus Christ. In after years the savages blessed her as their benefactress.

Nearly a hundred summers have passed since the occurrence of the events we have been describing. The war-whoop of the cruel Mohawk sounds no more from the forest-ambush, nor in the clearing; the dews and rains have washed away the red stains on the

soft sward, and green and peaceful in the sunshine lies
the turf by the beautiful river and on the grave where
the patriot mother is sleeping; but still in the memory of the sons and daughters of the region she once
blessed, lives the courage, the firmness, and the goodness of Nancy Van Alstine, the guardian of the Mohawk Valley.

CHAPTER VI.

PATRIOT WOMEN OF THE REVOLUTION.

DURING the dangers and trials of early colonial
life, the daughters learned from the example of
their mothers the lesson and the power of self-trust;
they learned to endure what their parents endured, to
face the perils which environed the settlement or the
household, and grew up to woman's estate versed in
that knowledge and experience of border-life which
well fitted them to repeat, in wilder and more perilous
scenes, the heroism of their forefathers and fore-
mothers.

The daughters again taught these, and added other
lessons, to their children. The grand-daughters of the
first emigrants seemed to possess—with the traits and
virtues of woman—the wisdom, courage, and strength
of their fathers and brothers. Each succeeding generation seemed to acquire new features of character,
added force, and stronger virtues, and thus woman
became a heroine endowed with manly vigor and

capable of performing deeds of masculine courage and resolution.

The generation of daughters, fourth in descent from the first settlers, lived during the stormy days of the Revolution; and right worthily did they perform their part on that stage of action, and prove by their deeds that they were lineal descendants of the first mothers of the Republic.

If we were to analyze the characters and motives of the women who lived and acted in that great crisis of our history, we should better understand and appreciate, in its nature, height, and breadth, their singular patriotism. Untainted by selfish ambition, undefiled by greed of gain, and purged of the earthy dross that too often alloys the lofty impulses of soldiers and statesmen in the path of fame, hers was a love of country that looked not for gain or glory, imperiled much, and was locked fast in a bitter companionship with anxiety, fear, and grief. Her heroism was not sordid or secular. Dearly did she prize the blessings of peace—household calm, the security of her loved ones, and the comforts and amenities of an unbroken social status. But she cheerfully surrendered them all at the call of her country in its hour of peril. For one hundred and fifty years she had toiled and suffered. She had won the right to repose, but this was not yet to be hers. A new ordeal awaited her which would test her courage and fortitude still more keenly, especially if her lot was cast in the frontier settlements.

It is easy to see that border-life in—

———"the times that tried men's souls "—

was surrounded by double dangers and hardships.
Indeed it is difficult to conceive of a more trying situation than that of woman in the outlying settlements
in the days of the Revolution. Left alone by her
natural protector, who had gone far away to fight the
battles of his country; exposed to attacks from the
red men who lurked in the forest, or from the British
soldiers marching up from the coast; wearied by the
labors of the farm and the household; harassed by
the cares of motherhood; for long years in the midst
of dangers, privations, and trials; with serene patience,
and with dauntless courage, she went on nobly doing
her part in the great work which resulted in the
glorious achievement of American Independence.

The wonder is that the American wives and mothers
of that day did not sink under their burdens. Their
patient endurance of accumulated hardships did not
arise from a slavish servility or from insensibility to
their rights and comforts. They justly appreciated
the situation and nobly encountered the difficulties
which could not be avoided.

Possessing all the affections of the wife, the tenderness of the mother, and the sympathies of the woman,
their tears flowed freely for others' griefs, while they
bore their own with a fortitude that none but a woman
could display. In the absence of the father the entire
education devolved upon the mother, who, in the
midst of the labors and sorrows of her isolated existence, taught them to read, and instructed them in the
principles of Christianity.

The countless roll of these unnamed heroines is
inscribed in the Book of the Most Just. Their record
is on high. But the names and deeds of not a few

are preserved as a bright example to the men and women of to-day.

While the husbands and fathers of Wyoming were on public duty the wives and daughters cheerfully assumed a large portion of the labor which women could perform. They assisted to plant, to make hay, to husk, and to garner the corn. The settlement was mainly dependent on its own resources for powder. To meet the necessary demand, the women boiled together a ley of wood-ashes, to which they added the earth scraped from beneath the floors of their house, and thus manufactured saltpeter, one of the most essential ingredients. Charcoal and sulphur were then mingled with it, and powder was produced "for the public defense."

One of the married sisters of Silas Deane, that eminent Revolutionary patriot, while her husband, Captain Ebenezer Smith, was with the army, was left alone with six small children in a hamlet among the hills of Berkshire, Massachusetts. Finding it difficult to eke out a subsistence from the sterile soil of their farm, and being quick and ingenious with her needle, she turned tailoress and made garments for her little ones, and for all the families in that region. She wrote her husband, telling him to be of good cheer, and not to give himself anxiety on his wife's or his children's account, adding that as long as her fingers could hold a needle, food should be provided for them. "Fight on for your country," she said; "God will give us deliverance."

Each section of the country had its special burdens, trials, and dangers. The populous districts bore the first brunt of the enemy's attack; the thinly settled regions were drained of men, and the women were left in a pitiable condition of weakness and isolation. This was largely the condition of Massachusetts and Connecticut, where nearly every family sent some, if not all, of its men to the war. In the South the patriots were forced to practice continual vigilance in consequence of the divided feeling upon the question of the propriety of separation from the mother-country. New York, New Jersey, and Pennsylvania were battle grounds, and here, perhaps more fully than elsewhere, were experienced war's woes and desolation. But in every State throughout the thirteen colonies, and in every town, hamlet, or household, where there were patriot wives, mothers, or daughters, woman's claims to moral greatness in that crisis were gloriously vindicated.

If we were to search for traits and incidents to illustrate the whole circle of both the stronger and the gentler virtues, we might find them in woman's record during the American Revolution.

In scenes of carnage and death women not seldom displayed a cool courage which made them peers of the bravest soldiers who bore flint-locks at Bunker Hill or Trenton. Of such bravery, the following quartette of heroines will serve as examples.

During the attack on Fort Washington, Mrs. Margaret Corbin, seeing her husband, who was an artillery man, fall, unhesitatingly took his place and heroically performed his duties. Her services were appreciated by the officers of the army, and honorably noticed by Congress. This body passed the following resolution in July, 1779:

Resolved, That Margaret Corbin, wounded and disabled at the battle of Fort Washington while she heroically filled the post of her husband, who was killed by her side, serving a piece of artillery, do receive during her natural life, or continuance of said disability, one half the monthly pay drawn by a soldier in the service of these States; and that she now receive out of public store one suit of clothes, or value thereof in money.

Soon after the commencement of the Revolutionary War, the family of a Dr. Channing, being in England, removed to France, and shortly afterwards sailed for the United States. The vessel, said to be stout and well armed, was attacked on the voyage by a privateer, and a fierce engagement ensued. During its continuance, Mrs. Channing stood on the deck, exhorting the crew not to give up, encouraging them with words of cheer, handing them cartridges and aiding such of them as were disabled by wounds. When at length the colors of the vessel were struck, she seized her husband's pistol and side arms and flung them into the sea, declaring that she would prefer death to the spectacle of their surrender into the hands of the foe.

At the siege of one of the forts of the Mohawk Valley, it is related by the author of the "Border Wars of the American Revolution," that an interesting young woman, whose name yet lives in story among her own mountains, perceiving, as she thought, symptoms of fear in a soldier who had been ordered to fetch water from a well, without the ranks and within range of the enemy's fire, snatched the bucket from his hands and ran to the well herself. Without changing color or giving the slightest evidence of fear, she drew and brought back bucket after bucket to the thirsty soldiers, and providentially escaped without injury.

Four or five miles north of the village of Herkimer, N. Y., stood the block-house of John Christian Shell, whose wife acted a heroic part when attacked by the Tories, in 1781. From two o'clock in the afternoon until twilight, the besieged kept up an almost incessant firing, Mrs. Shell loading the guns for her husband and older sons .to discharge. During the siege, McDonald, the leader of the Tories, attempted to force the door with a crow-bar, and was shot in the leg, seized by Shell, and drawn within doors. Exasperated by this bold feat, the enemy soon attempted to carry the fortress by assault; five of them leaping upon the walls and thrusting their guns through the loop-holes. At that moment the cool courageous woman, Mrs. Shell, seized an axe, smote the barrels, bent and spoiled them. The enemy soon after shouldered their guns, crooked barrels and all, and quickly buried themselves in the dense forest.

Heroism in those days was confined to no section of our country. Moll Pitcher, at Monmouth, battle-stained, avenged her husband by the death-dealing cannon which she loaded and aimed. Cornelia Beekman, at Croton, faced down the armed Tories with the fire of her eye; Angelica Vrooman, at Schoharie, moulded bullets amid the war and carnage of battle, while Mary Hagidorn defended the fort with a pike; Mrs. Fitzhugh, of Maryland, accompanied her blind and decrepit husband when taken prisoner at midnight and carried into the enemy's lines.

Dicey Langston, of South Carolina, also showed a "soul of love and bravery." Living in a frontier settlement, and in the midst of Tories, and being patriotically inquisitive, she often learned by accident, or discovered by strategy, the p tings so common in those days against the Whigs. Such intelligence she was accustomed to communicate to the friends of freedom on the opposite side of the Ennosee river.

Learning one time that a band of loyalists—known in those days as the "Bloody Scouts"—were about to fall upon the "Elder Settlement," a place where a brother of hers and other friends were residing, she resolved to warn them of their danger. To do this she must hazard her own life. Regardless of danger she started off alone, in the darkness of the night; traveled several miles through the woods, over marshes, across creeks, through a country where foot-logs and bridges were then unknown; came to the Tyger, a rapid and deep stream, into which she plunged and waded till the water was up to her neck. She then became bewildered, and zigzagged the channel for some time, finally reaching the opposite shore, for a helping hand was beneath, a kind Providence guided her. She then hastened on, reached the settlement, and her brother and the whole community were saved.

She was returning one day from another settlement of Whigs, in the Spartanburg district, when a company of Tories met her and questioned her in regard to the neighborhood she had just left; but she refused to communicate the desired information. The leader of the band then put a pistol to her breast, and threatened to shoot her if she did not make the wished-for disclosure.

"Shoot me if you dare! I will not tell you!" was her dauntless reply, as she opened a long handkerchief that covered her neck and bosom, thus manifesting a willingness to receive the contents of the pistol, if the officer insisted on disclosure or life.

The dastard, enraged at her defying movement, was in the act of firing, but one of the soldiers threw up the hand holding the weapon, and the uncovered heart of the girl was permitted to beat on.

The brothers of Dicey were no less patriotic than she; and they having, by their active services on the side of freedom, greatly displeased the loyalists, these latter were determined to be revenged. A desperate band accordingly went to the house of their father, and finding the sons absent, were about to wreak vengeance on the old man, whom they hated for the sons' sake. With this intent one of the party drew a pistol; but just as it was aimed at the breast of the aged and infirm old man, Dicey rushed between the two, and though the ruffian bade her get out of the way or receive in her own breast the contents of the pistol, she regarded not his threats, but flung her arms round her father's neck and declared she would receive the ball first, if the weapon must be discharged. Such fearlessness and willingness to offer her own life for the sake of her parent, softened the heart of the "Bloody Scout," and Mr. Langston lived to see his noble daughter perform other heroic deeds.

At one time her brother James, while absent, sent to the house for a gun which he had left in Dicey's care, with orders to deliver it to no. one, except by his direction. On reaching the house one of the party who were directed to call for it, made known their errand. Whereupon she brought and was about to deliver the weapon. At this moment it occurred to her that she had not demanded the countersign agreed on between

9

herself and brother. With the gun still in her hand, she looked the company sternly in the face, and remarking that they wore a suspicious look, called for the countersign. Thereupon one of them, in jest, told her she was too tardy in her requirements; that both the gun and its holder were in their possession. "Do you think so," she boldly asked, as she cocked the disputed weapon and aimed it at the speaker. "If the gun is in your possession," she added, "take charge of it!" Her appearance indicated that she was in earnest, and the countersign was given without further delay.

In these women of the Revolution were blended at once the heroine and the " Ministering Angel." To defend their homes they were men in courage and resolution, and when the battle was over they showed all a woman's tenderness and devotion. Love was the inspiring principle which nerved their arm in the fight, and poured balm into the wounds of those who had fallen. Should we have ever established our Independence but for the countless brave, kind, and self-sacrificing acts of woman?

After the massacre of Fort Griswold, when it was found that several of the prisoners were still alive, the British soldiers piled their mangled bodies in an old cart and started it down the steep and rugged hill, towards the river, in order that they might be there drowned. Stumps and stones however obstructed the passage of the cart, and when the enemy had retreated —for the aroused inhabitants of that region soon compelled them to that course—the friends of the wounded came to their aid, and thus several lives were saved.

One of those heroic women who came the next morning to the aid of the thirty-five wounded men, who lay all night freezing in their own blood, was Mrs. Mary Ledyard, a near relative of the Colonel. "She brought warm chocolate, wine, and other refreshments, and while Dr. Downer, of Preston, was dressing the wounds of the soldiers, she went from one to another, administering her cordials, and breathing gentle words of sympathy and encouragement into their ears. In these labors of kindness she was assisted by another relative of the lamented Colonel Ledyard—Mrs. John Ledyard—who had also brought her household stores to refresh the sufferers, and lavished on them the most soothing personal attentions. The soldiers who recovered from their wounds, were accustomed, to the day of their death, to speak of these ladies in terms of fervent gratitude and praise."

Another "heroine and ministering angel" at the same massacre was Anna Warner, wife of Captain Bailey. She received from the soldiers the affectionate *sobriquet* of "Mother Bailey." Had "Mother Bailey" lived in the palmy days of ancient Roman glory no matron in that mighty empire would have been more highly honored. Hearing the British guns, at the attack on Fort Griswold, she hurried to the scene of carnage, where she found her uncle, one of the brave defenders, mortally wounded. With his dying lips he prayed to see his wife and child—once more; hastening home, she caught and saddled a horse for the feeble mother, and taking the child in her arms ran three miles and held it to receive the kisses and blessing of its dying father. At a later period flannel being needed to use for cartridges, she gave her own undergarment for that purpose. This patriotic surrender showed the noble spirit which always actuated "Mother Bailey" and was an appropriation to her country of which she might justly be proud.

The combination of manly daring and womanly kindness was admirably displayed in the deeds of a maiden, Miss Esther Gaston, and of a married lady, Mrs. Slocum, whose presence upon battlefields gave aid and comfort, in several ways, to the patriot cause.

On the morning of July 30th, 1780, the former, hearing the firing, rode to the scene of conflict in company with her sister-in-law. Meeting three skulkers retreating from the fight, Esther rebuked them sharply, and, seizing the gun from the hands of one of them, exclaimed, " Give us your guns, and we will stand in your places!" The cowards, abashed and filled with shame, thereupon turned about, and, in company with the females, hurried back to face the enemy.

While the battle was raging, Esther and her companion busied themselves in dressing and binding up the wounds of the fallen, and in quenching their thirst, not even forgetting their helpless enemies, whose bodies strewed the ground.

During another battle, which occurred the following week, she converted a church into a hospital, and administered to the wants of the wounded.

Our other heroine, Mrs. Slocum, of Pleasant Green, North Carolina, having a presentiment that her husband was dead or wounded in battle, rose in the night, saddled her horse, and rode to the scene of conflict. We continue the narrative in the words of our heroine.

" The cool night seemed after a gallop of a mile or

two, to bring reflection with it, and I asked myself where I was going, and for what purpose. Again and again I was tempted to turn back; but I was soon ten miles from home, and my mind became stronger every mile I rode that I should find my husband dead or dying —this was as firmly my presentiment and conviction as any fact of my life. When day broke I was some thirty miles from home. I knew the general route our army expected to take, and had followed them without hesitation. About sunrise I came upon a group of women and children, standing and sitting by the road-side, each one of them showing the same anxiety of mind which I felt.

" Stopping a few minutes I enquired if the battle had been fought. They knew nothing, but were assembled on the road-side to catch intelligence. They thought Caswell had taken the right of the Wilmington road, and gone toward the northwest (Cape Fear). Again was I skimming over the ground through a country thinly settled, and very poor and swampy; but neither my own spirit nor my beautiful nag's failed in the least. We followed the well-marked trail of the troops.

" The sun must have been well up, say eight or nine o'clock, when I heard a sound like thunder, which I knew must be a cannon. It was the first time I ever heard a cannon. I stopped still; when presently the cannon thundered again. The battle was then fighting. What a fool! my husband could not be dead last night, and the battle only fighting now! Still, as I am so near, I will go on and see how they come out. So away we went again, faster than ever; and I soon found, by the noise of the guns, that I was near the fight. Again I stopped. I could hear muskets, rifles, and shouting. I spoke to my horse and dashed on in the direction of the firing and the shouts, which were louder than ever.

"The blind path I had been following, brought me into the Wilmington road leading to Moore's creek bridge, a few hundred yards below the bridge. A few yards from the road, under a cluster of trees, were lying perhaps twenty men. They were wounded. I knew the spot; the very tree; and the position of the men I knew as if I had seen it a thousand times. I had seen it all night! I saw *all* at once; but in an instant my whole soul centered in one spot; for there wrapped in a bloody guard cloak, was my husband's body! How I passed the few yards from my saddle to the place I never knew. I remember uncovering his head and seeing a face crusted with gore from a dreadful wound across the temple. I put my hand on the bloody face; 'twas warm; and an *unknown voice* begged for water; a small camp-kettle was lying near, and a stream of water was close by. I brought it; poured some in his mouth, washed his face; and behold—it was not my husband but Frank Cogdell. He soon revived and could speak. I was washing the wound in his head. Said he, 'It is not that; it is the hole in my leg that is killing me.' A puddle of blood was standing on the ground about his feet. I took the knife, and cut away his trousers and stockings, and found the blood came from a shot hole through and through the fleshy part of his leg. I looked about and could see nothing that looked as if it would do for dressing wounds, but some heart-leaves. I gathered a handful and bound them tight to the holes; and the bleeding stopped. I then went to others; I dressed the wounds of many a brave fellow who did good service long after that day! I had not enquired for my husband; but while I was busy Caswell came up. He appeared very much surprised to see me; and was with his hat in hand about to pay some compliment; but I interrupted him by asking—'Where is my husband?'

"'Where he ought to be, madam; in pursuit of the enemy. But pray,' said he, 'how came you here?'

"'O, I thought,' replied I, 'you would need nurses as well as soldiers. See! I have already dressed many of these good fellows; and here is one—and going up to Frank and lifting him up with my arm under his head so that he could drink some more water—'would have died before any of you men could have helped him.'

"Just then I looked up, and my husband, as bloody as a butcher, and as muddy as a ditcher, stood before me.

'Why, Mary!' he exclaimed, 'what are you doing there? Hugging Frank Cogdell, the greatest reprobate in the army?'

'I don't care,' I said. 'Frank is a brave fellow, a good soldier, and a true friend of Congress.'

'True, true! every word of it!' said Caswell. 'You are right, madam,' with the lowest possible bow.

"I would not tell my husband what brought me there. I was so happy; and so were all! It was a glorious victory; I came just at the height of the enjoyment. I knew my husband was surprised, but I could see he was not displeased with me. It was night again before our excitement had at all subsided.

Many prisoners were brought in, and among them some very obnoxious; but the worst of the Tories were not taken prisoners. They were, for the most part, left in the woods and swamps wherever they were overtaken. I begged for some of the poor prisoners, and Caswell told me none should be hurt but such as had been guilty of murder and house-burning.

"In the middle of the night I again mounted my horse and started for home. Caswell and my husband wanted me to stay till next morning, and they would send a party with me; but no! I wanted to see my child, and I told them they could send no party who could keep up with me. What a happy ride I had back! and with what joy did I embrace my child as he ran to meet me!"

The winter at Valley Forge was the darkest season in the Revolutionary struggle. The American army were sheltered by miserable huts, through which the rain and sleet found their way upon the wretched cots where the patriots slept. By day the half-famished soldiers in tattered regimentals wandered through their camp, and the snow showed the bloody tracks of their shoeless feet. Mutinous mutterings disturbed the sleep of Washington, and one dark, cold day, the soldiers at dusk were on the point of open revolt. Nature could endure no more, and not from want of patriotism, but from want of food and clothes, the patriotic cause seemed likely to fail. Pinched with cold and wasted with hunger, the soldiers pined beside their dying camp-fires. Suddenly a shout was heard from the sentinels who paced the outer lines, and at the same time a cavalcade came slowly through the snow up the valley. Ten women in carts, each cart

FOOD AND CLOTHING SUPPLIED TO THE REVOLUTIONARY ARMY BY PATRIOTIC WOMEN.   Page 136.

drawn by ten pairs of oxen, and bearing tons of meal and other supplies, passed through the lines amid cheers that rent the air. Those devoted women had preserved the army, and Independence from that day was assured.

Fortitude and patience were exemplified in a thousand homes from which members of the family had gone to battle for Independence. Straitened for means wherewith to keep their strong souls in their feeble bodies, worn with toil, tortured with anxiety for the safety of the soldier-father or son, or husband or brother, and fighting the conflict of life alone, woman· proved in that great ordeal her claim to those virtues which are by common consent assigned to her as her peculiar characteristics.

We may well suppose, too, that ready wit and address had ample scope for their exercise in those perilous times. And who but woman could best display those qualities?

While Ann Elliott, styled by her British admirers, "the beautiful rebel," was affianced to Col. Lewis Morris, of New York, the house where he was visiting her was suddenly surrounded by a detachment of "Black Dragoons." They were in pursuit of the Colonel, and it was impossible for him to escape by flight. What to do he knew not, but, quick as thought, she ran to the window, opened it, and, fearlessly putting her head out, in a composed manner demanded what was wanted. The reply was, "We want the rebel." "Then go," said she, "and look for him in the American army;" adding, "how dare you disturb a family under the protection of both armies?" She was so cool, self-possessed, firm, and resolute, as to triumph over the dragoons, who left without entering the house.

While the conflict was at its height in South Carolina, Captain Richardson, of Sumter district, was obliged to conceal himself for a while in the thickets of the Santee swamp. One day he ventured to visit his family—a perilous movement, for the British had offered a reward for his apprehension, and patrolling parties were almost constantly in search of him. Before his visit was ended a small party of soldiers presented themselves in front of the house. Just as they were entering, with a great deal of composure and presence of mind, Mrs. Richardson appeared at the door, and found so much to do there at the moment, as to make it inconvenient to leave room for the uninvited guests to enter. She was so calm, and appeared so unconcerned, that they did not mistrust the cause of her wonderful diligence, till her husband had rushed out of the back door, and safely reached the neighboring swamp.

The bearing of important dispatches through an enemy's country is an enterprise that always requires both courage and address. Such a feat was performed by Miss Geiger, under circumstances of peculiar difficulty.

At the time General Greene retreated before Lord Rawdon from Ninety-Six, when he passed Broad river, he was desirous to send an order to General Sumter, who was on the Wateree, to join him, that they might attack Rawdon, who had divided his force. But the General could find no man in that part of the state who was bold enough to undertake so dangerous mission. The country to be passed through for many miles was full of blood-thirsty Tories, who, on every occasion that offered, imbrued their hands in the blood of the Whigs. At length Emily Geiger presented herself to General Greene, and proposed to act as his messenger: and the general, both surprised and delighted, closed with her proposal. He accordingly wrote a letter and delivered it, and at the same time communicated the contents of it verbally, to be told to Sumter in case of accidents.

She pursued her journey on horseback, and on the second day was intercepted by Lord Rawdon's scouts. Coming from the direction of Greene's army and not being able to tell an untruth without blushing, Emily was suspected and confined to a room; and the officer sent for an old Tory matron to search for papers upon her person. Emily was not wanting in expedients, and as soon as the door was closed and the bustle a little subsided, she *ate up the letter*, piece by piece. After a while the matron arrived, and upon searching carefully, nothing was found of a suspicious nature about the prisoner, and she would disclose nothing. Suspicion being then allayed, the officer commanding the scouts suffered Emily to depart. She then took a route somewhat circuitous to avoid further detentions and soon after struck into the road leading to Sumter's camp, where she arrived in safety. Emily told her adventure, and delivered Greene's verbal message to Sumter, who in consequence, soon after joined the main army at Orangeburgh.

The salvation of the army was due more than once to the watchfulness and tact of woman.

When the British army held possession of Philadelphia, a superior officer supposed to have been the Adjutant General, selected a back chamber in the house of Mrs. Lydia Darrah, for private conference. Suspecting that some important movement was on foot, she took off her shoes, and putting her ear to the key-hole of the door, overheard an order read for all the British troops to march out, late in the evening of the fourth, and attack General Washington's army, then encamped at White Marsh. On hearing this, she returned to her chamber and laid herself down. Soon after, the officers knocked at her door, but she rose only at the third summons, having feigned to be asleep. Her mind was so much agitated that, from this moment, she could neither eat nor sleep, supposing it to be in her power to save the lives of thousands of her countrymen, but not knowing how she was to carry the necessary information to General Washington, nor daring to confide it even to her husband. The time left was short, and she quickly determined to make her way as soon as possible, to the American outposts. She informed her family, that, as they were in want of flour, she would go to Frankfort for some; her husband insisted that she should take with her the servant maid; but, to his surprise, she positively refused. Gaining access to General Howe, she solicited what he readily granted—a pass through the British troops on the lines. Leaving her bag at the mill, she hastened towards the American lines, and encountered on her way an American, Lieutenant Colonel Craig, of the light horse, who, with some of his men, was on the lookout for information. He knew her, and inquired whither she was going. She answered, in quest of her son, an officer in the American army; and prayed the Colonel to alight and walk with her. He did so, ordering his troops to keep in sight. To him she disclosed her momentous secret, after having obtained from him the most solemn promise never to betray her individually, since her life might be at stake. He conducted her to a house near at hand, directed a female in it to give her something to eat, and hastened to head-quarters, where he made General Washington acquainted with what he had heard. Washington made, of course, all preparation for baffling the meditated surprise, and the contemplated expedition was a failure.

Mrs. Murray of New York, the mother of Lindley Murray, the grammarian, by her ceremonious hospitality detained Lord Howe and his officers, while the British forces were in pursuit of General Putnam, and thus prevented the capture of the American army. In fine, not merely the lives of many individuals, but the safety of the whole patriot army, and even the cause of independence was more than once due to feminine address and strategy.

Patriotic generosity and devotion were displayed without stint, and women were ready to submit to any sacrifice in behalf of their country.

These qualities are well illustrated by the three following instances.

Mrs. William Smith, when informed that in order to dislodge the enemy then in possession of Fort St. George, Long Island, it would be necessary to burn or batter down her dwelling-house, promptly told Major Tallmadge to proceed without hesitation in the work of destruction, if the good of the country demanded the sacrifice.

While General Greene was retreating, disheartened

and penniless, from the enemy, after the disastrous defeat at Camden, he was met at Catawba ford by Mrs. Elizabeth Steele, who, in her generous ardor in the cause of freedom, drew him aside, and, taking two bags of specie from under her apron, presented them to him, saying, " Take these, for you will want them, and I can do without them."

While Fort Motte, on the Congaree River, was in the hands of the British, in order to effect its surrender, it became necessary to burn a large mansion standing near the center of the trench. The house was the property of Mrs. Motte. Lieut. Colonel Lee communicated to her the contemplated work of destruction with painful reluctance, but her smiles, half anticipating his proposal, showed at once that she was willing to sacrifice her property if she could thereby aid in the least degree towards the expulsion of the enemy and the salvation of the land.

Pennsylvania had the honor of being the native State of Mrs. McCalla, whose affectionate and devoted efforts to liberate her invalid husband, languishing in a British dungeon, have justly given her a high rank among the patriot women of the Revolution.

Weeks elapsed after the capture of Mr. McCalla, before she was able, with the most assiduous inquiries, to ascertain the place of his confinement. In the midst of her torturing anxiety and suspense her children fell sick of small-pox. She nursed them alone and unaided, and as soon as they were out of danger, resumed her search for her husband.

Mounting her horse, she succeeded in forcing her way to the head-quarters of Lord Rawdon, at Camden, and obtained reluctant permission to visit her husband for ten minutes only in his wretched prison-pen. Though almost overcome by the interview, she hastened home, having altogether ridden through the wilderness one hundred miles in twenty-four hours.

She proceeded immediately to prepare clothing and provisions for her husband and the other prisoners. Her preparations having been completed, she set out on her return to Camden, in company with one of her neighbors, Mrs. Mary Nixon. Each of the brave women drove before her a pack-horse, laden with clothes and provisions for the prisoners. These errands of mercy were repeated every month, often in company with other women who were engaged in similar missions, and sometimes alone.

Meanwhile she did not relax her efforts to effect the release of her husband. After many months she succeeded in procuring an order for the discharge of her husband with ten other prisoners, whose handcuffs and ankle chains were knocked off, and who left the prison in company with their heroic liberator.

Examples are not wanting, in our Revolutionary annals, of a stern and lofty spirit of self-sacrifice in behalf of country, that will vie with that displayed by the first Brutus.

We are told by the orator of the Society of the Cincinnati that when the British officers presented to Mrs. Rebecca Edwards the mandate which arrested her sons as "objects of retaliation, less sensitive of private affection than attached to her honor and the interest of her country, she stifled the tender feelings of the mother and heroically bade them despise the threats of their enemies, and steadfastly persist to support the glorious cause in which they had engaged—

that if the threatened sacrifice should follow they would carry a parent's blessing, and the good opinion of every virtuous citizen with them, to the grave; but if from the frailty of human nature — of the possibility of which she would not suffer an idea to enter her mind—they were disposed to temporize and exchange this liberty for safety, they must forget her as a mother, nor subject her to the misery of ever beholding them again."

As among the early Puritan settlers, so among the women of the Revolution, nothing was more remarkable than their belief in the efficacy of prayer.

In the solitude of their homes, in the cool and silence of the forest, and in the presence of the foe, Christian women knelt down and prayed for peace, for victory, for rescue from danger, and for deliverance from the enemies which beset them. Can we doubt that the prayers of these noble patriot women were answered?

Early in the Revolutionary War, the historian of the border relates that "the inhabitants of the frontier of Burke County, North Carolina, being apprehensive of an attack by the Indians, it was determined to seek protection in a fort in a more densely populated neighborhood, in an interior settlement. A party of soldiers was sent to protect them on their retreat. The families assembled; the line of march was taken towards their place of destination, and they proceeded some miles unmolested—the soldiers forming a hollow square with the refugee families in the center. The Indians had watched these movements, and had laid a plan for the destruction of the migrating party. The road to be traveled lay through a dense forest in the fork of a river, where the Indians concealed themselves and waited till the travelers were in the desired spot.

Suddenly the war-whoop sounded in front and on either side; a large body of painted warriors rushed in, filling the gap by which the whites had entered, and an appalling crash of fire-arms followed. The soldiers, however, were prepared. Such as chanced to be near the trees darted behind them, and began to ply the deadly rifle; the others prostrated themselves upon the earth, among the tall grass, and crawled to trees. The families screened themselves as best they could. The onset was long and fiercely urged; ever and anon, amid the din and smoke, the braves would rush out, tomahawk in hand, towards the center; but they were repulsed by the cool intrepidity of the backwoods riflemen. Still they fought on, determined on the destruction of the destined victims who offered such desperate resistance. All at once an appalling sound greeted the ears of the women and children in the center; it was a cry from their defenders—a cry for powder! "Our powder is giving out!" they exclaimed. "Have you any? Bring us some, or we can fight no longer."

A woman of the party had a good supply. She spread her apron on the ground, poured her powder into it, and going round from soldier to soldier, as they stood behind the trees, bade each who needed powder put down his hat, and poured a quantity upon it. Thus she went round the line of defense till her whole stock, and all she could obtain from others, was distributed. At last the savages gave way, and, pressed by their foes, were driven off the ground. The victorious whites returned to those for whose safety they

10

had ventured into the wilderness. Inquiries were made as to who had been killed, and one, running up, cried, " Where is the woman that gave us the powder? I want to see her!" "Yes! yes!—let us see her!" responded another and another; "without her we should have been all lost!" The soldiers ran about among the women and children, looking for her and making inquiries. Others came in from the pursuit, one of whom, observing the commotion, asked the cause, and was told.

" You are looking in the wrong place," he replied.

"Is she killed? Ah, we were afraid of that!' exclaimed many voices.

"Not when I saw her," answered the soldier. "When the Indians ran off, she was *on her knees in prayer* at the root of yonder tree, and there I left her."

There was a simultaneous rush to the tree—and there, to their great joy, they found the woman safe and still on her knees in prayer. Thinking not of herself, she received their applause without manifesting any other feeling than gratitude to Heaven for their great deliverance.

An eminent divine whose childhood was passed upon our New England frontier, during the period of the Revolution, narrated to the writer many years since, the story of his mother's life while her husband was absent in the patriot army. Their small farm was on the sterile hill-side, and with the utmost pains, barely yielded sufficient for the wants of the lone wife and her three little ones. There was no house within five miles, and the whole region around was stripped of its male inhabitants, such was the patriotic ardor of the people.

All the labors in providing for the household fell upon the mother. She planted and hoed the corn, milked the cow and tended the farm, at the same time not neglecting the inside duties of the household, feeding and clothing the children, nursing them when sick and instructing them in the rudiments of education.

"I call to mind, though after the lapse of eighty years," said the venerable man, "the image of my mother as distinctly as of yesterday, and she moves before me as she did in my childhood's home among those bleak hills—cheerful and serene through all, though even with my young eyes I could see that a brooding sorrow rested upon her spirit. I remember the day when my father kissed my brothers and me, and told us to be good boys, and help mother while he was gone: I remember too, that look upon my mother's face as she watched him go down the road with his musket and knapsack.

"When evening came, that day, and she had placed us in our little beds, I saw her kneeling and praying in a low tone, long and fervently, and heard her after she had pleaded that victory might crown our arms, intercede at the throne of grace for her absent husband and the father of her children.

"Then she rose and kissed us good-night, and as she bent above us I shall never forget till my latest hour the angelic expression upon her face. Sorrow, love, resignation, and holy trust were blended and beamed forth in that look which seemed to transfigure her countenance and her whole bearing.

"During all those trying years while she was so patiently toiling to feed and clothe us, and bearing the burdens and privations of her lonely lot, never did she omit the morning and evening prayer for her country and for the father of her children.

" One day we saw her holding an open letter in her hand and looking pale and as if she were about to faint. We gathered about her knees and gazed with wondering eyes, silently into her sad and care-worn face, for even then we had been schooled to recognize and respect the sorrows of a mother. Two weeks before that time, a battle had been fought in which father had been severely wounded. The slow mail of those days had only just brought this sad intelligence. As we stood beside her she bent and clasped us to her heart, striving to hide the great tears that coursed down her wasted cheeks.

" We begged her not to cry and tried to comfort her with our infantile caresses. At length we saw her close her eyes and utter a low prayer. Ere her lips had ceased to intercede with the Father of mercies, a knock was heard at the door and one of the neighboring settlers entered. He had just returned from the army and had come several miles on foot from his home, expressly to tell us that father was rapidly recovering from his wounds. It seemed as if he were a messenger sent from heaven in direct answer to the silent prayers of a mother, and all was joy and brightness in the house."

The patriot father returned to his family at the close of the war with the rank of Captain, which he had nobly won by his bravery in the battle's van. The sons grew up and became useful and honored citizens of a Republic which their father had helped to make free; and ever during their lives they fondly cherished the memory of the mother who had taught them so many examples of brave self-denial and pious devotion.

And still as we scan the pages of Revolutionary history, or revive the oral evidence of family tradition, the names and deeds of these brave and good women fill the eye and multiply in the memory. Through the fires, the frosts, the rains, the suns of one hundred years, they come back to us *now*, in the midst of our great national jubilee, vivid as with the life of yesterday. That era, which they helped to make glorious, is " with the years that are beyond the flood."

" Another race shall be, and other palms are won ; "

but never, while our nation or our language endures, shall the memory of those names and deeds pass away. In every succeeding year that registers the history of the Republic which they contributed to build, brighter and brighter shall grow the record of the Patriot Women of the Revolution.

CHAPTER VII.

MOVING WEST—PERILS OF THE JOURNEY.

IN regarding or in enjoying an end already accomplished by others, we are too apt to pass by the means through which that end was reached. America of to-day represents a grand result. We see that our land is great, rich, and powerful; we see that the flag waves from ocean to ocean, over a people furnished with all the appliances of civilization, and happy in their enjoyment; we are conscious that all this has come from the toils and the sufferings of many men and of many women who have lived and loved before us, and passed away, leaving behind them their country growing greater and richer, happier and more powerful, for what they have borne and done. But our views of the means by which that mighty end was reached are apt to be altogether too vague and general. While we are enjoying what others have worked to attain, let us not selfishly and forgetfully pass by the toils, the struggles, the firm endurance of those who went before us and accomplished this vast aggregate of results.

Each stage in the process by which these results were wrought out, had its peculiar trials, its special service. Looking back to that far-off past, and in the light of our own knowledge and conceptions, we find it almost impossible to decide which stage was encompassed with the deadliest dangers, the severest labors, the keenest sorrows, the largest list of discomforts. But certainly to woman, the breaking up of her eastern home, and the removal to the far west, was not the least burdensome and trying.

No characteristic of woman is more remarkable than the strength of her local associations and attachments. In making the home she learns to love it, and this feeling seems to be often strongest when the surroundings are the bleakest, the rudest, and the most comfortless. The Highlander and the Switzer pine amid the luxuriant scenes of tropical life, when their thoughts revert to the smoky shieling or to the rock-encompassed *chalet* of their far-off mountains. Such, too, doubtless, was the clinging fondness with which the women regarded their rude cabins on the frontier of the Atlantic States. They had toiled and fought to make these rude abodes the homes for those dearest to them; here children, the first-born of the Republic, had been nurtured; here, too, were the graves of the first fathers and mothers of America. Humble and comfortless as those dwelling-places would have seemed to the men and women of to-day, they were dear to the wives and mothers of colonial times.

Comprehending, as we may, this feeling, and knowing the peculiar difficulties of long journeys in those days, into a wild and hostile country, we can understand why the westward march of emigration and settlement was so slow during the first one hundred and fifty or sixty years of our history. New England had, it is true, been largely subjugated and reclaimed; a considerable body of emigrants, wedge-like, were driving slowly up through the Mohawk Valley towards Niagara; a weak, thin line, was straggling with diffi-

culty across the Alleghanies in Pennsylvania, towards
the Ohio, and a more compact and confident battalion
in Virginia, was pushing into Kentucky. But how
scattered and feeble that picket-line compared to the
army which was soon to follow it.

For a season, and while the British were trying to
force their yoke on the reluctant colonists, the westward movement had a check. The danger was in the
rear. His old home in the east was threatened, and
the pioneer turned about and faced the rising sun,
until the danger was past and he could pursue his
journey.

The close of the Revolutionary struggle gave a new
impulse to the westward march of the American people, which had been arrested for the time being by
the War of Independence.

The patriot soldiers found themselves, upon the
advent of peace, impoverished in fortune; but with
high hopes and stout hearts they immediately set
about repairing the ravages of the long war. Nurtured in the rugged school of danger and hardship,
they had ceased to regard the West with dread. Curiosity, blended with the hope of bettering their condition, turned their faces to that " fresh, unbounded,
magnificent wilderness." Accustomed to camp life
and scenes of exciting interest, the humdrum days at
the old homestead became distasteful. The West was
the hunter's paradise. The soil held beneath it the
potency of harvests of extraordinary richness, and the
soldier who had faced the disciplined battalions of
Great Britain recked little of the prowling red man.

During the Revolution, the women, left alone by
their husbands and fathers, who were with the army,

were more than ever thrown on their own resources. They tilled the farm, reared their swarthy and nimble broods of children, and sent the boys in blue and buff all they could spare from their slender store. During all this trying period they were fitting themselves for that new life in the western wilds which had been marked out for them by the hand of an overruling Providence.

And yet, hard and lonely as the lives of these devoted women must have been in their eastern homes, and bright as their imaginations may have pictured the richness of the West, it must have given them many a pang when the husband and father told them that the whole family must be removed at once from their beloved homestead, which they or their fathers had redeemed from the wilderness after so many years of toil. We may imagine the resolution that was required to break up the old attachments which bind women to their homes and firesides.

It must have required a heroic courage to do this for the purpose of seeking a new home, not only among strangers, but among wild beasts and savages. But the fathers and mothers a hundred years ago possessed a spirit which rose above the perils of their times. They went forward, unhesitatingly, in their long and toilsome journeys westward, driving their slow-footed oxen and lumbering-wagons hundreds of miles, over ground where no road was; through woods infested with bears and wolves, panthers and warlike tribes of Indians; settling in the midst of those dangerous enemies, and conquering them all.

The army of pioneers, like the skirmishers who had preceded them, moved forward in three columns; the northernmost passed through New York State; the middle column moved westward through Pennsylvania; the southernmost marched through Virginia. Within ten years after the treaty of Versailles, the three columns had met in Ohio and Kentucky, and spreading out over that beautiful region, were fighting with nature and savage men to subjugate both and bring them within the bounds of civilization. No more sublime spectacle has ever greeted the eye of the historian than the march of that army. Twenty or thirty thousand men and women, bearing, like the Israelites of old, their ark across the desert and waste places— that ark which bore the blessings of civilization and religion within its holy shrine! Aged matrons, nursing mothers, prattling infants, hoary patriarchs, and strong veterans fresh from the fields of their country's glory, marching to form a mighty empire in the wilderness!

In this present age of rapid and easy transition from place to place, it is difficult to form a just conception of the tediousness, hardships, and duration of those early emigrations to the West. The difference in conveyance is that between a train of cars drawn by a forty-ton locomotive and a two horse wagon, without springs, and of the most lumbering and primitive construction. This latter was the best conveyance that the emigrant could command. A few were so fortunately situated on the banks of rivers that they could float down with the current in flat-boats, while their cattle were being driven along the shore; or, if it was necessary to ascend toward the head-waters of a river, they could work their way up-stream with setting-poles. But most of the emigrants traveled with teams. Some of those who went part of the way in boats had to begin or end their journey in wagons. The vehicles which they provided on such occasions for land carriage were curiosities of wheel-craft—I speak of the Jersey wagons.

The old-fashioned Jersey wagon has, years ago, given place to more showy and flexible vehicles; but long before such were invented the Jersey wagon was an established institution, and was handed down, with the family name, from father to son. It was the great original of the modern emigrant wagon of the West; but as I have elsewhere pictured its appearance upon the arrival of a band of pioneers at their final destination, it is unnecessary to enter here upon any further description.

The spring of the year was the season usually selected for moving, and during many weeks previous to the appointed time, the emigrants had been actively providing against the accidents and discomforts of the road. When all was ready, the wagon was loaded, the oxen yoked and hooked to the neap; the women and children took their places on the summit of the huge load, the baby in its mother's lap, the youngest boy at his grandmother's feet, and off they started. The largest boy walked beside and drove the team, the other boys drove the cows, the men trudged behind or ahead, and the whole cavalcade passed out of the great gate, the grandmother peering through her spectacles, and the mother smiling through her tears and looking back more than once at the home which she had made but was now to leave for ever.

In this manner the earlier emigrants went forward, driving their heavily laden wagon by day and sleeping at night by the camp. After they had passed the region of roads and bridges they had to literally hew their way; cutting down bushes, prying their wagon out of bog-holes, building bridges or poling themselves across streams on rafts. But, in defiance of every obstacle, they pressed forward.

Neither rivers nor mountains stayed the course of the emigrant. Guiding his course by the sun, and ever facing the West, he went slowly on. When that luminary set, his parting rays lit the faces of the pioneer family, and when it rose it threw their long shadows before them on the soft, spongy turf of the forest glades. Sweating through the undergrowth; climbing over fallen trees; sinking knee-deep in marshes; at noon they halted to take a rest in the shade of the primeval forest, beside a brook, and there eat their mid-day meal of fried pork and corn cakes, which the women prepared; then on again, till the shadows stretched far back toward their old homes.

Sometimes a storm burst upon them, and the women and children huddled beneath the cart as the thunderbolts fell, shivering the huge trunks of the forest monarchs; and the lightning crimsoned the faces of the forlorn party with its glare. Then the heavens cleared; the sun came out; and the ox-cart went rumbling and creaking onward. No doubt the first days of that weary tramp had in them something of pleasurable excitement; the breezes of spring fanned the brows of the wayfarers, and told of the health and freedom of woodland life; the magnificence of the forest, the summits of the mountains, tinged with blue, the sparkling waters of lake and stream, must have given joy to even the most stolid of these households. But emotions of this description soon became strangers to their souls.

But the emigrants ere long found that the wilderness had lost the charms of novelty. Sights and sounds that were at first pleasing, and had lessened the sense of discomfort, soon ceased to attract attention. Their minds, solely occupied with obstacles, inconveniences, and obstructions, at every step of the way, became sullen, or, at least, indifferent.

To the toils and discomforts incident to their journey were often added casualties and great personal risks. An unlucky step might wrench an ankle; the axe might glance from a twig and split a foot open; and a broken leg, or a severed artery, is a frightful thing where no surgeon can be had. Exposure to all the changes of the weather—sleeping upon the damp ground, frequently brought on fevers; and sickness, at all times a great calamity, was infinitely more so to the pioneer. It must have been appalling in the woods. Many a mother has carried her wailing, languishing child in her arms, to lessen the jolting of the wagon, without being able to render it the necessary assistance. Many a family has paused on the way to gather a leafy couch for a dying brother or sister. Many a parent has laid in the grave, in the lonely wilderness, the child they should meet no more till the morning of the resurrection. Many a heart at the West has yearned at the thought of the treasured one resting beneath the spreading tree. After-comers have stopped over the little mound, and pondered upon the rude memorial carved in the bark above it; and those who had sustained a similar loss have wrung their hands and wept over it, for their own wounds were opened afresh.

Among the chapters of accident and casualty which make up the respective diaries of the families who left their eastern homes after the Revolution and joined the ranks of the Western immigrants there is none more interesting than that of Mrs. Jameson. She was the child of wealthy parents, and had been reared in luxury in the city of New York. Soon after peace was declared she was married to Edward Jameson, a brave soldier in the war, who had nothing but his stout arms and intrepid heart to battle with the difficulties of life. Her father, dying soon after, his estate was discovered to have been greatly lessened by the depreciation in value which the war had produced. Gathering together the remains of what was once a large fortune, the couple purchased the usual outfit of the emigrants of that period and set out to seek their fortunes in the West.

All went well with them until they reached the Alleghany River, which they undertook to cross on a raft. It was the month of May; the river had been swollen by rains, and when they reached the middle of the stream, the part of the raft on which Mr. Jameson sat became detached, the logs separated, and he sank to rise no more. The other section of the raft, containing Mrs. Jameson, her babe of eight months, and a chest of clothing and household gear, floated down-stream at the mercy of the rapid current.

Bracing herself against the shock, Mrs. Jameson managed to paddle to the side of the river from which she had just before started. She was landed nearly a

PERILOUS CROSSING OF THE ALLEGHANY RIVER.

mile below the point where had been left the cattle, and also the ox-cart in which their journey had been hitherto performed, and which her husband expected to carry over the river on the raft, returning for them as soon as his wife and babe had been safely landed on the western bank. The desolate mother succeeded in mooring the remains of the raft to the shore; then clasping her babe to her bosom, followed the bank of the river till she reached the oxen and cart, which she drove down to the place where she landed, and by great exertions succeeded in hauling the chest upon the bank. Her strength was now exhausted, and, lying down in the bottom of the cart, she gave way to grief and despair.

Her situation may be easily imagined : alone in the forest, thirty miles from the nearest settlement, her husband torn from her in a moment, and her babe smiling as though he would console his mother for her terrible loss. In her sad condition self-preservation would have been too feeble a motive to impel her to make any further effort to save herself; but maternal love—the strongest instinct in a woman's heart— buoyed her up and stimulated her to unwonted exertions.

The spot where she found herself was a dense forest, stretching back to a rocky ledge on the east, and terminated on the north by an alluvial meadow nearly bare of trees. Along the banks of the river was a thick line of high bushes and saplings, which served as a screen against the observations of savages passing up and down the river in their canoes. The woods were just bursting into leaf; the spring-flowers filled the air with odor, and chequered the green foliage

and grass; the whole scene was full of vernal freshness, life, and beauty.   The track which the Jamesons
had followed was about midway between the northern
and southern routes generally pursued by emigrants,
and it was quite unlikely that others would cross the
river at that point.   The dense jungle that skirted the
river bank was an impediment in the way of reaching
the settlements lower down, and there was danger of
being lost in the woods if the unfortunate woman
should start alone.

"On this spot," she said, "I must remain till some
one comes to my help."

The first two years of her married life had been
spent on a farm in Westchester County, New York,
where she had acquired some knowledge of farming
and woodcraft, by assisting her husband in his labors,
or by accompanying him while hunting and fishing.
She was strong and healthy; and quite unlike her
delicate sisters of modern days, her lithe frame was
hardened by exercise in the open air, and her face
was tinged by the kisses of the sun.

Slowly recovering from the terrible anguish of her
loss, she cast about for shelter and sustenance.   The
woods were swarming with game, both large and
small, from the deer to the rabbit, and from the wild
turkey to the quail.   The brooks were alive with trout.
The meadow was well suited for Indian corn, wheat,
rye, or potatoes.   The forest was full of trees of every
description.   To utilize all these raw materials was
her study.

A rude hut, built of boughs interlaced, and covered
thickly with leaves and dry swamp grass, was her first
work.   This was her kitchen.   The cart, which was

covered with canvas, was her sleeping-room. A shot-gun, which she had learned the use of, enabled her to keep herself supplied with game. She examined her store of provisions, consisting of pork, flour, and Indian meal, and made an estimate that they would last eight months, with prudent use. The oxen she tethered at first, but afterwards tied the horns to one of their fore feet, and let them roam. The two cows having calved soon after, she kept them near at hand by making a pen for the calves, who by their bleating called their mothers from the pastures on the banks of the river. In the meadow she planted half an acre of corn and potatoes, which soon promised an amazing crop.

Thus two months passed away. In her solitary and sad condition she was cheered by the daily hope that white settlers would cross her track or see her as they passed up and down the river. She often thought of trying to reach a settlement, but dreaded the dangers and difficulties of the way. Like the doe which hides her fawn in the secret covert, this young mother deemed herself and her babe safer in this solitude than in trying unknown perils, even with the chance of falling in with friends. She therefore contented herself with her lot, and when the toils of the day were over, she would sit on the bank and watch for voyagers on the river. Once she heard voices in the night on the river, and going to the bank she strained her eyes to gaze through the darkness and catch sight of the voyagers; she dared not hail them for fear they might be Indians, and soon the voices grew fainter in the distance, and she heard them no more. Again, while sitting in a clump of bushes on the bank

11

one day, she saw with horror six canoes with Indians, apparently directing their course to the spot where she sat. They were hideously streaked with war-paint, and came so near that she could see the scalping knives in their girdles. Turning their course as they approached the eastern shore they silently paddled down stream, scanning the banks sharply as they floated past. Fortunately they saw nothing to attract their attention; the cart and hut being concealed by the dense bushes, and there being no fire burning.

Fearing molestation from the Indians, she now moved her camp a hundred rods back, near a rocky ledge, from the base of which flowed a spring of pure water. Here, by rolling stones in a circle, she made an enclosure for her cattle at night, and within in it built a log cabin of rather frail construction; another two weeks was consumed in these labors, and it was now the middle of August.

At night she was at first much alarmed by the howling of wolves, who came sniffing round the cart where she slept. Once a large grey wolf put its paws upon the cart and poked its nose under the canvas covering, but a smart blow on the snout drove it yelping away. None of the cattle were attacked, owing to the bold front showed to these midnight intruders. The wolf is one of the most cowardly of wild beasts, and will rarely attack a human being, or even an ox, unless pressed by hunger, and in the winter. Often she caught glimpses of huge black bears in the swamps, while she was in pursuit of wild turkeys or other game; but these creatures never attacked her, and she gave them a wide berth.

One hot day in August she was gathering berries

on the rocky ledge beside which her house was situated, when seeing a clump of bushes heavily loaded with the finest blackberries, she laid her babe upon the ground, and climbing up, soon filled her basket with the luscious fruit. As she descended she saw her babe sitting upright and gazing with fixed eyeballs at some object near by; though what it was she could not clearly make out, on account of an intervening shrub. Hastening down, a sight met her eyes that froze her blood. An enormous rattlesnake was coiled within three feet of her child, and with its head erect and its forked tongue vibrating, its burning eyes were fixed upon those of the child, which sat motionless as a statue, apparently fascinated by the deadly gaze of the serpent.

Seizing a stick of dry wood she dealt the reptile a blow, but the stick being decayed and brittle, inflicted little injury on the serpent, and only caused it to turn itself towards Mrs. Jameson, and fix its keen and beautiful, but malignant eyes, steadily upon her. The witchery of the serpent's eyes so irresistibly rooted her to the ground, that for a moment she did not wish to remove from her formidable opponent.

The huge reptile gradually and slowly uncoiled its body; all the while steadily keeping its eye fixed on its intended victim. Mrs. Jameson could only cry, being unable to move, "Oh God! preserve me! save me, heavenly Father!" The child, after the snake's charm was broken, crept to her mother and buried its little head in her lap.

We continue the story in Mrs. Jameson's own words:—

" The snake now began to writhe its body down a

fissure in the rock, keeping its head elevated more than a foot from the ground. Its rattle made very little noise. It every moment darted out its forked tongue, its eyes became reddish and inflamed, and it moved rather quicker than at first. It was now within two yards of me. By some means I had dissipated the charm, and, roused by a sense of my awful danger, determined to stand on the defensive. To run away from it, I knew would be impracticable, as the snake would instantly dart its whole body after me. I therefore resolutely stood up, and put a strong glove on my right hand, which I happened to have with me. I stretched out my arm; the snake approached slowly and cautiously towards me, darting out its tongue still more frequently. I could now only recommend myself fervently to the protection of Heaven. The snake, when about a yard distant, made a violent spring. I quickly caught it in my right hand, directly under its head; it lashed its body on the ground, at the same time rattling loudly. I watched an opportunity, and suddenly holding the animal's head, while for a moment it drew in its forked tongue, with my left hand I, by a violent contraction of all the muscles in my hand, contrived to close up effectually its jaws!

"Much was now done, but much more was to be done. I had avoided much danger, but I was still in very perilous circumstances. If I moved my right hand from its neck for a moment, the snake, by avoiding suffocation, could easily muster sufficient power to force its head out of my hand; and if I withdrew my hand from its jaws, I should be fatally in the power of its most dreaded fangs. I retained, therefore, my hold with both my hands; I drew its body between my

feet, in order to aid the compression and hasten suffocation. Suddenly, the snake, which had remained
quiescent for a few moments, brought up its tail, hit
me violently on the head, and then darted its body
several times very tightly around my waist. Now
was the very acme of my danger. Thinking, therefore, that I had sufficient power over its body, I
removed my right hand from its neck, and in an
instant drew my hunting-knife. The snake, writhing
furiously again, darted at me; but, striking its body
with the edge of the knife, I made a deep cut, and
before it could recover its coil, I caught it again by
the neck; bending its head on my knee, and again
recommending myself fervently to Heaven, I cut its
head from its body, throwing the head to a great
distance. The blood spouted violently in my face;
the snake compressed its body still tighter, and I
thought I should be suffocated on the spot, and laid
myself down. The snake again rattled its tail and
lashed my feet with it. Gradually, however, the
creature relaxed its hold, its coils fell slack around
me, and untwisting it and throwing it from me as far
as I was able, I sank down and swooned upon the
bank.

"When consciousness returned, the scene appeared
like a terrible dream, till I saw the dead body of my
reptile foe and my babe crying violently and nestling
in my bosom. The ledge near which my cabin was
built was infested with rattlesnakes, and the one I
had slain seemed to be the patriarch of a numerous
family. From that day I vowed vengeance against
the whole tribe of reptiles. These creatures were in
the habit of coming down to the spring to drink, and

I sometimes killed four or five in a day. Before the summer was over I made an end of the whole family."

In September, two households of emigrants floating down the river on a flatboat, caught sight of Mrs. Jameson as she made a signal to them from the bank, and coming to land were pleased with the country, and were persuaded to settle there. The little community was now swelled to fifteen, including four women and six children. The colony throve, received accessions from the East, and, surviving all casualties, grew at last into a populous town. Mrs. Jameson was married again to a stalwart backwoodsman and became the mother of a large family. She was always known as the "Mother of the Alleghany Settlement."

Not a few of the pioneer women penetrated the West by means of boats. The Lakes and the River Ohio were the water-courses by which the advance guard of the army of emigrants was enabled to reach the fertile regions adjacent thereto. This mode of travel, while free from many of the hindrances and hardships of the land routes, was subject to other casualties and dangers. Storms on the lakes, and snags and shoals on the rivers, often made the pioneers regret that they had left the forests for the waters. The banks of the rivers were infested with savages, who slaughtered and scalped the men and carried the women and children into a captivity which was worse than death. The early annals of the West are full of the sad stories of such captivities, and of the women who took part in these terrible scenes.

The following instances will be interesting to the reader:

In the latter part of April, 1784, one Mr. Rowan,

with his own and five other families, set out from Louisville, in two flat-bottomed boats, for the Long Falls of Green River. Their intention was to descend the Ohio to the mouth of Green River, then ascend that stream to their place of destination. At that time there were no settlements in Kentucky within one hundred miles of Long Falls, afterwards called Vienna.

Having driven their cattle upon one of the boats they loaded the other with their household goods, farming implements, and stores. The latter was provided with covers under which the six families could sleep, with the exception of three of the men who took charge of the cattle boat.

The first three days of their journey were passed in ease and gaiety. Floating with the current and using the broad oars only to steer with, they kept their course in the main channel where there was little danger of shoals and snags. The weather was fine and the scenery along the banks of the majestic river had that placid beauty that distinguishes the country through which the lower Ohio rolls its mighty mass of waters on their way to the Mississippi. These halcyon days of the voyage were destined, however, to be soon abruptly terminated. They had descended the river about one hundred miles, gliding along in peace and fancied security; the women and children had retired to their bunks, and all of the men except those who were steering the boat were composing themselves to sleep, when suddenly the placid stillness of the night was broken by a fearful sound which came from the river far below them. The steersmen at first supposed it was the howling of wolves. But as they neared the spot from which the sound proceeded, on rounding a bend in the river, they saw the glare of fires in the darkness; the sounds at the same time redoubled in shrillness and volume, and they knew then that a large body of Indians were below them and would almost inevitably discover their boats. The numerous fires on the Illinois shore and the peculiar yells of the savages led them to believe that a flatboat which preceded them had been captured and that the Indians were engaged in their cruel orgies of torture and massacre. The two boats were immediately lashed together, and the best practical arrangements were made for defending them. The men were distributed by Mr. Rowan to the best advantage in case of an attack; they were seven in number. The boats were neared to the Kentucky shore, keeping off from the bank lest there might be Indians on that shore also. When they glided by the uppermost fire they entertained a faint hope that they might escape unperceived. But they were discovered when they had passed about half of the fires and commanded to halt. They however remained silent, for Mr. Rowan had given strict orders that no one should utter any sound but that of the rifle; and not that until the Indians should come within reach. The savages united in a most terrific yell, rushed to their canoes and pursued them. They floated on in silence—not an oar was pulled. The enemy approached the boats within a hundred yards, with a seeming determination to board them.

Just at this moment Mrs. Rowan rose from her seat, collected the axes and placed one by the side of each man, where he stood with his gun, touching him on the knee with the handle of the axe as she leaned it up beside him against the edge of the boat, to let him know it was there. She then retired to her seat, retaining a hatchet for herself.

None but those who have had a practical acquaintance with Indian warfare, can form a just idea of the terror which their hideous yelling is calculated to inspire. When heard that night in the mighty solitude through which those boats were passing, we are told that most of the voyagers were panic-stricken and almost nerveless until Mrs. Rowan's calm resolution and intrepidity inspired them with a portion of her own undaunted spirit. The Indians continued hovering on their rear and yelling, for nearly three miles, when awed by the inference which they drew from the silence of the party in the boat, they relinquished farther pursuit.

Woman's companionship and influence are nowhere more necessary than on the long and tedious journey of the pioneer to the West. Man is a born rover. He sails over perilous seas and beneath unfamiliar constellations. He penetrates the trackless forest and scales the mountains for gain or glory or out of mere love of motion and adventure. A life away from the fetters and conventionalities of civilized society also has its charms to the manly heart. The free air of the boundless wilderness acts on many natures as a stimulus to effort, but it seems also to breed a spirit of unrest. "I will not stay here! whither shall I go?" Thus the spirit whispers to itself. Motion, only motion! Onward! ever onward! The restless foot of the pioneer has reached and climbed the mountains. He pauses but a moment to gaze at the valley and

presses forward.   The valley reached and he must
cross the river, and now the unbounded expanse of
the plain spreads before him.   Traversing this after
many weary days he stands beneath a mightier moun-
tain-range towering above him.   Up! up! Struggling
upward but ever onward he has reached the snowy
summit and gazes upon wider valleys lit by a kinglier
sun and spanned by kindlier skies ; and far off he sees
sparkling in the evening light another and grander
ocean on whose shores he must pause.   Thus by various motives and impulses the line which bounds the
area of civilized society is constantly being extended.

But all through this tumult of the mind and heart,
through this rush of motion and life there is heard another voice.   Soft and penetrating it sounds in the
hour of calm and stillness and tells of happiness and
repose.   As in the beautiful song one word is its burden, Home! Home! Sweet Home! where the lonely
heart and toil-worn feet may find rest.   That voice
must have its answer, that aspiration must be reached
by the aid of woman.   It is she, and only she that
makes the home.   Around her as a beaming nucleus
are attracted and gather the thousand lesser lights of
the fireside.   She is the central figure of the domestic
group, and where she is not, there is no home.   Man
may explore a continent, subjugate nature and conquer savage races, but no permanent settlement can
be made nor any new empire formed without the alliance of woman.

She must therefore be the companion of the restless
rover on his westward march, in order that the secret
cravings of his soul may be at last satisfied in that

home of happiness and rest, which woman alone can form.

Nothing will better illustrate the restless and indomitable spirit that inspires the western pioneer, and at the same time display the constant companionship and tireless energy of woman, than the singular history of a family named Moody. The emigrant ancestors of this family lived and died in eastern Massachusetts, where after arriving from England, in 1634, they first settled. In 1675, two of the daughters were living west of the Connecticut river. A grand-daughter of the emigrant was settled near the New York boundary line in 1720. *Her* daughter marrying a Dutch farmer of Schoharie made her home in the valley of the Mohawk during the French and Indian wars and the Revolution. In 1783, although an aged woman, she moved with her husband and family to Ohio, where she soon after died, leaving a daughter who married a Moody, a far away cousin, and moved first into Indiana and finally into Illinois, where she and her husband died leaving a son, J. G. Moody, who inherited the enterprising spirit of his predecessors, and, marrying a female relative who inherited the family name and spirit, before he was of age resumed the family march towards the Pacific.

The first place where the family *halted* was in the territory of Iowa. Here they lived for ten years tilling a noble farm on the Des Moines river. Then they sold their house and land, and pushed one hundred miles further westward. Here again new toils and triumphs awaited them. With the handsome sum derived from the sale of their farm on the Des Moines, they were enabled to purchase an extensive domain of both prairie and woodland. In ten years they had a model farm, and the story of their successful labors attracted other settlers to their neighborhood. A large price tempted them and again they disposed of their farm.

We have traced genealogically the successive stages in the history of this pioneer family for the purpose of noting, not merely the cheerfulness with which so many generations of daughters accompanied their husbands on their westward march, but the energy which they displayed in making so many homes in the waste places, and preparing the way for the less bold and adventurous class of settlers who follow where the pioneer leads.

The family, after disposing of their second Iowa farm, immediately took up their line of march for Nebraska, where they bought and cultivated a large tract of land on one of the tributaries of the Platte. In due time the current of emigration struck them. A favorable offer for their house and cattle ranche was speedily embraced, and again they took up their line of march which extended this time into the heart of the Rocky Mountains, in Colorado, of which State they were among the earliest settlers.

Here Mr. Moody died; but his widow with her large family successfully maintained her cattle and sheep ranche till a rich gold mine was discovered upon her land. A sale was soon effected of both the mine and the ranche. In two weeks after the whole family, mother, sons, and daughters were *en route* to California, where their long wanderings terminated. There they are now living and enjoying the rich fruits of their energy and enterprise, proving for once the fal-

WAGON TRAIN ON THE PRAIRIE.   Page 173.

sity of the proverb that " a rolling stone gathers no moss."

The women of this family are types of a class—soldiers, scouts, laborers, nurses in the " Grand Army," whose mission it is to reclaim the waste places and conquer uncivilized man.

If they fight, it is only for peace and safety. If they destroy, it is only to rebuild nobler structures in the interest of civilization. If they toil and bleed and suffer, it is only that they may rest on their arms, at last, surrounded by honorable and useful trophies, and look forward to ages of home-calm which have been secured for their posterity.

CHAPTER VIII.

HOMESTEAD-LIFE IN THE BACKWOODS AND ON THE PRAIRIE.

THE first stage in pioneer-life is nomadic : a half-score of men, women, and children faring on day after day, living in the open air, encamping at night beside a spring or brook, under the canopy of the forest, it is only when they reach their place of destination, that the germ of a community fixes itself to the soil, and rises obedient to those laws of social and civil order which distinguish the European colonist from the Asiatic nomad.

The experiences of camp life form the initial steps to the thorough backwoods education which a woman must at length acquire, to fit her for the duties and trials incident to all remote settlements. Riding, driving, or tramping on, now through stately groves, now over prairies which lose themselves in the horizon, now fording shallow streams, or poling themselves on rafts across rivers, skirting morasses or wallowing through them, and climbing mountains, as they breathe the fresh woodland air and catch glimpses of a thousand novel scenes and encounter the dangers or endure the hardships of this first stage in their pilgrimage, they learn those first hard lessons which stand them in such good stead when they have settled in their permanent abodes in the heart of the wilderness which it is the work of the pioneer to subdue.

To the casual observer there is an air of romance and wild enjoyment in this journey through that magnificent land. Many things there doubtless are to give zest and enjoyment to the long march of the pioneer and his family. The country through which they pass deserves the title of " the garden of God." The trees of the forest are like stately columns in some verdurous temple ; the sun shines down from an Italian sky upon lakes set like jewels flashing in the beams of light, the sward is filled with exaggerated velvet, through whose green the purple and scarlet gleams of fruit and flowers appear, and everything speaks to the eye of the splendor, richness, and joy of wild nature. Traits of man in this scene are favorite themes for the painter's art. The fire burning under the spreading oak or chestnut, the horses, or oxen, or mules picketed in the vistas, Indian wigwams and squaws with children watching curiously the pioneer household sitting by their fire and eating their evening meal; this is the picture framed by the imagination of a poet or artist; but this is but a superficial sketch,—a mere glimpse of one of them any thousand phases of the long and weary journey. The reality is quite another thing.

The arrival of the household at their chosen seat marks the second stage in backwoods-life, a stage which calls for all the powers of mind and body, tasks the hands, exercises the ingenuity, summons vigilance, and awakens every latent energy. Woman steps at once into a new sphere of action, and hand in hand, shoulder to shoulder, with her stronger but not more resolute companion, enters on that career which looks to the formation of communities and states. It is the household which constitutes the primal atom, the aggregation whereof makes the village, town, or city; the state itself rests upon the household finally, and the household is what the faithful mother makes it.

The toilsome march at length ended, we see the great wagon, with its load of household utensils and farming implements, bedsteads walling up the sides, a wash-tub turned up to serve as a seat for the driver, a broom and hoe-handle sticking out behind with the handles of a plough, pots and kettles dangling below, bundles of beds and bedding enthroning children of all the smaller sizes, stopping at last "for good," and the whole cortege of men, women, and boys, cattle, horses, and hogs, resting after their mighty tramp.

Shelter and food are the first wants of the settler; the log-cabin rises to supply the one; the axe, the plough, the spade, the hoe, prepare the other.

The women not seldom joined in the work of felling

trees and trimming logs to be used in erecting the cabins.

Those who have never witnessed the erection of log-cabins, would be surprised to behold the simplicity of their mechanism, and the rapidity with which they are put together. The axe and the auger are often the only tools used in their construction, but usually the drawing-knife, the broad-axe, and the crosscut-saw are added.

The architecture of the body of the house is sufficiently obvious, but it is curious to notice the ingenuity with which the wooden fireplace and chimney are protected from the action of the fire by a lining of clay, to see a smooth floor formed from the plain surface of hewed logs, and a door made of boards split from the log, hastily smoothed with the drawing-knife, united firmly together with wooden pins, hung upon wooden hinges, and fastened with a wooden latch. Not a nail nor any particle of metal enters into the composition of the building—all is wood from top to bottom, all is done by the woodsman without the aid of any me-chanic. These primitive dwellings are by no means so wretched as their name and rude workmanship would seem to imply. They still frequently constitute the dwelling of the farmers in new settlements; they are often roomy, tight, and comfortable. If one cabin is not sufficient, another and another is added, until the whole family is accommodated, and thus the homestead of a respectable farmer often resembles a little village. The dexterity of the backwoodsman in the use of the axe is also remarkable, yet it ceases to be so regarded when we reflect on the variety of uses to which this implement is applied, and that in fact it enters into almost all the occupations of the pioneer, in clearing land, building houses, making fences, providing fuel; the axe is used in tilling his fields; the farmer is continually obliged to cut away the trees that have fallen in his enclosure, and the roots that impede his plough; the path of the surveyor is cleared by the axe, and his lines and corners marked by this instrument; roads are opened and bridges made by the axe, the first court houses and jails are fashoned of logs with the same tool. In labor or hunting, in traveling by land or water, the axe is ever the companion of the backwoodsman.

Most of these cabins were fortresses in themselves, and were capable of being defended by a family for several days. The thickness of the walls and numerous loop-poles were sometimes supplemented by a clay covering upon the roof, so as to resist the fiery arrows of the savages. Sometimes places of concealment were provided for the women and children beneath the floor, with a closely fitting trap door leading to it. Such a place of refuge was provided by Mrs. Graves, a widow who lost her husband in Braddock's retreat. In a large pit beneath the floor of the cabin every night she laid her children to sleep upon a bed of straw, and there, replacing one of the floor logs, she passed the weary hours in darkness, seated by the window which commanded a view of the clearing through which the Indians would have to approach. When her youngest child required nursing she would lift the floor-log and sit on the edge of the opening until it was lulled to sleep, and then deposit the nursling once more in its secret bed.

Once, while sitting without a light, knitting, before

12

the window, she saw three Indians approaching stealthily. Retreating to the hiding place beneath the floor, she heard them enter the cabin, and, having struck a light, proceed to help themselves to such eatables as they found in the pantry. After remaining for an hour in the house, and appropriating such articles as Indians most value, viz., knives, axes, etc., they took their departure.

More elaborate fortresses were often necessary, and, for purposes of mutual defence in a country which swarmed with Indians, the settlers banded together and erected stations, forts, and block-houses.

*A *station* may be described as a series of cabins built on the sides of a parallelogram and united with palisades, so as to present on the outside a continuous wall with only one or two doors, the cabin doors opening on the inside into a common square.

A fort was a stockade enclosure embracing cabins, etc., for the accommodation of several families. One side was formed by a range of cabins separated by divisions or partitions of logs; the walls on the outside were ten or twelve feet high, with roofs sloping inward. Some of these cabins were provided with puncheon-floors, i. e., floors made of logs split in half and smoothed, but most of the floors were earthen. At the angles of these forts were built the block-houses, which projected about two feet beyond the outer walls of the cabins and stockade; these upper stories were about eighteen feet, or two inches every way larger than the under one, leaving an opening at the commencement of the second story, to prevent the enemy from making a lodgment under the walls.

These block-houses were devised in the early days

* DeHass.

of the first settlements made in our country, and furnished rallying points for the settlers when attacked by the Indians. On the Western frontier they were enlarged and improved to meet the military exigencies arising in a country which swarmed with savages.

* In some forts, instead of block-houses, the angles were furnished with bastions; a large folding gate, made of thick slabs nearest the spring, closed the forts; the stockade, bastion, cabin, and block-house walls were furnished with port-holes at proper heights and distances. The whole of the outside was made completely bullet-proof; the families belonging to these forts were so attached to their own cabins on their farms that they seldom moved into the forts in the spring until compelled by some alarm, i. e., when it was announced by some murder that Indians were in the settlement.

We have described thus in detail the fortified posts established along the frontier for the purpose of showing that the life of the pioneer woman, from the earliest times, was, and now is, to a large extent, a military one. She was forced to learn a soldier's habits and a soldier's virtues. Eternal vigilance was the price of safety, and during the absence of the male members of the household, which were frequent and sometimes protracted, the women were on guard-duty, and acted as the sentinels of their home fortresses. Watchful against stratagem as against violent attack, they passed many a night all alone in their isolated cabins, averting danger with all a woman's fertility of resource, and meeting it with all the courage of a man.

On one occasion a party of Indians approached a solitary log-house with the intention of murdering the

* Doddridge's Notes.

inmates. With their usual caution, one of their number was sent forward to reconnoiter, who, discovering the only persons within to be a woman, two or three children, and a negro man, rushed in by himself and seized the negro. The woman caught up the axe and with a single blow laid the savage warrior dead at her feet, while the children closed the door, and, with ready sagacity, employed themselves fastening it. The rest of the Indians came up and attempted to force an entrance, but the negro and the children kept the door closed, and the intrepid mother, having no effective weapon, picked up a gun-barrel which had neither stock nor lock and pointed it at the savages through the apertures between the logs. The Indians deceived by the appearance of a gun, and daunted by the death of their companion, retired.

The station, the fort, and the block-house were the only refuge of the isolated settlers when the Indians became bolder in their attacks.

When the report of the four-pounder, or the ringing of the fort bell, or a volley of musketry sounded the alarm, the women and children hurried to the fortification. Sometimes, while threading the mazes of the forest, the hapless mother and her children would fall into an ambush. Springing from their cover, the prowling savages would ply their tomahawks and scalping knives amid the shrieks of their helpless victims, or bear them away into a captivity more cruel than death.

One summer's afternoon, while Mrs. Folsom, with her babe in her arms, was hasting to Fort Stanwig in the Black River Country, New York, after hearing the alarm, she caught sight of a huge Indian lying behind a log, with his rifle leveled apparently directly at her. She quickly sprang to one side and ran through the woods in a course at right angles with the point of danger, expecting every moment to be pierced with a rifle ball. Casting a horror-stricken glance over her shoulder as she ran, she saw her husband hastening on after her, but directly under the Indian's rifle. Shrieking loudly, she pointed to the savage just in time to warn her husband, who stepped behind a tree as the report of the rifle rang through the forest. In an instant he drew a bead upon the lurking foe, who fell with a bullet through his brain.

Before the family could reach the fort a legion of savages, roused by the report of the rifles, were on their trail. The mother and child fled swiftly towards their place of refuge, which they succeeded in reaching without harm; but the brave father, while trying to keep the savages at bay, was shot and scalped almost under the walls of the fort.

Ann Bush, another of these border heroines, was still more unfortunate than Mrs. Folsom. While she and her husband were fleeing for safety to one of the stations on the Virginia borders, they were overtaken and captured by the Indians, who shot and scalped her husband; and although she soon escaped from captivity, yet in less than twelve months after, while again attempting to find refuge in the same station, she was captured a second time, with an infant in her arms. After traveling a few hours the savages bent down a young hickory, sharpened it, seized the child, scalped it and spitted it upon the tree; they then scalped and tomahawked the mother and left her for dead. She lay insensible for many hours; but it was the will of Providence that she should survive the shock. When she recovered her senses she bandaged her head with her apron, and, wonderful to tell, in two days staggered back to the settlement with the dead body of her infant.

The transitions of frontier life were often startling and sad. From a wedding to a funeral, from a merrymaking to a massacre, were frequent vicissitudes. One of these shiftings of the scene is described by an actor and eye-witness as follows:

"Father had gone away the day before and mother and the children were alone. About nine o'clock at night we saw two Indians approaching. Mother immediately threw a bucket of water on the fire to prevent them from seeing us, made us lie on the floor, bolted and barred the door, and posted herself there with an axe and rifle. We never knew why they desisted from an attack or how father escaped. In two or three days all of us set out for Clinch Mountain to the wedding of Happy Kincaid, a clever young fellow from Holston, and Sally McClure, a fine girl of seventeen, modest and pretty, yet fearless. We knew the Shawnees were about; that our fort and household effects must be left unguarded and might be destroyed; that we incurred the risk of a fight or an ambuscade, a capture, and even death, on the route; but in those days, and in that wild country, folks did not calculate consequences closely, and the temptation to a frolic, a wedding, a feast, and a dance till daylight and often for several days together, was not to be resisted. Off we went. Instead of the bridal party, the well spread table, the ringing laughter, and the sounding feet of buxom dancers, we found a pile of ashes and six or seven ghastly corpses tomahawked and scalped." Mrs. McClure, her infant, and three other children, including Sally, the intended bride, had been carried off by the savages. They soon tore the poor infant from the mother's arms and killed and scalped it, that she might travel faster. While they were scalping this child, Peggy McClure, a girl twelve years old, perceived a sink-hole immediately at her feet and dropped silently into it. It communicated with a ravine, down which she ran and brought the news to the settlement. The same night Sally, who had been tied and forced to lie down between two warriors, contrived to loosen her thongs and make her escape. She struck for the canebrake, then for the river, and to conceal her trail resolved to descend it. It was deep wading, and the current was so rapid she had to fill her petticoat with gravel to steady herself. She soon, however, recovered confidence, returned to shore, and finally reached the still smoking homestead about dark next evening. A few neighbors well armed had just buried the dead; the last prayer had been said, when the orphan girl stood before them.

Yielding to the entreaties of her lover, who was present, and to the advice and persuasion of her friends, the weeping girl gave her consent to an immediate marriage ; and beside the grave of the household and near the ruins of the cabin they were accordingly made one.

These perilous adventures were episodes, we should remember, in a life of extraordinary labor and hardship. The luxuries and comforts of older communities were unknown to the settlers on the border-line, either in New England two centuries ago or in the West within the present generation. Plain in every way was the life of the borderer—plain in dress, in manners, in equipage, in houses. The cabins were furnished in the most primitive style. Blocks or stumps of trees served for chairs and tables. Bedsteads were made by laying rows of saplings across two logs, forming a spring-bed for the women and children, while the men lay on the floor with their feet to the fire and a log under their heads for a pillow.

The furniture of the cabin in the West, for several years after the settlement of the country, consisted of a few pewter dishes, plates, and spoons, but mostly of wooden bowls, trenchers, and noggins; if these last were scarce, gourds and hard-shell squashes made up the deficiency; the iron pots, knives, and forks were brought from the East, with the salt and iron on pack-horses. The articles of furniture corresponded very well with the articles of diet. "Hog and hominy" was a dish of proverbial celebrity; Johnny cake or pone was at the outset of the settlement the only form of bread in use for breakfast or dinner; at supper, milk and mush was the standard dish; when milk was scarce the hominy supplied its place, and mush was frequently eaten with sweetened water, molasses, bear's oil, or the gravy of fried meat.

In the display of furniture, delft, china, or silver were unknown; the introduction of delft-ware was considered by many of the backwoods people as a wasteful innovation; it was too easily broken, and the plates dulled their scalping and clasp knives.

The costume of the women of the frontier was suited to the plainness of the habitations where they lived and the furniture they used. Homespun, linsey-woolsey and buckskin were the primitive materials out of which their everyday dresses were made, and only on occasions of social festivity were they seen in braver robes. Rings, broaches, buckles, and ruffles were heir-looms from parents or grand-parents.

But this plainness of living and attire was a preparation for, and almost necessary antecedent of hardihood, endurance, courage, patience, qualities which made themselves manifest in the heroic acting of these women of the border. With such a state of society we can readily associate assiduous labor, a battling with danger in its myriad shapes, a subjugation of the hostile forces of nature, and a developing of a strange and peculiar civilization.

Here we see woman in her true glory, not a doll to carry silks and jewels, not a puppet to be dandled by fops, an idol of profane adoration reverenced to-day, discarded to-morrow, admired but not respected, desired but not esteemed, ruling by passion not affection, imparting her weakness not her constancy, to the sex she should exalt—the source and marrow of vanity. We see her as a wife partaking of the cares and guiding the labors of her husband and by domestic diligence spreading cheerfulness all around for his sake; sharing the decent refinements of civilization without being injured by them; placing all her joy, all her happiness in the merited approbation of the man she loves; as a mother, we find her affectionate, the ardent instructress of the children she has reared from infancy and trained up to thought and to the practice of virtue, to meditation and benevolence and to become strong and useful men and women.

"Could there be happiness or comfort in such

dwellings and such a state of society. To those who are accustomed to modern refinement the truth appears like fable. The lowly occupants of log cabins were often among the most happy of mankind. Exercise and excitement gave them health, they were practically equal; common danger made them mutually dependent; brilliant hopes of future wealth and distinction led them on, and as there was ample room for all, and as each new comer increased individual and general security, there was little room for that envy, jealousy, and hatred which constitutes a large portion of human misery in older societies. Never were the story, the joke, the song, and the laugh better enjoyed than upon the hewed blocks or puncheon-stools around the roaring log-fire of the early western settler. The lyre of Apollo was not hailed with more delight in primitive Greece than the advent of the first fiddler among the dwellers of the wilderness, and the polished daughters of the East never enjoyed themselves half so well moving to the music of a full band upon the elastic floor of their ornamented ball-room, as did the daughters of the western emigrants keeping time to the self-taught fiddler on the bare earth or puncheon floor of the primitive log cabin : the smile of the polished beauty is the wave of the lake where the breeze plays gently over it, and her movement the gentle stream which drains it; but the laugh of the log cabin is the gush of nature's fountain and its movement the leaping water."

Amid the multifarious toils of pioneer-life, woman has often proved that she is the last to forget the stranger that is within the gates. She welcomes the coming as she speeds the parting guest.

Let us suppose travelers caught in a rain storm, who reach at last one of these western homes. There is a roof, a stick chimney, drenched cattle crowding in beneath a strawy barrack, and some forlorn fowls huddling under a cart. The log-house is a small one, though its neat corn-crib and chicken-coop of slender poles bespeaks a careful farmer. No gate is seen, but great bars which are let down or climbed over, and the cabin has only a back door.

Within, everything ministers to the useful; nothing to the beautiful. Flitches of bacon, dried beef, and ham depend from the ceiling; pots and kettles are ranged in a row in the recess on one side the fireplace; and above these necessary utensils are plates and heavy earthen nappies. The axe and gun stand together in one corner.

The good woman of the house is thin as a shadow, and pinched and wrinkled with hard labor. Little boys and girls are playing on the floor like kittens.

A free and hospitable welcome is given to the travelers; their wet garments are ranged for drying on those slender poles usually seen above the ample fireplace of a log-cabin in the West, placed there for the purpose of drying sometimes the week's wash when the weather is rainy, sometimes whole rows of slender circlets of pumpkins for next spring's pies, or festoons of sliced apples.

The good woman, after busying herself in those little offices which evince a desire to make guests welcome, puts an old cloak on her head and flies out to place tubs, pails, pans, and jars under the pouring eaves, intimating that as soap was scarce, she "must try and catch rain water anyhow."

The "old man" has the shakes, so the woman has all to do; throws more wood on the fire and fans it with her apron; cuts rashers of bacon, runs out to the hen-coop and brings in new-laid eggs; mixes a johnny-cake and sets it in a pan upon the embers.

While the supper is cooking the rain subsides to a sprinkle, and the travelers look at the surroundings of this pioneer household.

The cabin stands in a prairie, skirted by a forest. A stream gurgles by. The prairie is broken with patches of corn and potatoes, which are just emerging from the rich black mould. Pig-pens, a barn, and corn-houses, a half-dozen sheep in an enclosure, cows and calves and oxen in a barn-yard, a garden patch, and hen-coops, and stumps of what were once mighty trees, tell the story of the farmer's labors; and the cabin, with all its appurtenances and surroundings, show how much the good woman has contributed to make it the abode of rustic plenty, all provided by the unaided toil of this pioneer couple.

They had come from the East ten years before, and their cabin was the initial point from which grew up a numerous settlement. Other cabins sent up their smoke in the prairie around them. A school-house and church had been built, and a saw-mill was at work on the stream near by, and surveyors for a railroad had just laid out a route for the iron horse.

Two little boys come in now, skipping from school, and at the same time the good woman, who is all patience and civility, announces supper. Sage-tea, johnny-cake, fried eggs, and bacon, seasoned with sundry invitations of the hostess to partake freely, and then the travelers are in a mood for rest.

The sleeping arrangements are of a somewhat perplexing character. These are one large bed and a trundle bed; the former is given up to the travelers, the trundle bed suffices for the little ones; the hostess prepares a cotton sheet partition for the benefit of those who choose to undress, and then begins to prepare herself for the rest which she stands sorely in need of. She and her good man repose upon the floor, with buffalo robes for pillows, and with their feet to the fire.

The hospitality of the frontier woman is bounded only by their means of affording it. Come when you may, they welcome you; give you of their best while you remain, and regret your departure with simple and unfeigned sincerity. If you are sick, all that sympathy and care can devise is done for you, and all this is from the heart.

Homestead-life, and woman's influence therein, is modified to some extent by the different races that contributed their quotas to the pioneer army. The early French settlements in our western States furnish a picture somewhat different from those of the emigrants of English blood: a patriarchal state of society, self-satisfied and kindly, with bright superficial features, but lacking the earnest purpose and restless aggressive energy of the Anglo-American, whose very amusements and festivals partook of a useful character.

Those French pioneer-women made thrifty and industrious housewives, and entered, with all the gaiety and enthusiasm of their race, into all the merry-makings and social enjoyments peculiar to those neighborhoods. On festive occasions, the blooming damsels wound round their foreheads fancy-colored handkerchiefs, streaming with gay ribbons, or plumed with flowers. The matrons wore the short jacket or petticoat. The foot was left uncovered and free, but on holidays it was adorned with the light moccasin, brilliant with porcupine quills, shells, beads, and lace.

A faithful picture of life in these French settlements possesses an indescribable charm, such as that conveyed by the perusal of Longfellow's Acadian Romance of " Evangeline," when we see in a border settlement the French maiden, wife, and widow.

Different types, too, of homestead-life are of course to be looked for in different sections. On the ocean's beach, on the shores of the inland seas, on the banks of great rivers, in the heart of the forest, on the rugged hills of New England, on southern Savannas, on western prairies, or among the mountains beyond, the region, the scenery, the climate, the social laws may be diverse, yet homestead-life on the frontier, widely varying as it does in its form and outward surroundings, is in its spirit everywhere essentially the same. The sky that bends over all, and the sun that sheds its light for all, are symbols of the oneness of the animating principle in the home where woman is the bright and potent genius.

We have spoken of the western form of homestead-life because the frontier-line of to-day lies in the occident. But in each stage of the movement that carried our people onward in their destined course from ocean to ocean, the wife and the mother were centers from which emanated a force to impel forward, and to fix firmly in the chosen abode those organisms of society which forms the molecular atoms out of which, by the laws of our being, is built the compact structure of civilization.

In approximating towards some estimate of woman's peculiar influence in those lonely and far-off western homes, we must not fail to take into account the humanizing and refining power which she exerts to soften the rugged features of frontier-life. Different classes of women all worked in their way towards this end.

" The young married people, who form a considerable part of the pioneer element in our country, are simple in their habits, moderate in their aspirations, and hoard a little old-fashioned romance—unconsciously enough—in the secret nooks of their rustic hearts. They find no fault with their bare loggeries; with a shelter and a handful of furniture, they have enough." If there is the wherewithal to spread a warm supper for the " old man " when he comes in from work, the young wife forgets the long, solitary, wordless day and asks no greater happiness than preparing it by the help of such materials and utensils as would be looked at with utter contempt in the comfortable kitchens of the East.

They have youth, hope, health, occupation, and amusement, and when you have added " meat, clothes, and fire," what more has England's queen ? "

We should, however, remember that there is another large class of women who, for various reasons, have left comfortable homes in older communities, and risked their happiness and all that they have in enterprises of pioneer life in the far West. What wonder that they should sadly miss the thousand old familiar means and appliances ! Some utensil or implement necessary to their husbandry is wanting or has been lost or broken, and cannot be replaced. Some comfort or luxury to which she has been used from childhood is lacking, and cannot be furnished. The multifarious materials upon which household art can employ itself are reduced to the few absolute essentials. These difficulties are felt more by the woman than the man. To quote the words of a writer who was herself a pioneer housewife in the West:

"The husband goes to his work with the same axe or hoe which fitted his hand in his old woods and fields; he tills the same soil or perhaps a far richer and more hopeful one; he gazes on the same book of nature which he has read from his infancy and sees only a fresher and more glowing page, and he returns home with the sun, strong in heart and full of self-congratulation on the favorable change in his lot. Perhaps he finds the home bird drooping and disconsolate. She has found a thousand difficulties which her rougher mate can scarcely be taught to feel as evils. She has been looking in vain for any of the cherished features of her old fireside. What cares he if the time-honored cupboard is meagerly represented by a few oak boards lying on pegs called shelves. His tea equipage shines as it was wont, the biscuits can hardly stay on the brightly glistening plates. His bread never was better baked. What does he want with the great old-fashioned rocking chair? When he is tired he goes to bed, for he is never tired till bed-time. The sacrifices in moving West have been made most largely by women."

It is this very dearth of so many things that once made her life easy and comfortable which throws her back upon her own resources. Here again is woman's strength. Fertile in expedients, apt in device, an artisan to construct and an artist to embellish, she proceeds to supply what is lacking in her new home. She has a miraculous faculty for creating much out of little, and for transforming the coarse into the beautiful. Barrels are converted into easy chairs and washstands; spring beds are manufactured with rows of slender, elastic saplings; a box covered with muslin stuffed with hay serves for a lounge. By the aid of considerable personal exertion, while she adds to the list of useful and necessary articles, she also enlarges the circle of luxuries. An hour or two of extra work now and then enables her to hoard enough to buy a new looking-glass, and to make from time to time small additions to the showy part of the household.

After she has transformed the rude cabin into a cozy habitation, she turns her attention to the outside surroundings. Woodbine and wild cucumber are trailed over the doors and windows; little beds of sweet-williams and marigolds line the path to the clearing's edge or across the prairie-sward to the well; and an apple or pear tree is put in here and there. In all these works, either of use or embellishment, if not done by her own hand she is at least the moving spirit. Thus over the rugged and homely features of her lot she throws something of the magic of that ideal of which the poet sings:

> " Nymph of our soul and brightener of our being :
> She makes the common waters musical—
> Binds the rude night-winds in a silver thrall,
> Bids Hybla's thyme and Tempe's violet dwell
> Round the green marge of her moon-haunted cell."

13

It is the thousand nameless household offices performed by woman that makes the home : it is the home which moulds the character of the children and makes the husband what he is. Who can deny the vast debt of gratitude due from the present generation of Americans to these offices of woman in refining and ameliorating the rude tone of frontier life? It may well be said that the pioneer women of America have made the wilderness bud and blossom like the rose. Under their hands even nature itself, no longer a wild, wayward mother, turns a more benign face upon her children. A land bright with flowers and bursting with fruitage testifies to the labors and influence of those who embellish the homestead and make it attractive to their husbands and children.

A traveler on the vast prairies of Kansas and Nebraska will often see cabins remote from the great thoroughfares embowered in vines and shrubbery and bright with beds of flowers. Entering he will discern the rugged features of frontier life softened in a hundred ways by the hand of woman. The steel is just as hard and more serviceable after it is polished, and the oak-wood as strong and durable when it is trimmed and smoothed. The children of the frontier are as hardy and as manly though the gentle voice of woman schools their rugged ways and her kind hand leads them through the paths of refinement and moulds them in the school of humanity.

CHAPTER IX.

SOME REMARKABLE WOMEN.

OF all the tens of thousands of devoted women who have accompanied the grand army of pioneers into the wilderness, not one but that has been either a soldier to fight, or a laborer to toil, or a ministering angel to soothe the pains and relieve the sore wants of her companions. Not seldom has she acted worthily in all these several capacities, fighting, toiling, and ministering by turns. If a diary of the events of their pioneer-lives had been kept by each of these brave and faithful women, what a record of toil and warfare and suffering it would present. How many different types of female character in different spheres of action it would show—the self-sacrificing mother, the tender and devoted wife, the benevolent matron, the heroine who blenched not in battle! Unnumbered thousands have passed beautiful, strenuous and brave lives far from the scenes of civilization, and gone down to their graves leaving only local, feeble voices, if any, to celebrate their praises and to-day we know not the place of their sepulcher. Others have had their memories embalmed by the pens of faithful biographers, and a few also have left diaries containing a record of the wonderful vicissitudes of their lives.

Woman's experience of life in the wilderness is never better told than in her own words. More impressible than man, to passing events; more susceptible to pain

and pleasure; enjoying and sorrowing more keenly
than her sterner and rougher mate, she possesses often
a peculiarly graphic power in expressing her own
thoughts and feelings, and also in delineating the
scenes through which she passes.

A woman's diary of frontier-life, therefore, possesses an intrinsic value because it is a faithful story,
and at the same time one of surpassing interest, in
consequence of her personal and active participation
in the toils, sufferings, and dangers incident to such a
life.

Such a diary is that of Mrs. Williamson which in
the quaint style of the olden time relates her thrilling
experience in the wilds of Pennsylvania. We see her
first as an affectionate, motherless girl accompanying
her father to the frontier, assisting him to prepare a
home for his old age in the depths of the forest and
enduring with cheerful resolution the manifold hardships and trials of pioneer-life, and finally closing her
aged parent's eyes in death. Then we see her as a
wife, the partner of her husband's cares and labors,
and as a mother, the faithful guardian of her sons;
and again as a widow, her husband having been torn
from her arms and butchered by a band of ruthless
savages. After her sons had grown to be sturdy men
and had left her to make homes for themselves, she
shows herself the strong and self-reliant matron of
fifty still keeping her outpost on the border, and culti-
vating her clearing by the assistance of two negroes.
At last after a life of toil and danger she is attacked
by a band of savages, and defends her home so bravely
that after making her their captive they spare her life
and in admiration of her courage adopt her into their

tribe. She dissembles her reluctance, humors her savage captors and forces herself to accompany them on their bloody expeditions wherein she saves many lives and mitigates the sufferings of her fellow-captives.

The narrative of her escape we give in her own quaint words.

" One night the Indians, very greatly fatigued with their day's excursion, composed themselves to rest as usual. Observing them to be asleep, I tried various ways to see whether it was a scheme to prove my intentions or not, but, after making a noise, and walking about, sometimes touching them with my feet, I found there was no fallacy. My heart then exulted with joy at seeing a time come that I might, in all probability be delivered from my captivity ; but this joy was soon dampened by the dread of being discovered by them, or taken by any straggling parties; to prevent which, I resolved, if possible, to get one of their guns, and, if discovered, to die in my defense, rather than be taken. For that purpose I made various efforts to get one from under their heads (where they always secured them), but in vain.

" Frustrated in this my first essay towards regaining my liberty, I dreaded the thought of carrying my design into execution : yet, after a little consideration, and trusting myself to the divine protection, I set forward, naked and defenceless as I was; a rash and dangerous enterprise ! Such was my terror, however, that in going from them, I halted and paused every four or five yards, looking fearfully toward the spot where I had left them, lest they should awake and miss me ; but when I was about two hundred yards from them, I mended my pace, and made as much haste as I could

to the foot of the mountains; when on sudden I was
struck with the greatest terror and amaze, at hearing
the wood-cry, as it is called, they make when any accident happens them.   However, fear hastened my
steps, and though they dispersed, not one happened
to hit upon the track I had taken.   When I had run
near five miles, I met with a hollow tree, in which I
concealed myself till the evening of the next day,
when I renewed my flight, and next night slept in a
canebrake.   The next morning I crossed a brook,
and got more leisurely along, returning thanks to
Providence, in my heart, for my happy escape, and
praying for future protection.   The third day, in the
morning, I perceived two Indians armed, at a short
distance, which I verily believed were in pursuit of
me, by their alternately climbing into the highest
trees, no doubt to look over the country to discover
me.   This retarded my flight for that day; but at
night I resumed my travels, frightened and trembling
at every bush I passed, thinking each shrub that I
touched, a savage concealed to take me.   It was moonlight nights till near morning, which favored my escape.   But how shall I describe the fear, terror and
shock that I felt on the fourth night, when, by the
rustling I made among the leaves, a party of Indians,
that lay round a small fire, nearly out, which I did
not perceive, started from the ground, and seizing their
arms, ran from the fire among the woods.   Whether
to move forward, or to rest where I was, I knew not,
so distracted was my imagination.   In this melancholy
state, revolving in my thoughts the now inevitable
fate I thought waited on me, to my great astonishment
and joy, I was relieved by a parcel of swine that

made towards the place where I guessed the savages
to be; who, on seeing the hogs, conjectured that their
alarm had been occasioned by them, and directly returned to the fire, and lay down to sleep as before. As
soon as I perceived my enemies so disposed of, with
more cautious step and silent tread, I pursued my
course, sweating (though the air was very cold) with
the fear I had just been relieved from. Bruised,
cut, mangled and terrified as I was, I still, through
divine assistance, was enabled to pursue my journey
until break of day, when, thinking myself far off from
any of those miscreants I so much dreaded, I lay
down under a great log, and slept undisturbed until
about noon, when, getting up, I reached the summit
of a great hill with some difficulty; and looking out
if I could spy any inhabitants of white people, to my
unutterable joy I saw some, which I guessed to be
about ten miles distance. This pleasure was in some
measure abated, by my not being able to get among
them that night; therefore, when evening approached
I again re-commended myself to the Almighty, and
composed my weary mangled limbs to rest. In the
morning I continued my journey towards the nearest
cleared lands I had seen the day before; and about
four o'clock in the afternoon I arrived at the house of
John Bell."

Mrs. Daviess was another of these women who,
like Mrs. Williamson, was a born heroine, of whom
there were many who acted a conspicuous part in the
territorial history of Kentucky. Large and splendidly
formed, she possessed the strength of a man with the
gentle loveliness of the true woman. In the hour of
peril, and such hours were frequent with her, she was

firm, cool, and fertile of resource; her whole life, of
which we give only a few episodes, was one continuous
succession of brave and noble deeds. Both she and
Mrs. Williamson appear to have been real instances of
the poet's ideal:

> "A perfect woman nobly planned
> To warn, to comfort, and command."

* Her husband, Samuel Daviess, was an early settler
at Gilmer's Lick, in Lincoln County, Kentucky. In
the month of August, 1782, while a few rods from his
house, he was attacked early one morning by an
Indian, and attempting to get within doors he found
that his house was already occupied by the other
Indians. He succeeded in making his escape to his
brother's station, five miles off, and giving the alarm
was soon on his way back to his cabin in company
with five stout, well armed men.

Meanwhile, the Indians, four in number, who had
entered the house while the fifth was in pursuit of
Mr. Daviess, roused Mrs. Daviess and the children
from their beds and gave them to understand that
they must go with them as prisoners. Mrs. Daviess
occupied as long a time as possible in dressing, hoping
that some relief would come. She also delayed the
Indians nearly two hours by showing them one article
of clothing and then another, explaining their uses
and expatiating on their value.

While this was going on the Indian who had been
in pursuit of her husband returned with his hands
stained with pokeberries, waving his tomahawk with
violent gestures as if to convey the belief that he had
killed Mr. Daviess. The keen-eyed wife soon dis-

---

* Collins' Historical Sketches.

covered the deception, and was satisfied that her husband had escaped uninjured.

After plundering the house, the savages started to depart, taking Mrs. Daviess and her seven children with them. As some of the children were too young to travel as rapidly as the Indians wished, and discovering, as she believed, their intention to kill them, she made the two oldest boys carry the two youngest on their backs.

In order to leave no trail behind them, the Indians traveled with the greatest caution, not permitting their captives to break a twig or weed as they passed along, and to expedite Mrs. Daviess' movements one of them reached down and cut off with his knife a few inches of her dress.

Mrs. Daviess was accustomed to handle a gun and was a good shot, like many other women on the frontier. She contemplated as a last resort that, if not rescued in the course of the day, when night came and the Indians had fallen asleep, she would deliver herself and her children by killing as many of the Indians as she could, believing that in a night attack the rest would fly panic-stricken.

Mr. Daviess and his companions reaching the house and finding it empty, succeeded in striking the trail of the Indians and hastened in pursuit. They had gone but a few miles before they overtook them. Two Indian spies in the rear first discovered the pursuers, and running on overtook the others and knocked down and scalped the oldest boy, but did not kill him. The pursuers fired at the Indians but missed. The latter became alarmed and confused, and Mrs. Daviess taking advantage of this circumstance jumped into a sink-hole with her infant in her arms. The Indians fled and every child was saved.

Kentucky in its early days, like most new countries, was occasionally troubled with ·men of abandoned character, who lived by stealing the property of others, and after committing their depredations, retired to their hiding-places, thereby eluding the operation of the law. One of these marauders, a man of desperate character, who had committed extensive thefts from Mr. Daviess, as well as from his neighbors, was pursued by Daviess and a party whose property he had taken, in order to bring him to justice.

While the party were in pursuit, the suspected individual, not knowing that any one was pursuing him, came to the house of Daviess, armed with his gun and tomahawk,—no person being at home but Mrs. Daviess and her children. After he had stepped into the house, Mrs. Daviess asked him if he would drink something; and having set a bottle of whiskey upon the table, requested him to help himself. The fellow not suspecting any danger, set his gun by the door, and while he was drinking Mrs. Daviess picked it up, and placing herself in the doorway had the weapon cocked and leveled upon him by the time he turned around, and in a peremptory manner ordered him to take a seat or she would shoot him. Struck with terror and alarm, he asked what he had done. She told him he had stolen her husband's property, and that she intended to take care of him herself. In that condition she held him prisoner until the party of men returned and took him into their possession.

These are only a few out of many similar acts which show the character of Mrs. Daviess. She became

noted all through the frontier settlements of that region during the troublous times in which she lived, not only for her courage and daring, but for her shrewdness in circumventing the stratagems of the wily savages by whom her family were surrounded. Her oldest boy inherited his mother's character, and promised to be one of the most famous Indian fighters of his day, when he met his death at the hands of his savage foes in early manhood.

If Mrs. Williamson and Mrs. Daviess were representative women in the more stormy and rugged scenes of frontier life, Mrs. Elizabeth Estaugh may stand as a true type of the gentle and benevolent matron, brightening her forest home by her kindly presence, and making her influence felt in a thousand ways for good among her neighbors in the lonely hamlet where she chose to live.

Her maiden name was Haddon; she was the oldest daughter of a wealthy and well educated but humble-minded Quaker of London. She was endowed by nature with strength of mind, earnestness, energy, and with a heart overflowing with kindness and warmth of feeling. The education bestowed upon her, was, after the manner of her sect, a highly practical one, such as might be expected to draw forth her native powers by careful training of the mind, without quenching the kindly emotions by which she was distinguished from her early childhood.

At the age of seventeen she made a profession of religion, uniting herself with the Quakers. During her girlhood William Penn visited the house of her father, and greatly interested her by describing his adventures with the Indians in the wilds of Pennsylvania. From that hour her thoughts were directed towards the new world, where so many of her sect had emigrated, and she longed to cross the ocean and take up her abode among them. She pictured to herself the toils and privations of the Quaker-pioneers in that new country, and ardently desired to join them and share their labors and dangers, and alleviate their sufferings by charitably dispensing a portion of that wealth which she was destined to possess.

Her father sympathized with her views and aims, and was at length induced to buy a large tract of land in New Jersey, where he proposed to go and settle in company with his daughter Elizabeth, and there carry out the plans which she had formed. His affairs in England took such a turn that he decided to remain in his native land.

This was a sad disappointment to Elizabeth. She had arrived at the conviction that among her people in the new world was to be her sphere of duty; she felt a call thither which she could not disregard; and when her father, who was unwilling that the property should lie unimproved, offered the tract of land in New Jersey to any relative who would settle upon it, she gladly availed herself of the proffer, and begged that she might go herself as a pioneer into that far-off wilderness.

It was a sore trial for her parents to part with their beloved daughter; but her character was so stable, and her convictions of duty so unswerving, that at the end of three months and after much prayer, they consented tearfully that Elizabeth should join "the Lord's people in the new world."

Arrangements were accordingly made for her departure, and all that wealth could provide or thoughtful affection devise, was prepared, both for the long voyage across that stormy sea and against the hardships and trials in the forest home which was to be hers. In the spring of 1700 she set sail, accompanied by a poor widow of good sense and discretion, who had been chosen to act as her friend and housekeeper, and two trustworthy men-servants, members of the Society of Friends.

Among the many extraordinary manifestations of strong faith and religious zeal connected with the early settlement of this country, few are more remarkable than this enterprise of Elizabeth Estaugh. Tenderly reared in a delightful home in a great city, where she had been surrounded with pleasing associations from infancy, and where as a lovely young lady she was the idol of the circle of society in which she moved, she was still willing and desirous at the call of religious duty, to separate herself from home, friends, and the pleasures of civilization, and depart to a distant clime and a wild country. Hardly less remarkable and admirable was the self-sacrificing spirit of her parents in giving up their child in obedience to the promptings of her own conscience. We can imagine the parting on the deck of the vessel which was spreading its sails to bear this sweet missionary away from her native land and the beloved of her old home. Angelic love beams and sorrow darkles from the serene countenances of the father, and mother, and daughter, and yet no tear is shed on either side. The vessel drops down the harbor, and the family stand on the wharf straining their eyes to catch the last look from the departing maiden, who leans on the bulwark and answers the silent and sorrowful faces with a heavenly smile of love and pity. Even during the long and tedious voyage Elizabeth never wept. Her sense of duty controlled every other emotion of her soul, and she maintained her martyr-like cheerfulness and serenity to the end.

That part of New Jersey where the Haddon tract lay was at that period an almost unbroken wilderness. Scarcely more than twenty years had then elapsed since the twenty or thirty cabins had been built which formed the germ-settlement out of which grew the city of Brotherly Love, and nine miles of dense forest and a broad river separated the maiden and her household from the people in the hamlet across the Delaware.

The home prepared for her reception stood in a clearing of the forest, three miles from any other dwelling. She arrived in June, when the landscape was smiling in youthful beauty, and it seemed to her as if the arch of heaven was never before so clear and bright, the carpet of the earth never so verdant. As she sat at her window and saw evening close in upon her in that broad forest home, and heard for the first time the mournful notes of the whippoorwill, and the harsh scream of the jay in the distant woods, she was oppressed with a sense of vastness, of infinity, which she never before experienced, not even on the ocean. She remained long in prayer, and when she lay down to sleep beside her matron-friend, no words were spoken between them. The elder, overcome with fatigue, soon sank into a peaceful slumber; but the young enthusiast lay long awake, listening to the lone voice of the whippoorwill complaining to the night. Yet, notwithstanding this prolonged wakefulness, she arose early and looked out upon the lovely landscape. The rising sun pointed to the tallest trees with his golden finger, and was welcomed with a gush of song from a thousand warblers. The poetry in Elizabeth's soul, repressed by the severe plainness of her education, gushed up like a fountain. She dropped on her knees, and with an outburst of prayer, exclaimed fervently, " Oh, Father, very beautiful hast thou made this earth! How beautiful are thy gifts, O Lord!"

To a spirit less meek and brave, the darker shades of the picture would have obscured these cheerful gleams; for the situation was lonely, and the inconveniences innumerable. But Elizabeth easily triumphed over all obstacles, by practical good sense and by the quick promptings of her ingenuity. She was one of those clear, strong natures, who always have a definite aim in view, and who see at once the means best suited to the end. Her first inquiry was, what grain was best adapted to the soil of her farm; and being informed that rye would yield the best, " Then I shall eat rye bread," was the answer.

When winter came, and the gleaming snow spread its unbroken silence over hill and plain, was it not dreary then? It would have been dreary indeed to one who entered upon this mode of life for mere love of novelty, or a vain desire to do something extraordinary. But the idea of extended usefulness, which had first lured this remarkable girl into a path so unusual, sustained her through all her trials. She was too busy to be sad, and leaned too trustingly on her Father's hand to be doubtful of her way. The neighboring Indians soon loved her as a friend, for they always

found her truthful, just, and kind. From their teachings she added much to her knowledge of simple medicines. So efficient was her skill, and so prompt her
sympathy, that for many miles round, if man, woman,
or child were alarmingly ill, they were sure to send
for Elizabeth Haddon; and wherever she went, her
observing mind gathered some hint for the improve-
ment of farm or dairy. Her house and heart were
both large, and as her residence was on the way to the
Quaker meeting-house in Newtown, it became a place
of universal resort to Friends from all parts of the
country traveling that road, as well as an asylum for
benighted wanderers.

Late one winter's evening a tinkling of sleigh-bells
was heard at the entrance of the clearing, and soon the
hoofs of horses were crunching the snow as they passed
through the great gate towards the barn. The arrival
of strangers was a common occurrence, for the home
of Elizabeth Haddon was celebrated far and near as
the abode of hospitality. The toil-worn or benighted
traveler there found a sincere welcome, and none who
enjoyed that friendly shelter and abundant cheer ever
departed without regret. But now there was an unwonted stir in that well-ordered family; great logs
were piled in the capacious fireplace, and hasty preparations were made as if to receive guests who were
more than ordinarily welcome. Elizabeth, looking
from the window, had recognized one of the strangers
in the sleigh as John Estaugh, with whose preaching
years before in London she had been deeply impressed,
and ever since she had treasured in her memory many
of his words. It was almost like a glimpse of her dear
old English home to see him enter, and stepping for-

ward with more than usual cordiality she greeted him, saying,

"Thou art welcome, friend Estaugh, the more so for being entirely unexpected."

"And I am glad to see thee, Elizabeth," he replied, with a friendly shake of the hand, "it was not until after I had landed in America that I heard the Lord had called thee hither before me; but I remember thy father told me how often thou hadst played the settler in the woods, when thou wast quite a little girl."

"I am but a child still," she replied, smiling.

"I trust thou art," he rejoined; "and as for those strong impressions in childhood, I have heard of many cases when they seemed to be prophecies sent from the Lord. When I saw thy father in London, I had even then an indistinct idea that I might sometime be sent to America on a religious visit."

"And hast thou forgotten, friend John, the ear of Indian corn which my father begged of thee for me? I can show it to thee now. Since then I have seen this grain in perfect growth; and a goodly plant it is, I assure thee. See," she continued, pointing to many bunches of ripe corn which hung in their braided husks against the wall of the ample kitchen; "all that, and more, came from a single ear, no bigger than the one thou didst give my father. May the seed sown by thy ministry be as fruitful!" "Amen," replied both the guests.

That evening a severe snow-storm came on, and all night the blast howled round the dwelling. The next morning it was discovered that the roads were rendered impassable by the heavy drifts. The home of

14

Elizabeth had already been made the center of a settlement composed mainly of poor families, who relied
largely upon her to aid them in cases of distress.
That winter they had been severely afflicted by the
fever incident to a new settled country, and Elizabeth
was in the habit of making them daily visits, furnish-
ing them with food and medicines.

The storm roused her to an even more energetic
benevolence than ordinary. Men, oxen, and sledges
were sent out, and pathways were opened; the whole
force of Elizabeth's household, under her immediate
superintendence, joining in the good work. John
Estaugh and his friend tendered their services joy-
fully, and none worked harder than they. His countenance glowed with the exercise, and a cheerful
childlike outbeaming honesty of soul shone forth, at-
tracting the kind but modest regards of the maiden.
It seemed to her as if she had found in him a partner
in the good work which she had undertaken.

When the paths had been made, Elizabeth set out
with a sled-load of provisions to visit her patients, and
John Estaugh asked permission to accompany her.

While they were standing together by the bedside
of the aged and suffering, she saw her companion in
a new and still more attractive guise. His countenance
expressed a sincerity of sympathy warmed by rays of
love from the Sun of mercy and righteousness itself. He
spoke to the feeble and the invalid words of kindness
and consolation, and his voice was modulated to a
deep tone of tenderness, when he took the little
children in his arms.

The following "first day," which world's people call
the Sabbath, meeting was attended at Newtown by the

whole family, and then John Estaugh was moved by the Spirit to speak words that sank into the hearts of his hearers. It was a discourse on the trials and temptations of daily life, drawing a contrast between this course of earthly probation, with its toils, sufferings, and sorrows, and that higher life, with its rewards to the faithful beyond the grave.

Elizabeth listened to the preacher with meek attention; he seemed to be speaking to her, for all the lessons of the discourse were applicable to herself. As the deep tones of the good man ceased to vibrate in her ears, and there was stillness for a full half hour in the house, she pondered over it deeply. The impression made by the young preacher seemed to open a new window in her soul; he was a God-sent messenger, whose character and teachings would lift still higher her life, and sanctify her mission with a holier inspiration.

A few days of united duties and oneness of heart made John and Elizabeth more thoroughly acquainted with each other than they could have been by years of ordinary fashionable intercourse.

They were soon obliged to separate, the young preacher being called to other meetings of his sect in New Jersey and Pennsylvania. When they bade each other farewell, neither knew that they would ever meet again, for John Estaugh's duty might call him from the country ere another winter, and his avocations in the new world were absorbing and continuous. With a full heart, but with the meekness characteristic of her sect, Elizabeth turned away to her daily round of good works with a new and holier zeal.

In May following they met again. John Estaugh,

in company with numerous other Friends, stopped at her house to lodge while on their way to the quarterly meeting at Salem. The next day a cavalcade started from her hospitable door on horseback, for that was before the days of wagons in Jersey.

John Estaugh, always kindly in his impulses, busied himself with helping a lame and very ugly old woman, and left his hostess to mount her horse as she could. Most young women would have felt slighted; but in Elizabeth's noble soul the quiet, deep tide of feeling rippled with an inward joy. "He is always kindest to the poor and neglected," thought she; "verily he is a good youth."

She was leaning over the side of her horse, to adjust the buckle of the girth, when he came up on horseback and enquired if anything was out of order. She thanked him, with slight confusion of manner, and a voice less calm than her usual utterance. He assisted her to mount, and they trotted along leisurely behind the procession of guests, speaking of the soil and climate of this new country, and how wonderfully the Lord had here provided a home for his chosen people. Presently the girth began to slip, and the saddle turned so much on one side that Elizabeth was obliged to dismount. It took some time to readjust the girth, and when they again started, the company were out of sight. There was brighter color than usual in the maiden's cheeks, and unwonted radiance in her mild, deep eyes.

After a short silence, she said, in a voice slightly tremulous, "Friend John, I have a subject of importance on my mind, and one which nearly interests thee. I am strongly impressed that the Lord has sent thee

to me as a partner for life. I tell thee my impression
frankly, but not without calm and deep reflection, for
matrimony is a holy relation, and should be entered
into with all sobriety. If thou hast no light on the
subject, wilt thou gather into the stillness and rever-
ently listen to thy own inward revealings? Thou art
to leave this part of the country to-morrow, and not
knowing when I should see thee again, I felt moved
to tell thee what lay upon my mind."

The young man was taken by surprise. Though
accustomed to that suppression of emotion which
characterizes his religious sect, the color came and
went rapidly in his face, for a moment. But he soon
became calmer, and replied, "This thought is new to
me, Elizabeth, and I have no light thereon. Thy
company has been right pleasant to me, and thy countenance ever reminds me of William Penn's title-page,
'*Innocency with her open face.*' I have seen thy kindness to the poor, and the wise management of thy
household. I have observed, too, that thy warm-
heartedness is tempered with a most excellent discretion, and that thy speech is ever sincere. Assuredly,
such is the maiden I would ask of the Lord as a most
precious gift; but I never thought of this connection
with thee. I came to this country solely on a
religious visit, and it might distract my mind to entertain this subject at present. When I have discharged
the duties of my mission, we will speak further."

"It is best so," rejoined the maiden, "but there is
one thing disturbs my conscience. Thou hast spoken
of my true speech; and yet, friend John, I have
deceived thee a little, even now, while we conferred
together on a subject so serious. I know not from

what weakness the temptation came, but I will not
hide it from thee. I allowed thee to suppose, just
now, that I was fastening the girth of my horse
securely; but, in plain truth, I was loosening the girth,
John, that the saddle might slip, and give me an
excuse to fall behind our friends; for I thought thou
wouldst be kind enough to come and ask if I needed
thy services."

They spoke no further upon this topic; but when
John Estaugh returned to England in July, he pressed
her hand affectionately, as he said, "Farewell, Elizabeth: if it be the Lord's will I shall return to thee
soon."

The young preacher made but a brief sojourn in
England. The Society of Friends in London appreciated his value as a laborer among them and would
have been pleased to see him remain, but they knew
how fruitful of good had been his labors among the
brethren in the wilderness, and deemed it a wise resolution when he informed them that he should shortly
return to America. Early in September he set sail
from London and reached New York the following
month. A few days after landing he journeyed on
horseback to the dwelling where Elizabeth was awaiting him, and they were soon after married at Newtown
Meeting according to the simple form of the Society
of Friends. Neither of them made any change of
dress for the occasion; there was no wedding feast;
no priest or magistrate was present; in the presence
of witnesses they simply took each other by the hand
and solemnly promised to be kind and faithful to each
other. The wedded pair then quietly returned to
their happy home, prepared to resume together that

life of good words and kind deeds which each had thus far pursued alone.

Thrice during the long period of their union did she cross the Atlantic to visit her aged parents, and not seldom he left her for a season when called to preach abroad. These temporary separations were hard for her to bear, but she cheerfully gave him up to follow in the path of his duty wherever it might lead him. Amid her cares and pleasures as a wife she neither grew self-absorbed nor, like many of her sex, bounded her benevolence within the area of the household. Her heart was too large, her charity too abounding, to do that, and her sense of duty to her fellow-men always dominated that narrow feeling which concentrates kindness on self or those nearest to one. While her husband performed his noble work in the care of souls, she pursued her career within the sphere where it was so allotted. As a housewife she was notable; to her might be applied the words of King Lemuel, in the Proverbs of Solomon, celebrating and describing the good wife, "and her works praised her in the gates." As a neighbor she was generous and sympathetic; she stretched out her hand to the poor and needy; she was at once a guardian and a minister of mercy to the settlement.

When, after forty years of happiness in wedlock, her husband was taken from her, she gave evidence of her appreciation of his worth in a preface which she published to one of his religious tracts entitled, "Elizabeth Estaugh's testimony concerning her beloved husband, John Estaugh." In this preface she says:

"Since it pleased Divine Providence so highly to

favor me with being the near companion to this dear worthy, I must give some small account of him. Few, if any, in a married state, ever lived in sweeter harmony than we did. He was a pattern of moderation in all things; not lifted up with any enjoyments, nor cast down at disappointments; a man endowed with many good gifts, which rendered him very agreeable to his friends, and much more to me, his wife, to whom his memory is most dear and precious."

Elizabeth survived her excellent husband twenty years, useful and honored to the last. The monthly meeting of Haddonfield, in a published testimonial, speaks of her thus:

"She was endowed with great natural abilities, which, being sanctified by the Spirit of Christ, were much improved; whereby she became qualified to act in the affairs of the church, and was a serviceable member, having been clerk to the woman's meeting nearly fifty years, greatly to their satisfaction. She was a sincere sympathizer with the afflicted; of a benevolent disposition, and in distributing to the poor, was desirous to do it in a way most profitable and durable to them, and, if possible, not to let the right hand know what the left did. Though in a state of affluence as to this world's wealth, she was an example of plainness and moderation. Her heart and house were open to her friends, whom to entertain seemed one of her greatest pleasures. Prudently cheerful and well knowing the value of friendship, she was careful not to wound it herself nor to encourage others in whispering supposed failings or weaknesses. Her last illness brought great bodily pain, which she bore with much calmness of mind and sweetness of spirit. She departed this life as one falling asleep, full of days, "like unto a shock of corn fully ripe.' "

The maiden name of this gentle and useful woman has been preserved in Haddonfield, thus appropriately commemorating her manifold services in the early days of the settlement of which she was the pioneer-mother.

———•••———

CHAPTER X.

ROMANCE OF THE BORDER.

THE romance of border-life is inseparably associated with woman, being her natural attendant during her wanderings through the wilderness. A distinguished American orator has suggested that a series of novels might be written founded upon the true stories of the border-women of our country. Such a contribution to our literature has thus far been made only to a limited extent. The reason for this deficiency will be obvious on a moment's reflection. The *true stories* of the pioneer-wives and mothers are often as interesting as any work of fiction, and need no embellishment from the imagination of a writer, because they are crowded with incidents and situations as thrilling as those which form the staple out of which novels are fabricated; love and adventure, hair-breadth escapes, heart-rending tragedies on the frontier, are thus woven into a narrative of absorbing and permanent interest, *permanent* because it is part of the history and biography of America. Some of the truest of these stories are those which are most deeply fraught with tenderness and romance. What is more calculated to move the mind and heart of man for example than a story of two lovers environed by some deadly danger, or of separation and reunion, or a love faithful unto death?

Many years ago a young pioneer traveling across the plains met a lady to whom he became attached, and after a short courtship they were united in marriage. A trip over the plains in those days was not one to be chosen for a honey-moon excursion but the pair bore their labors and privations cheerfully; perils and hardships only seemed to draw them closer together, and they were looking forward to a home on the Pacific slope where in plenty and repose they would be indemnified for the pains and fatigues of the journey. But their life's romance was destined, alas! to a sudden and mournful end. While crossing one of the rapid mountain streams their boat filled with water, and though the young man struggled manfully to gain the shore with his bride, the rush of the torrent bore them down and they sank to rise no more. An hour later their bodies were found locked together in a last embrace. The rough mountaineers had not the heart to unclasp that embrace but buried them by the side of the river in one grave.

The Indian was of course an important factor in the composition of these border romances. He was generally the villain in the plot of the story, and too often a successful villain whose wiles or open attacks were the means of separating two lovers. These tales have

TWO KENTUCKY GIRLS CAPTURED BY INDIANS.

Page 220.

often a tragical catastrophe, but sometimes the *denouement* is a happy one, thanks to the courage and constancy of the heroine or hero.

*Among the adventurers whom Daniel Boone the
famous hunter and Indian fighter of Kentucky, de-
scribes as having re-inforced his little colony was a
young gentleman named Smith, who had been a major
in the militia of Virginia, and possessed a full share of
the gallantry and noble spirit of his native State. In
the absence of Boone he was chosen, on account of his
military rank and talent, to command the rude citadel
which contained all the wealth of this patriarchal band,
their wives, their children, and their herds. It held
also an object particularly dear to this young soldier—
a lady, the daughter of one of the settlers, to whom
he had pledged his affections. It came to pass upon
a certain day when a siege was just over, tranquillity
restored, and the employment of husbandry resumed,
that this young lady, with a lady companion, strolled
out, as young ladies in love are very apt to do, along
the bank of the Kentucky River.

Having rambled about for some time they espied a
canoe lying by the shore, and in a frolic stepped into
it, with the determination of visiting a neighbor on the
opposite bank. It seems that they were not so well
skilled in navigation as the Lady of the Lake who
paddled her own canoe very dexterously; for instead
of gliding to the point of destination they were whirled
about by the stream, and at length thrown on a sand-
bar from which they were obliged to wade to the shore.
Full of the mirth excited by their wild adventure they
hastily arranged their dresses and were proceeding to
climb the bank, when three Indians rushed from a

* Potter's Life of Daniel Boone.

neighboring covert, seized the fair wanderers, and forced them away. Their savage captors evincing no sympathy for their distress, nor allowing them time for rest or reflection, hurried them along during the whole day by rugged and thorny paths. Their shoes were worn off by the rocks, their clothes torn, and their feet and limbs lacerated and stained with blood. To heighten their misery one of the savages began to make love to Miss ———, (the intended of Major S.) and while goading her along with a pointed stick, promised in recompense for her sufferings to make her his squaw. This at once roused all the energies of her mind and called its powers into action. In the hope that her friends would soon pursue them she broke the twigs as she passed along and delayed the party as much as possible by tardy and blundering steps. The day and the night passed, and another day of agony had nearly rolled over the heads of these afflicted girls, when their conductors halted to cook a hasty repast of buffalo meat.

The ladies meanwhile were soon missed from the garrison. The natural courage and sagacity of Smith now heightened by love, gave him the wings of the wind and the fierceness of the tiger. The light traces of feminine feet led him to the place of embarkation; the canoe was traced to the opposite shore; the deep prints of the moccasin in the sand told the rest of the story.

The agonized Smith, accompanied by a few of his best woodsmen, pursued the spoil-encumbered foe. The track once discovered they kept it with that unerring sagacity so peculiar to our hunters. The bended grass, the disentangled briars, and the compressed shrubs afforded the only, but to them the certain indication of the route of the enemy. When they had sufficiently ascertained the general course of the retreat of the Indians, Smith quitted the trace, assuring his companions that they would fall in with them at the pass of a certain stream-head for which he now struck a direct course, thus gaining on the foe who had taken the most difficult paths.

Having arrived at the stream, they traced its course until they discovered the water newly thrown upon the rocks. Smith, leaving his party, now crept forward upon his hands and knees, until he discovered one of the savages seated by a fire, and with a deliberate aim shot him through the heart. The women rushed towards their deliverer, and recognizing Smith, clung to him in the transport of newly awakened joy and gratitude; while a second Indian sprang towards him with his tomahawk. Smith, disengaging himself from the ladies, aimed a blow at his antagonist with his rifle, which the savage avoided by springing aside, but at the same moment the latter received a mortal wound from another hand. The other and only remaining Indian fell in attempting to escape. Smith with his interesting charge returned in triumph to the fort where his gallantry no doubt was repaid by the sweetest of all rewards.

The May flower, or trailing arbutus, has been aptly styled our national flower. It lifts its sweet face in the desolate and rugged hillside, and flourishes in the chilly air and earth of early spring. So amid the rude scenes of frontier-life, love and romance peep out, and courtship is conducted in log cabins and even in more untoward places.

A tradition of the early settlement of Auburn, New York, relates that while Captain Hardenberg, the stout young miller, was busy with his sacks of grain in his little log-mill, he was unexpectedly assaulted and overwhelmed with the arrows not of the savages but of love. The sweet eyes as well as the blooming health and courage of the daughter of Roeliffe Brinkerhoff who had been sent by her father to the mill, made young Hardenberg capitulate, and during the hour while she was waiting for the grist he managed thoroughly to assure her of the state of his affections; the courtship thus well begun resulted soon after in a wedding.

The imagination of the poet garnering the anecdotes and early traditions of the frontier around which lingers an aroma of love, has clothed them with new life, adorned them with bright colors, endowed them with fresh and vernal perfume and then woven them into a wreath with the magic art of poesy. From out of a group of stern features on Plymouth rock, graven with the deep lines of austere and almost cruel duty, the sweet face of Rose Standish looks winningly at us. The rugged captain of the Pilgrim band wooes Priscilla Mullins, through his friend John Alden, and finds too late that love does not prove fortunate when made by proxy; and Evangeline, maid, wife and widow comes back to us in beauty and sorrow from the far Acadian border. These romances of our eastern country have been fortunate in having a poet to make them immortal. But the West is equally fruitful in incidents which furnish material, and only lack the poet or novelist to work them up into enduring form.

The western country seems naturally fitted in many

ways for love and romance. In that region the mind
is uncramped and unfettered by the excessive schooling and over-training which prevails in the older settlements of the East. The heart beats more freely
and warmly when its current is unchecked by conventionalities. Life is more intense in the West. The
transitions of life are more frequent and startling.
Both men and things are continually changing. In
such a society impulse governs largely: the cooler and
more selfish faculties of man's nature are less domi-
nant. When we add to these conditions, the changes,
hardships, and enforced separations of the frontier as
frequent concomitants, we have exactly a state of society which is fruitful in romantic incidents—brides
torn from their husband's embrace and hurried away;
but restored as suddenly and strangely; two faithful
lovers parted forever or re-united miraculously; and
thrilling scenes in love's melodrama acted and re-acted
on different stages but always with startling effect.

The effects of the romantic incidents in the lives of
our pioneer women are also heightened by the extraordinary freshness and ever-changing scenery of the
wilderness. Nature there spreads out like a mighty
canvas: the forest, the mountains, and the prairies
show clear and distinct through the crystal air so that
peak and tree and even the tall blades of grass are
outlined with a microscopic nearness. Over this vivid
surface bison are browsing, and antelopes gambolling;
plumed warriors flit by on their ponies, as the pioneer-
men and women with wagons, oxen and horses are
moving westward. This is the scene where love
springs spontaneously out of the close companionship
which danger enforces.

The story of the Chase family is an illustration of the adage that truth is often stranger than fiction, and might readily furnish the groundwork upon which the genius of some future Cooper could construct an American romance of thrilling interest.

The stage whereon this drama of real life was acted lay in that rich, broad expanse between the Arkansas and the South Platte Rivers. The time, 1847. The principal actors were the Chase family, consisting of old Mr. Chase, his wife, sons, and grandsons, Mary, his daughter, LaBonté and Kilbuck two famous hunters and mountaineers, Antoine a guide and Arapahoe Indians.

The scene opens with a view of three white-tilted Conestoga wagons or "prairie schooners," each drawn by four pair of oxen rumbling along through a plain enameled with the verdure and many tinted flowers of spring. The day is drawing to its close, and the rays of the sinking sun throw a mellow light over a waving sea of vernal herbage. The wagons are driven by the sons of Mr. Chase and contain the women and the household goods of the family. Behind the great swaying "schooners" walk the men with shouldered rifles, and a troup of mounted men have just galloped up to bid adieu to the departing emigrants. From out this group, the mild face of Mary Chase beams with a parting smile in response to rough but kindly farewells of these her old friends and neighbors. The last words of warning and God-speed are spoken by the mounted men, who gallop away and leave them making their first stage on a journey which will carry them northward and westward more than two thousand miles from their old home in Missouri.

And now the sun has set, and still in the twilight the train moves on, stopping as the darkness falls, at a rich bottom, where the loose cattle, starting some hours before them, have been driven and corralled. The oxen are unyoked, the wagons drawn up, so as to form the sides of a small square. A huge fire is kindled, the women descend and prepare the evening meal, boiling great kettles of coffee, and baking corncakes in the embers. The whole company stretch themselves around the fire, and having finished their repast, address themselves to sweet sleep, such as tired voyagers over the plains can so well enjoy. The men of the party are soon soundly slumbering; but the women, depressed with the thoughts that they are leaving their home and loved friends and neighbors, perhaps forever, their hearts filled with forebodings of danger and misfortune, cast only wakeful eyes upon the darkened plain or up to the inscrutable stars that are shining with marvelous brightness in the azure firmament. Far into the night they wake and watch, silently weeping until nature is exhausted, and a sleep, troubled with sad dreams, visits them.

With the first light of morning the camp is astir, and as the sun rises, the wagons are again rolling along across the upland prairies, to strike the trail leading to the south fork of the Platte. Slowly and hardly, fifteen miles each day, they toil on over the heavy soil. At night, while in camp, the hours are beguiled by Antoine, their Canadian guide, who tells stories of wild life and perilous adventures among the hunters and trappers who make the prairies and mountains their home. His descriptions of Indian fights and slaughters, and of the sufferings and priva-

15

tions endured by the hunters in their arduous life, fix the attention of the women of the party, and especially of Mary Chase, who listens with greater interest because she remembers that such was the life led by one very dear to her—one long supposed to be dead, and of whom, since his departure, fifteen years before, she has heard not a syllable. Her imagination now pictures him anew, as the most daring of these adventurous hunters, and conjures up his figure charging through the midst of yelling savages, or as stretched on the ground, perishing of wounds, or of cold and famine.

Among the characters that figure in Antoine's stories is a hunter named La Bonte, made conspicuous by his deeds of hardihood and daring. At the first mention of his name Mary's face is suffused with blushes; not that she for a moment dreamed that it could be her long lost La Bonte, for she knows that the name is a common one, but because from associations which still linger in her memory, it recalled a sad era in her former life, to which she could not revert without a strange mingling of pleasure and pain. She remembers the manly form of La Bonte as she first saw him, and the love which sprang up between them; and then the parting, with the hope of speedy reunion. She remembers how two years passed without tidings of her lover, when, one bitter day, she met a mountaineer, just returned from the far West to settle in his native State; and, inquiring tremblingly after La Bonte, he told how he had met his death from the Blackfeet Indians in the wild gorges of the Yellowstone country.

Now, on hearing once more that name, a spring of

sweet and bitter recollections is opened and a vague hope is raised in her breast that the lover of her youth is still alive. She questions the Canadian, "Who was this La Bonte who you say was such a brave mountaineer?" Antoine replies, "He was a fine fellow—strong as a buffalo-bull, a dead shot, cared not a rush for the Indians, left a girl that he loved in Missouri, said the girl did not love him, and so he followed the trail to the mountains. He hasn't gone under yet; be sure of that," says the good natured guide, observing the emotion which Mary showed, and suspecting that she took a more than ordinary interest in the young hunter.

As the guide ceased to speak, Mary turns away and bursts into a flood of tears. The mention of the name of one whom she had long believed dead, and the recital of his praiseworthy qualities, awake the strongest feelings which she had cherished towards one whose loss she still bewails.

The scene now changes to the camp of a party of hunters almost within rifle-shot of the spot where the Chase family are sitting around their evening fire. There are three in this party: one is Kilbuck, so known on the plains, another is a stranger who has chanced to join them, the third is a hunter named *La Bonte.*

The conversation turning on the party encamped near them, the stranger remarks that their name is Chase. La Bonte looks up a moment from the lock of his rifle, which he is cleaning, but either does not hear, or, hearing, does not heed, for he resumes his work. "Traveling alone to the Platte valley," continues the stranger, "they'll lose their hair, sure." "I hope not,"

rejoins Kilbuck, " for there's a girl among them worth
more than that." " Where does she come from,
stranger," inquires La Bonte. " Down below Missouri,
from Tennessee, I hear." " And·what's her name ? "
The colloquy is interrupted by the entrance into the
camp of an Arapahoe Indian. The hunters address
him in his own language. They learn from him that
a war-party of his people was out on the Platte-trail
to intercept the traders on their return from the North
Fork. He cautions them against crossing the divide,
as the braves, he says, are " a heap mad, and take
white scalp." The Indian, rewarded for his information with a feast of buffalo-meat, leaves the camp and
starts for the mountains. The hunters pursue their
journey the next day, traveling leisurely along, and
stopping where good grass and abundant game is
found, until, one morning, they suddenly strike a
wheel-track, which left the creek-bank and pursued a
course at right angles to it in the direction of the
divide. Kilbuck pronounces it but a few hours old,
and that of three wagons drawn by oxen. " These are
the wagons of old Chase," says the strange hunter
" they're going right into the Rapahoe trap," cries
Kilbuck. " I knew the name of Chase years ago,"
says La Bonte in a low tone, " and I should hate the
worst kind to have mischief happen to any one that
bore it. This trail is fresh as paint, and it goes against
me to let these simple critters help the Rapahoes to
their own hair. This child feels like helping them
out of the scrape. What do you say, old hos ? " " I
think with you, my boy," replies Kilbuck, " and go in
for following the wagon-trail and telling the poor critters that there's danger ahead of them. " What's

your talk, stranger?" "I'm with you," answered the latter; and both follow quickly after La Bonte, who gallops away on the trail.

Returning now to the Chase family, we see again the three white-topped wagons rumbling slowly over the rolling prairie and towards the upland ridge of the divide which rose before them, studded with dwarf pines and cedar thickets. They are evidently traveling with caution, for the quick eye of Antoine, the guide, has discovered recent Indian signs upon the trail, and with the keenness of a mountaineer he at once sees that it is that of a war-party, for there were no horses with them and after one or two of the moccasin tracks there was the mark of a rope which trailed upon the ground. This was enough to show him that the Indians were provided with the usual lassoes of skin with which to secure the horses stolen on the expedition. The men of the party accordingly are all mounted and thoroughly armed, the wagons are moving in a line abreast, and a sharp lookout is kept on all sides. The women and children are all consigned to the interior of the wagons and the former also hold guns in readiness to take part in the defense should an attack be made. As they move slowly on their course no Indians make their presence visible and the party are evidently losing their fears if not their caution.

As the shadows are lengthening they reach Black Horse Creek, and corrall their wagons, kindle a fire, and are preparing for the night, when three or four Indians suddenly show themselves on the bluff and making friendly signals approach the camp. Most of the men are away attending to the cattle or collecting fuel, and only old Chase and a grandson fourteen years of age are in the camp. The Indians are hospitably received and regaled with a smoke, after which they gratify their curiosity by examining the articles lying around, and among others which takes their fancy the pot boiling over the fire, with which one of them is about very coolly to walk off, when old Chase, snatching it from the Indian's hands, knocks him down. One of his companions instantly begins to draw the buckskin cover from his gun and is about to take summary vengeance for the insult offered to his companion, when Mary Chase, courageously advancing, places her left hand on the gun which he is in the act of uncovering and with the other points a pistol at his breast.

Whether daunted by this bold act of the girl, or admiring her devotion to her father, the Indian, drawing back with a deep grunt, replaces the cover on his piece and motioning to the other Indians to be peaceable, shakes hands with old Chase, who all this time looks him steadily in the face.

The other whites soon return, the supper is ready, and all hands sit down to the repast. The Indians then gather their buffalo-robes about them and quickly withdraw. In spite of their quiet demeanor, Antoine says they mean mischief. Every precaution is therefore taken against surprise; the mules and horses are hobbled, the oxen only being allowed to run at large; a guard is set around the camp; the fire is extinguished lest the savages should aim by its light at any of the party; and all slept with rifles and pistols ready at their side.

The night, however, passes quietly away, and nothing disturbs the tranquility of the camp except the mournful cry of the prairie wolf chasing the antelope. The sun has now risen; they are yoking the cattle to the wagons and driving in the mules and horses, when a band of Indians show themselves on the bluff and descending it approach the camp with an air of confidence. They are huge braves, hideously streaked with war-paint, and hide the malignant gleams that shoot from their snaky eyes with assumed smiles and expressions of good nature.

Old Chase, ignorant of Indian treachery and in spite of the warnings of Antoine, offering no obstruction to their approach, has allowed them to enter the camp. What madness! They have divested themselves of their buffalo-robes, and appear naked to the breech-clout and armed with bows and arrows, tomahawks, and scalping knives. Six or seven only come in at first, but others quickly follow, dropping in by twos and threes until a score or more are collected around the wagons.

Their demeanor, at first friendly, changes to insolence and then to fierceness. They demand powder and shot, and when they are refused begin to brandish their tomahawks. A tall chief, motioning to the band to keep back, now accosts Mr. Chase, and through Antoine as an interpreter, informs him that unless the demands of his braves are complied with he will not be responsible for the consequences; that they are out on the war-trail and their eyes red with blood so that they cannot distinguish between white man's and Utah's scalps; that the party and all their women and wagons are in the power of the Indian braves; and therefore that the white chief's best plan will be to make what terms he can; that all they require is that they shall give up their guns and ammunition on the prairie and all their mules and horses, retaining only the medicine-buffaloes (the oxen) to draw their wagons. By this time the oxen have been yoked to the teams and the teamsters stand whip in hand ready for the order to start. Old Chase trembles with rage at the insolent demand. "Not a grain of powder to save my life," he yells; "put out boys!" As he turns to mount his horse which stands ready saddled, the Indians leap upon the wagons and others rush against the men who make a brave fight in their defence. Mary, who sees her father struck to the ground, springs with a shrill cry to his assistance at the moment when a savage, crimson with paint and looking like a red demon, bestrides his prostrate body, brandishing a glittering knife in the air preparatory to plunging it into the old man's heart. All is wild confusion. The whites are struggling heroically against overpowering numbers. A single volley of rifles is heard and three Indians bite the dust. A moment later and the brave defenders are disarmed amid the shrieks of the women and the children and the triumphant whoops of the savages.

Mary, flying to her father's rescue, has been overtaken by a huge Indian, who throws his lasso over her shoulders and drags her to the earth, then drawing his scalping-knife he is about to tear the gory trophy from her head. The girl, rising upon her knees, struggles towards the spot where her father lies, now bathed in blood. The Indian jerks the lariat violently and drags her on her face, and with a wild yell rushes to complete the bloody work.

At that instant a yell as fierce as his own is echoed from the bluff, and looking up he sees La Bonte charging down the declivity, his long hair and the fringes of his garments waving in the breeze, his trusty rifle supported in his right arm, and hard after him Kilbuck and the stranger galloping with loud shouts to the scene of action. As La Bonte races madly down the side of the bluff, he catches sight of the girl as the ferocious savage is dragging her over the ground. A cry of horror and vengeance escapes his lips, as driving his spurs to the rowels into his steed he bounds like an arrow to the rescue. Another instant and he is upon his foe; pushing the muzzle of his rifle against the broad chest of the Indian he pulled the trigger, literally blowing out the savage's heart. Dropping his rifle, he wheels his trained horse and drawing a pistol from his belt he charges the enemy among whom Kilbuck and the stranger are dealing death-blows. The Indians, panic-stricken by the suddenness of the attack, turn and flee, leaving several of their number dead upon the field.

Mary, with her arms bound to her body by the lasso, and with her eyes closed to receive the fatal stroke, hears the defiant shout of La Bonte, and glancing up between her half-opened eyelids, sees the wild figure of the mountaineer as he sends the bullet to the heart of her foe. When the Indians flee, La Bonte, the first to run to her aid, cuts the skin-rope, raises her from the ground, looks long and intently in her face, and sees his never-to-be-forgotten Mary Chase. "What! can it be you, Mary?" he exclaims, gazing at the trembling maiden, who hardly believes her eyes as she returns his gaze and recognizes in her deliverer her former lover. She only sobs and clings closer to him in speechless gratitude and love.

Turning from these lovers reunited so miraculously, we see stretched on the battle-field the two grandsons of Mr. Chase, fine lads of fourteen or fifteen, who after fighting like men fall dead pierced with arrows and lances. Old Chase and his sons are slightly wounded, and Antoine shot through the neck and half scalped. The dead boys are laid tenderly beneath the prairie-sod, the wounds of the others are dressed, and the following morning the party continue their journey to the Platte. The three hunters guide and guard them on their way, Mary riding on horseback by the side of her lover.

For many days they pursued their journey, but with feelings far different from those with which they had made its earlier stages. Old Mr. Chase marches on doggedly and in silence; his resolution to seek a new home on the banks of the Columbia has been shaken more by the loss of his grandsons, than by the fatigues and privations incident to the march. The unbidden tears often steal down the cheeks of the women, who cast many a longing look behind them towards the southeastern horizon, far beyond whose purple rim lay their old home. The South Fork of the Platte has been passed, Laramie reached, and for a fortnight the lofty summits of the mountains which overhang the "pass" to California have been in sight; but when they strike the broad trail which would conduct them to their promised land in the valley of the Columbia, the party pause, gaze for a moment steadfastly at the mountain-summits, and then as if by a common impulse, the heads of the horses and oxen are faced to the east, and men, women, and children toss their hats and bonnets in the air, hurrahing lustily for home as the huge wagons roll down along the banks of the river Platte. The closing scene in this romantic melodrama was the marriage of Mary and La Bonte, in Tennessee, four months after the rescue of the Chase family from the Indians.

The following " romance of the forest " we believe has never before been published. The substance of it was communicated to the writer by a gentleman who received it from his grandfather, one of the early settlers of Michigan.

In the year 1762 the Great Pontiac, the Indian Napoleon of the Northwest, had his headquarters in a small secluded island at the opening of Lake St. Clair. Here he organized, with wonderful ability and secrecy, a wide-reaching conspiracy, having for its object the destruction of every English garrison and settlement in Michigan. His envoys, with blood-stained hatchets, had been despatched to the various Indian tribes of the region, and wherever these emblems of butchery had been accepted the savage hordes were gathering, and around their bale-fires in the midnight pantomimes of murder were concentrating their excitable natures into a burning focus which would light their path to carnage and rapine.

While these lurid clouds, charged with death and destruction, were gathering, unseen, about the heads of the adventurous pioneers, who had penetrated that beautiful region, a family of eastern settlers, named Rouse, arrived in the territory, and, disregarding the admonitions of the officers in the fort at Detroit, pushed on twenty miles farther west and planted themselves in the heart of one of those magnificent oak-openings which the Almighty seems to have designed as parks and pleasure-grounds for the sons and daughters of the forest.

Miss Anna Rouse, the only daughter of the family, had been betrothed before her departure from New York State to a young man named James Philbrick, who had afterward gone to fight the French and Indians. It was understood that upon his return he was to follow the Rouse family to Michigan, where, upon his arrival, the marriage was to take place.

In a few months young Philbrick reached the appointed place, and in the following week married Miss Rouse in the presence of a numerous assemblage of soldiers and settlers, who had come from the military posts and the nearest plantations to join in the festivities.

All was gladness and hilarity; the hospitality was bounteous, the company joyous, the bridegroom brave and manly, and the bride lovely as a wild rose. When the banquet was ready the guests trooped into the room where it was spread, and even the sentinels who had been posted beside the muskets in the door-yard, seeing no signs of prowling savages, had entered the house and were enjoying the feast. Scarcely had they abandoned their post when an ear-piercing war-whoop silenced in a moment the joyous sound of the revelers. The soldiers rushed to the door only to be shot down. A few succeeded in recovering their arms, and made a desperate fight. Meanwhile the savages battered down the doors, and leaped in at the windows. The bridegroom was shot, and left for dead, as he was assisting to conceal his bride, and a gigantic warrior, seizing the latter, bore her away into the darkness. After a short but terrific struggle, the savages were driven out of the house, but the defenders were so crippled by their losses and by the want of arms which the enemy had carried away, that it was judged best not to attempt to pursue the Indians, who had disappeared as suddenly as they came.

When the body of the bridegroom was lifted up it was discovered that his heart still beat, though but faintly. Restoratives were administered, and he slowly came back to life, and to the sad consciousness that all that could make life happy to him was gone for ever.

The family soon after abandoned their new home and moved to Detroit, owing to the danger of fresh attacks from Pontiac and his confederates. Years rolled away; young Philbrick, as soon as he recovered from his wounds, took part in the stirring scenes of the war, and strove to forget, in turmoil and excitement, the loss of his fair young bride. But in vain. Her remembrance in the fray nerved his arm to strike, and steadied his eye to launch the bullet at the heart of the hated foes who had bereft him of his dearest treasure; and in the stillness of the night his imagination pictured her, the cruel victim of her barbarous captors.

Peace came in 1763, and he then learned that she had been carried to Canada. He hastened down the St. Lawrence and passed from settlement to settlement, but could gain no tidings of her. After two years, spent in unavailing search, he came back a sad and almost broken-hearted man.

Her image, as she appeared when last he saw her,

all radiant in youth and beauty, haunted his waking hours, and in his dreams she was with him as a visible presence.   Months, years rolled away; he gave her up as dead, but he did not forget his long-lost bride.

One summer's day, while sitting in his cabin in Michigan, in one of those beautiful natural parks, where he had chosen his abode, he heard a light step, and, looking up, saw his bride standing before him, beautiful still, but with a chastened beauty which told of years of separation and grief.

Her story was a long one.   When she was borne away from the marriage feast by her savage captor, she was seen by an old squaw, the wife of a famous chief who had just lost her own daughter, and being attracted by the beauty of Miss Rouse, she protected her from violence, and finally adopted her.   Twice she escaped, but was recaptured.   The old squaw afterwards took her a thousand miles into the wilderness, and watched her with the ferocious tenderness that the tigress shows for her young.   At length, after nearly six years, her Indian mother died.   She succeeded then in making her escape, traveled four hundred miles on foot, reached the St. Lawrence, and after passing through great perils and hardships, arrived at Detroit.   There she soon found friends, who relieved her wants and conveyed her to her husband, whom she had remembered with fondness and loved with constancy during all the weary years of her captivity.

CHAPTER XI.

A HUNDRED ills brood over the cabin in the wilderness. Some are ever-present; others lie in wait, and start forth at intervals.

Labor, Solitude, Fear; these are the companions of woman on the border: to these come other visitants—weariness, and that longing, yearning, pining of the heart which the Germans so beautifully term *sehn-sucht*—hunger, vigils, bodily pain and sickness, the biting cold, the drenching storm, the fierce heat, with savage eyes of man and beast glaring from the thicket. Then sorrow takes bodily shape and enters the house: loved ones are borne away—the child, or the father, or saddest of all, the mother; the long struggle is over, and the devoted woman of the household lays her wasted form beneath the grassy sod of the cabin yard.

Bereavement is hard to bear in even the houses where comfort, ease, and luxury surround the occupants, where friends and kinsfolk crowd to pour out sympathy and consolation. But what must it be in the rude cabin on the lonely border? The grave hollowed out in the hard soil of the little inclosure, the rough shell-coffin hewn with tears from the forest tree, the sorrowing household ranged in silence beside the form which will gladden the loneliness of that stricken

(239)

family no longer, and then the mourners turn away and go back to their homely toils.

If from the time of the landing we could recall the long procession of the actors and the events of border-life, and pass them before the eye in one great moving panorama, how somber would be the colors of that picture! All along the grand march what scenes of captivity, suffering, bereavement, sorrow, and in these scenes, woman the most prominent figure, for she was the constant actress in this great drama of woe!

The carrying away and the return of captives in war has furnished themes by which poets and artists in all ages have moved the heart of man. The breaking up of homes, the violent separations of those who are kindred by blood, and the sundering for ever of family ties were ordinary and every day incidents in the border-wars of our country: but the frequency of such occurrences does not detract from the mournful interest with which they are always fraught.

At the close of the old French and Indian War, Colonel Henry Bouquet stipulated with the Indian tribes on the Ohio frontier as one of the conditions of peace that they should restore all the captives which they had taken. This was agreed to, and on his return march he was met by a great company of settlers in search of their lost relatives. "Husbands found their wives and parents their children, from whom they had been separated for years. Women frantic between hope and fear, were running hither and thither, looking piercingly into the face of every child, to find their own, which, perhaps, had died—and then such shrieks of agony! Some of the little captives shrank from their own forgotten mothers, and hid in terror in the blankets of the squaws that had adopted them. Some that had been taken away young, had grown up and married Indian husbands or Indian wives, and now stood utterly bewildered with conflicting emotions. A young Virginian had found his wife ; but his little boy, not two years old when captured, had been torn from her, and had been carried off, no one knew whither. One day a warrior came in, leading a child. No one seemed to own it. But soon the mother knew her offspring and screaming with joy, folded her son to her bosom. An old woman had lost her grand-daughter in the French war, nine years before. All her other relatives had died under the knife. Searching, with trembling eagerness, in each face, she at last recognized the altered features of her child. But the girl who had forgotten her native tongue, returned no answer, and made no sign. The old woman groaned, wept, and complained bitterly, that the daughter she had so often sung to sleep on her knees, had forgotten her in her old age. Soldiers and officers were alike overcome. 'Sing,' whispered Bouquet, 'sing the song you used to sing.' As the low, trembling tones began to ascend, the wild girl gave one sudden start, then listening for a moment longer, her frame shaking like an ague, she burst into a passionate flood of tears. That was sufficient. She was the lost child. All else had been effaced from her memory, but the music of the nursery-song. During her captivity she had heard it in her dreams."

Another story of the same character is that of Frances Slocum, the "Lost child of Wyoming," which though perhaps familiar to some of our readers, will bear repeating.

16

In the time of the Revolution the house of Mr. Slocum in the Wyoming valley, was attacked by a party of Delawares. The inmates of the house, at the moment of the surprise, were Mrs. Slocum and four young children, the eldest of whom was a son aged thirteen, the second, a daughter aged nine, the third, Frances Slocum, aged five, and a little son aged two and a half.

The girl, aged nine years old, appears to have had the most presence of mind, for while the mother ran into a copse of wood near by, and Frances attempted to secrete herself behind a staircase, the former seized her little brother, the youngest above mentioned, and ran off in the direction of the fort. True she could not make rapid progress, for she clung to the child, and not even the pursuit of the savages could induce her to drop her charge. The Indians did not pursue her far, and laughed heartily at the panic of the little girl, while they could not but admire her resolution. Allowing her to make her escape, they returned to the house, and after helping themselves to such articles as they chose, prepared to depart.

The mother seems to have been unobserved by them, although, with a yearning bosom, she had so disposed of herself that while she was screened from observation she could notice all that occurred. But judge of her feelings at the moment when they were about to depart, as she saw her little Frances taken from her hiding place, and preparations made to carry her away into captivity. The sight was too much for maternal tenderness to endure. Rushing from her place of concealment, she threw herself upon her knees at the feet of the captors, and with the most earnest entreaties pleaded for the restoration of the child. But their bosoms were made of sterner stuff than to yield even to the most eloquent and affectionate entreaties of a mother, and with characteristic stoicism they prepared to depart. Deaf alike to the cries of the mother, and the shrieks of the child, Frances was slung over the shoulder of a stalwart Indian with as much indifference as though she were a slaughtered fawn.

The long, lingering look which the mother gave to her child, as her captors disappeared in the forest, was the last glimpse of her sweet features that she ever had. But the vision was for many a long year ever present to her fancy. As the Indian threw the child over his shoulder, her hair fell over her face, and the mother could never forget how the tears streamed down her cheeks, when she brushed it away as if to catch a last sad look of the mother from whom, her little arms outstretched, she implored assistance in vain.

These events cast a shadow over the remaining years of Mrs. Slocum. She lived to see many bright and sunny days in that beautiful valley—bright and sunny, alas! to her no longer. She mourned for the lost one, of whom no tidings, at least during her pilgrimage, could be obtained. After her sons grew up, the youngest of whom, by the way, was born but a few months subsequent to the events already narrated, obedient to the charge of their mother, the most unwearied efforts were made to ascertain what had been the fate of the lost sister. The forest between the Susquehanna and the Great Lakes, and even the most distant wilds of Canada, were traversed by the brothers in vain, nor could any information respecting her be derived from the Indians. Once, indeed, during an excursion of one of the brothers into the vast wilds of the West, a white woman, long ago captive, came to him in the hopes of finding a brother; but after many anxious efforts to discover evidences of relationship, the failure was as decisive as it was mutually sad.

There was yet another kindred occurrence, still more painful. One of the many hapless female captives in the Indian country becoming acquainted with the inquiries prosecuted by the Slocum family, presented herself to Mrs. Slocum, trusting that in her she might find her long lost mother. Mrs. Slocum was touched by her appearance, and fain would have claimed her. She led the stranger about the house and yards to see if there were any recollections by which she could be identified as her own lost one. But there was nothing written upon the pages of memory to warrant the desired conclusion, and the hapless captive returned in bitter disappointment to her forest home. In process of time these efforts were all relinquished as hopeless. The lost Frances might have fallen beneath the tomahawk or might have proved too tender a flower for transplantation into the wilderness. Conjecture was baffled, and the mother, with a sad heart, sank into the grave, as did also the father, believing with the Hebrew patriarch that the "child was not."

Long years passed away and the memory of little Frances was forgotten, save by two brothers and a sister, who, though advanced in the vale of life, could not forget the family tradition of the lost one. Indeed it had been the dying charge of their mother that they must never relinquish their exertions to discover Frances.

Fifty years and more had passed since the disappearance of little Frances, when news came to the surviving members of the bereaved family that she was still alive. She had been adopted into the tribe of the Miami Indians, and was passing her days as a squaw in the lodges of that people.

The two surviving brothers and their sister undertook a journey to see, and if possible, to reclaim, the long lost Frances. Accompanied by an interpreter whom they had engaged in the Indian country, they reached at last the designated place and found their sister. But alas! how changed! Instead of the fair-haired and laughing girl, the picture yet living in their imagination, they found her an aged and thorough-bred squaw in everything but complexion. She was sitting when they entered her lodge, composed of two large log-houses connected by a shed, with her two daughters, the one about twenty-three years old, and the other about thirty-three, and three or four pretty grandchildren. The closing hours of the journey had been made in perfect silence, deep thoughts struggling in the bosoms of all. On entering the lodge, the first exclamation of one of the brothers was,—" Oh, God! is that my sister!" A moment afterward, and the sight of her thumb, disfigured in childhood, left no doubt as to her identity. The following colloquy, conducted through the interpreter, ensued:

" What was your name when a child ? "

" I do not recollect."

" What do you remember ? "

" My father, my mother, the long river, the staircase under which I hid when they came."

" How came you to lose your thumb-nail ? "

" My brother hammered it off a long time ago, when I was a very little girl at my father's house."

" Do you know how many brothers and sisters you had ? "

She then mentioned them, and in the order of their ages.

" Would you know your name if you should hear it repeated ? "

" It is a long time since, and perhaps I should not."

" Was it Frances ? "

At once a smile played upon her features, and for a moment there seemed to pass over the face what might be called the shadow of an emotion, as she answered, " *Yes.*"

Other reminiscences were awakened, and the recognition was complete. But how different were the emotions of the parties! The brothers paced the lodge in agitation. The civilized sister was in tears. The other, obedient to the affected stoicism of her adopted race, was as cold, unmoved, and passionless as marble.

The brothers and sister returned unable, after urgent and loving entreaties, to win back their tawny sister from her wilds. Her Indian husband and children were there; there was the free, open forest, and she clung to these; and yet the love of her kinsfolk for her, and her's for them, was not quenched.

Transporting ourselves far from the beautiful valley of Wyoming, where the grief-stricken mother will wake never more to the consciousness of the loss of

PARTED FOR EVER.   Page 276.

her sweet Frances, we stand on the prairies of Kansas. The time is 1856. One of the settlers who, with his wife, was seeking to build up a community in the turmoil, which then made that beautiful region such dangerous ground, has met his death at the hands of a rival faction. We enter the widow's desolated home. A shelter rather than a house, with but two wretched rooms, it stands alone upon the prairie. The darkness of a stormy winter's evening was gathering over the snow-clad slopes of the wide, bare prairie, as, in company with a sympathizing friend, we enter that lonely dwelling.

In the scantily-furnished apartment into which we are shown, two or three women and as many children are crowding around a stove, for the night is bitter cold, and even the large wood-fire scarcely heated a space so thinly walled. Behind a heavy pine table, on which stands a flickering tallow-candle, and leaning against a half-curtained window on which the sleet and winter's blast beat drearily, sits a woman of some forty years of age, clad in a dress of dark, coarse stuff, resting her head on her hand, and seeming unmindful of all about her.

She was the widow of Thomas W. Barber, one of the victims of the Kansas war. The attenuated hand supporting the aching head, and half shielding the tear-dimmed eyes, the silent drops trickling down the wasted cheeks, told but too well the sad story.

"They have left me," she cried, "a poor, forsaken creature, to mourn all my days! Oh, my husband, my husband, they have taken from me all that I hold dear! one that I loved better than I loved my own life!"

Thomas W. Barber was a careful and painstaking

farmer, a kind neighbor, and an inoffensive, amiable man. His "untimely taking off" was indeed a sad loss to the community at large, but how much more to his wife! She had loved him with a love that amounted to idolatry. When he was returning from his daily toil she would go forth to meet him. When absent from home, if his stay was prolonged, she would pass the whole night in tears; and when ill, she would hang over his bed like a mother over her child. With a presentiment of evil, when he left his home for the last time, after exhausting every argument to prevent him from going, she had said to him, "Oh, Thomas! if you should be shot, I shall be left all alone, with no child and nothing in the wide world to fill your place!" This was their last parting.

The intelligence of his death was kept in mercy from her, through the kindness of friends, who hoped to break it to her gently. This thoughtful and sympathetic purpose was marred by the unthinking act of a young man, who had been sent with a carriage to convey her to the hotel where her husband's body lay. As he rode up he shouted, "Thomas Barber is killed!" His widow half-caught the dreadful words, and rushing to the door cried, "Oh, God! What do I hear?" Seeing the mournful and sympathetic faces of the bystanders, she knew the truth and filled the house with her shrieks. When they brought her into the apartment where her husband lay, she threw herself upon his corpse, and kissing the dead man's face, called down imprecations on the heads of those who had bereaved her of all she held dear.

The prairies of the great West resemble the ocean in more respects than in their level vastness, and the

travelers who pass over them are like mariners who
guide themselves only by the constellations and the
great luminaries of heaven.   The trail of the emigrant,
like the. track of the ship, is often uncrossed for days
by others who are voyaging over this mighty expanse.
Distance becomes delusive, and after journeying for
days and failing to reach the foot-hills of the mountains, whose peaks have shone to his eyes in so many
morning suns, the tired emigrant is tempted by the
abounding richness of the country to pause.   He is
one hundred miles from the nearest settlement.   Beside a stream he builds his cabin.   He is like a
voyager whose ship has been burned, leaving him in a
strange land which he must conquer or die.

   Such was the situation of that household on the
prairie of Illinois, concerning whom is told a story full
of mournful pathos.   We should note, in passing on
to our story, one of the dangers to which prairie-
dwellers are exposed.   They live two or three months
every year in a magazine of combustibles.   One of the
peculiarities of the climate in those regions is the dry-
ness of its summers and autumns.   A drought often
commences in August which, with the exception of a
few showers towards the close of that month, continues, with little interruption, throughout the full season.
The immense mass of vegetation with which the fertile soil loads itself during the summer is suddenly
withered, and the whole earth is covered with com-
bustible materials.   A single spark of fire falling
anywhere upon these plains at such a time, instantly
kindles a blaze that spreads on every side, and continues its destructive course as long as it finds fuel, these

fires sweeping on with a rapidity which renders it hazardous even to fly before them.

The flames often extend across a wide prairie and advance in a long line; no sight can be more sublime than to behold at night a stream of fire several miles in breadth advancing across these plains, leaving behind it a black cloud of smoke, and throwing before it a vivid glare which lights up the whole landscape with the brilliancy of noonday. A roaring and crackling sound is heard like the rushing of the hurricane; the flame, which, in general, rises to the height of about twenty feet, is seen sinking and darting upward in spires precisely as the waves dash against each other, and as the spray flies up into the air; the whole appearance is often that of a boiling and flaming sea violently agitated. Woe to the farmer whose ripe corn-field extends into the prairie, and who has carelessly suffered the tall grass to grow in contact with his fences; the whole labor of a year is swept away in a few hours.

More than sixty years since, and before the beautiful wild gardens of Illinois had been tilled by the hand of the white man, an emigrant with his family came thither from the East in search of a spot whereon to make his home. One bright spring day his white-topped wagon entered a prairie richer in its verdure and more brilliant in its flowers, than any that had yet met his eyes. At night-fall it halted beside a clump of trees not far from a creek. On this site a log-cabin soon rose and sent its smoke curling through the overhanging boughs.

The only neighbors of the pioneers were the rambling Indians. Their habitation was the center of a vast circle not dwelt in, and rarely even crossed by white settlers; oxen, cows, and a dog were their only domestic animals. For many months after their cabin was built they depended on wild game and fruits for subsistence; the rifle of the father, and traps set by the boys, brought them an abundant supply of meat. The wife and mother wrought patiently for those she loved. Her busy hands kept a well-ordered house by day, and at night she plied the needle to repair the wardrobe of her little household band. It was already growing scanty, and materials to replace it could only be procured at a distance, and means to procure it were limited. Patching and darning until their garments were beyond repair, she then supplied their place with skins stripped from the deer which the father had shot. Far into the night, by the flickering light of a single candle, this gentle housewife plied "her busy care," while her husband, worn out with his day's work, and her children, tired by their rambles, were slumbering in the single chamber of the cabin.

October came, and a journey to the nearest settlement for winter goods and stores, must be made. After due preparation the father and his eldest son started in the emigrant wagon, and expected to be absent many days, during which the mother and her children, with only the dog for their protection, looked hourly forth upon the now frost-embrowned prairie, and fondly hoped for their return.

Day after day passed, and no sign of life was visible upon the plain save the deer bounding over the sere herbage, or the wolf loping stealthily against the wind which bore the scent of his prey. A rising haze began to envelope the landscape, betokening the approach of the Indian summer,

"The melancholy days had come,
The saddest of the year,"

and the desolation of nature found an answering mood in the soul of that lone woman. One day she was visited by a party of Indian warriors, and from them she learned that there was a war between the tribes through whose country the journey of her husband lay. A boding fear for his safety took possession of her, and after the warriors had partaken of her hospitality and departed, and night came, she laid her little ones in their bed, and sat for hours on the threshold of the cabin door, looking out through the darkness and praying silently for the return of her loved ones. The wind was rising and driving across the sky black masses of clouds which looked like misshapen specters of evil. The blast whistled through the leafless trees and howled round the cabin. Hours passed, and still the sorrowful wife and mother sat gazing into the gloom as if her eyes would pierce it and lighten on the wished-for object.

But what is that strange light which far to the north gleams on the blackened sky? It was not the lightning's flash, for it was a steady brightening glow. It was not the weird flash of the aurora borealis, but a redder and more lurid sheen; nor was it the harbinger of the rising sun which lit that northern sky. From a tinge it brightens to a gleam, and deepened at last into a broad glare. That lonely heart was overwhelmed with the dreadful truth. The prairie is on fire! Often had they talked of prairie fires as a spectacle of grandeur. But never had she dreamed of the red demon as an enemy to be encountered in that dreadful solitude.

Her heart sank within her as she saw the danger leaping toward her like some fiery and maddened race-horse. Was there no escape ? Her children were sweetly sleeping, and the faithful dog, her only guardian, was gazing as if with mute sympathy into her face. Within an hour she calculates the conflagration would be at her very door. All around her is one dry ocean of combustibles. She cannot reach the tree-tops, and if she could, to cling there would be impossible amid those towering flames. The elements seemed to grow madder as the fire approached ; fiercer blew the blast, intermitting for a moment only to gather fresh potency and mingle its own strength with that of the flames. She still had a faint hope that a creek a few miles away would be a barrier over which the blaze could not leap. She saw by the broad light which made even the distant prairie like noonday, the tops of the trees that fringed the creek but for a few moments, and then they were swallowed up in that crimson furnace. Alas ! the stream had been crossed by the resistless flames, and her last hope died away.

Bewildered and half stupefied by the terrors of her situation, she had not yet wakened her children. But now no time was to be lost. Already in imagination she felt the hot breath of her relentless foe. It was with much difficulty that she awoke them and aroused them to a sense of their awful danger. Hastily dressing them she encircled them in her arms and kissed and fondled them as if for a last farewell. Now for the first time she missed the dog, the faithful companion and guardian of her solitude, and on whose aid she still counted in the hour of supreme peril. She called him loudly, but in vain. Turning her face northward she saw one unbroken line of flame as far as the eye could reach, and forcing its way towards her like an infuriated demon, roaring, crackling, sending up columns of dun-colored smoke as it tore along over the plain. A few minutes more and her fate would be decided. Falling on her knees she poured out her heart in prayer, supplicating for mercy and commending herself and her helpless babes to Almighty God As she rose calmed and stayed by that fervent supplication a low wistful bark fell on her ear; the dog came bounding to her side; seizing her by the dress as if he would drag her from the spot, he leaped away from her, barking and whining, looking back towards her as he ran. Following him a few steps and seeing nothing, she returned and resumed her seat, awaiting death beside her children.

Again the dog returned, pawing, whining, howling, and trying in every way to attract her attention. What could he mean? Then for the first time flashed upon her the thought which had already occurred to the sagacious instinct of the dumb brute! The ploughed field! Yes, there alone was hope of safety! Clasping the two youngest children with one arm she almost dragged the eldest boy as she fled along the trodden path, the dog going before them showing every token of delight. The fire was at their heels, and its hot breath almost scorched their clothes as they ran. They gained the herbless ploughed field and took their station in its center just as the flames darted round on each side of them.

The exhausted mother, faint with the sudden deliverance, dropped on the ground among her helpless babes. Father of mercies! what an escape!

In a few moments the flames attacked the haystack, which was but a morsel to its fury, and then seizing the house devoured it more slowly, while the great volume of the fire swept around over the plain. Long did the light of the burning home blight the eye of the lone woman after the flames had done their worst on the prairie around her and gone on bearing ruin and devastation to the southern plains and groves.

The vigils and the terrors of that fearful night wrought their work on the lonely woman, and she sank into a trance-like slumber upon the naked earth, with her babes nestling in her lap and the dog, her noble guardian, crouching at her feet. She awoke with the first light of morning to the terrible realities from which for a few brief hours she had had a blessed oblivion. She arose as from a dream and cast a dazed look southward over a charred and blackened expanse stretching to the horizon, over which the smoke was hanging like a pall. Turning away, stunned by the fearful recollection, her eyes fell upon the smouldering ruins of her once happy home. She tottered with her chilled and hungry children towards the heap of smoking rafters and still glowing embers of the cabin, with which the morning breezes were toying as in merry pastime, and sat down upon a mound which stood before what had once been the door. Here, at least, was warmth, but whither should she go for shelter and food. There was no house within forty miles and the cruel flames had spared neither grain nor meat. There was no shelter but the canopy of heaven and no food but roots and half-burned nuts.

Wandering hither and thither under the charred and leafless trees, she picked up with her numb and nerveless fingers the relics of the autumn nuts or feebly dug in the frost-stiffened ground for roots. But these were rare; here and there she found a nut shielded by a decayed log, and the edible roots were almost hidden by the ashes of the grass. She returned to the fire, around which her innocent children had begun to frolic with childlike thoughtlessness. The coarse morsels which she gave them seemed for the moment to quiet their cravings, and the strange sight of their home in ruins diverted their minds. The mother saw with joy that they were amusing themselves with merry games and had no part in her bitter sorrows and fears. Long and earnestly did she bend her eyes on the wide, black plains to see if she could discern the white-topped wagon moving over that dark expanse. Noon came and passed but brought not the sight for which she yearned: only the brown deer gamboling and the prairie hen wheeling her flight over the scorched waste!

Night came with its cold, its darkness, its hunger, its dreadful solitude! The chilled and shelterless woman sat with the heads of her sleeping children pillowed in her lap, and listened to the howling of the starved wolves, the dog her only guardian. She had discovered a few ground-nuts, which she had divided among the children, reserving none for herself; she had stripped off nearly all her clothing in order to wrap them up warmly against the frosty air, and with pleasant words, while her head was bursting, she had soothed them to sleep beside the burning pile; and there, through the watches of the long night, she gazed fondly at them and prayed to the Father of mercies that they, at least, might be spared.

The night was dark: beyond the circle of the burning embers nothing could be discerned. At intervals, her blood was curdled by the long, mournful howl of the gaunt gray wolf calling his companions to their prey. The cold wind whistled around her thinly clad frame and chilled it to the core. As the night grew stiller a drowsiness against which she contended in vain, overcame her, her eyelids drooped, her shivering body swayed to and fro, until by the tumbling down of the embers she was again aroused, and would brace herself for another hour's vigil. At last the darkness became profoundly silent and even the wind ceased to whisper, the nocturnal marauders stole away, and night held her undisputed reign. Then came a heavy dreamless sleep and overpowered the frame of the watcher, chilled as it was, and faint with hunger, and worn with fatigue and vigils: she curled her shivering limbs around her loved ones and became oblivious to all.

It was the cry of her babes that waked her from slumber. The fire was slowly dying; the sun was looking down coldly from the leaden sky; slowly his beams were obscured by dark, sullen masses of vapor, which at last curtained the whole heavens. Rain! When she sat watching in the darkness, a few hours before, she thought nothing could make her condition worse. But an impending rain-storm which, thirty-six hours before, would have been hailed as merciful and saving, would now only aggravate their situation.

17

Darker and darker grew the sky. She must hasten for food ere the clouds should burst. Her limbs were stiff with cold, her sight was dim, and her brain reeled as she rose to her feet and tottered to the grove to search for sustenance to keep her wailing babes alive. Her own desire for food was gone, but all exhausted as she was she could not resist the pleadings of the loved ones who hung upon her garments and begged for food.

Gleaning a few more coarse morsels on the ground so often searched, she tottered back to the spot which still seemed home though naught of home was there. Strange, racking pains wrung her wasted body, and sinking down beside her children she felt as if her last hour had come. Yes! she would perish there beside those consecrated ashes with her little ones around her. A drizzling rain was falling faster and faster. The fire was dying and she pushed the brands together, and gathered her trembling babes about her knees, and between the periods of her agony told them not to forget their mamma nor how they had lost her; she gave the eldest boy many tender messages to carry to her husband and to her first born. With wondering and tearful face he promised to do as she desired, but begged her to tell him where she would be when his father came and whether his little brother would go with her and leave him all alone.

The rain poured down mercilessly and chilly blew the blast. The embers hissed and blackened and shed no more warmth on the suffering group. Keener and heavier grew the mother's pangs, and there beside the smoking ruins of her home, prone on the drenched soil, with the pitiless sky bending above her, her help-

less children wailing around her writhing form, the
hapless woman gave birth to a little babe, whose eyes
were never opened to the desolation of its natal home.

Unconscious alike to the cries of the terror stricken
children and of the moaning caresses of her dumb
friend, that poor mother's eyes were only opened
on the dreadful scene when day was far advanced.
Through the cold rain, still pouring steadily down, the
twilight seemed to her faint eyes to be creeping over
the earth. Sweet sounds were ringing in her ears.
These were but dreams that deluded her weakened
mind and senses. She strove to rise, but fell back
and again relapsed into insensibility. Once again her
eyes opened. This time it was no illusion. The
eldest of the little watchers was shouting in her ear,
" Mother, I see father's wagon ! " There it was close
at hand. All day it had been slowly moving across
the blackened prairie. The turf had been softened
by the rain and the last few miles had been inconceiv-
ably tedious. The charred surface of the plain had
filled the heart of both father and son with terror,
which increased as they advanced.

When they were within a mile of the spot where
the cabin stood and could see no house, they both
abandoned the wagon, and leaving the animals to
follow as they chose, they flew shouting loudly as
they sped on till they stood over the perishing group.
They could not for the moment comprehend the dreadful calamity, but stared at the wasted faces of the
children, the infant corpse, the dying wife, the desolate home.

Cursing the day that he had been lured by the
festal beauty of those prairies, the father lifted the

dying woman in his arms, gazed with an agonized face upon her glassy eyes, and felt the faint fluttering in her breast that foretold the last and worst that could befall him. Slowly, word˙ by word, with weak sepulchral voice, she told the dreadful story.

He slipped off his outer garments and wrapped them around her, and wiping off the rain-drops from her face drew her to his heart. But storm or shelter was all the same to her now, and the death-damp on her brow was colder than the pelting shower. He accused himself of her cruel murder and wildly prayed her forgiveness. From these accusations she vindicated him, besought him not to grieve for her, and with many prayers for her dear children and their father, she resigned her breath with the parting light of that sad autumnal day.

After two days and nights of weeping and watching, he laid her remains deep down below the prairie sod, beside the home which she had loved and made bright by her presence.

CHAPTER XII.

NO portion of our country has been the scene of more romantic and dangerous adventures than that region described under the broad and vague term the "Southwest." Texas, New Mexico, and Arizona, are vast, remote, and varied fields with which danger and hardship, wonder and mystery are ever associated. The country itself embraces great contrarieties of scenery and topography—the rich farm, the expansive cattle ranch, the broad lonely prairie watered by majestic rivers, the barren desert, the lofty plateau, the secluded mining settlement, and vast mountain ranges furrowed by torrents into black cañons where sands of gold lie heaped in inaccessible, useless riches.

The forms of human society are almost equally diverse. Strange and mysterious tribes, each with different characteristics, here live side by side. Vile mongrel breeds of men multiply to astonish the ethnologist and the moralist. Here roam the Comanches and the Apaches, the most remorseless and bloodthirsty of all the North American aboriginal tribes. Mexican bandits traverse the plains and lurk in the mountain passes, and American outlaws and desperadoes here find a refuge from justice.

As the Anglo-Saxon after fording the Sabine, the Brazos, and the Colorado River of Texas, advances westward, he is brought face to face with these differ-

(261)

ent races with whom is mixed in greater or less proportion the blood of the old Castilian conquerors. Each of these races is widely alien from, and most of them instinctively antagonistic to the North European people.

Taking into view the immense distances to be traversed, the natural difficulties presented by the face of the country, the remoteness of the region from civilization, and the mixed, incongruous and hostile character of the inhabitants, we might naturally expect that its occupation by peaceful settlers,—by those forms of household life in which woman is an essential element—would be indefinitely postponed. But that energy and ardor which marks alike the men and the women of our race has carried the family, that germ of the state, over all obstacles and planted it in the inhospitable soil of the most remote corners of this region, and there it will flourish and germinate doubtless till it has uprooted every neighboring and noxious product.

The northeastern section of this extensive country is composed of that stupendous level tract known as the "Llano Estacado," or "Staked Plain." Stretching hundreds of miles in every direction, this sandy plain, treeless, arid, with only here and there patches of stunted herbage, whitened by the bones of horses and mules, and by the more ghastly skeletons of too adventurous travelers, presents an area of desolation scarcely more than paralleled by the great African Desert.

In the year 1846, after news had reached the States that our troops were in peaceful occupation of New Mexico, a party of men and women set out from the upper valley of the Red River of Louisiana, with the intention of settling in the valley of the river Pecos, in the eastern part of the newly conquered territory. The company consisted of seven persons, viz: Mr. and Mrs. Benham and their child of seven years, Mr. and Mrs. Braxton and two sons of fifteen and eighteen years respectively.

They made rapid and comfortable progress through the valley of the Red River, and in two weeks reached the edge of the "Staked Plain," which they now made preparations to cross, for the difficulties and dangers of the route were not unknown to them. Disencumbering their pack-mules of all useless burdens and supplying themselves with water for two days, they pushed forward on their first stage which brought them on the evening of the second day to a kind of oasis in this desert where they found wood, water, and grass. From this point there was a stretch of ninety miles perfectly bare of wood and water, and with rare intervals of scanty herbage for the beasts. After this desolate region had been passed they would have a comparatively easy journey to their destination.

On the evening of the second day of their passage across this arid tract they had the misfortune to burst their only remaining water cask, and to see the thirsty sands drink up in a moment every drop of the precious liquid. They were then forty miles from the nearest water. Their beasts were jaded and suffering from thirst. The two men were incapacitated for exertion by slight sun-strokes received that day, and one of the boys had been bitten in the hand by a rattlesnake while taking from its burrow a prairie dog which he had shot.

The next day they pursued their march only with the utmost difficulty; the two men were barely able to sit on their horses, and the boy which had been bitten was faint and nerveless from the effect of the poison. The heat was felt very severely by the party as they dragged themselves slowly across the white expanse of sand, which reflected the rays of the sun with a painful glare into the haggard eyes of the wretched wanderers. Before they had made fifteen miles, or little more than one-third of the distance that would have to be accomplished before reaching water, the horses and mules gave out and at three o'clock in the afternoon the party dismounted and panting with heat and thirst stretched themselves on the sand. The sky above them was like brass and the soil was coated with a fine alkali deposit which rose in clouds at their slightest motion, filling their nostrils and eyes, and increasing the agonies they were suffering.

Their only hope was that they would be discovered by some passing train of hunters or emigrants. This hope faded away as the sun declined and nothing but the sky and the long dreary dazzling expanse of sand met their eyes.

The painful glare slowly softened, and with sunset came coolness; this was some slight mitigation to their sufferings; sleep too, promised to bring oblivion; and hope, which a merciful Providence has ordained to cast its halo over the darkest hours, told its flattering tale of possible relief on the morrow.

The air of that desert is pellucid as crystal, and the last beams of the sun left on the unclouded azure of the sky a soft glow, through which every thing in the western horizon was outlined as if drawn by some magic pencil. Casting their eyes in that direction the wretched wayfarers saw far away a dun-colored haze through which small black specks seemed to be moving. Growing larger and more distinct it approached them slowly over the vast expanse until its true nature was apparent. It was a cloud of dust such as a party of horsemen make when in rapid motion over a soil as fine and light as ashes. Was it friend or foe? Was it American cavalry or was it a band of Mexican guerrillas that was galloping so fiercely over that arid plain? These torturing doubts were soon solved. Skimming over the ground like swallows, six sunburnt men with hair as black as the crow's wing, gaily dressed, and bearing long lances, soon reined in their mustangs within twenty paces of the party and gazed curiously at them. One of the band then rode up and asked in broken English if they were "Americans:" having thus made a reconnoisance and seeing their helplessness, without waiting for a reply, he beckoned to his companions who approached and demanded the surrender of the party. Under other circumstances a stout resistance would have been made; but in their present forlorn condition they could do nothing.

Their guns, a part of their money, and whatever the unfortunate families had that pleased the guerrillas, was speedily appropriated, the throats of their horses and mules were cut, Mrs. Braxton and Mrs. Benham were seized, and in spite of their struggles and shrieks each of them was placed in front of a swarthy bandit, and then the Mexicans rode away cursing "Los Americanos," and barbarously leaving them to die of hunger and thirst.

After a four hours' gallop, the marauders reached

an adobe house on Picosa Creek, a tributary of the
Rio Pecos. This was the headquarters of the gang,
and here they kept relays of fresh horses, mustangs,
fiery, and full of speed and bottom. Mrs. Benham
and Mrs. Braxton were placed in a room by themselves on the second story, and the door was barricaded so that escape by that avenue was impossible;
but the windows were only guarded by stout oaken
bars, which the women, by their united strength,
succeeded in removing. Their captors were plunged
in a profound slumber, when Mrs. Benham and her
companion dropped themselves out of the window,
and succeeded in reaching the stable without discovery. Here they found six fresh horses ready saddled
and bridled, the others on which the bandits had made
their raid being loose in the enclosure.

It was a cruel necessity which impelled our brave
heroines to draw their knives across the hamstrings of
the tired horses, thus disabling them so as to prevent
pursuit. Then softly leading out the six fresh mustangs, each of our heroines mounted one of the horses
man-fashion and led the others lashed together with
lariats; walking the beasts until out of hearing, they
then put them to a gallop, and, riding all night, came,
at sunrise, to the spot where their suffering friends
lay stretched on the sand, having abandoned all hope.

After a brief rest, the whole party pushed rapidly
forward on their journey, arriving that evening at a
place of safety. Two days after, they reached the
headwaters of the Pecos. Here they purchased a
large adobe house, and an extensive tract, suitable
both for grazing and tillage.

These events occurred early in the autumn. During the following winter the Mexicans revolted, and massacred Governor Bent and his military household. On the same day seven Americans were killed at Arroyo Hondo; a large Mexican force was preparing to march on Santa Fé, and for a time it seemed as if the handful of American soldiers would be driven out of the territory. This conspiracy was made known to the authorities by an American girl, who was the wife of one of the Mexican conspirators, and becoming, through her husband, acquainted with the plan of operations, divulged them to General Price in season to prevent a more general outbreak. As it was, the American settlers were in great danger.

The strong and spacious house in which the Benhams and Braxtons lived had formerly been used as a stockade and fortification against Indian attack. Its thick walls were pierced with loop-holes, and its doors, of double oak planks, were studded with wrought-iron spikes, which made it bullet-proof. A detachment of United States troops were stationed a short distance from their ranch, and the two families, in spite of the disturbed condition of the country, felt reasonably secure. The troops were withdrawn, however, after the revolt commenced, leaving the new settlers dependent upon their own resources for protection. Their cattle and horses were driven into the enclosure, and the inmates of the house kept a sharp lookout against hostile parties of marauders, whether Indian or Mexican.

Early on the morning of January 24th a mounted party of twelve Mexicans made their appearance in front of the enclosure, which they quickly scaled, and discharged a volley of balls, one of which passed through a loop-hole, and, entering Mr. Braxton's eye as he was aiming a rifle at the assailants, laid him dead at the feet of his wife. Mrs. Braxton, with streaming eyes, laid the head of her husband in her lap and watched his expiring throes with agony, such as only a wife and mother can feel when she sees the dear partner of her life and the father of her sons torn in an instant from her embrace. Seeing that her husband was no more, she dried her tears and thought only of vengeance on his murderers.

The number of the besieged was twelve at the start, viz: Mr. and Mrs. Braxton, Mr. and Mrs. Benham and their children, three Irish herders, and a half-breed Mexican and his wife, who were house servants. The death of Mr. Braxton had reduced their number to eleven. A few moments later the Mexican half-breed disappeared, but was not missed in the excitement of the defense.

The besieged returned with vigor the fire of their assailants, two of whom had already bit the dust. The women loaded the guns and passed them to the men, who kept the Mexicans at a respectful distance by the rapidity of their fire. Mrs. Benham was the first to mark the absence of Juan the Mexican half-breed, and, suspecting treachery, flew to the loft with a hatchet in one hand and a revolver in the other. Her suspicion was correct. Juan had opened an upper window, and, letting down a ladder, had assisted two of the attacking party to ascend, and they were preparing to make an assault on those below by firing through the cracks in the floor, when the intrepid woman despatched Juan with a shot from her revolver and clove the skull of another Mexican; the third leaped from the window and escaped.

As Mrs. Benham was about to descend from the loft, after drawing up the ladder and closing the window, she was met by the wife of the treacherous half-breed, who aimed a stroke at her breast with a *machete* or large knife, such as the Mexicans use. She received a flesh wound in the left arm as she parried the blow, and it was only with the mixed strength of Mrs. Braxton and one of the herders, who had now ascended to the loft, that the infuriated Mexican whom Mrs. Benham had made a widow, could be mastered and bound.

Three of the attacking party had now been killed and three others placed *hors de combat;* the remnant were apparently about to retire from the siege, when six more swarthy desperadoes, mounted on black mustangs, came galloping up and halted on a hill just out of rifle shot.

Mrs. Braxton and Mrs. Benham, looking through a field glass, at once recognized them as the band which had made them captives a few months before.

After a few moments of consultation one of the band, who appeared to be only armed with a bow and arrow, advanced towards the house waving a white flag. Within thirty paces of the door stood a large tree, and behind this the envoy, bearing the white flag, ensconced himself, and, striking a light, twanged his bow and sent a burning arrow upon the roof of the house, which, being dry as tinder, in a moment was in a blaze.

Both of the women immediately carried water to the roof and extinguished the flames. Another arrow, wrapped in cotton steeped in turpentine, again set the roof on fire, and as one of the intrepid matrons threw a bucket of water upon the blaze, the dastard stepped from behind the tree and sent a pistol ball through her right arm, but at the same moment received two rifle balls in his breast, and fell a corpse.

Mrs. Benham, for it was she who had been struck, was assisted by her husband to the ground floor, where her wound was examined and found to be fortunately not a dangerous one. A new peril, however, now struck terror to their hearts; the water was all exhausted. The fire began to make headway. Mrs. Braxton, calling loudly for water to extinguish it, and meeting no response, descended to the ground floor, where the defenders were about to give up all hope, and either resign themselves to the flames, or by emerging from the house, submit to massacre at the hands of the now infuriated foe. As Mrs. Braxton rolled her eyes hither and thither in search of some substitute for water, they fell on the corpse of her husband. His coat and vest were completely saturated with blood. It was only the sad but terrible necessity which immediately suggested to her the use to which these garments could be put. Shuddering, she removed them quickly but tenderly from the body, flew to the roof and succeeded, by these dripping and ghastly tokens of her widowhood, in finally extinguishing the flames.

The attack ceased at night-fall, and the Mexicans withdrew. The outbreak having been soon quelled by the United States forces, the territory was brought again into a condition of peace and comparative security.

At the close of the war in 1848, Mrs. Braxton married a discharged volunteer named Whitley, and having disposed of the late Mr. Braxton's interest in the New Mexican ranche, removed, in 1851, with her husband and family, to California, where they lived for two years in the Sacramento valley.

Whitley was possessed of one of those roving and adventurous spirits which is never happy in repose, and when he was informed by John Crossman, an old comrade, of the discovery of a rich placer which he had made during his march as a United States soldier across the territory of Arizona, at that time known as the Gadsden purchase, he eagerly formed a partnership with the discoverer, who was no longer in the army, and announced to his wife his resolution to settle in Arizona. She endeavored by every argument she could command to dissuade him from this rash step, but in vain, and finding all her representations and entreaties of no avail, she consented, though with the utmost reluctance, to accompany him. They accordingly sold their place and took vessel with their household goods, for San Diego, from which point they purposed to advance across the country three hundred miles to the point where Crossman had located his placer.

The territory of Arizona may be likened to that wild and rugged mountain region in Central Asia, where, according to Persian myth, untold treasures are guarded by the malign legions of Ahriman, the spirit of evil. Two of the great elemental forces have employed their destructive agencies upon the surface of the country until it might serve for an ideal picture of desolation. For countless centuries the water has

seamed and gashed the face of the hills, stripping them
of soil, and cutting deep gorges and cañons through
the rocks.   The water then flowed away or disappeared in the sands, and the sun came with its parch-
ing heat to complete the work of ruin.   Famine and
thirst stalk over those arid plains, or lurk in the wa-
terless and gloomy cañons; as if to compensate for
these evils, the soil of the territory teems with mineral wealth.   Grains of gold glisten in the sandy *débris* of ancient torrents, and nuggets are wedged in
the faces of the precipices.   Mountains of silver and
copper are waiting for the miner who is bold enough
to venture through that desolate region in quest of
these metals.

The journey from San Diego was made with pack-
mules and occupied thirty days, during which nearly
every hardship and obstacle in the pioneer's catalogue
was encountered.   When they reached the spot described by Crossman they found the place, which lay
at the bottom of a deep ravine, had been covered with
boulders and thirty feet of sand by the rapid torrents
of five rainy seasons.   They immediately commenced
"prospecting."   Mrs. Braxton had the good fortune to
discover a large " pocket," from which Crossman and
her husband took out in a few weeks thirty thousand
dollars in gold.   This contented the adventurers, and
being disgusted with the appearance of the country,
they decided to go back to California.

Instead of returning on the same route by which
they came, they resolved to cross the Colorado river
higher up and in the neighborhood of the Santa Maria.
They reached the Colorado river after a toilsome
march, but while searching for a place to pass over,

Crossman lost his footing and fell sixty feet down a precipice, surviving only long enough to bequeath his share of the treasure to his partner. Here, too, they had the misfortune to lose one of their four pack-mules, which strayed away. Pressing on in a north-westerly direction they passed through a series of deep valleys and gorges where the only water they could find was brackish and bitter, and reached the edge of the California desert. They had meanwhile lost another mule which had been dashed to pieces by falling down a cañon. Mr. Whitley's strength becoming exhausted his wife gave up to him the beast she had been riding, and pursued her way on foot, driving before her the other mule, which bore the gold-dust with their scanty supply of food and their only remaining cooking utensils. Their tents and camp furniture having been lost they had suffered much from the chilly nights in the mountains, and after they had entered the desert, from the rays of the sun. Before they could reach the Mohave river Mr. Whitley became insane from thirst and hunger, and nothing but incessant watchfulness on the part of his wife could prevent him from doing injury to himself. Once while she was gathering cactus-leaves to wet his lips with the moisture they contained, he bit his arm and sucked the blood. Upon reaching the river he drank immoderately of the water and in an hour expired, regaining his consciousness before death, and blessing his devoted wife with his last breath. Ten days later the brave woman had succeeded in reaching Techichipa in so wasted a condition that she looked like a specter risen from the grave. Here by careful nursing she was at length restored to health. The

18

gold-dust which had cost so dearly was found after a long search, beneath the carcass of the mule, twenty miles from Techichipa.

The extraordinary exploits of Mrs. Braxton can only be explained by supposing her to be naturally endowed with a larger share of nerve and hardihood than usually falls to the lot of her sex. Some influence, too, must be ascribed to the peculiarly wild and free life that prevails in the southwest. Living so much of the time in the open air in a climate peculiarly luxuriant and yet bracing, and environed with dangers in manifold guise, all the latent heroism in woman's nature is brought out to view, her muscular and nervous tissues are hardened, and her moral endurance by constant training in the school of hardship and danger, rests upon a strong and healthy physique. Upon this theory we may also explain the following incident which is related of another border-woman of the southwest.

* Beyond the extreme outer line of settlements in western Texas, near the head waters of the Colorado River, and in one of the remotest and most sequestered sections of that sparsely populated district, there lived in 1867, an enterprising pioneer by the name of Babb, whose besetting propensity and ambition consisted in pushing his fortunes a little farther toward the setting sun than any of his neighbors, the nearest of whom, at the time specified, was some fifteen miles in his rear.

The household of the borderer consisted of his wife, three small children, and a female friend by the name of L———, who, having previously lost her husband,

---

* Marcy's Border Reminiscences.

was passing the summer with the family. She was a veritable type of those vigorous, self-reliant border women, who encounter danger or the vicissitudes of weather without quailing.

Born and nurtured upon the remotest frontier, she inherited a robust constitution, and her active life in the exhilarating prairie air served to develop and mature a healthy womanly physique. From an early age she had been a fearless rider, and her life on the frontier had habituated her to the constant use of the horse until she felt almost more at home in the saddle than in a chair.

Upon one bright and lovely morning in June, 1867, the adventurous borderer before mentioned, set out from his home with some cattle for a distant market, leaving his family in possession of the ranch, without any male protectors from Indian marauders.

They did not, however, entertain any serious apprehensions of molestation in his absence, as no hostile Indians had as yet made their appearance in that locality, and everything passed on quietly for several days, until one morning, while the women were busily occupied with their domestic affairs in the house, the two oldest children, who were playing outside, called to their mother, and informed her that some mounted men were approaching from the prairie. On looking out, she perceived, to her astonishment, that they were Indians coming upon the gallop, and already very near the house. This gave her no time to make arrangements for defense; but she screamed to the children to run in for their lives, as she desired to bar the door, being conscious of the fact that the prairie warriors seldom attack a house that is closed, fearing, doubtless, that it may be occupied by armed men, who might give them an unwelcome reception.

The children did not, however, obey the command of their mother, believing the strangers to be white men, and the door was left open. As soon as the alarm was given, Mrs. L—— sprang up a ladder into the loft, and concealed herself in such a position that she could, through cracks in the floor, see all that passed beneath.

Meantime the savages came up, seized and bound the two children outdoors, and, entering the house, rushed toward the young child, which the terror-stricken mother struggled frantically to rescue from their clutches; but they were too much for her, and tearing the infant from her arms, they dashed it upon the floor; then seizing her by the hair, they wrenched back her head and cut her throat from ear to ear, putting her to death instantaneously.

Mrs. L——, who was anxiously watching their proceedings from the loft, witnessed the fiendish tragedy, and uttered an involuntary shriek of horror, which disclosed her hiding-place to the barbarians, and they instantly vaulted up the ladder, overpowered and tied her; then dragging her rudely down, they placed her, with the two elder children, upon horses, and hurriedly set off to the north, leaving the infant child unharmed, and clasping the murdered corpse of its mangled parent.

In accordance with their usual practice, they traveled as rapidly as their horses could carry them for several consecutive days and nights, only making occasional short halts to graze and rest their animals, and get a little sleep themselves, so that the unfortunate captives necessarily suffered indescribable tortures from harsh treatment, fatigue, and want of sleep and food. Yet they were forced by the savages to continue on day after day, and night after night, for many, many weary miles toward the "Staked Plain," crossing *en route* the Brazos, Wachita, Red, Canadian, and Arkansas Rivers, several of which were at swimming stages.

The warriors guarded their captives very closely, until they had gone so great a distance from the settlements that they imagined it impossible for them to make their escape and find their way home, when they relapsed their vigilance slightly, and they were permitted to walk about a little within short limits from the bivouacs; but they were given to understand by unmistakable pantomime that death would be the certain penalty of the first attempt to escape.

In spite of this, Mrs. L———, who possessed a firmness of purpose truly heroic, resolved to seize the first favorable opportunity to get away, and with this resolution in view, she carefully observed the relative speed and powers of endurance of the different horses in the party, and noted the manner in which they were grazed, guarded, and caught; and upon a dark night, after a long, fatiguing day's ride, and while the Indians were sleeping soundly, she noiselessly and cautiously crawled away from the bed of her young companions, who were also buried in profound slumber, and going to the pasture-ground of the horses, selected the best, leaped upon his back *à la garçon*, with only a lariat around his neck, and without saddle or bridle, quietly started off at a slow walk in the direction of the north star, believing that this course would lead

her to the nearest white habitations.   As soon as she
had gone out of hearing from the bivouac, without
detection or pursuit, she accelerated the speed of the
horse into a trot, then to a gallop, and urged him
rapidly forward during the entire night.

At dawn of day on the following morning she rose
upon the crest of an eminence overlooking a vast area
of bald prairie country, where, for the first time since
leaving the Indians, she halted, and, turning round,
tremblingly cast a rapid glance to the rear, expecting
to see the savage blood-hounds upon her track ; but,
to her great relief, not a single indication of a living
object could be discerned within the extended scope
of her vision.   She breathed more freely now, but still
did not feel safe from pursuit ; and the total absence
of all knowledge of her whereabouts in the midst
of the wide expanse of dreary prairie around her,
with the uncertainty of ever again looking upon a
friendly face, caused her to realize most vividly her
own weakness and entire dependence upon the Almighty, and she raised her thoughts to Heaven in fervent supplication.

The majesty and sublimity of the stupendous works
of the great Author and Creator of the Universe,
when contrasted with the insignificance of the powers
and achievements of a vivified atom of earth modeled
into human form, are probably under no circumstances
more strikingly exhibited and felt than when one becomes bewildered and lost in the almost limitless am-
plitude of our great North American " pampas," where
not a single foot-mark`or other trace of man's pres-
ence or action can be discovered, and where the soli-

tary wanderer is startled at the sound even of his own
voice.

The sensation of loneliness and despondency resulting from the appalling consciousness of being really
and absolutely lost, with the realization of the fact
that but two or three of the innumerable different
points of direction embraced within the circle of the
horizon will serve to extricate the bewildered victim
from the awful doom of death by starvation, and in
entire ignorance as to which of these particular directions should be followed, without a single road, trail,
tree, bush, or other landmark to guide or direct—the
effects upon the imagination of this formidable array
of disheartening circumstances can be fully appreciated only by those who have been personally subjected to their influence.

A faint perception of the intensity of the mental
torture experienced by these unfortunate victims may,
however, be conjectured from the fact that their senses
at such junctures become so completely absorbed and
overpowered by the cheerless prospect before them,
that they oftentimes wander about in a state of temporary lunacy, without the power of exercising the
slightest volition of the reasoning faculties.

The inflexible spirit of the heroine of this narrative did not, however, succumb in the least to the
imminent perils of the situation in which she found
herself, and her purposes were carried out with a
determination as resolute and unflinching as those of
the Israelites in their protracted pilgrimage through
the wilderness, and without the guidance of pillars of
fire and cloud.

The aid of the sun and the broad leaves of the

pilot-plant by day, with the light of Polaris by night, enabled her to pursue her undeviating course to the north with as much accuracy as if she had been guided by the magnetic needle.

She continued to urge forward the generous steed she bestrode, who, in obedience to the will of his rider, coursed swiftly on hour after hour during the greater part of the day, without the least apparent labor or exhaustion.

It was a contest for life and liberty that she had undertaken, a struggle in which she resolved to triumph or perish in the effort: and still the brave-hearted woman pressed on, until at length her horse began to show signs of exhaustion, and as the shadows of evening began to appear he became so much jaded that it was difficult to coax or force him into a trot, and the poor woman began to entertain serious apprehensions that he might soon give out altogether and leave her on foot.

At this time she was herself so much wearied and in want of sleep that she would have given all she possessed to have been allowed to dismount and rest; but, unfortunately for her, those piratical quadrupeds of the plains, the wolves, advised by their carnivorous instincts that she and her exhausted horse might soon fall an easy sacrifice to their voracious appetites, followed upon her track, and came howling in great numbers about her, so that she dared not set her feet upon the ground, fearing they would devour her; and her only alternative was to continue urging the poor beast to struggle forward during the dark and gloomy hours of the long night, until at length she became so exhausted that it was only with the utmost effort

AN EQUESTRIAN FEAT.   Page 281.

of her iron will that she was enabled to preserve her balance upon the horse.

Meantime the ravenous pack of wolves, becoming more and more emboldened and impatient as the speed of her horse relaxed, approached nearer and nearer, until, with their eyes flashing fire, they snapped savagely at the heels of the terrified horse, while at the same time they kept up their hideous concert like the howlings of ten thousand fiends from the infernal regions.

Every element in her nature was at this fearful juncture taxed to its greatest tension, and impelled her to concentrate the force of all her remaining energies in urging and coaxing forward the wearied horse, until, finally, he was barely able to reel and stagger along at a slow walk; and when she was about to give up in despair, expecting every instant that the animal would drop down dead under her, the welcome light of day dawned in the eastern horizon, and imparted a more cheerful and encouraging influence over her, and, on looking around, to her great joy, there were no wolves in sight.

She now, for the first time in about thirty-six hours, dismounted, and knowing that sleep would soon overpower her, and the horse, if not secured, might escape or wander away, and there being no tree or other object to which he could be fastened, she, with great presence of mind, tied one end of the long lariat to his neck, and, with the other end around her waist, dropped down upon the ground in a deep sleep, while the famished horse eagerly cropped the herbage around her.

She was unconscious as to the duration of her

slumber, but it must have been very protracted to have compensated the demands of nature, for the exhaustion induced by her prodigious ride.

Her sleep was sweet, and she dreamed of happiness and home, losing all consciousness of her actual situation until she was suddenly startled and aroused by the pattering sound of horses' feet, beating the earth on every side.

Springing to her feet in the greatest possible alarm, she found herself surrounded by a large band of savages, who commenced dancing around, flouting their war-clubs in terrible proximity to her head, while giving utterance to the most diabolical shouts of exultation.

Her exceedingly weak and debilitated condition at this time, resulting from long abstinence from food, and unprecedented mental and physical trials, had wrought upon her nervous system to such an extent that she imagined the moment of her death had arrived, and fainted.

The Indians then approached, and, after she revived, placed her again upon a horse, and rode away with her to their camp, which, fortunately, was not far distant. They then turned their prisoner over to the squaws, who gave her food and put her to bed; but it was several days before she was sufficiently recovered to be able to walk about the camp.

She learned that her last captors belonged to "Lone Wolf's" band of Kiowas.

Although these Indians treated her with more kindness than the Comanches had done, yet she did not for an instant entertain the thought that they would ever voluntarily release her from bondage; neither had she the remotest conception of her present locality, or of the direction or distance to any white settlement; but she had no idea of remaining a slave for life, and resolved to make her escape the first practicable moment that offered.

During the time she remained with these Indians a party of men went away to the north, and were absent six days, bringing with them, on their return, some ears of green corn. She knew the prairie tribes never planted a seed of any description, and was therefore confident the party had visited a white settlement, and that it was not over three days' journey distant. This was encouraging intelligence for her, and she anxiously bided her time to depart.

Late one night, after all had become hushed and quiet throughout the camp, and every thing seemed auspicious for the consummation of her purposes, she stole carefully away from her bed, crept softly out to the herd of horses, and after having caught and saddled one, was in the act of mounting, when a number of dogs rushed out after her, and by their barking, created such a disturbance among the Indians that she was forced, for the time, to forego her designs and crawl hastily back to her lodge.

On a subsequent occasion, however, fortune favored her. She secured an excellent horse and rode away in the direction from which she had seen the Indians returning to camp with the green corn. Under the certain guidance of the sun and stars she was enabled to pursue a direct bearing, and after three consecutive days of rapid riding, anxiety, fatigue, and hunger, she arrived upon the border of a large river, flowing directly across her track. The stream was swollen to the top of its banks; the water coursed like a torrent through its channel, and she feared her horse might not be able to stem the powerful current; but after surmounting the numerous perils and hardships she had already encountered, the dauntless woman was not to be turned aside from her inflexible purpose by this formidable obstacle, and she instantly dashed into the foaming torrent, and, by dint of encouragement and punishment, forced her horse through the stream and landed safely upon the opposite bank.

After giving her horse a few moments' rest, she again set forward, and had ridden but a short distance when, to her inexpressible astonishment and delight, she struck a broad and well-beaten wagon-road, the first and only evidence or trace of civilization she had seen since leaving her home in Texas.

Up to this joyful moment the indomitable inflexibility of purpose of our heroine had not faltered for an instant, neither had she suffered the slightest despondency, in view of the terrible array of disheartening circumstances that had continually confronted her, but when she realized the hopeful prospect before her of a speedy escape from the reach of her barbarous captors, and a reasonable certainty of an early reunion with people of her own sympathizing race, the feminine elements of her nature preponderated, her stoical fortitude yielded to the delightful anticipation, and her joy was intensified and confirmed by seeing, at this moment, a long train of wagons approaching over the distant prairie.

The spectacle overwhelmed her with ecstasy, and she wept tears of joy while offering up sincere and heartfelt thanks to the Almighty for delivering her from a bondage more dreadful than death.

She then proceeded on until she met the wagons in charge of Mr. Robert Bent, whom she entreated to give her food instantly, as she was in a state bordering upon absolute starvation. He kindly complied with her request, and after the cravings of her appetite had been appeased he desired to gratify his curiosity, which had been not a little excited at the unusual exhibition of a beautiful white woman appearing alone in that wild country, riding upon an Indian saddle, with no covering on her head save her long natural hair, which was hanging loosely and disorderly about her shoulders. Accordingly, he inquired of her where she lived, to which she replied, "In Texas." Mr. B. gave an incredulous shake of his head at this response, remarking at the same time that he thought she must be mistaken, as Texas happened to be situated some five or six hundred miles distant. She reiterated the assurance of her statement, and described to him briefly the leading incidents attending her capture and escape; but still he was inclined to doubt, believing that she might possibly be insane.

He informed her that the river she had just crossed was the Arkansas, and that she was then on the old Santa Fé road, about fifteen miles west of Big Turkey Creek, where she would find the most remote frontier house. Then, after thanking him for his kindness, she bade him adieu, and started away in a walk toward the settlements, while he continued his journey in the opposite direction.

On the arrival of Mr. Bent at Fort Zara, he called upon the Indian agent, and reported the circumstance of meeting Mrs. L———, and, by a singular coincidence, it so happened that the agent was at that very time holding a council with the chiefs of the identical band of Indians from whom she had last escaped, and they had just given a full history of the entire affair, which seemed so improbable to the agent that he was not disposed to credit it until he received its confirmation through Mr. Bent. He at once dispatched a man to follow the woman and conduct her to Council Grove, where she was kindly received, and remained for some time, hoping through the efforts of the agents to gain intelligence of the two children she had left with the Comanches, as she desired to take them back to their father in Texas; but no tidings were gained for a long while.

The two captive children were afterwards ransomed and sent home to their father.

It will readily be seen, by a reference to the map of the country over which Mrs. L——— passed, that the distance from the place of her capture to the point where she struck the Arkansas river could not have been short of about five hundred miles, and the greater part of this immense expanse of desert plain she traversed alone, without seeing a single civilized human habitation.

It may well be questioned whether any woman either in ancient or modern times ever performed such a remarkable equestrian feat, and the story itself would be almost incredible were we not in possession of so many well authenticated instances of the hardihood and powers of endurance shown by woman on the frontiers of our country.

CHAPTER XIII.

WOMAN'S EXPERIENCE ON THE NORTHERN BORDER.

THE vanguard of the "Great Army" which for nearly three centuries has been hewing its pathway across the continent, may be divided into certain *corps d'armée*, each of which moves on a different line, thus acting on the Napoleonic tactics, and subjugating in detail the various regions through which it passes. One corps, spreading out in broad battalions, marches across the great prairies and winding through the gorges of the Rocky mountains, encamps on the shore of Peaceful sea: another, skirting the waves of the gulfs and fording the wide rivers of the South, plants its outposts on the Rio Grande; a third cuts its way through the trackless forests on the northern border till it strikes the lakes, and then crossing these inland seas or passing round them, pauses and breathes for a season in that great expanse known as the country of the Red River of the North.

Each of these mighty pioneer divisions has its common toils, dangers, and sufferings. Each, too, has toils, dangers, and sufferings peculiar to itself. The climate is the deadly foe of the northern pioneer. The scorching air of a brief summer is followed closely by the biting frost of a long winter. The snow, piled in drifts, blocks his passage and binds him to his threshold. Sometimes by a sudden change in the temperature a thaw converts the vast frozen mass into

(287)

slush. In the depth of those arctic winters sometimes fire, that necessary but dangerous serf, breaks its chains and devastates its master's dwelling; then frost allies its power to that of fire, and the household often succumbs to disaster, or barely survives it.

Fire, frost, starvation, and wild beasts made frantic by winter's hunger, are the imminent perils of the northern pioneer!

The record of woman in these regions on the northern frontier is crowded with incidents which display a heroism as stern, a hardihood as rugged, a fortitude as steadfast, as was ever shown by her sex under the most trying situations into which she is brought by the exigencies of border life.

Such a record is that of Mrs. Dalton, who spent her life from early womanhood in that region.

Naturally of a frail and delicate organization, reared in the ease and luxury of an eastern home, and possessed of those strong local attachments which are characteristic of females of her temperament, it was with the utmost reluctance that she consented to follow her husband into the wilderness. Having at last consented, she showed the greatest firmness in carrying out a resolution which involved the loss of a happy home at the place of her nativity, and consigned her to a life of hardship and danger.

Her first experience in this life was in the wilds of northern New York, her husband having purchased a small clearing and a log-cabin in that region on the banks of the Black river. She was transported thither, reaching her destination one cold rainy evening early in May, after a wearisome journey, for this was before the days of rapid transit.

Her first impressions must have been gloomy indeed. Without was pouring rain and a black sky; the forest was dark as Erebus; within no fire blazed on the hearth in the only room on the first floor of the cabin, and the flickering light of a tallow candle made the darkness but the more visible; a rude table and settles made out of rough planks, were all the furniture the cabin could boast; there was no ladder to reach the loft which was to be her sleeping room; the only window, without sash or glass, was a mere opening in the side of the cabin; the rain beat in through the cracks in the door and through the open window, and trickled through the roof, which was like a sieve, while the wind blew keenly through a hundred seams and apertures in the log-walls.

The night, the cold, the storm, the dark and cheerless abode, were too much to bear; the delicate young wife threw herself upon a settle and burst into a flood of tears. This was but a momentary weakness. Rising above the depression produced by the dreary scene, the woman's genius for creating comfort out of the slenderest materials and bringing sunshine into darkness, soon began to manifest itself.

We will not detail the various trials and cares by which that forlorn cabin was transformed into a comfortable home, nor how fared Mrs. Dalton the first rather uneventful year of her life in the woods. The second spring saw her a mother, and the following autumn she became again a homeless westward wanderer. Her husband had sold the cabin and clearing in New York, and having purchased an extensive tract of forest-land a few miles south of Georgian Bay in Upper Canada, decided to move thither.

19

The family with their household goods took sloop on Lake Ontario late in October, and sailed to Toronto; from this place on the 15th day of November, they proceeded across the peninsula in sleighs. Their party consisted of Mr. and Mrs. Dalton and their child, and John McMurray, their hired man, and his wife.

The first forty miles of their journey lay over a well-beaten road, and through a succession of clearings, which soon began to diminish until they reached a dense forest, which rose in solemn stillness around them and cast across their path a shadow which seemed to the imagination of Mrs. Dalton an omen of coming evil.

The sun had now set, but the party still drove on through the forest-shadows; the moon having risen giving a new and strange beauty to the scenery. The infant had fallen asleep. A deep silence fell upon the party; night was above them with her mysterious stars; the ancient forest stretched around them on every side; nature lay wrapped in a snowy winding sheet; the wind was rising, and a drifting scud of clouds from the northeast passed across the moon, and gave a still more weird and somber character to the scene. A boding sadness sank into the heart of Mrs. Dalton as the sleighs drove up to the cabin in the clearing where they were to pass the night. It was occupied by an old negro and his wife, who had found in the Canadian woods a safe refuge from servitude.

Hardly had they and their horses been safely bestowed under shelter when the sky became entirely overcast, the wind rose to a gale, and a driving storm of snow and sleet filled the air. All night, and the following day the tempest raged without intermission, and on the morning of the second day the sun struggling through the clouds looked down on the vast drifts of snow, some of them nearly twenty feet in depth, completely blocking their farther passage, and enforcing a sojourn of some days in their present quarters.

During this time the babe fell ill, and grew worse so rapidly that Mr. Dalton determined to push through the snow-drifts on horseback to the nearest settlement, which lay eight miles south of them, and procure the services of a physician. He started early in the morning, expecting to return in the afternoon. But afternoon and evening passed, and still Mr. Dalton did not return. His course was a difficult one through forest and thicket, and when evening came, and night passed with its bitter cold, Mrs. Dalton's anxiety was increased to torture. Her only hope was that her husband had reached the settlement in safety, and had been induced to remain there till the following morning before undertaking to return.

Soon after the sun rose that morning, Mrs. Dalton and the hired man set out on horseback in search of the missing one. Tracing his course through the snow for four miles they at length caught sight of him standing up to his waist in a deep drift, beside his horse. His face was turned toward them. So lifelike and natural was his position that it was only when his wife grasped his cold rigid fingers that she knew the terrible truth. Her husband and the horse were statues of ice thus transformed by the deadly cold as they were endeavoring to force a passage through those immense drifts.

From the speechless, tearless trance of grief into which Mrs. Dalton was thrown by the shock of her awful loss, she was roused only by the recollection of the still critical condition of her child and the necessity that she should administer to its wants. Its recovery from illness a few days after, enabled the desolate widow to cast about her in grief and doubt, and decide what course she should pursue.

As her own marriage portion as well as the entire fortune of her late husband was embarked in the purchase of the forest tract, she concluded to continue her journey twenty miles farther to the point of her original destination, and there establish herself in the new house which had been provided for her in the almost unbroken wilderness.

A thaw which a few days after removed a large body of the snow, enabled her with her companions, the McMurrays, to reach her destination, a large and commodious cabin built of cedar-logs in a spacious clearing by the former owner of the tract.

Her first impressions of her new home were scarcely more prepossessing than those experienced upon reaching the dreary cabin on the banks of the Black river. A small lake hard by was hemmed in by a somber belt of pine-woods. The clearing was dotted by charred and blackened stumps, and covered with piles of brushwood. The snowy shroud in which lifeless nature was wrapped and the utter stillness and solitude of the scene, completed the funereal picture which Mrs. D. viewed with eyes darkened by grief and disappointment.

The cares and labors of pioneer-life are the best antidotes to the corrosion of sorrow and regret, and Mrs.

Dalton soon found such a relief in the myriad toils and distractions which filled those wintry days. A thousand duties were to be discharged: a thousand wants to be provided for: night brought weariness and blessed oblivion: morning again supplied its daily tasks and labor grew to be happiness.

Midwinter was upon them with its bitter cold and drifting snows; but with abundant stores of food and fuel, Mrs. D. was thanking God nightly for his many mercies, little dreaming that a new calamity impended over her household.

One bitter day in January the two women were left alone in the cabin, McMurray having gone a mile away to fell trees for sawing into boards. Mrs. McM. had stuffed both the stoves full of light wood; the wind blowing steadily from the northwest, produced a powerful draught, and in a few moments the roaring and crackling of the fire and the suffocating smell of burning soot attracted Mrs. Dalton's attention. To her dismay, both the stoves were red hot from the front plates to the topmost pipes which passed through the plank-ceiling and projected three feet above the roof. Through these pipes the flames were roaring as if through the chimney of a blast furnace.

A blanket snatched from the nearest bed, that stood in the kitchen, and plunged into a barrel of cold water was thrust into the stove, and a few shovels full of snow thrown upon it soon made all cool below. The two women immediately hastened to the loft and by dashing pails full of water upon the pipes, contrived to cool them down as high as the place where they passed through the roof. The wood work around the pipes showed a circle of glowing embers, the water was nearly exhausted and both the women running out of the house discovered that the roof which had been covered the day before by a heavy fall of snow, showed an area of several square feet from which the intense heat had melted the snow; the sparks falling upon the shingles had ignited them, and the rafters below were covered by a sheet of flame.

A ladder, which, for some months, had stood against the house, had been moved two days before to the barn which stood some thirty rods away; there seemed no possibility of reaching the fire. Moving out a large table and placing a chair upon it, Mrs. D. took her position upon the chair and tried to throw water upon the roof, but only succeeded in expending the last dipper full of water that remained in the boiler, without reaching the fire.

Mrs. McMurray now abandoned herself to grief and despair, screeching and tearing her hair. Mrs. D., still keeping her presence of mind, told her to run after her husband, and to the nearest house, which was a mile away, and bring help.

Mrs. McM., after a moment's remonstrance, on account of the depth of the snow, regained her courage, and, hastily putting on her husband's boots, started, shrieking "fire!" as she passed up the road, and disappeared at the head of the clearing.

Mrs. D. was now quite alone, with the house burning over her head. She gazed at the blazing roof, and, pausing for one moment, reflected what should first be done.

The house was built of cedar-logs, and the suns and winds of four years had made it as dry as tinder; the breeze was blowing briskly and all the atmospheric conditions were favorable to its speedy destruction. The cold was intense, the thermometer registering eighteen degrees below zero. The unfortunate woman thus saw herself placed between two extremes of heat and cold, and apprehended as much danger from the one as from the other.

In the bewilderment of the moment, the direful extent of the calamity never struck her, though it promised to put the finishing stroke to her misfortune, and to throw her naked and houseless upon the world.

"What shall I first save?" was the question rapidly asked, and as quickly answered. Anything to serve for warmth and shelter—bedding, clothing, to protect herself and babe from that cruel cold! All this passed her mind like a flash, and the next moment she was working with a right good will to save what she could of these essential articles from her burning house.

Springing to the loft where the embers were falling from the burning roof, she quickly threw the beds and bedding from the window, and emptying trunks and chests conveyed their contents out of reach of the flames and of the burning brands which the wind was whirling from the roof. The loft was like a furnace, and the heat soon drove her, dripping with perspiration, to the lower room, where, for twenty minutes, she strained every nerve to drag out the movables. Large pieces of burning pine began to fall through the boarded ceiling about the lower rooms, and as the babe had been placed under a large dresser in the kitchen, it now became absolutely necessary to remove it. But where? The air was so bitter that nothing but the fierce excitement and rapid motion

had preserved Mrs. Dalton's hands and feet from freez
ing.   To expose the tender nursling to that direful
cold was almost as cruel as leaving it to the mercy of
the fire.

A mother's wit is not long at fault where the safety
of her child is concerned.   Emptying out all the
clothes from a large drawer which she had dragged a
safe distance from the house, she lined it with blankets and placed the child inside, covering it well over
with bedding, and keeping it well wrapped up till help
should arrive.

The roof was now burning like a brush heap; but aid
was near at hand.   As she passed out of the house for
the last time, dragging a heavy chest of clothes, she
looked once more despairingly up the clearing and
saw a man running at full speed.   It was McMurray.
Her burdened heart uttered a deep thanksgiving, as
another and another figure came skipping over the
snow towards her burning house.

She had not felt the intense cold, although without
bonnet or shawl, and with hands bare and exposed to
the biting air.   The intense anxiety to save all she
could had so diverted her thoughts from herself that
she took no heed of the peril in which she stood from
fire and frost.   But now the reaction came; her knees
trembled under her, she grew giddy and faint, and
dark shadows swam before her.

The three men sprang on the roof and called for
water in vain; it had long been exhausted.   "Snow!
snow! Hand us up pails full of snow!" they
shouted.

It was bitter work filling the pails with frozen snow,
but the two women (for Mrs. McMurray had now

returned) scooped up pails full of snow with their bare hands and passed them to the men on the roof.

By spreading this on the roof, and on the floor of the loft, the violence of the fire was checked. The men then cast away the smoldering rafters and flung them in the snow-drifts.

The roof was gone, but the fire was at last subdued before it had destroyed the walls. Within one week from the time of the fire the neighboring settlers built a new roof for Mrs. Dalton in spite of the intense cold, and while it was building Mrs. D. and her household were sheltered at the nearest cabin.

The warm breath of spring brought with it some halcyon days, as if to reconcile Mrs. Dalton to her life of solitude and toil. The pure beauty of the crystal waters, the august grandeur of the vast forest, and the aromatic breezes from the pines and birches, cast a magic spell upon her spirit. She soon learned the use of the rifle, the paddle, and the fishing rod. Charming hours of leisure and freedom were passed upon the water of the lake, or in rambles through the arches of the forest. In these pleasures, enhanced by the needful toils of the household or the field, the summer sped away.

August came, and the little harvest of oats and corn were all safely housed. For some days the weather had been intensely hot, although the sun was entirely obscured by a bluish haze, which seemed to render the unusual heat of the atmosphere more oppressive. Not a breath of air stirred the vast forest, and the waters of the lake took on a leaden hue.

Before the sun rose on the morning of the 12th the heavens were covered with hard looking clouds of a

deep blue-black color, fading away to white at their
edges, and in form resembling the long, rolling waves
of a heavy sea, but with the difference that the clouds
were perfectly motionless, piled in long curved lines,
one above the other.

As the sun rose above the horizon, the sky presented a magnificent spectacle. Every shade of saffron,
gold, rose-color, scarlet, and crimson, mottled with the
deepest violet, were blended there as on some enormous tapestry. It was the storm-fiend who shook that
gorgeous banner in the face of the day-god!

As the day advanced the same blue haze obscured
the sun, which frowned redly through his misty veil.
At ten o'clock the heat was suffocating. The thermometer in the shade ranged after midday from ninety-six to ninety-eight degrees. The babe stretched
itself upon the floor of the cabin, unable to jump
about or play, the dog lay panting in the shade, the
fowls half-buried themselves in the dust, with open
beaks and outstretched wings. All nature seemed to
droop beneath the scorching heat. At three o'clock
the heavens took on a sudden change. The clouds,
that had before lain so still, were now in rapid motion,
hurrying and chasing each other round the horizon.
It was a strangely awful sight. Before a breath had
been felt of the mighty blast that had already burst
on the other side of the lake, branches of trees, leaves,
and clouds of dust were whirled across the water,
which rose in long, sharp furrows, fringed with foam,
as if moved in their depths by some unseen but powerful agent.

The hurricane swept up the hill, crushing and overturning everything in its course. Mrs. Dalton, stand-

ing at the open door of her cabin, speechless and motionless, gazed at the tremendous spectacle. The babe crept to its mother's feet, its cheeks like marble, and appealed to her for protection. Mrs. McMurray, in helpless terror, had closed her eyes and ears to the storm, and sat upon a chest, muffled in a shawl.

The storm had not yet reached its acme. The clouds, in huge cumuli, were hurrying as to some great rendezvous, from which they were to be let loose for their work of destruction. The roaring of the blast and the pealing of the thunder redoubled in violence. Turning her eyes to the southwest, Mrs. Dalton now saw, far down the valley, the tops of the huge trees twisted and bowed, as if by some unseen but terrible power. A monstrous dun-colored cloud marked the course of this new storm-titan. Nearer and nearer it came, with a menacing rumble, and swifter than a race-horse.

The cabin lay directly in its track. In a moment it would be upon them. Whither should they fly? One place of safety occurred on the instant to the unfortunate woman; clasping her babe to her breast and clutching the gown of her companion, she ran to the trap-door which conducted to the cellar and raising it pushed Mrs. McMurray down the aperture and quickly following her, Mrs. Dalton closed the trap.

Not five seconds later the hurricane struck the cabin with such force that every plank, rafter, beam, and log was first dislocated and then caught up in the whirlwind and scattered over the forest in the wake of the storm. As the roar of the blast died away the rain commenced pouring in torrents accompanied by vivid flashes of lightning and loud peals of thunder.

The air in the close shallow cellar, where the women were, soon grew suffocating, and as the fury of
the tempest was spent, they took courage and pushed
at the trap.   It stuck fast; again they both applied
their shoulders to it but only succeeded in raising it
far enough to see that the trunk of an enormous tree
lay directly across the door.

The cellar in which they were, was little more than
a large pit, eight feet by six, and served as a recepta-
cle for their winter's stores; as it lay directly in the
center of the floor which was formed of large logs
split in halves and their surfaces smoothed, there was
no mode of egress except by digging underneath the
floor as far as the walls of the cabin and so emerging;
but this was a work of extreme difficulty, owing to the
fact that the soil was full of the old roots of trees
which had been cut down to make room for the cabin.

The first danger, however, was from suffocation; to
meet this Mrs. Dalton and her companion pried open
the door as far as the fallen trunk would allow, and
kept it in position by means of a large chip which they
found in the pit.   This gave them sufficient air through
a chink three inches in width; and they next looked
about them for means of egress.   After trying in vain
to dislodge one of the floor logs, they proceeded to
dig a passage through the earth underneath the floor.
Discouraged by the slowness of their progress in this
undertaking, and drenched with the rain which poured
in through the crevice in the door, they began to give
themselves up for lost.   Their only hope was that
McMurray or some one of the neighbors would come
to their relief.

The rain lasted only one hour, and the sun soon

made its appearance. This was after six o'clock, as the prisoners judged from the shadows cast over the ruins of the cabin. The shades of evening fell and at last utter darkness; still no one came. No sound was borne to the ears of the women in their earthly dungeon save that of the rushing waters of the creek and the mournful howling of wolves who, like jackals, were prowling in the track of the tempest. Several of these animals, attracted by the infant's cries, came and put their noses at the door of the pit and finding that it held prey, paced the floor above it all night: but with the first light of morning they scampered away into the woods.

Meanwhile the women resumed their efforts to burrow their way out, taking turns in working all night. By daybreak the passage lacked only four feet of the point where an outlet could be had. Ere noon, if their strength held out, they would reach the open air.

But after four hours more of severe toil they met an unexpected obstacle: their progress was blocked by a huge boulder embedded in the soil. Weary with their protracted toil and loss of sleep, and faint from want of food, they desisted from further efforts and sat down upon the damp earth of that dungeon which now promised to be their tomb.

Sinking upon her knees Mrs. Dalton lifted her heart to God in prayer that he might save her babe, her faithful domestic and herself from the doom which threatened them. Hardly had she risen from her knees, when, as if a messenger had been sent in answer to her prayer, voices were heard and steps sounded upon the floor above them. The party had come from a neighboring settlement for the express purpose of relieving the sufferers from the recent storm.   A few blows with an axe and the prisoners were free.   Recognizing their preservation as a direct answer to prayer, and with deep gratitude both of the women fell on their knees and lifted up their hearts in humble thanksgiving to that God who had saved them by an act of his providence from an awful death. When all hope was gone His hand was stretched forth, making his strength manifest in the weakness of those hapless women and that helpless babe.

Before the first of October a new cabin had been built for Mrs. D. by her generous neighbors, and the other ravages of the storm had been repaired.   Once more fortune, so often adverse, turned a smiling face upon the household.   Two weeks sped away and then the fickle goddess frowned again upon this much enduring family.

A long continued drought had parched the fields and woods until but a spark was needed to kindle a conflagration.   Two parties of hunters on the 16th of October, had rested one noon on opposite sides of Mrs. Dalton's clearing and carelessly dropped sparks from their pipes into the dried herbage.   Two hours after their departure, the flames, fanned by a gentle breeze, had formed a junction and encircled the cabin with a wall of fire.   A dense canopy of smoke hung over the clearing, and as it lifted, tongues of flame could be seen licking the branches of the tall pines.   Showers of sparks fell upon the roof.   The atmosphere grew suffocating with the pitchy smoke and it became a choice of deaths, either that of choking or that of burning.

Only one avenue of escape was left open to the family; if they could reach the lake and embark in the canoe which lay moored near the shore they would be safe : a single passage conducted to the water, and that was a burning lane lined with trees and bushes which were bursting into fiercer flames every moment as they gazed down it.

Nearer and nearer crept the fire, and hotter and hotter grew the choking air. There was no other choice. McMurray threw water on the gowns of his wife and Mrs. Dalton until they were drenched; then wrapping the baby in a blanket and enveloping their heads in shawls, the whole party abandoned their house to destruction, and ran the gauntlet of the flames. They passed the spot of ordeal in safety, reached the canoe and embarking pushed off into the lake. From this point of security they caught glimpses of the element as it crept steadily on its way towards the cabin. Through the rifts in the smoke they saw the fiery tongues licking the lower timbers and darting themselves into the cracks between the logs like some gluttonous monster preparing to gorge himself. The women clasped their hands and looked up. Both were supplicating the Father of All that their home might be spared.

A rescue was coming from an unlooked for source. While Mrs. Dalton's face was upturned to heaven in silent prayer, a large drop splashed upon her brow; another followed—the first glad heralds of a pouring rain which extinguished the fire just as it had begun to feed on that unlucky habitation.

After such an almost unbroken series of disasters and losses, we might well inquire whether the subsequent life of Mrs. Dalton was saddened and darkened by similar experiences.

"Every cloud has a silver lining." The hardest and saddest lives have their hours of softness, their gleams of sunshine. It is a wise and beautiful arrangement in the economy of Divine Providence that the law of physical and moral compensation is always operating to equalize the pains and the pleasures, the hardships and the comforts, the joys and the sorrows of human life. Before continuous, patient, and conscientious endeavors, the obstacles that fill the pathway of the pioneer through the wilderness are surmounted, the rough places are made smooth, and the last days of the dwellers in the desert and forest become like the latter days of the patriarch, "more blessed than the beginning."

We may truly say of Mrs. Dalton, that her "latter days were more blessed than the beginning." A happy marriage which she entered into the following spring, and a long life of prosperity and peace after her escape from the last great danger, as we have narrated, were the fitting reward of the courage, diligence, and devotion displayed during the two first summers and winters which she passed in the northern wilderness.

The wide region lying between the sources of the Mississippi and the bends of the Missouri in Dakota, and stretching thence far up to the Saskatchewan in the north, has been appropriately styled "the happy hunting ground." The *rendezvous* to which the mighty nimrods of the northwest return from the chase are huge cabins, built to stand before the howling blasts, and give shelter against the arctic regions of the winter. In these abodes dwell the wives and children of many of those rugged men, and create even there, by their devoted toils and gentle companionship, at least the semblance of a home. Almost whelmed in the snow, and when even the mercury freezes in the bulb of the thermometer, these anxious and loving housewives feed the lamp and keep the fire burning on the hearth. Dressing the skins of the deer, they keep their husbands well shod and clothed. The long winter of eight months passes monotonously away; the men, accustomed to a life of excitement, chafe and grow surly under their enforced imprisonment; but the women, by their kind offices and sweet words, act as a constant sedative upon these morose outbreaks. The hunters, it is said, grow softer in their manners as the winter wanes. They are unconscious scholars in the refining school of woman.

Among the diversions which serve to while away the tediousness of those winter nights are included the narration of personal adventures passed through by the different hunters in their wild life. Tales of narrow escapes, of Indian fights, of desperate encounters with beasts of the forests; and through the rough texture of these narratives now and then appears a pathetic incident in which woman is the prominent figure. Sometimes it is a hunter's wife who is the heroine, and again the scene is laid in the home of the settler, where woman faces some dreadful danger for her loved ones, or endures extraordinary suffering faithfully to the end. Such an incident as the following was preserved in the memory of a hunter, who recently communicated the essential facts to the writer.

Minnesota well deserves the name of the pioneer's

20

paradise. Occupying as it does that high table-land
out of which gush into the pure bracing air, the thousand fountains of the Father of waters and of the majestic Red river; studded with lakes that glisten like
molten silver in the sunshine; shadowed by primeval forests; now stretching out in prairies which lose
themselves in the horizon; now undulating with hills
and dales dotted with groves and copses, nature here,
like some bounteous and imperial mother, seems to
have prepared with lavish hand a royal park within
which her roving sons and daughters may find a permanent abode.

The country through which the Red river flows
from Otter Tail lake towards Richville, is unsurpassed
for rural beauty. Trending northward it then passes
along towards Pembina, a border town on our northern boundary, through a plain of vast extent, dotted
with groves of oak planted as if by hand. Voyaging
down this noble river in midsummer, between its
banks embowered with wild roses we breathe an air
loaded with perfume and view a scene of wild but en-
chanting loveliness. Here summer celebrates her
brief but splendid reign, then lingering for a while in
the lap of dreamy, balmy autumn, flies at length into
southern exile, abdicating her throne to winter, which
stalks from the frozen zone and rules the region with
undisputed and rigorous sway.

In the month of March, 1863, a party of four hunters set out from Pembina, where they had passed
the winter, and undertook to reach Shyenne, a small
trading post on the west bank of the Red river, in the
territory of Dakota. A partial thaw, followed by a
cold snap, had coated the river in many places with

ice, and by the alternate aid of skates and snow-shoes,
they reached on the third evening after their departure, Red Lake river in Minnesota, some eighty miles
distant from Pembina. Clearing away the snow in a
copse, they scooped a shallow trench in the frozen
soil with their hatchets, and kindling a fire so as to
cover the length and breadth of the excavation, they
prepared their frugal repast of hunters' fare. Then
removing the fire to the foot of the trench and piling logs upon it, they lay down side by side on the
warmed soil, and wrapping their blankets around
them slept soundly through the still cold night, until
the sun's edge showed itself above the rim of the vast
plain that stretched to the east. As the hunters rose
from their earthy couch and stretched their cramped
limbs, casting their eyes hither and thither over the
boundless expanse, they descried upon the edge of a
copse some quarter of a mile to the south a bright-red
object, apparently a living thing, crouched upon the
snow as if sunning itself. Rising simultaneously and
with awakened curiosity they approached the spot.
Before they had taken many steps the object disappeared suddenly. Fixing their eyes steadily on the
point of its last appearance, they slowly advanced
with cocked rifles until they reached a large tree with
arching roots, around which were the traces of small
shoeless feet. An orifice barely large enough to admit
a man showed them beneath the tree a cave. One of
the hunters, peering through the aperture, spied
within, a girl of ten years crouched in the farthest
corner of the recess, covered with a thick red flannel
cloak, and shivering with cold and terror. Speaking
kind words to the little stranger they succeeded at

length in reassuring her. She came out from her hiding-place, and the hunters with rugged kindness wrapped her feet and limbs in their coats and bore her to the fire. The first words she uttered were, " mother! go for mother!" She had gone away to shoot game the night before, the little girl said, and had not returned.

Two of the hunters hastened back and succeeded in tracing the mother's course a mile up the river to a thicket; there, covered thinly with leaves and with her rifle in her stiffened hand, they found the hapless wanderer, but alas! cold in death. Her set and calm features, her pinched and wasted face, her scantily robed form, mutely but eloquently told a tale of fearful suffering borne with unflinching fortitude. Weak and weary, the deadly cold had stolen upon her in the darkness and with its icy grip had stilled for ever the beating of her brave true heart. Excavating a grave in the snow they decently straightened her limbs, and piling logs and brush upon her remains to keep them from the beasts of prey, silently and sorrowfully left the scene.

Who were these lonely wanderers in that wild and wintry waste! The presence of the rifle and of the large high boots which she wore, together with other circumstances, were evidences which enabled the shrewd hunters to guess a part of their story. It appeared that the family must have consisted originally of three persons, a man and wife, with the child now the sole survivor of the party. Voyaging down the Red river during the preceding summer and autumn; lured onward by the fatal beauty of the region, and deluded by the ease with which their wants could be supplied, they had evidently neglected to provide against the winter, which at length burst upon them all unprepared to encounter its rigors.

The rest of this heart-rending story was gathered from the lips of their little protege. Her father, mother, and herself had started from Otter Tail lake in September, 1862, after the quelling of the Sioux outbreak, and voyaged down the Red river in a canoe, intending to settle in the wild-rice region a few miles southeast of the spot where they then were. Their canoe with most of their household goods had broken from its moorings in November, one night while they were encamped on the shore. The father had gone to bring it back, and being overtaken by a terrible snow-storm, had never returned. [His body was found the following spring.] The mother had managed to procure barely sufficient game during the winter to keep herself and her child alive. The cave, their only shelter, was strewed with the beaks and feathers of birds, and with the teeth and claws of small animals; all the other portions of the game she had shot had been devoured in the extremity to which hunger had reduced them. Her mother, the little girl said, was very weak the last day, and could hardly walk. "I begged to go with her when she took her gun and went out to shoot something for supper, but she told me I must stay at *home* and keep warm." Home! could that wretched shelter be a home for the hapless mother and her child? Tears were wrung from those rugged sons of the wilderness, and coursed down their iron cheeks when they visited the spot where parental tenderness had striven to shield the object of its affection from the bitter blast. The snow banked about the roots of the tree and showing the marks of her numbed fingers, the crevices stuffed with moss, the bed of dried leaves and the bedding which she had stripped from her own person to cover her child, were proofs and tokens of the love which would have created comfort in the midst of desolation and given even that miserable nook in winter's dreary domain the semblance of a home. In the heart of that frozen waste, far from human fellowship, with hunger gnawing at her vitals and the frost curdling the genial current in her veins, still burned brightly in that poor lonely heart the pure and deathless flame of maternal love.

CHAPTER XIV.

ENCOUNTERS WITH WILD BEASTS—COURAGE AND DARING.

THE inhabitants of the frontier from the earliest times have had to face the fiercest and most ravenous wild beasts which prowl in the forests of this continent; and the local histories of the various sections and single settlements on our border-land abound in thrilling accounts of combats between those pests of the forest and individual men and women.

Wolves, like the poor, were always with the frontiersmen. Bears, both black and brown, were familiar visitors. The cougar, American lion, catamount, or "*painter*" (panther), as it is variously styled, was a denizen of every forest from Maine to Georgia, and from the St. Croix River to the Columbia. Wild cats, and even deer, when brought to bay, proved themselves dangerous combatants. Last, but not the least terrible in the catalogue, comes the grizzly bear, the monarch of the rocky waste that lies between the headwaters of the Platte and the Missouri rivers, and the sierras of the Pacific slope.

The stories of *rencontres* and combats between pioneer women and these savage rangers of the woods, are numerous and thrilling. Sometimes they seem almost improbable, especially to such as have only known Woman as she appears to the dwellers of our eastern cities, and in homes where luxury and ease have softened the sex.

A story like the following, for example, as told by one of our most veracious travelers, may be listened to with at least some degree of incredulity by gentlemen and ladies of the lounge and easy chair. A woman living on the Saskatchewan accompanied her husband on a hunting expedition into the forest. He had been very successful, and having killed one more deer than they could well carry home, he went to the house of a neighboring settler to dispose of it, leaving his wife to take care of the rest until his return. She sat carelessly upon the log with his hunting knife in her hand, when she heard the breaking of branches near her, and turning round, beheld a great bear only a few paces from her.

It was too late to retreat, and, seeing that the animal was very hungry and determined to come to close quarters, she rose, and placed her back against a small tree, holding her knife close to her breast, and in a straight line with the bear.

The shaggy monster came on. She remained motionless, her eyes steadily fixed upon her enemy's, and, as his huge arms closed around her, she slowly drove the knife into his heart. The bear uttered a hideous cry, and sank dead at her feet. When her husband returned, he found the courageous woman taking the skin from the carcass of the formidable brute. "How," some of our readers will exclaim, "can a woman possess such iron nerves as to dare and do such a deed as this?" And yet, evidence of masculine courage and daring, displayed by women in this and multitudes of other cases where confronted by danger in this form, is direct and unimpeachable.

Such stories, however startling and extraordinary, become credible when we remember the circumstances by which woman is surrounded in pioneer life, and how those circumstances tend to strengthen the nerves and increase the hardihood of the softer sex. Hunting is there one of the necessary avocations, in which women often become practiced, in order to supply the wants of existence. On our northwestern frontier, especially, female hunters have, from the start, been noted for their courage and skill.

One of the famous huntresses of the northwest, while returning home from the woods with a wild turkey which she had shot, unexpectedly encountered a large moose in her path, which manifested a disposition to attack her. She tried to avoid it, but the animal came towards her rapidly and in a furious manner. Her rifle was unloaded, and she was obliged to take shelter behind a tree, shifting her position from tree to tree as the brute made at her.

At length, as she fled, she picked up a pole, and

quickly untying her moccasin strings, she bound her knife to the end of the pole. Then, placing herself in a favorable position, as the moose came up, she stabbed him several times in the neck and breast. At last the animal, exhausted with the loss of blood, fell. She then dispatched it, and cut out its tongue to carry home as a trophy of victory. When they went back to the spot for the carcass, they found the snow trampled down in a wide circle, and copiously sprinkled with blood, which gave the place the appearance of a battle-field. It proved to be a male of extraordinary size.

The gray wolf species, two centuries ago and later, was spread over the Atlantic States from Maine to Georgia, and was in most newly-settled regions a frequent and obnoxious visitor to cattle yards and sheep-folds. We are told that the first Boston immigrants were obliged to build high and strong fences around their live stock to keep them from the depredations of these marauders.

Less bold than his European kindred, the gray wolf of North America is still an extremely powerful and dangerous animal, as may be proved by recalling the frequent encounters of the early settlers—both men and women—with these prowling pests. When pinched with hunger or driven to extremities, they will attack men or women and fight desperately, either to satiate their appetites or to save their skins from an assailant. A great number of stories and incidents concerning collisions between women and these savage brutes are scattered through the local histories of our early times, and illustrate the nerve and daring which, as we have shown, were habitual to the women in the border settlements.

About the middle of the last century, a household in the hill country of Georgia was greatly vexed by the frequent incursions of a large animal of this species which prowled about the cow-yard, and carried off calves and sheep, sometimes even venturing up to the door of the cabin. The family consisted of a man and his wife and three daughters, all grown up. Each one of the five had shot ineffectually at the brute, which seemed to bear a charmed life. A strong steel trap was finally set near the calf-pen, in a stout enclosure, and in a few days the trappers were delighted to hear a commotion in that quarter which indicated the success of their stratagem. His wolf-ship, sure enough, had been caught by one of his hind legs, and was found to be furiously gnawing at the trap and the chain which held him. The womenkind, rejoicing in the capture of their old enemy, all entered the enclosure and stood watching the struggles of the fierce beast, while the father was loading his gun to dispatch it.

In one of his leaps, the staple that held the chain gave way, and the wolf would have bounded over the fence, and made his escape to the woods, but for the ready courage of the eldest daughter of the family, a large, powerful woman of twenty-five. Seizing the chain, she held it firmly in both her hands; the wolf snapped at her arms, and at last, in his desperation, sprang at her throat with such force that he overthrew her, but still she did not relax her grip of the chain, though the animal, in his struggles, dragged her on the ground across the enclosure. Her father, at this critical moment, returned with his loaded gun and dispatched the brute. The young woman, barring a few bruises and scratches, was entirely uninjured.

The speed and endurance of these animals, when in pursuit of their prey,

> "With their long gallop, which can tire
> The hound's deep hate, the hunter's fire,"

makes them very dangerous assailants, when ravenous with hunger. We recall, in this connection, the thrilling story of a brave Kentucky girl, who, with her sisters, was pursued by a pack of black wolves.

The pluck and ready wit for which the Kentucky girls have been so celebrated is well illustrated by this adventure, which, after threatening consequences of the most tragical nature, had finally a comical *denouement*.

In the year 1798, a family of Virginia emigrants settled in central Kentucky in the midst of a dense forest, where, by the aid of three negro men whom they had brought with them, a spacious cabin was soon erected and a large clearing made. The family consisted of Mr. and Mrs. Carter, three daughters, well grown, buxom girls, full of life and fun, and a son, who, though only fourteen years of age, was a fine rider and versed in forest-craft.

The country where they lived was rich and beautiful. One could ride on horseback for miles through groves of huge forest trees, beneath which the turf lay firm and green. Through this open wood a wagon could be driven without difficulty; but locomotion in those days and regions was largely on horseback. There were no roads, except between the larger settlements; unless those passage-ways through the woods could be called roads. These were made by cutting down a tree or clearing away the undergrowth here and there, and "blazing" the trees along the passage by chopping off a portion of the bark as high as a man could reach with an axe.

At that period Kentucky was a famous hunting-ground! All kinds of game abounded in those magnificent forests and beneath that genial clime. Wild turkeys roosted in immense flocks in the chestnut, beach, and oak trees; pigeons by the million darkened the air; deer could be shot by any hunter by stopping a few moments in the forest where they came to feed.

The fiercer and more ravenous beasts abounded in proportion. Bears, catamounts, and wolves swarmed in the denser parts of the forests, and in the winter the two last named beasts were a great annoyance to the settlers by the boldness with which they invaded the cattle and poultry-yards and pig-pens.

The black wolf of the Western country was and is a very destructive and fierce animal, hunting in large packs, which, after using every stratagem to circumvent their prey, attacked it with great ferocity.

Like the Indian, they always endeavored to surprise their victims and strike the mortal blow without exposing themselves to danger. They seldom attack a man except when asleep or wounded, or otherwise taken at a disadvantage.

As the Carter homestead was ten miles from any settlement, it was fairly haunted by these wild beasts, which considered the cattle, calves, colts, sheep, and pigs of the new comers their legitimate prey.

Young Carter and his sisters having emigrated from

the most populous part of Virginia where social enter-
tainments were frequent, found the time during the
winter months hang heavy on their hands, and as the
young ladies' favorite colts and pet lambs had often
suffered from incursions of the wolves and panthers,
they amused themselves by setting traps for them and
occasionally giving them a dose of cold lead, for they
were all good shots with the rifle,—the girls as well as
their brother.

Two or three years passed in the forest taught them
to despise the wolves and panthers as cowardly brutes,
and the girls were not afraid to pass through the forest
at any time of the day or night. Often just at dusk,
when returning from a picnic or walk, they would see
half a dozen or more wolves prowling in the woods;
the girls would run towards them screaming and shaking their mantles, and the whole pack would scurry
away through the undergrowth.

This cowardly conduct of the wolves taught their
fair pursuers to underestimate the ferocious nature of
the beasts, as we shall hereafter see.

The winter of 1801 was a severe one. Heavy
snows fell, and the passage through the woods was
difficult, either by reason of the snows or from the
thaws which succeeded them. Never before had the
wolves been so bold and ferocious. It happened that
in the depth of this winter a merry-making was
announced to take place in the nearest settlement,
ten miles distant.

The Carter girls were of course among the invited
guests, for their beauty and spirit were famed through
the whole region. Their parents having perfect confidence in the ability of the girls to take care of

themselves, and also considering that their brother was to accompany them on horseback, Mr. Carter, the elder, ordered their house-servant, an old negro named Hannibal, to tackle up a pair of stout roadsters to a two-seated wagon and drive his daughters to the merry-making.

Hannibal was a fiddler of renown and that of course formed a double reason why he should go to the ball.

The snow was not so deep as to delay the party materially.   They were determined under any circumstances to reach the scene of Christmas festivities, where the young ladies, as well as their partners, anticipated a " good time " in the dance, and perchance "*possibilities*" which might be protracted until a late hour upon the following morning, when the guests would disperse upon the understanding that they were to meet and continue their amusements the same evening.

In spite of the urgent invitations of their friends that the young ladies should pass the night at the settlement, they set out on their way home, to which they were lighted by a full moon, whose light was reflected from the snow and filled the air with radiance.

The girls were assisted into the old two-seated wagon, Hannibal, rolling his eyes and showing his teeth, clambered on the front seat, placing his fiddle in its case between his knees, and grasping the reins shouted to the horses, which started off at a rattling pace, young Carter and an escort of admiring cavaliers riding behind as a guard of honor.

After accompanying them on their way for three miles, the escort took leave of them amid much doffing of hats and waving of handkerchiefs.

The wagon was passing through the dense forest which it had traversed the night before, when a deep, mournful howl was borne to the ears of the party. Another followed, and then a succession of similar sounds, till the forest resounded with the bayings as if of a legion of wolves.

Upon the departure of the escort, young Carter, with youthful impetuosity and thoughtlessness, had put spurs to his horse, a beast of blood and mettle, and was now far in advance of the wagon, which was moving slowly through the forest, barely lighted by the moon, which cast its beams through the interlacing boughs.

The girls were not in the least scared by the wolfish concert. Not so Hannibal, who rolled his eyes up and down the woods, whipped up the horses, and uttered sundry ejaculations in the negro dialect expressive of his alarm and apprehension on the young ladies' account.

An open space in the forest soon showed to the party a half dozen dark, gaunt objects squatted on their haunches, whining and sniffing, directly in the track of the wagon. They rose and ranged themselves by the side of the road, the vehicle passing so near that Hannibal was able to give them with his whip two or three cuts which sent them snarling to the rear.

The howling ceased, and for a few moments the girls thought their disagreeable visitors had bid them good night. Looking back, however, one of the girls saw a dozen or more loping stealthily behind them. They soon reached the wagon, and one of the boldest of the pack leaped up behind and tore away a piece of the shawl in which one of the girls was wrapped, but a smart blow on the snout from the hand of the brave girl sent him yelping back to his fellows.

The horses becoming frightened, tore, snorting, through the woods, lashed by the old negro, half beside himself with terror: but the wolves only loped the faster and grew the bolder in proportion to the speed of the wagon. Sometimes they would throw their forepaws as high as the hind seat, and snap at the throats of the girls, who thereupon gave their wolfships severe buffets with their fists and thus drove them back.

The wolves were increasing in number and ferocity every moment, and but for a happy thought of the oldest Miss Carter, the whole party would have undoubtedly fallen a prey to the ferocious animals.

An old deserted cabin stood in the forest close to the track which they were following. Seizing the reins from the hands of the affrighted darkey, she guided the wagon up to the door of the cabin, and the whole party dismounting rushed into the door. Here Miss Carter stood with a stout stick, while the negro helped her sisters up into a loft by means of a ladder.

The pack again squatted on their haunches and whined wistfully, but were kept at bay by the daring maiden. After her sisters had been safely housed in the loft, with Hannibal who had in his fright quite forgotten her, she immediately joined them and had scarcely ascended the ladder when more than twenty of the wolves rushed pell-mell into the cabin.

The rest of the pack made an attack on the horses, which by their kicking and plunging broke loose from the harness, and dashed homewards through the woods followed by the yelling pack.

While this was going on, the young women recovered their equanimity, and hearing the horses break away from their assailants, directed the negro to close the door; which after some difficulty he succeeded in doing. Twenty wolves were thus snugly trapped.

One of the girls soon proposed that the old fiddler should play a few tunes to the animals, which were now whining in their cage.

The darkey accordingly took his violin, which he had clung to through all their mad drive, and struck up "Money Musk," which he played as correctly and in as good time as was possible under the circumstance. Soon collecting his nerve and coolness as he went on, he scraped out his whole *répertoire* of dancing tunes, "*St. Patrick's day in the morning*," "*The Irish Washerwoman*," "*Pop goes the Weasel*," winding up with a "*Breakdown* and *Fishers' Hornpipe.*"

The effect of the music, while it cheered and amused the girls in their strange situation, seemed to have a directly contrary effect on the wolves, who crouched, yelped, and trembled until they seemed utterly powerless and harmless. What threatened to be a tragedy was in this way turned into something that resembled a comedy.

By daylight Mr. Carter, with his son and two negroes, arrived on the scene, armed to the teeth with guns and axes, and made short work with the brutes climbing on the roof of the cabin and descending into the loft from which place they shot them in detail. The bounty which at that time was paid for wolves'

21

heads was awarded to Miss Carter by whose ingenuity
the brutes were trapped.

The wild cat of this continent is said to be the
lineal descendant of "the harmless, necessary cat,"
which the early emigrants brought over with them
from Europe, among their other four-footed friends and
companions. Certain depraved and perverse representatives of this domestic creature took to the woods,
and, becoming outlaws from society, reverted to their
original savage state. Their offspring waxed in size
and fierceness beyond their progenitors. They became
at last proverbial for their fighting qualities, and to
be able to "whip one's weight in wild cats," is a terse
expression signifying strength.

The fecundity of this animal, as well as its predatory
skill, makes it an extremely frequent and annoying
poacher on the poultry-yards of the backwoods settlers,
especially in the hill districts of the Southern States,
where the climate and the abundance of game appear
to have developed them to an uncommon size and
fierceness.

Their strength and ferocity was fully tested by a
settler's wife, in the upper part of Alabama, some fifty
years ago, as will appear from the following account:

Mrs. Julia Page, a widow, with three small children,
occupied a house in a broken and well-wooded country,
some miles west of the present town of Huntsville,
where the only serious annoyance and drawback
was the immense number of these animals which
prowled through the woods and decimated the poultry.
Stumpy tailed, green eyed, they strolled through the
clearing and sunned themselves on the limbs of neighboring trees, blinking calmly at the clucking hens

which they marked for their prey, and even venturing to throw suspicious glances at the infant sleeping in its cradle. Sociable in their disposition, they appeared to even claim a kind of proprietary interest in the premises and in the appurtenances thereof.

Shooting a dozen and trapping as many more, made little appreciable difference in the numbers of the feline colony. The dame at last constructed with much labor a close shed, within which her poultry were nightly housed. This worked well for a season. But one evening a commotion in the hennery informed her that the depredators were again at work. Hastily seizing an axe in one hand and carrying a lighted pitch pine knot in the other, she hurried to the scene of action, and found Grimalkin feasting sumptuously on her plumpest pullet. The banqueters were evidently a mother and her well-grown son, whom she was instructing in the predatory art and practice.

The younger animal immediately clambered to the hole where it had made its entrance, and was about to make a successful exit, when the matron, sticking the lighted knot in the ground, struck the animal with the axe, breaking its back and bringing it to the ground. Without an instant's warning, the mother cat sprang upon Mrs. Page, and fastening its powerful claws in her breast, tore savagely at her neck with its teeth.

The matron, shrieking with terror, strove with all her might to loosen the animal's hold, but in vain. The maternal instinct had awakened all its fierceness, and as the blood commenced to flow in streams from the deep scratches and bites inflicted by its teeth and claws, its ferocious appetency redoubled. It tore and bit as if nothing would appease it but the luckless victim's death.   Mrs. Page would doubtless have fallen a prey to its savage rage, but for a happy thought which flashed across her mind in her desperate straits.

Snatching the pine knot from the earth, she applied it to the hindquarters of the wild cat. The flame instantly singed off the thick fur and scorched its flesh. With a savage screech, it relaxed its hold and fell to the ground, where she succeeded at last in dispatching the creature. It proved to be one of the largest of its species, measuring nearly three feet from its nose to the tip of its tail, and weighing over thirty pounds.

For many years this colony of pioneer wild cats continued to "make things hot" for the settlers in that region, but most of them were finally exterminated, and the remnant emigrated to some more secluded region.

The character of the common black bear is a study for the naturalist, and the hunter. He is fierce or good-natured, sullen or playful, lazy or energetic, bold or cowardly, "all by turns and nothing long." He is the clown of the menagerie, the laughing stock rather than the dread of the hunter, and the abhorrence of border house-wives, owing to his intrusive manners, his fondness for overturning beehives, and his playful familiarity with the contents of their larders in the winter season.

Incidents are related where in consequence of these contrarieties of bear-nature, danger and humor are singularly blended.

While the daughters of one of the early settlers of Wisconsin was wandering in "maiden meditation," through the forest by which her father's home was surrounded, she was suddenly startled from her reverie by a hoarse, deep, cavernous growl, and as she lifted her eyes, they were opened wide with dismay and terror. Not twenty paces from her, rising on his huge iron clawed hind feet, was a wide-mouthed, vicious looking black bear, of unusual size, who had evidently been already "worked up," and was "spoiling for a fight." That the bear meant mischief was plain, but the girl was a pioneer's daughter, and her fright produced no symptoms of anything like fainting.

Bears could climb, she knew that very well; but then if she got out of his way quickly enough he might not take the trouble to follow her.

It was the only chance, and she sprang for the nearest tree. It was of medium size, with a rough bark and easy to climb. All the better for her, if none the worse for the bear, and in an instant she was perched among the lower branches. For two or three minutes the shaggy monster seemed puzzled and as if in doubt what course he had best pursue; then he came slowly up and began smelling and nuzzling round the roots of the tree as if to obtain the necessary information in order to enable him to decide this important question.

The young woman in the tree was no coward, but little as was the hope of being heard in that forest solitude she let her fears have their own way and screamed loudly for help. As if aroused and provoked by the sound of her voice, bruin began to try the bark with his foreclaws while his fierce little eyes looked up carnivorously into the face of the maiden, and his little tongue came twisting spirally from his half opened jaws as if he were gloating over a choice titbit.

A neighboring settler, attracted by the cries of distress, soon reached the scene of action. Though completely unarmed he did not hesitate to come to close quarters with bruin, and seizing a long heavy stick he commenced to vigorously belabor the hind quarters of the brute, who, however, only responded to these attentions by turning his head and winking viciously at his assailant, still pursuing his upward gymnastics in the direction of the girl, who on her part was clambering towards the upper branches of the tree.

The young man redoubled his blows and for a moment bruin seemed disposed to turn and settle matters with the party in his rear, but finally to the dismay of both the maiden and her champion, and evidently deeming his readiest escape from attack would be to continue his ascent, he resumed his acrobatic performance and was about to place his forefeet on the lower limbs, when his foe dropping his futile weapon, seized the stumpy tail of the beast with his strong hands, and bracing his feet against the trunk of the tree pulled with all his might. The girl seeing the turn that matters had taken, immediately broke off a large limb and stoutly hammered the bear's snout. This simultaneous attack in front and rear was too much for bruin : with an amusing air of bewilderment he descended in a slow and dignified manner and galloped off into the forest.

There are but few instances on record where female courage has been put to the severe test of a hand to hand combat with grizzly bears. The most remarkable conflict of this description is that which we will endeavor to detail in the following narrative, which brings out in bold relief the traits of courage, hardi-

TREED BY A BEAR.   Page 356.

hood, and devotion, all displayed by woman in most trying and critical situations, wherein she showed herself the peer of the stoutest and most skillful of that hardy breed of men—the hunters of the far west.

In the summer of 1859 a party of men and women set out from Omaha, on an exploring tour of the Platte valley, for the purpose of fixing upon some favorable location for a settlement, which was to be the head-quarters of an extensive cattle-farm. The leader in the expedition was Col. Ansley, a wealthy Englishman. He was accompanied by Joseph Dagget, his agent, whose business had carried him several times across the Rocky Mountains to California; Mrs. Dagget and a daughter of sixteen, both of whom had crossed the plains before with Mr. D.—two half-breeds also accompanied the party as guides, hunters, muleteers, and men of all work.

As Mrs. Dagget is the heroine of our story, she deserves a description in detail. Her early life had been spent in the wilds of Northern New York, where she became versed in fishing, hunting, and wood-craft. She grew up in that almost unbroken wilderness to more than woman's ordinary stature, and with a masculine firmness of nerve and fiber. We need hardly add that she was an admirable *equestrienne.*

At the age of seventeen she was married to Joseph Dagget, who possessed those qualities which she was naturally most inclined to admire in a man.

The seventeen years that followed her marriage she spent with her husband in the wilds of the North and West, where she obtained all the further experience necessary to complete her education as a practical Woman of the Border. It is unnecessary to state

that such a woman as Mrs. Dagget was an exceedingly useful member of frontier society. Several
times she and her husband had been the leading spirits in starting new settlements far in advance of the
main stream of immigration: after the courage and
experience of Mr. and Mrs. D. had helped on the infant settlement for a season, the restless spirit of adventure would seize them, and selling out, they would
push on further west.

Miss Jane Dagget was a girl after her father's and
mother's own heart, and was their constant companion in their expeditions and journeys over prairie and
mountain.

The party started in June from Omaha, and journeyed along the north bank of the Platte river as far
as the North Fork of that stream.   They were well-
mounted on blooded horses, furnished by Col. Ansley,
and were followed by four pack-mules with such
baggage as the party needed, under the care of the
half-breed guides.

Two weeks sufficed to locate the ranch, after which
they pursued their way along the North Platte, as far
as Fort Laramie, intending from that post to advance
northward to strike the North Fork of the Cheyenne,
and following that stream to the Missouri river, there
take the steamboat back to Omaha. This diversion
in their proposed route was made at the suggestion of
Col. Ansley, who was a keen and daring sportsman,
and wished to add a fight with grizzlies to his *répertoire* of hunting adventures.

The first day's journey, after leaving Fort Laramie,
was barren of incident.   Pursuing their route due-
north, over a rolling and well-grassed country, inter-

spersed with sandy stretches, they reached, on the evening of the second day, some low hills, covered with thickets and small trees, between which ran valleys thickly carpeted with grass. Here they were preparing their camp, when one of the half-breeds cried out, "Voila Greezly!"

The whole party turned their eyes, and saw, sure enough, an enormous mouse-colored grizzly sitting on his haunches beside a tree, regarding them with strong marks of curiosity.

The half-breeds straightway began to prepare for action, after the California fashion, that is to say, they coiled their "lariats," and rode slowly up to the brute, who stood his ground, only edging up until his flank nearly rested against the tree, a stout sapling some four inches in diameter.

The rest of the party stood ready with their rifles, not excepting even the ladies. The horses snorted and trembled, while their hearts beat so loudly that the riders could plainly hear them.

Meanwhile François, one of the half-breeds, had let slip his lasso, which fell squarely over the head of the grizzly; then drawing it "taut." he kept it so while he slowly walked his horse around the tree, binding the grizzly firmly to it.

The whole party now advanced with rifles poised, ready to give the *coup de grâce* to his bearship ; when, with a thundering growl, *another* "grizzly" came shambling swiftly out from the bushes, and made directly for François. Before the party recovered from their surprise at this new appearance on the scene, the brute reared up and seized François by the leg, which he crunched and shattered.

Only one of the party dared to fire, for fear of wounding the guide ; that one was Mrs. Dagget, who, poising her carbine, would have sent a ball through the monster's heart but for a sudden start of her high-mettled horse. As it was, her shot only wounded the beast, which immediately left François and dashed at our heroine, who drew a navy-revolver from her holsters, gave the infuriated animal two more shots, and then wheeled her horse and galloped away, making a circuit as she rode, so as to reach the other side of the tree from which the first grizzly had now disengaged himself, and attacking Michael, the remaining guide, had broken his horse's leg with a blow of his paw ; the horse fell, and Michael's arm was fractured, and the bear then dashing at Col. Ansley and Mr. Dagget, put them to flight, together with Miss Dagget. The Colonel's horse, stumbling, threw his rider, and leaving him with a dislocated shoulder, galloped away across the plain.

Mr. Dagget and his daughter quickly dismounted, and led the Colonel, groaning, to a thicket, where they placed him in concealment, and then returned to the combat. Mrs. Dagget meanwhile, having diverted both the grizzlies by repeated shots from her revolver, also drew them after her, away from the unfortunate half-breeds, who lay with shattered limbs on the ground where they had first fallen. By skillfully manœuvring her horse, she had been completely successful in drawing her antagonists some forty rods away. But although she had emptied her revolvers, making every shot tell in the bodies of the grizzlies, and the blood was streaming from their huge forms, they showed no abatement in their strength and fero-

city, and it was with an indescribable feeling of relief
that she saw her husband and daughter now advancing
to her own rescue. This feeling was, however, blended
with a wife's and mother's fears lest her beloved husband and daughter should take harm from the savage
monsters.

Mr. Dagget and his daughter, having carefully re-
loaded their rifles, had now crept up cautiously behind,
and watching their opportunity, had planted a ball
squarely in each of the bears, just behind their fore-
shoulders. This appeared to be the finishing stroke,
and the brutes stretched themselves on the plain—to
all appearance lifeless.

François and Michael were then placed in as comfortable a position as possible; the Colonel was brought
out of the thicket; the mules and stray horses were
brought back to camp; and then a consultation was
held between the Daggets as to what should be done
for the sufferers. Refreshment was given them; some
attempts at rude surgery were made in the way of
bandaging and setting the broken limbs and dislocated
shoulders. It was sixty miles to Fort Laramie; the
night was on them, and the best course seemed to be
to rest their jaded steeds and start for a surgeon early
in the morning.

This course would have been pursued, but for another disaster, which occurred just as they were preparing to rest for the night. Mr. Dagget, from pure
curiosity, was prompted to examine the carcasses of the
bears. He noticed that one of them had dragged
itself some distance from where it fell towards a
thicket, but lay on its side as if dead. With a hunter's
curiosity, he lifted one of its forepaws to examine the

position of the death-wound, when the brute rose with a terrific growl and struck Mr. Dagget's arm with its paw, breaking it like a pipe-stem, and then, rolling over, groaned away its life, which it had thus far clung to with such fatal tenacity.

This was too much for the equanimity of Mrs. Dagget. The moans of the guides, with broken limbs, which had already swelled to a frightful size, and the pain which Col. Ansley and her husband strove in vain to conceal, were too harrowing to her woman's nature to permit her to rest quietly in camp that night. She was not long in adopting the seemingly desperate resolution of riding to the Fort and bringing back a nurse and surgeon.

Whispering to her daughter, she informed her of her determination, and quickly saddling the swiftest and freshest of the horses, she led him softly out from the camp, and, mounting, set her face southward, and touched the horse lightly with the whip. The generous beast seemed, by instinct, to understand his rider's errand, and bounded over the wild plain with a kind of cheerful alacrity that rendered unnecessary any further urging.

The sky was overcast, so that she had no stars to guide her course, and was obliged to guess the route which the party had followed from the Fort. By-and-by she struck a trail, which she thought she recognized as the one over which they had come after leaving the Platte River. For four hours she rode forward, the horse not flagging in his steady gallop. According to her calculations, she must have made forty miles of her journey, and she was anticipating that by the break of day she would have made the

Fort, when, turning her eyes upward to the left, she saw—through the clouds that had rifted for the first time—the great dipper, and knew at once that instead of riding southward, she had been riding eastward, and must be now at least seventy miles from the Fort, instead of being within twenty miles of it, as she had supposed.

Her horse began to show symptoms of fatigue. She slowed him to a walk as she turned his head to the southwest, and pursued her course sluggishly across the plains. Erelong the blackness of night faded into gray, and then came twilight streaks, which showed her the dreary country she was passing through. It was a vast sandy plain, thinly dotted with sage-bush and other stunted shrubs. The sun rose bright and hot, and, until ten o'clock, she pursued her way not faster than two miles an hour. Her horse now gave out, and refused to move a step. She dismounted and sat down on the sand beside a sage-bush, which partially sheltered her from the sun's rays.

We continue our narrative with Mrs. Dagget's own account of her perilous adventure :—

"For nearly two hours I sat on the ground, while my poor horse feebly staggered from bush to bush, and nibbled at the stunted herbage. I then remounted him and pursued my way, at a snail's pace, towards the Fort. The most serious apprehension I entertained at this moment was that of sun-stroke, as my head was only shielded from the rays by a white handkerchief; my hat had blown off in the conflict with the bears, and, in my distress and anxiety to start for assistance, I had not stopped to look for it. I felt no hunger, but

a little after noon, when the burning heat of the sun
was reflected with double violence from the hot sand,
and the distant ridges of the hills, seen through the
ascending vapor, seemed to wave and fluctuate like the
unsettled sea, I became faint with thirst, and climbed
a tree in hopes of seeing distant smoke or other
appearance of a human habitation. But in vain;
nothing appeared all around but thick underwood and
hillocks of white sand.

"My thirst by this time became insufferable; my
mouth was parched and inflamed; a sudden dimness
would frequently come over my eyes with other symptoms of fainting; and my horse, being barely able to
walk, I began seriously to apprehend that I should
perish of thirst. To relieve the burning pain in my
mouth or throat, I chewed the leaves of different
shrubs, but found them all bitter, and of no real service
to me.

"A little before sunset, having reached the top of a
gentle rising, I climbed a high tree, from the topmost
branches of which I cast a melancholy look over the
barren wilderness, but without discovering the most
distant trace of a human dwelling. The same dismal
uniformity of shrubs and sand everywhere presented
itself, and the horizon was as level and uninterrupted
as that of the sea.

"Descending from the tree, I found my horse devouring the stubble and brushwood with great avidity, and
as I was now too faint to attempt walking, and my
horse too fatigued to carry me, I thought it but an act
of humanity, and perhaps the last I should ever have
it in my power to perform, to take off his bridle and
let him shift for himself; in doing which I was sud-

denly affected with sickness and giddiness, and falling upon the sand, I felt as if the hour of death was fast approaching.

" ' Here then,' thought I, after a short but ineffectual struggle, 'terminates all my hopes of being useful in my day and generation; here must the short span of my life come to an end! I cast (as I believed) a last look on the surrounding scene, and whilst I reflected on the awful change that was to take placé, this world with its enjoyments seemed to vanish from my recollection. Nature, however, at length resumed its functions; and on recovering my senses, I found myself stretched upon the sand, with the bridle still in my hand, and the sun just sinking behind the trees. I now summoned all my resolution, and determined to make another effort to prolong my existence. And as the evening was somewhat cool, I resolved to travel as far as my limbs would carry me, in hopes of reaching (my only resource) a watering-place.

"With this view, I put the bridle on my horse, and driving him before me, went slowly along for about an hour, when I perceived some lightning from the northeast; a most delightful sight; for it promised rain. The darkness and lightning increased rapidly; and in less than an hour I heard the wind roaring among the bushes. I had already opened my mouth to receive the refreshing drops which I expected; but I was instantly covered with a cloud of sand, driven with such force by the wind as to give a very disagreeable sensation to my face and arms; and I was obliged to mount my horse and stop under a bush, to prevent being suffocated. The sand continued to fly in amazing quantities for near an hour; after which I again set forward, and traveled with difficulty, until ten o'clock. About this time, I was agreeably surprised by some very vivid flashes of lightning, followed by a few heavy drops of rain.

"In a little time the sand ceased to fly, and I alighted and spread out all my clean clothes to collect the rain, which at length I saw would certainly fall. For more than an hour it rained plentifully, and I quenched my thirst by wringing and sucking my clothes. A few moments after I fell into a profound slumber, in spite of the rain which now fell in torrents.

"The sky was clear and the sun was well up when I woke: drenched to the skin I rose as soon as my stiffened limbs would permit, and cast a look at the southern horizon. A line of black dots was distinctly visible, slowly moving westward. Mounting my horse, which was now freshened by his rest and the scanty provender which he had gathered in the night, I pushed on and succeeded in overtaking the party which was a detachment of United States cavalry. Before night we reached the Fort, and early next morning I accompanied a surgeon and two attendants, with an ambulance, to the camp where we found all as we had left them, and overjoyed at my return. When the fractures had been reduced, and Col. Ansley's shoulder put into place, the whole party were brought back to the Fort, quite content to wait awhile before engaging again in a ' grizzly-bear hunt.' "

The strength of nerve and fortitude which maternal love will inspire, is brilliantly illustrated by the story of an adventure with an American lion which happened not long since in the remote territory of Wyoming.

A Mrs. Vredenbergh one night, during the absence of her husband, had retired with her three children, to rest, in a chamber, on the first floor of the cabin where she lived, when an enormous mountain-lion leaped into the room through an open window placed at some distance from the ground for purposes of ventilation. The brute after entering the apartment whined and shook itself, and then lay down upon the floor in a watchful attitude with its eyes fixed upon the bed where lay Mrs. V., almost paralyzed with fright at this dangerous visitor. Her children were her first thought. Two of them were in a cot beyond the bed, where she lay; the third, an infant of six months, was reposing in its mother's arms.

Mrs. Vredenbergh remembered in an instant that perfect silence and stillness might prevent the brute from springing upon them; and accordingly she suppressed every breath and motion on her own part, while her children luckily were sleeping so profoundly that their breathing could not be heard. After a few minutes the monster began to relax the steady glare of his great green orbs, and winked lazily, purring loudly as though in good humor. The first powerful impulse to scream and fly to the adjoining apartment having been repressed, the matron's heart became calmer and her mind employed itself in devising a thousand plans for saving herself and her children. Her husband's gun hung loaded above the head of the bed, but it could not be reached without rising: if she woke her children she feared her action in so doing or the noise they would make would bring the monster upon them. She had heard that the mountain-lion would not attack human beings when his

22

hunger had been appeased, and from a noise she had heard in the cow-house just after retiring, she surmised that the brute had made a raid upon the cattle and glutted himself; this conjecture received confirmation from the placidity of the animal's demeanor. Resting upon this theory she finally maintained her original policy of perfect stillness, trusting that her husband would soon return. Her greatest fear now was that the infant might wake and cry, for she was well aware that the ferocity of the mountain-lion is roused by nothing so quickly as the cry of a child.

A full hour passed in this manner. The moon was at its full, and from her position on the couch, Mrs. Vredenbergh could, without turning her head, see every motion of the creature. It lay with its head between its forepaws in the posture assumed by the domestic cat when in a state of semi-watchfulness, approaching to a doze. The senses of the matron were strung to an almost painful acuteness. The moonlight streaming in at the window was to her eyes like the glare of the sun at noonday: the ticking of the clock on the wall fell on her ears, each tick like a sharply pointed hammer seeming to bruise the nerve. A keen thrill ran like a knife through her tense frame when the infant stirred and moaned in his sleep. The lion roused himself in an instant, and fixing his eyes upon the bed came towards it arching his back and yawning. He rubbed himself against the bedstead and stood for a moment so near that Mrs. V. could have touched him with her hand, then turned back and commenced pacing up and down the room. The infant fortunately ceased its moaning and sighing gently fell back into its slumbers; and again the beast, purring and winking, lay down and resumed its former position.

The quick tread of the lady's husband at this moment was heard; as he put his hand upon the latch to enter, Mrs. V. could contain herself no longer, and uttered a series of loud shrieks. The lion, rising, bounded over the head of Mr. Vredenbergh as he entered the cabin, and disappeared in the forest.

The safety of the family consisted partly perhaps in the fact that the intruder before entering the house had satiated his appetite by gorging himself upon a calf, the remains of which were next day discovered in the cow-house; but the preservation of herself and children was also due to the self-control with which Mrs. Vredenbergh maintained herself in that trying situation.

CHAPTER XV.

ACROSS THE CONTINENT.—ON THE PLAINS.

THE movement of emigration westward since the early part of the seventeenth century resembles the great ocean billows during a rising tide. Sweeping over the watery waste with a steady roll, dragged by the lunar force, each billow dashes higher and higher on the beach, until the attractive influence has been spent and the final limit reached. The spirit of religious liberty and of adventure carried the European across the Atlantic. This was the *first* wave of emigration. The achievement of our Independence gave the next great impetus to the movement. The acquisition of California and the discovery of gold was the third stimulus that carried our race across the continent. The final impulse was communicated by the completion of the Pacific railroad.

At the close of the Mexican War in 1848, our frontier States were, Texas, Arkansas, Missouri, Iowa, and Wisconsin. With the exception of a few forts, trading-posts, missionary stations, and hunters' camps, the territory extending from the line of furthest settlement in those States, westward to the Pacific Ocean, was for the most part an uninhabited waste. This tract, (including the Gadsden purchase,) covering upwards of seventeen hundred thousand square miles and nearly half as large as the whole of Europe, was now to be penetrated, explored, reclaimed, and added to the area of civilization.

The pioneer army of occupation who were to commence this mighty work moved through Missouri and Iowa, and crossing the turbid flood which formed one of the great natural boundaries of that wild empire, saw before them the vast plains of Nebraska and Kansas stretching with scarcely a break for five hundred miles as the crow flies to the foot-hills of the Rocky Mountains. The Platte, the Kansas, and the Arkansas, with their tributaries, indicated the general bearings of the march, the sun and moon were unerring guides.

The host divided itself: one part spread over and tilled the rich country which extends for two hundred miles west of the Missouri River; another part grazed its flocks and herds on the pasture ground beyond; another, crossing the belt of desert, settled in the picturesque region between the barrens and the foot-hills; another penetrated into the mountains and planted itself in the labyrinthian valleys and on the lofty table lands between the Black Hills and the California Sierras; another more boldly marched a thousand miles across a wilderness of mountain ranges, and settled on the slope which descends to the shores of the Pacific.

The rivers and streams between the Missouri and the mountains, and latterly the railroads, were the *axes* around which population gathered and turned itself. Here were the dwelling-places of the settlers; here woman's work was to be done and her influence to be employed in building up the empire on the plains.

We have stated how, by a series of processes extending through successive generations and the lapse of centuries, she grew more and more capable to fulfill her mission on this continent, and how, as the physical and moral difficulties that beset frontier-life multiplied, she gathered corresponding strength and faculties to meet them. In entering that new field of pioneer enterprise which lay beyond the Missouri River in 1848, there still, among others, remained that one great grief over the separation from her old home.

When the eastern woman bade farewell to her friends and started for the plains, it seemed to her, and often proved to be, a final adieu. We say nothing of that large class which, being more scantily endowed with this world's goods, were forced to make the long, wearisome journey with ox-teams from the older settlements of the East. We take the weaker case of the well-to-do emigrant wife who, by railroad, and by steamboat on the lakes or rivers, reached, after a journey of two thousand miles, the point upon the Missouri River where she was to enter the "prairie schooner" and move out into that vast expanse; even to *her* the pangs of separation must have then been felt with renewed and redoubled force. That "turbid flood" was the casting-off place. She was as one who ventures in a small boat into a wide, dark ocean, not knowing whether she would ever return or find within the murky waste a safe abiding place.

There was the uncertainty; the positive dangers of the route; the apprehended dangers which might surround the settlement; the new country, with all its difficulties, privations, labors, and trials; the possibilities of disease, with small means of relief; the utter solitude, with little prospect of solacing companionship.

And yet, with so dreary a picture presented to her mental vision, she did not shrink from the enterprise, nor turn back, until all hope of making a home for her family in that remote region had fled. We recall a few instances in which, after years of toil, sorrow, and suffering—when all had been lost, the heroine of the household has been driven back by a stress of circumstances with which human power was unavailing to cope. Such a case was that of Mrs. N——, of which the following are the substantial facts:

While a squad of United States cavalry were journeying in 1866 from the Great Bend of the Arkansas to Fort Riley, in Kansas, the commanding officer, as he was sweeping with his glass the horizon of the vast level plain over which they were passing, descried a small object moving towards their line of march through the tall grass some two miles to their left. No other living thing was visible throughout their field of vision, and conjecture was rife as to what this single moving object in that lonely waste could be. It moved in a slow and hesitating way, sometimes pausing, as if weary, and then resuming its sluggish course towards the East. They made it out clearly at last. It was a solitary woman. She had a rifle in her hand, and as the squad changed their course and approached her, she could be seen at the distance of half a mile putting herself in the posture of defense and making ready to use her rifle. The horsemen waved their hats and shouted loudly to advise her that they were friends. She kept her rifle at her shoulder and stood like a statue, until, seeming to be reassured, she changed her attitude and with tottering steps approached them.

She was a woman under thirty, who had evidently been tenderly reared; small and fragile, her pale, wasted face bore those lines which mutely tell the tale of long sorrow and suffering. Her appearance awoke all those chivalrous feelings which are the honor of the military profession. She was speechless with emotion. The officer addressed her with kind and respectful inquiries. Those were the first words of her mother tongue she had heard for four weeks. Like the breath of the " sweet south " blowing across the fabled lute, those syllables, speaking of home and friends, relaxed the tension to which her nerves had been so long strung and she wept. Twice she essayed to tell how she happened to be found in such a melancholy situation on that wild plain, and twice she broke down, sobbing with those convulsive sobs that show how the spirit can shake and over-master the frail body.

Weak, weary, and worn as she was, they ceased to question her, and preserved a respectful silence, while they did all that rough soldiers could do to make her comfortable. An army overcoat was wrapped around her, stimulants and food given her, and one of the soldiers, shortening a stirrup, and strapping a folded blanket over his saddle, made a comfortable seat upon his horse, which he surrendered to her. The following day she had acquired sufficient strength to tell her sad story.

Three years before, she, with her husband and four children, had left her childhood's home, in the eastern part of Ohio, and set out for Kansas. Her oldest boy sickened and died while passing through Illinois, and they laid him to rest beneath the waving prairie grass. After crossing the Missouri river, her second child, a lovely little girl of six years, was carried off by the scarlet fever, and they left her sleeping beneath the green meadow sward on the bank of the Kansas.

After a wearisome march of eighty days, they reached their destination on the Smoky Hill Branch of the Kansas River, and lying about three hundred miles west of Fort Leavenworth. Here, in a country suitable for grazing and tillage, they chose their home. Mr. N. devoted himself to the raising of cattle, tilling only land enough to supply the wants of himself and family.

She had toiled day and night to make their home comfortable and happy for her husband and children. Fortune smiled upon them. Their herds multiplied and throve upon the rich pasturage and in the mild air of the region where they grazed. Two more children were added to their flock. Their roof-tree sheltered all from the heats of summer and the bleak winds which sweep those plains in the winter season. Bounteous harvests blessed their store. They were visited by the red man only as a wayfarer and friend.

This bright sky was at last suddenly overclouded. A plague raged among their cattle. A swarm of grasshoppers ravaged their crops. A drought followed, which burned up the herbage. "Terrors," says, the poet, "come not as single spies, but in battalions." Pestilence at last came to complete the ruin of that hapless household. Her husband was first stricken down, and after a week of suffering, died in a delirium, which, while it startled and saddened the little flock, kept him all unapprehensive of the evils which might visit his bereaved family after his departure. The wife dug, with her own hands, a shallow grave on the bluff where their house stood, and bearing, with difficulty, in her slender arms the wasted remains, laid them, coffinless, in the trench, and covering them with earth, returned to the house to find her three oldest children suffering from the same malady. The pestilence made short but sure work with their little frames. One by one they breathed their last in their mother's arms. Kissing their waxen features, she bore them out all alone and laid them tenderly side by side with their father.

The little babe of four months was still the picture of health. All unconscious of its bereavements and of the bitter sorrows of her on whose bosom he lay, he throve upon the maternal bounty which poured for him, though her frail life seemed to be passing away with it.

Like some subtle but potent elixir, which erects the vital spirit, and holds it when about to flee from its tenement, so did that sweet babe keep the mother's heart pulsing with gentle beat during the days which followed those forlorn funeral rites.

A week passed, during which a great terror possessed her, lest she too should have the latent seeds of the pestilence in her frame, and should have imparted the dreadful gift to her babe through the fountain of motherhood.

A racking pain in her forehead, followed by lassitude, told her alas! that all she had shuddered to think of was coming to pass.   Weary and suffering, she laid herself upon the couch, which she prayed but for her infant might be her last resting place.   Too soon, as she watched with a keenness of vision which only a mother can possess, did she see the first shadow of the destroyer reflected on the face of her little one.   It faded like a flower in the hot blast of July,

"So softly worn, so sweetly weak,"

and before two suns had come and gone, it lay like a bruised lily on the fever-burning bosom which gave it life.

Unconsciousness came mercifully to the poor mother. For hours she lay in blessed oblivion.   But the vital principle, which often displays its wondrous power in the feeblest frames, asserted its triumph over death, and she awoke again to the remembrance of losses that could never be repaired this side the grave.

Three days passed before the fever left her.   She

arose from her couch, and, with shaking frame, laid her little withered blossom on its father's grave, and covering it with a mound of dried grass, crowned it with yellow autumn leaves.

The love of life slowly returned; but the means to sustain that life had been destroyed by murrain, the grasshoppers, and the drought. The household stores would suffice but for a few days longer. The only and precarious means of subsistence which would then remain, would be such game as she could shoot. The Indians becoming apprised of the death of Mr. N., had carried off the horses.

Only one avenue of escape was left her; casting many "a longing, lingering look" at the home once so happy, but now so swept and desolate, she took her husband's rifle and struck boldly out into the boundless plain, towards the trail which runs from the Arkansas River to Fort Riley, and after several days of great suffering fell in with friends, as we have already described.

The sad experience of Mrs. N. is fortunately a rare one at the present day. The vast area occupied by the plains of Kansas and Nebraska, is in many respects naturally fitted for those forms of social life in which woman's work may be performed under the most favorable circumstances; a country richly adapted to the various forms of agriculture and to pastoral occupations; a mild and generally equable climate are there well calculated to show the pioneer-housewife at her best.

Another great advantage has been the fact that this region was a kind of graduating school, into which the antecedent schools of pioneer-life. could send skilled pupils, who, upon a fair and wide field, and in a virgin soil, could build a civil and social fabric, reflecting past experiences and embodying a multi tude of separate results into a large and harmonious whole.

Visiting some years since the States of Kansas and Nebraska, we passed first through that rich and already populous region in the eastern part of the former State, which twenty-five years since was an uninhabited waste. Here were all the appliances of civilization: the school, the church, the town hall; improved agriculture, the mechanic arts, the varied forms of mercantile traffic, and at the base of the fabric the home made and ordered by woman. Here but yesterday was the frontier where woman was performing her oft before repeated task, and laying, according to her methods and habits, and within her appropriate sphere, the foundations of that which is to-day a great, rich, and prosperous social and civil State. Here, too, we saw many of the mothers, not yet old, who through countless trials, labors, and perils have aided in the noble work on which they now are looking with such honest pride and satisfaction.

For many successive afternoons we passed on from city to city, and from village to village. The sun preceded us westward; we steered our course directly towards it, and each day as it sank to the earth, brightly and more brightly glowed the sky as with the purest gold. The settlements became more scattered, the uninhabited spaces grew wider. *We were nearing one of the frontiers.*

In the spring the mead through which we were passing was a natural parterre, where in the midst of the lively vernal green, bloomed the oxlip, the white and blue violet, the yellow-cup dotted with jet, and many another fragile and aromatic member of the floral sisterhood.

Ascending a knoll crowned by a little wood which lay like a green shrub upon that treeless, grassy plain, we saw from this point the prairie stretching onward its loftily waving extent to the horizon. Here and there amidst the vast stretch arose small log-houses, which resembled little birds' nests floating upon the ocean. Here and there, also, were people harvesting grain.

Among the harvesters were three young women, who were nimbly binding sheaves, with little children around them. The vastness of the prairie made the harvesters themselves look like children playing at games.

Some distance beyond us, in the track we were pursuing, we saw what at first glance appeared to be a white dahlia. As we neared it, this huge white flower seemed to be moving; it was the snowy sun-bonnet of a young school-teacher, who was convoying a troop of children to the school-house, whose brown roof showed above the luxuriant herbage. She seemed to be beloved by her scholars, for they surrounded her and clung to her. She had been giving them, it appeared, a lesson in practical botany; their hats were adorned with scarlet and yellow blossoms, and they carried bunches of oxlips and violets. The school-mistress had a face like a sister of charity; the contour and lines showed resolution and patience; the whole expression blended with intelligence, a strong and lovely character. She entered the door of the log

school-house, and gently drew within it the youngest
of her charges.   Around the school-house we saw
other groups of sturdy boys and chubby girls, frisking
and shouting gaily as we drove by.

It is under the tuition of the women especially that
a vigorous, intelligent, and laborious race grows up
in these border settlements on the plains.   The children are taught the rudiments, and afterwards endeavor to improve their condition in life.   The boys
often enter upon political and public careers.   The
girls marry early, and contribute to make new societies in the wilderness.   These farms are the nurseries
from which the State will soon obtain its officials and
its teachers, both male and female.

The gardens, the cottages, and cabins nearly all
showed some external signs of the embellishing hand
of woman.   Entering one of these houses, we found
the men and young women out gathering the harvest.
An elderly woman acted as our hostess.   She was
maid of all-work, a chamber-maid, cook, dairy-woman,
laundress, and children's nurse ; and yet she found
time to make us a cordial welcome.   The house was
only one year old, and rather open to the weather,
but bore the marks of womanly thrift and even of
refinement.

The matron who entertained us displayed piety,
restless activity, humanity, intelligence, and a youth-
fully warm heart, all of which marked her as a type
of that large class of elderly housewives who are
using the education which they acquired in their girlhood in the East to form new and model communities
on these wide and rich plains.

We asked her about her life and thus came to hear,

without the least complaint on her part, of its many difficulties.   And yet when her husband and sons and daughters returned home from the field, we could see that it was a joyous and happy home.

The eldest daughter, Mrs. B———, then a widow of twenty-five or six, told us the story of her experience in border-life.   She was born in Wisconsin, when as a territory it had a population of only three thousand.   Soon after the removal of her father and mother to Kansas, and at the age of sixteen she had married one of the most adventurous of the race of young pioneers which drew their first breath upon the then frontier in Illinois.

Their wedding tour was in a prairie schooner from Atchison to the semi-fertile region which borders on the desert belt which stretches through western Nebraska and Kansas to New Mexico.   Here they made their first home.   Life in that particular section must be a pastoral rather than an agricultural one: her husband accordingly devoted himself almost entirely to the raising of cattle.

We hardly need say, that next to the hunter, the cattle-herder approximates most nearly to savage life; his wife must accordingly find her position under such circumstances, a peculiarly trying one.   The house in which Mrs. B——— and her husband lived was a simple hut constructed by digging away the side of a hill which formed the earthen rear and side walls of their dwelling, the top and front being of logs also covered with earth.   Their kitchen, sleeping-room, dining-room, and parlor were represented by a single apartment.   Three men with their wives were their companions in the enterprise, and all lived in similar houses.

As most of the men's time was occupied in looking after their herds and preventing them from wandering too far or from being stamped and stolen by thievish savages, a large share of the other out-door labors fell upon the women. Cheerfully accepting these burdens Mrs. B—— and her three female companions tilled the small patches of corn and potatoes which with pickled beef formed their only food. Much of the time they were left entirely alone and were alarmed as well as annoyed by frequent visits from Indians, who, however, abstained from violence, contenting themselves with eating what was given them and pilfering whatever stray articles they could find.

Three years were passed by the little colony in this wild pastoral life. Though the heats of summer and the sudden storms of wind in winter, were severe, disease was never added to their list of ordinary discomforts and privations. Two of the men twice a year drove their cattle two hundred and fifty miles to the nearest railway station, but none of the women accompanied them on these trips, which were always looked forward to by their husbands as a relief from the monotony of their life as herders.

The third summer after their arrival was extremely sultry, and the drought so common in that region, promised to be more than usually severe. The crops were rapidly being consumed by four weeks of continuous hot, dry weather, when one day late in July, the four housewives, who were sitting together in the cabin of Mrs. B——, observed a sudden darkening of the western sky, and felt sharp eddying gusts of wind which blew fitfully from the southwest. A succession of small whirlwinds carried aloft the sand in front of their houses, which were ranged not far apart on the hillside.

These phenomena, accompanied with various other atmospheric commotions, lasted for half an hour, and ceased to attract their attention. The wind, however, continued to increase, and the ears of the four matrons anon caught the sound of a dull, steady roar, which rose above the fitful howling of the blast. They ran to the door and saw a dark cloud shaped like a monstrous funnel moving swiftly towards them from the west. The point of this funnel was scarcely more than one hundred feet from the earth, and swayed like the car of a balloon descending from a great height.

Dismayed by this extraordinary spectacle they hastened in doors. Scarcely had they gained shelter when their ears were saluted by a sound louder than the broadside of a double decker, and the next moment the roof of the house was torn away with tremendous force and almost at the same instant a flood of water twenty feet deep swept the four women with the *débris* of the house down the hillside and whirled them away over the plain.

Three of the women, including Mrs. B———, severely bruised and half drowned, emerged from the torrent when it spread out and spent itself upon the level; the fourth stunned by a blow from one of the house-logs, and suffocated by the rush of the waters, could not be resuscitated. The water-spout, for such was the agent of the destruction which had been wrought, had fallen on the hillside and swept away two of the other houses besides that of Mrs. B———, and for ten days, while new dwellings could be con-

23

structed and the furniture and other articles carried away could be recovered, the three houseless families were quartered partly in the remaining house, and the rest encamped under the open sky, where they suffered additional discomfort from the thunder storms in the night, which followed the water-spout.

The next summer they were visited by another disaster in the shape of grasshoppers. Often had these terrible pests of the settlers in that and the adjacent regions, flown in immense clouds over their heads during former seasons, winging their way to the richer country which lay to the east, but never before had they been attracted to the scanty patches of corn and potatoes which skirted the hovels where the herders dwelt. But early in July of that year a swarm settled down almost ancle deep on the little strip of ploughed land, and within the space between the rising and the setting of the sun, every vestige of greenness had disappeared as if burned with fire.

After a short consultation that evening, the whole party determined to take time by the forelock, and abandoning their cabins remove with their household goods and herds of cattle before the insect plunderers had prepared the way for a famine which they were certain to do before many days. Hastily loading their carts with their household goods and stores, and collecting their cattle, five hundred in number, they set out for the Missouri River, three hundred miles distant.

Having reached their destination they sold all their cattle, and after resting a few days joined a company of five pioneers who were traveling over the military road, via Fort Kearney and through the Platte valley,

with the intention of settling in the picturesque and
well watered region east of the foot-hills of the Rocky
Mountains, and slaughtering buffaloes for their skins.

Mrs. B———, and her two female companions, with
a shrewd eye to profit, concluded an arrangement
with the hunters by which they were to board and
make the whole party comfortable, in their capacity
as housewives, for a certain share in the profits of the
buffalo skins, their husbands joining the party as
hunters.

All the necessary preparations having been made,
they set out on horse-back with ten pack-mules, and
made rapid progress, reaching the buffalo country without accident in twenty-two days.

Here the women occasionally joined in the hunt,
and being fearless riders as well as good shots added a
few buffalo robes to their own account. On one of
these hunts, Mrs. B———, becoming separated from
the party while following a stray bison with too much
ardor, reached a small valley which looked as if it
might be a favorite grazing ground for the brutes.
The wind blew in her face as she rode, and owing to
this circumstance, the bison being a quick scented animal, she was enabled to approach a solitary bull feeding by a stream at the foot of the hill and dispatched
it by a shot from her rifle.

Dismounting, she whipped out her hunting knife
and was proceeding to flay the carcass, when she was
attracted by a low rumbling sound which shook the
earth, and looking up the steep bluff at the foot
of which she stood, saw a herd which must have contained ten thousand bison, plunging madly down upon
her. Her horse taking fright broke away from the

bush to which he was fastened and galloped off. Mrs.
B——— ran after him at the top of her speed, but was
conscious that the black mass behind her would soon
overtake and trample her under foot, such was the impetus they had received in their course down the hill.

Not a tree was in sight, but remembering two or
three sink-holes which she had seen beside a clump
of bushes near the spot where she had taken aim at
the bull-bison, she hastened thither and succeeded in
dropping into one some ten feet in depth just as the
leaders of the herd were almost upon her. Lying
there panting and up to her waist in water, she heard
the shaggy battalions sweep over her, and, a moment
after they had passed, caught the sound of voices.
Emerging cautiously for fear of Indians, which were
swarming in the region, she saw four of the hunters
whom she had left an hour before galloping in hot
pursuit of the herd. The five other hunters coming
up in front of the herd as it was commencing to climb
the bluff on the other side of the valley, succeeding
in turning the terrified multitude to one side, and
when they came up with Mrs. B——— she saw they
had caught her horse, which had met them as it was
galloping homeward.

Thus supplied with a steed she mounted, and regaining her rifle which she had dropped in her flight,
nothing daunted by the danger she had so narrowly
escaped, joined in the hunt which ended in a perfect
battue. The hunters succeeded in driving a part of
the herd into a narrow gorge and strewing the ground
with carcasses.

Three months of this wild life made our heroine
pine for more quiet pursuits, and she induced her

husband to return to the frontier of eastern Nebraska, where, with the profits of the cattle enterprise and the hunt, a large tract was purchased on one of the tributaries of the Platte. Here, after six years of labor, they built up a model farm, well stocked with choice breeds of cattle, planted with nurseries of fruit trees, and laid down to grain. Attracted by the story of their success, other settlers flocked into the region. The completion of the Pacific Railroad soon after furnished them with an easy access to market. Every thing went on prosperously till the death of Mr. B—— from a casualty. But notwithstanding this loss, Mrs. B—— kept up the noble farm which her energy and perseverance had done so much to make what it was. She was then on a visit to her father's family in Kansas, where we met her, and had invited her father, mother, and sisters to remove to her home in Nebraska, which they were intending shortly to do.

The whole family showed evidence of the possession of the same bold and energetic character which the eldest daughter had displayed during her ten years' experience on the extreme frontier, beside those other qualities both of heart and mind which mark the true pioneer woman.

Heartfelt kindness and hospitality, seriousness and mirth in the family circle,—these characteristics of border life, when it is good, had all been transplanted into the western wilderness by these colonists. That day among the dwellers of the plain; that fine old lady; those handsome, fearless, warm-hearted, kind, and modest young women; that domestic life; that rich hospitality, combined to show how much happiness may be enjoyed in those frontier homes, where woman is the presiding genius.

CHAPTER XVI.

" HOW beautiful upon the mountains are the feet of him that bringeth good tidings: that publisheth peace: that bringeth good tidings of good: that publisheth salvation."

Among the faithful messengers who have borne this Gospel of peace to the benighted red man, there have been many devoted and pious women. The story of woman as a missionary in all climes and countries contains in itself the elements of the moral-sublime. History has not recorded,—poetry itself has seldom portrayed more affecting exhibitions of Christian fortitude, of feminine heroism, and of all the noble and generous qualities which constitute the dignity and glory of woman, than when it spreads before the wondering eyes of the world the picture of her toils, her sacrifices, and even her martyrdom, in this field of her glory.

We see her in the pestilential jungles of India, or beneath the scorching sun on Afric's burning sands, or amid the rigors of an Arctic winter, in the midst of danger, disease, and every trial or hardship that can crush the human heart; and through all presenting a character equal to the sternest trial, and an address and fertility of resource which has often saved her co-workers and herself from what seemed an inevitable doom.

(358)

Such an exhibition of heroic qualities, such a picture of toils, sacrifices, sufferings, and dangers, is also presented to our eyes in the record of woman as a missionary among the fierce and almost untamable aboriginal tribes which roam over our American continent. The trials, hardships, and perils which always environ frontier life, were doubled and intensified in that mission. Taking her life in her hand, surrounded by alien and hostile influences, often entirely cut off from communication with the civilized world, armed not with carnal weapons, but trusting that other armor—the sword of the Spirit, the shield of faith, and the helmet of salvation—with her heart full of love and pity for her dark-browed brethren, woman as a missionary to the Indians is a crowning glory of her age and sex.

The influence of woman in this field has been poured out through two channels—one direct, the other indirect; and it is sometimes difficult to decide which of these two methods have produced the greatest results. As an indirect worker, she has lightened her husband's labors as a missionary, has softened the fierce temper of the pagan tribes, and by her kind and placid ministrations has prepared their minds for the reception of Gospel truth.

As an example of such a worker, Mrs. Ann Eliot, the wife of the Rev. John Eliot, surnamed the "Apostle," stands conspicuous among a host. It was the prudence and skill of this good woman, exercised in her sphere as a wife, a mother, a housekeeper, and a doctress, that enabled her husband to carry out his devout and extensive plans and perform his labors in Christianizing the Indian tribes of New England.

In estimating the great importance of those pious and far-reaching plans, we must bear in mind the precarious condition of the New England Colonies in the days of the "Apostle" John and his excellent wife. The slender and ·feeble settlements on Plymouth and Massachusetts Bay had hardly yet taken root, and were barely holding their own against the adverse blasts that swept over them. A combination between the different savage tribes, by which they were surrounded, might have extinguished, in a day, the Puritan Colonies, and have set back, for generations, the destinies of the American continent.

The primary and unselfish purpose of the "Apostle" John Eliot was to convert these wild tribes to the doctrine and belief of Christ. One of the results of his labors in that direction was also, we can hardly doubt, the political salvation of those feeble colonies. The mind and heart of the "Apostle" were so absorbed in the great work wherein he was engaged that a skillful and practical partner was absolutely necessary to enable him to prepare for and fully discharge many duties which might properly devolve upon him, but from which his wife in his preoccupation now relieved him.

In her appropriate sphere she also exercised an important influence, indirectly, in carrying out her husband's plans. Amidst her devoted attentions to the care and nurture of her six children she found time for those many duties that devolved on a New England housekeeper of the olden time, when it was difficult and almost impossible to command the constant aid of domestics. To provide fitting apparel and food for her family, and to make this care justly comport with a small income, a free hospitality, and a large charity, required both efficiency and wisdom.

This she accomplished without hurry of spirit, fretfulness, or misgiving. But she had in view more than this: she aimed so to perform her own part as to leave the mind of her husband free for the cares of his sacred profession, and in this she was peculiarly successful. Her understanding of the science of domestic comfort, and her prudence—the fruit of a correct judgment—so increased by daily experience, that she needed not to lay her burdens upon him, or divert to domestic cares and employments the time and energy which he would fain devote to God. "The heart of her husband *did* safely trust in her," and his tender appreciation of her policy and its details was her sweet reward.

It was graceful and generous for the wife thus to guard, as far as in her lay, her husband's time and thoughts from interruption. For, in addition to his pastoral labors, in which he never spared himself, were his missionary toils among the heathen. His poor Indian people regarded him as their father. He strove to uplift them from the debasing habits of savage life.

Groping amid their dark wigwams, he kneeled by the rude bed of skins where the dying lay, and pointed the dim eye of the savage to the Star of Bethlehem. They wept in very love for him, and grasped his skirts as one who was to lead them to heaven. The meekness of his Master dwelt with him, and day after day he was a student of their uncouth articulations, until he could talk with the half-clad Indian children, and see their eyes brighten, for they understood what he said. Then he had no rest until the whole of the

Book of God, that "Word" which has regenerated the world, was translated into their language.

Not less remarkable was the assistance lent by Mrs. Eliot to her husband's labors in her capacity as a medical assistant. The difficulty of commanding the attendance of well educated physicians, by the sparse population of the colony, rendered it almost indispensable that a mother should be not unskillful in properly treating those childish ailments which beset the first years of life. Mrs. Eliot's skill and experience as a doctress soon caused her to be sought for by the sick and suffering. Among the poor, with a large charity, she dispensed safe and salutary medicines. Friends and strangers sought her in their sicknesses, and from such as were able she received some small remuneration, often forced upon her, and used to eke out the slender income of her husband.

The poor Indians, too, were among her patients. Often they would come to her house in pain and suffering, and she would cheerfully give them medicine and advice, and dismiss them healed and rejoicing. The red man in his wigwam, tossing on his couch of anguish, was visited by this angel of mercy, who bound up the aching brow, and cooled the sore fever. Who can question that many souls were won to Christ by these deeds of practical charity.

In the light of such acts and such a life, we ascribe to Mrs. Eliot no small share in the success of those heroic labors by which five thousand "praying Indians" in New England were brought to bear testimony to the truths of the Bible and the power of revealed religion.

While woman's work in the Indian missions has

been often indirect, in many other cases she has co-operated directly in efforts looking to the conversion of the red man. Prominent among the earlier pioneers in the missionary cause was Jemima Bingham. She came of a devout and God-fearing race, being a niece of Eleazur Wheelock, D. D., himself a successful laborer in the Indian missionary work, and was reared amid the religious privileges of her Connecticut home. There, in 1769, she married the Rev. Samuel Kirkland, who had already commenced among the Oneida Indians those active and useful labors which only terminated with his life.

Entering with a sustained enthusiasm into the plans of her husband, she shortly after her marriage, accompanied him to his post of duty in the wilderness near Fort Stanwix—now Rome. This was literally on the frontier, in the midst of a dense forest which extended for hundreds of miles in every direction, and was the abode of numerous Indian tribes, some of which were hostile to the white settlers.

Their forest-home was near the " Council House " of the Oneidas—in the heart of the forest. There, surrounded by the dusky sons of the wilderness, the devoted couple, alone and unaided, commenced their joint missionary labors. The gentle manners and the indomitable courage and energy of Mr. Kirkland, were nobly supplemented by the admirable qualities of his wife. With the sweetness, gentleness, simplicity, and delicacy so becoming to woman under all circumstances, were blended in her character, energy that was unconquerable, courage that danger could not blench, and firmness that human power could not bend.

Faithfully, too, in the midst of her missionary la-

bors, did she discharge her duties as a mother.   One
of her sons rewarded her careful teaching by rising
to eminence, and becoming President of Harvard
College.

Prior to his marriage Mr. Kirkland made his home
and pursued his missionary labors at the " Council
House ;" after a house had been prepared for Mrs.
Kirkland, he still continued to preach and teach at the
" Council House," addressing the Indians in their own
language, which both he and his wife had acquired.
Mrs. Kirkland visited the wigwams and instructed the
squaws and children, who in turn flocked to her house
where she ministered to their bodily and spiritual
wants.

The women and children of the tribe were her
chosen pupils.   Seated in circles on the greensward
beneath the spreading arches of giant oaks and maples,
they listened to her teachings, and learned from her
lips the wondrous story of Christ, who gave up his
life on the cross that all tribes and races of mankind
might live through Him.   Then she prayed for them
in the musical tongue of the Oneidas, and the " sounding aisles of the dim woods rang" with the psalms and
hymns which she had taught those dusky children of
the forest.

The change wrought by these ministrations of Mr.
and Mrs. Kirkland was magical.   A peaceful and well-
ordered community, whose citizens were red men,
rose in the wilderness, and many souls were gathered
into the fold of Christ.

During the years of her residence and labors among
the Oneidas, she won many hearts by her kind deeds
as a nurse and medical benefactor to the red men and

their wives and children. She was thus presented to them as a bright exemplar of the doctrines which she taught. Both she and her husband gained a wide influence among the Indians of the region, many of whom they were afterwards and during the Revolutionary contest, able to win over to the patriot cause.

The honor of having inaugurated Sunday-schools on the frontier, must be awarded to woman. Truly this class of religious enterprises, in view of the circumstances by which they were surrounded, and the results produced, may be placed side by side with that missionary work which looks to the conversion of the pagan. The impressing of religious truth on the minds of the young, and preparing them to build up Christian communities in the wilderness, is in itself a great missionary work, the value of which is enhanced by the sacrifices and difficulties it involves. It was in Ohio that one of the first Sunday-schools in our country was kept, with which the name of Mrs. Lake must ever be identified.

In 1787, a year made memorable by the framing of the Constitution of the United States, the Ohio Company was organized in Boston, and soon after built a stockade fort at Marietta, Ohio, and named it Campus Martius. The year it was completed, the Rev. Daniel Storey, a preacher at Worcester, Massachusetts, was sent out as a chaplain. He acted as an evangelist till 1797, when he became the pastor of a Congregational church which he had been instrumental in collecting in Marietta and the adjoining towns, and which was organized the preceding year. He held that relation till the spring of 1804. Probably he was the first

Protestant minister whose voice was heard in the vast wilderness lying to the northwest of the Ohio river.

In the garrison at Marietta, was witnessed the formation and successful operation of one of the first Sunday-schools in the United States. Its originator, superintendent, and sole teacher, was Mrs. Andrew Lake, an estimable lady from New York. Every Sabbath, after "Parson Storey had finished his public services," she collected as many of the children at her house as would attend, and heard them recite verses from the Scriptures, and taught them the Westminster catechism. Simple in her manner of teaching, and affable and kind in her disposition, she was able to interest her pupils—usually about twenty in number—and to win their affections to herself, to the school, and subsequently, in some instances, to the Saviour. A few, at least, of the little children that used to sit on rude benches, low stools, and the tops of meal bags, and listen to her sacred instructions and earnest admonitions, have doubtless ere this become pupils with her, in the "school of Christ" above.

Among the many names especially endeared to the friends of missions, there is another that we cannot forget—that of Sarah L. Smith. Like the Rev. Samuel Kirkland, she was a native of Norwich, Connecticut.

Her maiden name was Huntington. She was born in 1802; made a profession of religion in youth; became the wife of the Rev. Eli Smith in July, 1833; embarked with him for Palestine in the following September, and died at Boojah, near Smyrna, the last day of September, 1836.

Her work as a foreign missionary was quickly finished. She labored longer as a home missionary

among the Mohegans, who lived in the neighborhood of
Norwich, and there displayed most conspicuously the
moral heroism of her nature. In conjunction with
Sarah Breed, she commenced her philanthropic operations in the year 1827. "The first object that drew
them from the sphere of their own church was the
project of opening a Sunday-school for the poor Indian
children of Mohegan. Satisfied that this was a work
which would meet with the Divine approval, they
marked out their plans and pursued them with untiring energy. Boldly they went forth, and, guided by
the rising smoke or sounding axe, followed the Mohegans from field to field, and from hut to hut, till they
had thoroughly informed themselves of their numbers,
condition, and prospects. The opposition they encountered, the ridicule and opprobrium showered upon them
from certain quarters, the sullenness of the natives,
the bluster of the white tenants, the brushwood and
dry branches thrown across their pathway, could not
discourage them. They saw no 'lions in the way,' while
mercy, with pleading looks, beckoned them forward."

"The Mohegans then numbered a little more than
one hundred, only one of whom was a professor of
religion. She was ninety-seven years of age. In her
hut the first prayer-meeting and the first Sunday-
school gathered by these young ladies, was held.

Miss Breed soon removed from that part of the
country, and Miss Huntington continued her labors for
awhile alone. She was at that time very active in
securing the formation of a society and the circula-
tion of a subscription, having for their object the erection of a chapel. She found, ere long, a faithful co-
worker in Miss Elizabeth Raymond. They taught a

school in conjunction, and, aside from their duties as teachers, were, at times, "advisers, counsellors, law-givers, milliners, mantua-makers, tailoresses, and almoners."

"The school was kept in a house on Fort Hill, leased to a respectable farmer, in whose family the young teachers boarded by alternate weeks, each going to the scene of labor every other Sunday morning, and remaining till the evening of the succeeding Sunday, so that both were present in the Sunday-school, which was twice as large as the other.

A single incident will serve to show the dauntless resolution which Miss Huntington carried into her pursuits. Just at the expiration of one of her terms of service, during the winter, a heavy and tempestuous snow blocked up the roads with such high drifts that a friend, who had been accustomed to go for her and convey her home in bad weather, had started for this purpose in his sleigh, but turned back, discouraged. No path had been broken, and the undertaking was so hazardous that he conceived no woman would venture forth at such a time. He therefore called at her father's house to say that he should delay going for her till the next day. What was his surprise to be met at the door by the young lady herself, who had reached home just before, having walked the whole distance on the hard crust of snow, *alone*, and some of the way over banks of snow that entirely obliterated the walls and fences by the roadside."

While at Mohegan, Miss Huntington corresponded with the Hon. Lewis Cass, then Secretary of War, and secured his influence and the aid of that department. In 1832, a grant of nine hundred dollars was made

from the fund devoted to the Indian Department, five
hundred being appropriated towards the erection of
missionary buildings, and four for the support of a
teacher.

Before leaving the Mohegan for a wider field, this
devoted and courageous missionary had the happiness of
seeing a chapel, parsonage, and school-house standing
on "the sequestered land" of her forest friends, and
had thus partially repaid the debt of social and moral
obligation to a tribe who fed the first and famishing
settlers in Connecticut, who strove to protect them
against the tomahawk of inimical tribes, and whose
whoop was friendly to freedom when British aggress-
ors were overriding American rights.

In most of the missionary movements among the
Indian tribes on our frontier, from the time of the
Apostle, John Eliot, to the present, woman has taken,
directly or indirectly, an active part. In the mission
schools at Stockbridge and Hanover; among the Nar-
ragansetts, the Senecas, the Iroquois, the Cherokees,
the Choctaws, the Creeks, and many other tribes, we
see her, as a missionary's wife, with one hand sustain-
ing her husband in his trying labors, while with the
other she bears the blessed gospel — a light to the
tawny Gentiles of our American wilderness. This
passing tribute is due to these devout and zealous
sisters. Their lives were passed far from their homes
and kindred, amid an unceasing round of labors and
trials, and not seldom they met a martyr's death at the
hands of those whom they were seeking to benefit.

The following record of a passage in the life of a
faithful minister and his wife, when about to leave a
beloved people and enter on the missionary work, will

24

show how hard it is for woman to sunder the ties that
bind her to her home, and go she knows not where, and
yet with what childlike trust she enters that perilous
and difficult field of effort to which she is called.

"My dear good wife seems more than usually
depressed at the thought of leaving the many friends
who have endeared themselves to her by their kind
offices. It is hard enough for *me* to break the bands
of love that a year's tender intercourse with the
people has thrown around my heart. But this I could
bear, if other and gentler hearts than mine were not
made to suffer; if other and dearer ties than those I
have formed had not to be broken. My wife is warm
in her attachments. She loves companionship. On
every new field where our changing lot is cast, she
forms intimate friendships with those who are of a like
spirit with herself, if such are to be found. Sometimes she meets none to whom she can open her heart
of hearts—none who can sympathize with her. But
here it has been different. She has found companions
and friends—lovers of the good, true, and beautiful,
with whom she has often taken sweet counsel. To part
with these and go, where and among whom she cannot tell, is indeed a hard trial. I passed through her
room a little while ago, and saw her sitting by the bed,
leaning her arm upon it, with her head upon her
hand, and looking pensively out upon the beautiful
landscape that stretches far away in varied woodland,
meadow, glittering stream, and distant mountain.
There was a tear upon her cheek. This little messenger from within, telling of a sad heart, touched my
feelings.

"Mary," said I, sitting down by her side, and taking

her hand in one of mine, while with the other I
pointed upward, "He will go with us, and He is our
best and kindest friend. If we would wear the crown,
we must endure the cross. 'For our light affliction,
which is but for a moment, worketh for us a far more
exceeding weight of glory.' We are only pilgrims
and sojourners here; but our mission is a high and
holy one—ever to save the souls of our fellow-men.
Think of that, Mary. Would you linger here when
our Master calls us away, to labor somewhere else in
His vineyard? Think of the Lord, when upon earth.
Remember how He suffered for us. Hear Him say,
'The foxes have holes, and the birds of the air have
nests, but the Son of Man hath not where to lay his
head.' And shall the servant be greater than his
Master?"

"I know I am but a poor, weak, murmuring creature," she said, looking up into my face, with overflowing eyes. "But I ask daily for grace to make me
resigned to His holy will. I do not wish to remain here
when I know it is the Lord who calls me away. Still
my weak heart cannot help feeling pain at the thought
of parting from our dear little home and our good
friends who have been so kind to us, and going, I
know not whither. My woman's heart is weak, while
my faith is strong. Thus far the Lord has been better
to me than all my fears. Why, then, should I hold
back, and feel so reluctant to enter the path His wisdom points out? I know if He were to lead me to
prison, or to death, that it would be good for me. If
He were to slay me, yet would I trust in him."

When we compare the greatness of the ends secured,
with the smallness of the means employed, a review

of the results of the Moravian Missions, throughout the heathen world, will strike us with astonishment.

The character of the Moravian women peculiarly fitted them for the work. They were a mixed race. The fiery enthusiasm of the Sclaves was in them blended with the steadfast energy and patient docility of the Germans. The fire of their natures was a holy fire—a lambent flame which lighted but did not destroy. Their creed was one of love; it was a *joyful persuasion* of their interest in Christ and their title to His purchased salvation. Here, then, we have the key to the success which attended the Moravian Missions in all parts of the world. They brought the heathen to the feet of Christ by the spirit of love; they faced every danger and endured every hardship in the cause of their Master, for theirs' was a *joyful persuasion*. They were the " *Herrenhutters,*" the soldiers of the Lord, and yet in their lives they were representatives of the Prince of Peace, and sought to gather about them in this life the emblems of heaven.

It was before the middle of the last century that those gentle and pious brothers and sisters commenced their especial labors among the North American Indians, and to-day those labors have not ceased.

The story of these Moravian Missions for nearly a century is one long religious epic poem, full of action, suffering, battle, bereavement,—all illumined with the dauntless, fervent, Christ-like spirit which bore these gentle ministers along their high career. Their principal field of labor for the first forty years was Pennsylvania, where they established missionary stations at Bethlehem, Gnadenhutten, (tents of grace,) Nazareth,

Friedenshutten, (tents of peace,) Wechquetank, and many other places.

The settlement at Gnadenhutten was the most important and the most interesting, historically considered, of all the stations. Here the Moravian brothers and sisters showed themselves at their best, and that is saying much. Assuming every burden, making every sacrifice, and performing the hardest service, they at the same time displayed consummate tact and address in conciliating their red brethren, taking their meals in common with them, and even adopting the Indian costume.

In a short time Gnadenhutten became a regular and pleasant town. The church stood in a valley. On one side were the Indian houses, in the form of a crescent, upon a rising ground; on the other, the houses of the missionaries and a burying-ground. The Indians labored diligently in the fields, one of which was allotted to each family; and as these became too small, the brethren purchased a neighboring plantation and erected a saw-mill. Hunting, however, continued to be their usual occupation. As this is a precarious mode of subsistence, a supply of provisions was constantly forwarded from Bethlehem. The congregation increased by degrees to about five hundred persons. A new place of worship was opened and a school established. The place was visited by many heathen Indians, who were struck with the order and happiness of the converts, and were prepared to think favorably of the Christian religion.

Besides laboring with unwearied diligence at Gnadenhutten, the brethren made frequent journeys among the Indians in other parts. Several establishments were attempted, among which one was at Shomoken, on the Susquehanna river. This was attended with great expense, as every necessary of life was carried from Bethlehem. The missionaries were likewise in constant danger of their lives from the drunken frolics of the natives. They visited Onondaga, the chief town of the Iroquois, and the seat of their great council, and obtained permission for two of them to settle there and learn the language. They went, but suffered much from want, being obliged to hunt, or seek roots in the forest, for subsistence.

The missionaries' wives united with their husbands in these arduous labors in the wilderness, and their kind offices and gentle ways did much to render the missionary work entirely effectual.

Under such auspices for eight years, Gnadenhutten was the smiling abode of peace, happiness, and prosperity. The good work was bringing forth its legitimate fruits. A large Indian congregation was being instructed in the Word and prepared to disseminate the doctrines of Christ among their heathen brethren, when the din of the French and Indian war was heard on the border. The Moravians in their various settlements were soon surrounded literally with circles of blood and flame. Some of them fled eastward to the larger towns; others sought concealment in the depths of the forest or on the mountains.

The Brethren at Bethlehem and Gnadenhutten resolved to stand at their post. Slowly the fiery circles encompassed them closely and more closely till November, 1755, when the long expected bolt fell.

The missionaries with their wives and families were assembled in one house partaking of their evening meal, when a party of French Indians approached. Hearing the barking of the dogs, Senseman, one of the Brethren, went to the back door and others at the same time hearing the report of a gun rushed to the front door, where they were met by a band of hideously painted savages with guns pointed ready to fire the moment the door was opened.

The Rev. Martin Nitschman fell dead in the doorway. His wife and others were wounded, but fled with the rest up to the garret and barricaded the door with bedsteads. One of the Brethren escaped by jumping out of a back window, and another who was ill in bed did the same though a guard stood before his door. The savages now pursued those who had taken refuge in the garret, and strove hard to break in the door, but finding it too well secured, they set fire to the house. It was instantly in flames.

At this time a boy called Sturgeous, standing upon the flaming roof, ventured to leap off, and thus escaped. A ball had previously grazed his cheek, and one side of his head was much burnt. Mr. Partsch likewise leaped from the roof while on fire, unhurt and unobserved. Fabricius made the same attempt, but was brought down by two balls, seized alive and scalped. All the rest, eleven in number, were burned to death. Senseman, who first went out, had the inexpressible grief of seeing his wife perish in the flames.

Mrs. Partsch, who had escaped, could not, through fear and trembling, go far, but hid herself behind a tree upon a hill near the house. From this place the gentle sister of that forlorn band gazed trembling and with ghastly features upon that scene of fire and butchery. She saw her beloved brethren and sisters dragged forth and shot or tomahawked. Before the breath had left their bodies she saw the scalps torn from their heads, some of the wounded women kneeling and imploring for mercy in vain. The burning house was the funeral pyre from which the loving spirit of Mrs. Senseman took its flight to eternal rest. Gazing through the windows, which the fire now illumined with a lurid glare, she saw Mrs. Senseman surrounded by flames standing with arms folded and exclaiming— " 'Tis all well, dear Saviour !"

One of the closing scenes in the history of the protracted toils and sufferings of the missionaries of Gnadenhutten, is of thrilling and tragical interest. Ninety-six of the Indian converts having been treacherously lured from the settlement, and taken prisoners, by hostile Indians and white renegades, were told that they must prepare for death. Then was displayed a calmness and courage worthy of the early Christian martyrs. Kneeling down in that dreadful hour, those unfortunate Indian believers prayed fervently to the God of all; then rising they suffered themselves to be led unresistingly to the place appointed for them to die. The last sounds that could be heard before the awful butchery was finished were the prayers and praises of the Indian women, of whom there were forty, thus testifying their unfaltering trust in the promise taught them by their white sisters—the devoted Moravians of Gnadenhutten.

CHAPTER XVII.

OF all that devout and heroic bands of men and women who have undertaken to bear the hardships and face the dangers of our American wilderness, for the special purpose of carrying the Gospel of peace, love, and brotherhood to the benighted denizen of our American forests, none have exhibited more signal courage, patience, and devotion than the companies which first selected Oregon as their special field of labor.

In order to properly estimate the appliances and dangers of this enterprise, the Oregon field must be surveyed, not from our present point of view, when steam locomotive power on land and water has brought that distant region within comparatively easy reach; when the hands of the State and National Government have grown strong to defend, and can be stretched a thousand leagues in an hour to punish, if the lightning brings tidings of wrong; when a multitude of well-ordered communities have power and lawful authority to protect their citizens; and when peace and comfort are the accompaniments, and a competency is the reward of industry.

How different was the view of Oregon presented to the eye in 1834! A vast tract of wilderness, covering an area of more than three hundred thousand square miles, composed of sterile wastes, unbroken forests, and almost impassable ranges of mountains, presenting a constant succession of awful precipices, rugged crags, and yawning chasms, and traversed by rapid torrents, emptying into rivers full of perils to the navigator. This mighty expanse was roamed by more than thirty different Indian tribes; the only white inhabitants being at the few posts and settlements of the Hudson Bay Company. The different routes by which this region could be reached presented to the traveler a dilemma, either side of which was full of difficulty.

The water route was nearly twenty thousand miles in length, and involved a long and perilous voyage round Cape Horn. The land route was across the continent, through the gorges and over the precipices of the Rocky Mountains, up and down the dangerous rivers, and among numerous bloodthirsty tribes. Such was the opening prospect offered to the eye of religious enterprise, when the question of the mission to Oregon was first agitated.

It is something more than forty years since the "Macedonian Cry" was heard from the dark mountains and savage plains of that far country, startling the Christian church in America. The thrill of the appeal made by the delegation of Flathead Indians, was electric, and fired the churches of all the principal denominations with a spirit of noble emulation.

Dr. Marcus Whitman, and Mrs. Whitman, his wife, and Mr. and Mrs. Spaulding, were among the earliest to respond to the appeal. In 1836 they crossed the continent, scaled the Rocky Mountains, and penetrated to the heart of the wild region which was to be the scene of their heroic labors, crowned at length by a martyr's death.

Mrs. Whitman and Mrs. Spaulding, it should be remembered, were the first white women that ever crossed that mighty range which nature seems to have intended as a barrier against the aggressive westward march of the Anglo-Saxon race.

Strong indeed must have been the impelling motive which carried these two weak women over that rugged barrier!

Mr. and Mrs. Gray, Mr. and Mrs. Clark, Mr. and Mrs. Littlejohn, Mr. and Mrs. Smith, and the Lees came next, pursuing their toilsome march over the same mountain ranges, and closely behind them came Mr. and Mrs. Griffin and Mr. and Mrs. Munger.

The story of the adventures and difficulties passed through by these missionary bands in forcing their way over the mountains, would fill volumes. Their way lay sometimes over almost inaccessible crags, and at others, through gloomy and tangled forests, and as they descended, the snow increased in depth, and they felt the effects of the increasing cold very keenly. The only living things which they saw were a few mountain goats. Sometimes chasms yawned at their feet, and they were forced to go out of their course twenty miles before they could cross. Once one of the ladies wandered from the party in search of mountain ferns. She was soon missed, and one of the guides was sent back to search for her. After a short quest they found her tracks in the snow, which they followed till they came to a *crevasse*, through which she had slipped and fallen sixty feet into a monstrous drift, where she was floundering and shouting feebly for help.

With some difficulty she was extricated unhurt from this perilous situation.

When their day's journey was ended, they had also to encamp on the snow, beating down the selected spot previously, till it would bear a man on the surface without sinking. The fire was kindled on logs of green timber, and the beds were made of pine-branches. All alike laid on the snow.

One of the peculiar dangers to which they were exposed, were the mountain torrents, which in that region were impassable often for the stoutest swimmer; and this danger became magnified when they reached the upper Columbia River, which they were obliged to navigate in boats. At one particular spot in the course of their voyage they narrowly escaped a serious disaster.

The Columbia is, at the spot alluded to, contracted into a passage of one hundred and fifty yards, by lofty rocks on either side, through which it rushes with tremendous violence, forming whirlpools in its passage capable of engulphing the largest forest trees, which are afterwards disgorged with great force. This is one of the most dangerous places that boats have to pass. In going up the river the boats are all emptied, and the freight has to be carried about half a mile over the tops of the high and rugged rocks. In coming down, all remain in the boats; and the guides, in this perilous pass, display the greatest courage and presence of mind, at moments when the slightest error in managing their frail bark would hurl its occupants to certain destruction. On arriving at the head of

the rapids, the guide gets out on the rocks and sur-
veys the whirlpools. If they are filtering in—or
"making," as they term it—the men rest on their
paddles until they commence throwing off, when the
guides instantly reëmbark, and shove off the boat and
shoot through this dread portal with the speed of
lightning.

Sometimes the boats are whirled round in the vor-
tex with such awful rapidity that renders all management of the vessel impossible, and the boat and its
hapless crew are swallowed up in the abyss. One of
the party had got out of the boat, preparing to walk,
when looking back he saw one of the other boats containing two of the ladies, in a dangerous situation,
having struck, in the midst of the rapids, upon the
rocks, which had stove in her side.

The conduct of the men in this instance, evinced
great presence of mind. The instant the boat struck
they had sprung on the gunwale next the rock, and
by their united weight kept her lying upon it. The
water foamed and raged round them with fearful violence. Had she slipped off, they must all have been
dashed to pieces amongst the rocks and rapids below;
as it was, they managed to maintain their position until the crew of the other boat, which had run the rapids safely, had unloaded and dragged the empty boat
up the rapids again. They then succeeded in throwing a line to their hapless companions. But there was
still great danger to be encountered, lest in hauling
the empty boat towards them they might pull themselves off the rock. They, at length, however, succeeded by cautious management in getting the boat
alongside, and in embarking in safety. A moment

afterwards their own boat slipped from the rock, and was dashed to pieces. Everything that floated they picked up afterwards.

The same noble spirit which carried Mrs. Whitman, Mrs. Spaulding, Mrs. Gray, Mrs. Littlejohn, Mrs. Clark, Mrs. Smith, Mrs. Munger, Mrs. Griffin, and their coadjutors across our continent on their lofty errand, also inspired another band of gospel messengers to move in the same great enterprise.

Dr. White of New York, and his wife, were prominent in this latter movement. Their immediate company consisted of thirteen individuals, five of whom were women, *viz:* Mrs. White, Mrs. Beers, Miss Downing, Miss Johnson, and Miss Pitman. These ladies were all admirably fitted both physically and mentally for the enterprise in which they were embarked.

Mrs. White was a lady in whom were blended quiet resolution, a high sense of duty, and great sensibility. When her husband informed her one cold night, in the winter of 1836, that there was a call for them from Oregon; that the Board of Missions advertised for a clergyman, physician, &c., &c., and as he could act in the capacity of doctor, he thought it might be well to respond thereto. She did not immediately answer; and looking up, he was surprised to find her weeping. This seemed to him singular, as her disposition was so unusually cheerful, and it was seldom there was a trace of tears to be found upon her cheek, especially, as he thought, for so trivial a cause. In some confusion and mortification, he begged her not to allow his words to cause her uneasiness. Still she wept in silence, till, after a pause of several moments, she struggled for composure, seated herself by his

side, extended her hand for the paper, and twice looking over the notice, remarked, that if he could so ar-
range his affairs as to render it consistent for him to
go to Oregon, she would place no obstacle in his way,
and with her mother's consent would willingly accompany him.

Dr. White offered his services to the Board of Missions, they were accepted, and he was requested to be
in readiness to sail in a few weeks, from Boston via
the Sandwich Islands, to Oregon. Mrs. White still retained her determination to accompany her husband,
though till she saw the appointment and its publica-
tion, she scarcely realized the possibility of a necessity
for her doing so. The thought that they were now to
leave, probably for ever, their dear home, and dearer
friends, was a sad one, and she shed tears of regret
though not of reluctance to go. She pictured to herself her mother's anguish, at what must be very like
consigning her only daughter to the grave.

The anticipated separation from that mother, who
had nursed her so tenderly and loved her with that
tireless, changeless affection which the maternal heart
only knows, filled her with sorrow. However, by a
fortunate coincidence they were spared the painful
scene they had feared, and obtained her consent with
little difficulty. When they visited her, for that purpose, she had just been reading for the first time the
life of Mrs. Judson; and the example of this excellent lady had so interested her that when the project
was laid before her she listened with comparative calmness, and, though somewhat astonished, was willing
they should go where duty led them. This in some
measure relieved Mrs. White, and with a lightened

heart and more composure she set about the necessary preparations.

In a short time all was in readiness, the last farewell wept, rather than spoken, the last yearning look lingered on cherished objects, and they were on their way to Oregon.

On the day that their eldest son was one year old, they embarked from Boston.

That their adieus were sorrowful may not be doubted, indeed this or any other word in our language is inadequate to describe the emotions of the party. As the pilot-boat dropped at the stern of the vessel, its occupants waved their handkerchiefs and simultaneously began singing a farewell " Missionary Hymn." The effect was electric; some rushed to the side in agony as though they would recall the departed ones and return with them to their native land. Others covered their faces, and tears streamed through their trembling fingers, and sobs shook the frames of even strong men. They thought not of formalities in that hour; it was not a shame for the sterner sex to weep. The forms of their friends fast lessened in the distance, and at last their boat looked like a speck on the wave, and the sweet cadences of that beautiful song faintly rolling along to their hearing, like the sigh of an angel, were the last sounds that reached them from the home of civilization.

With hushed respiration, bowed heads, and straining ears, they listened to its low breathings now wafted gently and soothingly to them on the breeze, then dying away, and finally lost in the whisperings of wind and waves.

For weeks did it haunt their slumbers while tossing

upon the treacherous deep. And it came not alone; for with it were fair visions of parents, home, brothers, and sisters, joyous childhood and youth, and everything they had known at home floated in vivid pictures before them touching them as by the fairy pencil of the dream-angel.

The voyage was a protracted one. But the close relationship into which they were brought served to knit together the bonds of Christian fellowship, and inspire them with a oneness of purpose in carrying out their noble enterprise. Immediately on arriving at their field of labor they entered on their first work, *viz:* that of establishing communities. In that almost unbroken wilderness, cabins were erected, the ground prepared for tillage, and steps were taken towards the building of a saw and grist-mill. The Indians were conciliated, and a mission-school for their instruction was established. The party received constant accessions to their numbers as the months rolled away, and opened communication with the other mission-colonies in the territory.

During the summer the ladies divided their labors; the school of Indians was taught by Miss Johnson; Miss Downing (now Mrs. Shepherd) attended to the cutting, making, and repairing of the clothing for the young Indians, as well as those for the children of the missionaries; Mrs. White and Miss Pitman (now Mrs. Jason Lee) superintended the domestic matters of the little colony.

In September, Mr. and Mrs. Leslie, three daughters, and Mr. Perkins the *fiancé* of Miss Johnson, joined them. The family was now enlarged to sixty members. Dr. and Mrs. White removed into their new

25

cabin—a mile distant. Here ensued a repetition of trials, privations, and hardships, such as they had already endured in their former habitation.

Their cabin was a rude affair, scarcely more than a shanty, without a chimney, and with only roof enough to cover a bed; a few loose boards served for a floor; one side of the house was entirely unenclosed, and all their cooking had to be done in the open air, in the few utensils which they had at hand.

One by one these deficiencies, with much toil and difficulty, were supplied; a tolerably close roof and walls shielded them measurably from the autumn tempests; a new chimney carried up about half the smoke generated from the green fuel with which the fireplace was filled; the hearth, made of clay and wood-ashes, was, however, a standing eyesore to Mrs. White, who appears to have been a notable housewife, as it did not admit of washing, and had to be renewed every two or three months.

These were discomforts indeed, but nothing compared with another annoyance to which they were nightly subject—that part of the territory where they lived being infested by black wolves of the fiercest species. Their situation was so lonely, and Doctor White's absences were so frequent, that Mrs. White was greatly terrified every night by the frightful howlings of these ferocious marauders.

One night Doctor White left home to visit Mr. Shepherd, who was ill, and some of the sick mission children. Mrs. White, while awaiting his return, suddenly heard a burst of prolonged howling from the depths of the forest through which the Doctor would have to pass on his return homeward. The howls

RESCUING A HUSBAND FROM WOLVES. Page 387.

were continued with all the eagerness which showed that the brutes were close upon their prey. She flew to the yard, and in the greatest terror, besought the two hired men to fly to her husband's rescue.

They laughed at her fears, and endeavored to reason her into composure. But the horrid din continued. Through the wild chorus she fancied she heard a human voice faintly calling for help. Unable longer to restrain her excited feelings, she snatched up a long pair of cooper's compasses—the first weapon that offered itself—and sallied out into the woods, accompanied by the men, armed with rifles.

They ran swiftly, the diapason of the howls guiding them in the proper course, and in a few moments they came to a large tree, round which a pack of hungry monsters had collected, and were baying in full chorus, jumping up and snapping their jaws at a man who was seated among the branches.

The cowardly brutes, catching sight of the party, sneaked off with howls of baffled rage, and were soon beyond hearing. The doctor descended from his retreat, quite panic-stricken at his narrow escape. He informed them that on first starting from the mission, he had picked up a club, to defend himself from the wolves, should they make their appearance; but when one of the animals came within six feet of him, and by its call, gathered others to the pursuit, his valiant resolutions vanished—he dropped his stick and plied his heels, with admirable dexterity, till the tree offered its friendly aid, when he hallooed for help with all the power of his lungs; but for Mrs. White's appreciation of the danger, and her speedy appearance upon the scene, Dr. White's term of usefulness in the Oregon mission would have been greatly abridged.

The necessities of their missionary life compelled different members of their little band to make frequent journeys both by land and water. It was on one of these journeys, and while passing down the Columbia River in a canoe, that Mrs. White met with an accident that plunged the whole mission into mourning.

Mrs. White, with her babe, and Mr. Leslie, had embarked in a canoe on the river where the current was extremely rapid, and as they reached the middle of the stream, the canoe began to quiver and sway from side to side. The sense of her danger came upon Mrs. W., as with a presentiment of coming disaster. She trembled like a leaf as she remarked, "How very helpless is a female with an infant." At the instant that her voice ceased to echo from the rocky shores, and as if a spirit of evil stood ready to prove the truth of her exclamation, the canoe, which was heavily laden, gave a slight swing, and striking a rock, began to fill with water, and, in a few seconds, went down. As the water came up round them, the child started convulsively in its mother's arms and gave a piercing shriek, Mr. Leslie at the same time exclaiming, "Oh, God! we're lost!"

When the canoe rose, it was free from its burthen, and bottom upwards; and Mrs. White found herself directly beneath it, painfully endeavoring to extricate herself, enduring dreadful agony in her struggle for breath.

Despairingly she felt herself again sinking, and, coming in contact with the limbs of a person in the water, the reflection flitted across her brain, "I have done with my labors for these poor Indians. Well, all will be over in a moment; but how will my poor mother feel when she learns my awful fate?" Mr. Leslie afterwards stated that he had no recollection till he rose, and strove to keep above water, but again sank, utterly hopeless of succor.

He rose again just as the canoe passed around a large rock, and its prow was thrown within his reach. He clutched it with eager joy, and supported himself a moment, gasping for breath, when he suddenly thought of his fellow-passenger, and the exclamation ran through his mind,—"What will the doctor do?" He instantly lowered himself in the water as far as possible, and, still clinging with one hand, groped about as well as he was able, when, providentially, he grasped her dress, and succeeded in raising her to the surface. By this time the Indians—expert swimmers —had reached the canoe; and, with their assistance, he supported his insensible burden, and placed her head upon the bottom with her face just out of water. After a few moments, she gasped feebly, and, opening her eyes, her first words were, "Oh, Mr. Leslie, I've lost my child!"

"Pray, do dismiss the thought," said he, "and let us try to save ourselves."

They were wafted a long way down the river, no prospect offering for their relief. At length they espied, far ahead, the two canoes which had entered the river before them, occupied, as it proved, by an Indian chief and his attendants. Mr. Leslie hallooed to them with all his remaining strength, and they hastened towards them, first stopping to pick up the trunks and a few other things which had floated down stream.

When, at last, they reached the sufferers, finding them so much exhausted, the chief cautioned them to retain their hold, without in the least changing their position, while he towed them gently and carefully to the shore.   Here they rested, draining the water from their clothes, and Mr. Leslie from his head and stomach,—for he had swallowed a vast quantity.   In half an hour the Indians righted the canoe, which had been drawn on shore, and, to their amazement, and almost terror, they found beneath it the dead babe, wrapped in its cloak, having been kept in its place by the atmospheric pressure.

Mr. Leslie was now uncertain what course to pursue, and asked his companion's advice.   She told them she was desirous of proceeding immediately to Fort Vancouver, as they had nothing to eat, no fire, and, in short, had lost so many of their effects, that they had nothing wherewith to make themselves comfortable, if they remained there till even the next day.

Their canoe was a large one, being about twenty feet in length and four in breadth, and was laden with a bed, bedding, mats, two large trunks of clothing, kettles, and dishes, and provisions to last the crew throughout the journey, and also articles of traffic with the natives, and they lost all but their trunks, the contents of which were now thoroughly soaked.

They seated themselves in the canoe, and the chief threw his only blanket over Mrs. W——'s shoulders, both himself and men exerting themselves to render their charges comfortable during the thirty-six miles they were obliged to travel before reaching the fort, which was late in the evening.

They were met by Mr. Douglas, who was greatly shocked at the narrative, and whose first words were, " My God! what a miracle! Why, it is only a short time since, in the same place, we lost a canoe, with seven men, all good swimmers."

The following morning, the bereaved mother was quite composed. They started at eight o'clock, and with the little coffin, provided by Mr. Douglas, at their feet, traveled rapidly all day, and camped at night just above the falls of the Willamette. They took supper, the men pitched their borrowed tents, and, after a day of great fatigue, they lay quietly down to rest.

In a short time, however, they were disturbed by a loud paddling, and voices; and looking out, beheld about thirty Indians, men, women, and children, in canoes, who landed and camped very near them.

Their arrival filled Mrs. White with new apprehension. She feared now that she might be robbed of her dead treasure, and perhaps lose her own life, before she could consign it to its last resting-place. All through that restless, dreary night, she kept her vigils, with bursting heart, beside the corpse of her babe. The noises of the Indian camp, the guttural voices of the men, the chattering of the squaws, rang in her ears, while the cries and prattling of the children, by reminding her of the lost one, served to enhance the poignancy of her grief. What a situation for the desolate mother! All alone with death, far from her mother, husband, home, and friends, surrounded by a troop of barbarous, noisy savages weighed down with grief, tearless from its very weight, not knowing what next would befall her. What agony did she endure through that night's dreary vigils! She felt as though she were draining the cup of sorrow to its dregs, without the strength to pray that it might pass from her.

They set off as soon as it was light, that they might, if possible, reach the Mission before putrescency had discolored the body of the infant. They arrived at McKoy's about one o'clock, where, while they were dining, horses were prepared, and they went on without delay. It is impossible to describe the emotions of the doctor when he met them about twelve miles from the Mission, as, excepting a floating rumor among the natives, which he hardly credited, he had had no intimation of the accident. The sad presentiment was realized. Death had entered their circle and robbed them of their fair child! As he looked into the face of his wife, he comprehended in part her sufferings.

Amid these and similar sad experiences, this heroic band of Christian women abated not their zeal or efforts in the work to which they had put their hand.

In other parts of the territory, separate missionary establishments were superintended by the Whitmans, the Spauldings, and others. The blessings of civilization and religion were thus extended by these devoted men and women to the benighted red man.

For a period of eight years Dr. and Mrs. Whitman resided on the banks of the Walla-Walla River, doing all in their power to benefit the Indians. Such labors as theirs deserved a peaceful old age, and the enduring gratitude of their tawny protégés. Alas! that we have to record that such was not their lot! Melancholy indeed was the fate of that devoted band upon the Walla-Walla!

The measels had broken out among the Indians and spread with frightful rapidity through the neighboring tribes. Dr. Whitman did all he could to stay its progress, but great numbers of them died.

The Indians supposed that the doctor could have stayed the course of the malady if he had wished it, and accordingly concocted a plan to destroy him and his whole family. With this object in view about sixty of them armed themselves and came to his house.

The inmates, having no suspicion of any hostile intentions, were totally unprepared for resistance or flight. Dr. and Mrs. Whitman and their nephew—a youth of about seventeen or eighteen years of age— were sitting in the parlor in the afternoon, when Sil-aw-kite, the chief, and To-ma-kus, entered the room and addressing the doctor told him very coolly they had come to kill him. The doctor, not believing it possible that they could entertain any hostile intentions towards him, told him as much; but whilst in the act of speaking, To-ma-kus drew a tomahawk from under his robe and buried it deep in his brain. The unfortunate man fell dead in his chair. Mrs. Whitman and the nephew fled up stairs and locked themselves into an upper room.

In the meantime Sil-aw-kite gave the war-whoop, as a signal to his party outside, to proceed in the work of destruction, which they did with the ferocity and yells of so many fiends. Mrs. Whitman, hearing the shrieks and groans of the dying, looked out of the window and was shot through the breast by a son of the chief, but not mortally wounded. A party then rushed up stairs and dispatched the niece on the spot, dragged her down by the hair of her head and taking her to the front of the house, mutilated her in a shocking manner with their knives and tomahawks.

There was one man who had a wife bedridden. On the commencement of the affray he ran to her room, and, taking her up in his arms, carried her unperceived by the Indians to the thick bushes that skirted the river, and hurried on with his burden in the direction of Fort Walla-Walla. Having reached a distance of fifteen miles, he became so exhausted that, unable to carry her further, he concealed her in a thick clump of bushes on the margin of the river, and hastened to the Fort for assistance.

On his arrival, Mr. McBain immediately sent out men with him, and brought her in. She had fortunately suffered nothing more than fright. The number killed, (including Dr. and Mrs. Whitman,) amounted to fourteen. The other females and children were carried off by the Indians, and two of them were forthwith taken as wives by Sil-aw-kite's son and another. A man employed in the little mill, forming a part of the establishment, was spared to work the mill for the Indians. The day following the awful tragedy, a Catholic priest, who had not heard of the massacre, stopped on seeing the mangled corpses strewn round the house, and requested permission to bury them, which was readily granted.

On the priest leaving the place, he met, at a distance of five or six miles, a brother missionary of the deceased, Mr. Spaulding, the field of whose labors lay about a hundred miles off, at a place on the river Cold-water. He communicated to him the melancholy fate of his friends, and advised him to fly as fast as possible, or, in all probability, he would be another victim. He gave him a share of his provisions, and Mr. Spaulding hurried homeward, full of apprehensions for the safety of his own family ; but, unfortunately, his horse escaped from him in the night, and after a six days' toilsome march on foot, having lost his way, he at length reached the banks of the river, but on the opposite side to his own home.

In the dead of the night, in a state of starvation, having eaten nothing for three days, everything seeming to be quiet about his own place, he cautiously embarked in a small canoe, and paddled across the river. But he had no sooner landed than an Indian seized him, and dragged him to his own house, where he found all his family prisoners, and the Indians in full possession. These Indians were not of the same tribe with those who had destroyed Dr. Whitman's family, nor had they at all participated in the outrage; but having heard of it, and fearing the white man would include them in their vengeance, they had seized on the family of Mr. Spaulding for the purpose of holding them as hostages for their own safety. The family were uninjured; and he was overjoyed to find things no worse.

Notwithstanding this awful tragedy the heroic women remained at their posts in the different missionary stations in the territory, and long afterwards pursued those useful labors which, by establishing pioneer-settlements in the wilderness, and by civilizing and christianizing the wild tribes, prepared the way for the army of emigrants which is now converting that vast wilderness into a great and flourishing state.

CHAPTER XVIII.

WOMAN IN THE ARMY.

IN the great wars of American history, there are, in immediate connection with the army, two situations in which woman more prominently appears: the former is where, in her proper person, she accompanies the army as a *vivandiere*, or as the daughter of the regiment, or as the comrade and help-meet of her husband; the latter, and less frequent capacity, is that of a soldier, marching in the ranks and facing the foe in the hour of danger. During the war for Independence a large number of brave and devoted women served in the army, principally in their true characters as wives of regularly enlisted soldiers, keeping even step with the ranks upon the march, and cheerfully sharing the burdens, privations, hardships, and dangers of military life.

In some cases where both wife and husband took part in the struggle for independence, the wife even surpassed her husband in those heroic virtues which masculine vanity arrogates as its exclusive possession. The name of Mrs. Jemima Warner has been embalmed in history as one of those remarkable women in whom was seen at once the true wife, the heroine, and the patriot.

She appears to have been a native of Lancaster, Pennsylvania, and became the wife of James Warner, a private in Captain Smith's company, of Daniel Morgan's rifle corps.

In 1775 she followed her husband to the north, and joined him at Prospect Hill, Cambridge, in the fall of that year. Morgan's riflemen were picked men, and were sure to be placed in the posts where the greatest danger threatened.

But James Warner, though a stalwart man in appearance, possessed none of the qualities demanded in extraordinary emergencies. If ever man needed, in hardship and danger, a constant companion, superior to himself, it was private James Warner, and such a companion was his wife Jemima. She is described as gifted with the form and personal characteristics of a true heroine, and the heroic qualities which she displayed through all the romantic and tragic campaign against Canada proves that her spirit corresponded to the frame which it animated.

The Canadian campaign was in many respects the severest and most trying of any during the Revolution. General Arnold's march through the woods of Maine was attended with delays, misfortunes, and losses which would have discouraged any but the bravest, and most determined and hardy. The strength and fortitude of the men was tried to the utmost, by wearisome marches, floods, winter's cold and famine, and in these crises private Warner was one of those few whose soldiership failed to stand the test.

The advanced guard of the army of the wilderness was composed of Morgan's troops, who, with incredible labor and hardship, ascended the Dead river and crossed the highlands into the Canadian frontier, one hundred and twenty miles from Quebec, with their last rations in their knapsacks, and with their passage obstructed by a vast swamp overflowed with water from two to three feet deep. Smith's and Hendrick's companies reached it first, and halted to wait for stragglers. Mrs. Warner came up with another woman, the wife of Sergeant Grier, of Hendrick's company—as much a heroine as herself, though less unfortunate in her experience. The soldiers were entering the water, breaking the ice as they went with their gunstocks, and the women courageously wading after them, when some one shouted, "Where is Warner?" Jemima, who had not noticed her husband's disappearance, started back in search of him. Warner was no more enfeebled in body than many of the other men, but his fortitude had given out. Begging his comrades to delay their march for a while, she hurried back in search of her husband, but an hour passed, and his company marched without him. Utterly destitute of that forethought which is so necessary an element of endurance and resolution in extremity, he had eaten all his rations, which should have lasted him two days. Knowing that the supplies of the army were exhausted, his faint heart saw no hope ahead. His brave wife had had a sad trial with him. From the day that provisions had began to be scarce he had been the same improvident laggard. Familiar with his failings, she was in the habit of hoarding food, the price of her own secret fastings, against such need as this. She now exerted herself to the utmost to rouse him, and induce him to press on and rejoin his comrades. It was long before she prevailed, and at last, when they started, the army had gone on, and Warner and his heroic wife were forced to make their way through the wilderness alone. She realized that her husband's safety depended entirely upon herself, and took care of him as she would have taken care of a child. Refusing to entertain, for a moment, the thought of perishing in the wilderness, she did her best to cheer her husband and drive such thoughts from his mind. It was a thankless task, but her love and devotion were equal to everything. Endowed with a strong constitution, and free from disease, the young soldier could have survived the terrible march to Canada, had he possessed but a little of her courage and good sense. Taking the lead in the bitter journey, through swamps and snows, threading the tangled forests, climbing cliffs, and fording half-frozen creeks,—day after day the heroic woman pushed her faint-hearted husband on, feeding him from her own little store of ember-baked cakes, and eating almost nothing herself till they were more than half way to Sertigan on the Chaudiere river, toward Quebec.

Here Warner dropped down, completely discouraged, and resisted all his wife's entreaties to rise again. It was in vain that she appealed to every motive that could nerve a soldier, every sentiment that could inspire and stimulate a man. Relief, she said, *must* be before them, and not far away; for her sake, would he not try once more? Her pleadings and her tears were wasted. The faint-hearted soldier had made his last halt. Weak he undoubtedly was, but comparing the nourishment each had taken, she should have been physically worse off than he. It was the superiority of her mental and moral organization that kept her from sinking as low as her husband. Failing to stir him to make another effort to save himself, she filled his canteen with water, and placing that and the little remnant of her wretched bread between his knees, she turned away and went down the river, with a heavy but dauntless heart, in search of help. On her way she met a boat coming up the river, and in it were two army officers and two friendly Indians. Hailing the party, she told them of her distress and begged them to take her husband on board. They replied that it was impossible. They had been sent after Lieutenant Macleland, a sick officer left behind with an attendant, at Twenty-foot Falls, and the little birch bark canoe would only carry two more men. They could only spare her food enough to keep herself alive. Weeping, she turned back and sadly followed the canoe up the stream till it was lost to view. When she again reached the spot where she had left her discouraged husband, she found him alive but helpless, and sinking fast. While the devoted wife sat by his side, doing what little she could for his comfort, the canoe party came down the river, bearing the gallant Macleland, their loved but dying officer. Again the hapless wife begged, with piteous tears, that they would take her husband in. No! All her prayers were useless. Macleland was worth more than Warner.

When all hope had fled, Jemima staid faithfully by her husband till he had breathed his last. She could only close his eyes and try to cover his body from the wolves. Then, when love had done its best, she strapped his powder horn and pouch to her person, shouldered his rifle, and set out on her weary tramp toward Quebec. Melancholy as it was, one sees a certain sublimity in the woman's act of selecting and carrying with her those warlike keepsakes. It was in perfect keeping with those tragic times. Tender thoughtfulness of her poor husband's martial honor outlived her power to inspire him again to her heroism, and made her grand in the forlornness of her sorrow. She was determined that his arms should go to the war, if he could not.

The same brave mind that had made her so admirable as a soldier's helpmeet, upheld her through tedious hardships and continued perils on her lonely way to the settlement. Once there, it was necessary for her to wait till she could recover her exhausted strength, Her triumph over the severe tasking of all those bitter days in the wilderness, without chronic injury, or even temporary sickness, would be called now, in a woman, a miracle of endurance.

As she passed on from parish to parish, the simple Canadian peasant, always friendly to the American cause, welcomed with warm hospitality the handsome young woman, the story of whose singular bravery and devotion had reached their ears.

Her subsequent life and history is shrouded in obscurity. We know not whether she married a husband worthier of such a partner in those trying times, or whether she retired to brood alone over a sorrow with which shame for the object of her grief must have mingled. Whatever her lot may have been, her name deserves a place on the golden roll of our revolutionary heroines.

As we have already remarked, only a few instances are on record where women served in the army of the revolution as enlisted soldiers. Occasional services performed under the guise of men, were more frequent. As bearers of dispatches and disguised as couriers,

26

they glided through the enemy's lines. Donning their father's or brother's overcoats and hats, they deceived the besiegers of the garrison into the belief that soldiers were not lacking to defend it, and even ventured in male habiliments to perform more perilous feats; such, for example, as the following :

Grace and Rachel Martin, the wives of two brothers who were absent with the patriot army, receiving intelligence one evening that a courier under guard of two British officers, would pass their house on a certain night with important dispatches, resolved to surprise the party and obtain the papers.

Disguising themselves in their husband's outer garments, and providing themselves with arms, they waylaid the enemy. Soon after they took their station by the roadside, the courier and his escort made their appearance. At the proper moment the disguised ladies sprang from their bushy covert, and presenting their pistols, ordered the party to surrender their papers. Surprised and alarmed, they obeyed without hesitation or the least resistance. The brave women having put them on parole, hastened home by the nearest route, which was a bypath through the woods, and dispatched the documents to General Greene.

Perhaps the most remarkable case of female enlistment and protracted service in the patriot army, was that of Deborah Samson. The career of this woman shows that her motive in adopting and following the career of a soldier was a praiseworthy one. The whole country was aglow with patriotic fervor, and in no section did the flame burn with a purer luster than in that where Deborah was nurtured. It was not idle curiosity nor mere love of roving, that incited her, in those straitlaced days, to abandon her home and join in the perilous fray where the standard of freedom was "full high advanced." She had evidently counted the cost of the extraordinary step which she was about to take, but found in the difficulties and dangers which it entailed nothing to obstruct or daunt her purpose.

Her parents were in humble circumstances, and lived in Plymouth, Massachusetts, where Deborah grew up with but slender advantages for anything more than a practical education; and yet such was her diligence in the acquisition of knowledge, that before she was eighteen she had shown herself competent to take charge of a district school, in which duty she displayed some of the same qualities which made her after-career remarkable.

She seems for several months to have cherished the secret purpose of enlisting in the American army, and with that view laid aside a small sum from her scanty earnings as a school-teacher, with which she purchased a quantity of coarse fustian; out of this material, working at intervals and by stealth, she made a complete suit of men's clothes, concealing in a hay-stack each article as it was finished.

When her preparations had been completed, she informed her friends that she was going in search of higher wages for her labor. Tieing her new suit of men's attire in a bundle, she took her departure. She probably availed herself of the nearest shelter for the purpose of assuming her disguise. Her stature was lofty for a woman, and her features, though finely proportioned, were of a masculine cast. When at a subsequent period she had donned the buff and blue

regimentals and marched in the ranks of the patriot
army, she is said to have looked every inch the
soldier.

Pursuing her way she presented herself at the camp
of the American army as one of those patriotic young
men who desired to assist in opposing the British, and
securing the independence of their country.

Her friends, supposing that she was engaged at service at some distant point, made little inquiry as to
her whereabouts, knowing her self-reliance, and her
ability to follow out her own career without the aid of
their counsel or assistance.   Those who were nearest
to her appear to have never made such a search for
her as would have led to her discovery.

Having decided to enlist for the whole term of the
war, from motives of patriotism, she was received and
enrolled as one of the first volunteers in the company
of Captain Nathan Thayer, of Medway, Massachusetts,
under the name of Robert Shirtliffe.   Without friends
and homeless, as the young recruit appeared to be, she
interested Captain Thayer, and was received into his
family while he was recruiting his company.   Here she
remained some weeks, and received her first lessons
in the drill and duties of the young soldier.

"Accustomed to labor from childhood upon the
farm and in outdoor employment, she had acquired
unusual vigor of constitution; her frame was robust
and of masculine strength; and, having thus gained
a degree of hardihood, she was enabled to acquire
great expertness and precision in the manual exercise,
and to undergo what a female, delicately nurtured,
would have found it impossible to endure.   Soon after
they had joined the company, the recruits were sup-

plied with uniforms by a kind of lottery. That drawn by Robert did not fit, but, taking needle and scissors, he soon altered it to suit him. To Mrs. Thayer's expression of surprise at finding a young man so expert in using the implements of feminine industry, the answer was, that, his mother having no girl, he had been often obliged to practice the seamstress's art."

While in the family of Captain Thayer, she was thrown much into the society of a young girl then visiting Mrs. Thayer. She soon began to show much partiality for Deborah (or Robert), and as she seemed to be versed in the arts of coquetry, Robert felt no scruples in paying close attention to one so volatile and fond of flirtation; she also felt a natural curiosity to learn within how short a time a maiden's fancy might be won.

Mrs. Thayer regarded this little romance with some uneasiness, as she could not help perceiving that Robert did not entirely reciprocate her young friend's affection. She accordingly lost no time in remonstrating with Robert, and warning him of the serious consequences of his folly in trifling with the feelings of the maiden. The remonstrance and caution were good-naturedly received, and the departure of the blooming soldier soon after terminated all these love passages, though Robert received from his fair young friend some souvenirs, which he cherished as relics in after years.

For three years, and until 1781, our heroine appears as a soldier, and during this time she gained the approbation and confidence of the officers by her exemplary conduct and by the fidelity with which her duties were performed. When under fire, she showed an unflinching boldness, and was a volunteer in several hazardous enterprises. The first time she was wounded, was in a hand-to-hand fight with a British dragoon, when she received a severe sword-cut in the side of her head, laying bare her skull.

About four months after the first wound, she was again doomed to bleed in her country's cause, receiving another severe wound in her shoulder, the bullet burying itself deeply, and necessitating a surgical examination.

She described her first emotion when the ball struck her, as a sickening terror lest her sex should be discovered. The pain of the wound was scarcely felt in her excitement and alarm, even death on the battle-field she felt would be preferable to the shame that would overwhelm her in case the mystery of her life were unveiled. Her secret, however, remained undiscovered, and, recovering from her wound, she was soon able again to take her place in the ranks.

Some time after, she was seized with a brain fever, which was then prevalent in the army. During the first stages of her malady, her greatest suffering was the dread that consciousness would desert her and her carefully guarded secret be disclosed to those about her. She was carried to the hospital, where her case was considered a hopeless one. One day the doctor approached the bed where she lay, a corpse, as every one supposed. Taking her hand, he found the pulse feebly beating, and, attempting to place his hand on the heart, he discovered a female patient, where he had little expected one. The surgeon said not a word of his discovery, but with a prudence, delicacy, and generosity ever afterwards appreciated by the sufferer, he provided every comfort her perilous condition required, and paid her those medical attentions which soon secured her return to consciousness. As soon as her condition would permit, he had her removed to his own house, where she could receive the better care.

After her health was nearly restored, Doctor Binney, her generous benefactor, had a long conference with the commanding officer of the company in which Robert had served, and this was followed by an order to the youth to carry a letter to General Washington.

Ever since her removal into the doctor's family, she had entertained the suspicion that he had discovered the secret of her life. Often while conversing with him, she watched his face with anxiety, but never discovered a word or look to indicate that the physician knew or suspected that she was other than what she represented herself to be. But when she received the order to carry the letter to the commander-in-chief, her long cherished misgivings became at last a certainty.

The order must be obeyed. With a trembling heart she pursued her course to the headquarters of Washington. When she was ushered into the presence of the Chief, she was overpowered with dread and uncertainty, and showed upon her face the alarm and confusion which she felt. Washington, noticing her agitation, and supposing it to arise from diffidence, kindly endeavored to re-assure her. She was soon bidden to retire with an attendant, while he read the communication of which she had been the bearer.

In a few moments, she was again summoned to the

presence of Washington, who handed her in silence a
discharge from the service, with a note containing a
few brief words of advice, and a sum of money sufficient to bear her expenses to some place where she
might find a home. To her latest hour, she never
forgot the delicacy and forbearance shown her by that
great and good man.

After the war was over, she became the wife of
Benjamin Gannet, of Sharon. During the presidency
of General Washington, she was invited to visit the
seat of government, and, during her stay at the
capital, Congress granted her a pension and certain
lands in consideration of her services to the country
as a soldier.

In the War of 1812, woman shared more or less in
the hard and perilous duties of a soldier, especially
upon the Canadian border, and on the western frontier, where Indian hostilities now broke out afresh.
She stood guard in the homes exposed to attack all
along the thin line, which the savage or the British
soldier threatened to break through, and on more
than one battle-field proved her lineal descent from
the brave mothers of the Revolution.

To the female imagination, the war with Mexico
must have been clothed with peculiar hardships and
dangers. The length of the marches, the vast distance from home, the torrid heats, fell diseases that
prevailed in that clime, and the nature of the half-
civilized enemy, all conspired to warn the gentler
sex against taking part in that conflict. And yet all
these appalling difficulties and perils could not damp
the martial ardor of Mrs. Coolidge. She was born in
Missouri, where, at St. Louis, she married her husband,

who was a Mexican trader. Accompanying him on one of his yearly journeys to Santa Fé, she had the misfortune to see him meet his death, at the hands of a Mexican bravo, in the outskirts of that city.

Her life had been a stirring one from her early girlhood, and, when war broke out with Mexico, she attired herself in manly garments, and by her stature and rather masculine appearance readily passed muster with the recruiting officer. Under the name of James Brown, she was duly entered on the rolls of a Missouri company, which soon after took steamboat for Fort Leavenworth, the rendezvous. From this point, on the 16th of June, 1846, a force of sixteen hundred and fifty-eight men, including our heroine (or hero), took up their line of march to Santa Fé.

Most of this little army were mounted men, and of this number was Mrs. Coolidge, who was an admirable horsewoman. Their course lay over the almost boundless plains that stretch westward to the foot-hills of the Rocky Mountains, a distance of nearly one thousand miles.

In fifty days they reached Santa Fé, of which they took possession without opposition.. The soldierly bearing and quick intelligence of Mrs. Coolidge soon attracted the attention of Col. Kearney, the commanding officer, and she was selected by him to be one of the bearers of dispatches to the war department.

A picked mustang, of extraordinary mettle and endurance, was placed at her disposal; a strong and fleet horse of the messenger stock, crossed with the mustang, was selected for her guide, a sturdy Scotchman, formerly in the Santa Fé trade; and one bright day, early in September, they set out on their long and perilous journey for Leavenworth. The first sixteen miles, over a broken and hilly country, was void of incident. They had passed through Arroyo Hondo and reached the Cañon, (El Boca del Cañon,) one of the gateways to Santa Fé; as they were threading this narrow pass, they saw, on turning a short angle of the precipice that towered three hundred feet above them, four mounted Mexicans, armed to the teeth and prepared to dispute their passage. One of them dismounted, and, advancing towards our couriers, waved a white handkerchief, and demanded in Spanish and in broken English their surrender. The guide replied in very concise English, telling him to go to a place unmentionable to polite ears. The envoy immediately rejoined his companions and mounted his horse; the party then turned and trotted forward a few paces as if they were about to give Mrs. Coolidge and the guide a free passage, when they suddenly wheeled their horses, and, discharging their pieces, seized their lances and dashed down full tilt upon our heroine and her guide. A shot from the guide's rifle hurled one of the Mexicans out of his saddle, like a stone from a sling. Mrs. Coolidge was less fortunate in her aim; missing the rider, her bullet struck a horse full in the forehead, but such was the speed with which it was approaching, that it was carried within twenty paces of the spot where she stood before it fell; the rider, uninjured, quickly extricated himself, and, seizing from his holster a horse-pistol, shot Mrs. Coolidge's horse, which nevertheless still kept his legs, and, as her assailant rushed towards her with his *machete*, or large knife, she leveled a pistol and sent a ball through one of his

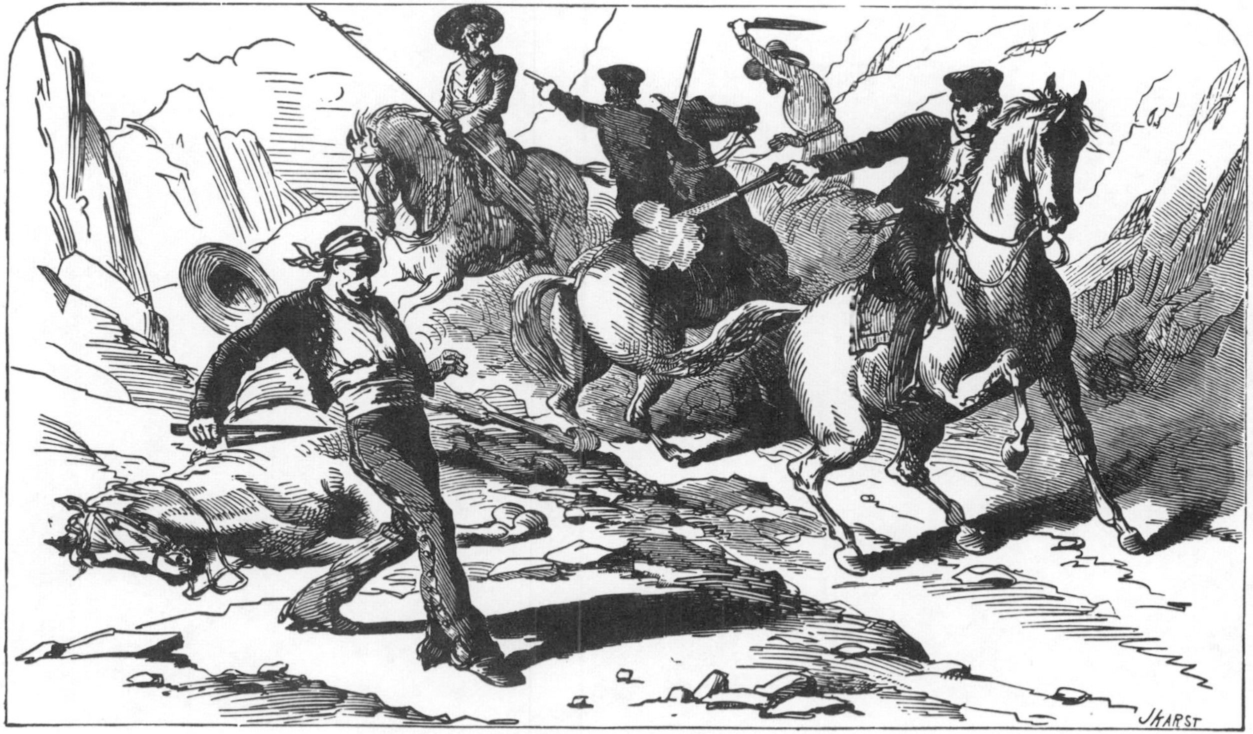

DEFEAT OF GUERILLAS. Page 410.

legs, breaking it and bringing him to the ground. Dismounting from her horse, which was reeling and staggering with loss of blood, she held her other pistol to the head of the prostrate guerrilla, who surrendered at discretion.

Meanwhile, the guide had dispatched one of the two remaining Mexicans, and, though he had a shot in the fleshy part of his leg, he had succeeded in compelling the other to surrender by shooting his horse.

Mrs. Coolidge now, for the first time, discovered blood dripping from a wound made by a musket-ball in her bridle-arm. Hastily winding her scarf about it, she bound the arms of her prisoner with a piece of rope, and broke his lance and the locks of his pistols and carbine. The other prisoner was served in the same fashion. The arms of the two dead Mexicans were also broken or disabled. The fleetest and best of the two remaining horses was taken by Mrs. Coolidge in lieu of her own gallant little mustang, which was now gasping out his life on the rocky bottom of the pass. Our gallant couriers then paroled the two prisoners, and galloped rapidly down the cañon, taking the other mustang with them, and leaving the guerrillas to find their way home as they best might. As they mounted their horses, the guide remarked to Mrs. Coolidge that he had heretofore entertained the suspicion that she might be a woman, but that now he knew she was a man.

A swift ride brought them to old Pecos, a distance of ten miles, where they supped and passed the night. Their wounds were mere scratches and did not necessitate any delay, and the next day, after a long, slow gallop, they reached Los Vegas. Then, keeping their course to the northwest and pushing rapidly forward, they passed the present site of Fort Union, and, having secured a large supply of dried buffalo meat, crossed the wonderful *mesa* or table-land west of the Canadian River, and encamped for a night and day on the east bank of that stream.

The next stretch for two hundred miles lay through a country infested with Utah and Apache Indians. Three or four days of swift riding would carry them through this dangerous region to a place of security on the Arkansas River. If they should meet a hostile band, it was agreed that they would trust for safety in the swiftness of their steeds, which had already proved themselves capable of both speed and endurance.

They had crossed Rabbit-ear Creek and reached the Cimarron, without seeing even the sign of a foe, when, early one morning, the guide, looking eastward over the vast sandy plain, from the camp where they had passed the night, saw far away a body of fifty mounted Indians, whom, after examining with his glass, he pronounced to be Uta' 'ng rapidly towards them. There was no escape, and, in accordance with their programme, they mounted their horses and rode slowly to meet them.

The Indians, spying them, formed a semicircle and galloped towards the fearless couple, who put their horses to a canter, and, riding directly against the center of the line of warriors, dashed through it on the run. The Indians, quickly recovering from the astonishment produced by this daring manœuver, wheeled their horses and dashed after them. All but ten of the Indians were soon distanced; these ten

continued the pursuit, but in an hour and a half this
number was reduced to seven, and in another hour
only five remained.   They were evidently young
braves, who were hoping to distinguish themselves
by taking two American soldiers' scalps.

On they sped—the pursuers and the pursued—over
the wild plain.   A space of barely half a mile divided
them.   The horses, however, of each party seemed so
evenly matched in speed and endurance that neither
gained on the other.   The mustangs, the one ridden
by our heroine, the other with only a ninety pound
pack on its back, though glossy with sweat, and their
nostrils crimson and expanded with the terrible strain
upon them, showed no sign of flagging.   The guide's
horse, a heavier animal, began at length to show
symptoms of fatigue.   If there had been time, he
would have shifted his saddle on the pack-mustang,
but this was not to be thought of.   By dint of spur-
ring and lashing the smoking flanks of the now drooping steed, he barely kept his place by the side of his
companion.

They were now near a small creek, an affluent of
the Arkansas, when the guide, turning his eyes, saw
that only three of the Indians were on their trail, the
two others were galloping slowly back.   Just as he
announced this fact to Mrs. Coolidge, his tired horse
fell heavily, throwing him forward upon his head and
stunning him senseless.

Our heroine, dismounting, dragged her unconscious
comrade to the bank of the creek, and, throwing
water in his face, quickly restored him to his senses;
but, before he could handle his gun, the Indians had
come within a hundred paces, whooping fiercely to

call back their companions, who just before abandoned the pursuit. They were luckily only armed with bows and arrows, and, circling about the fearless pair, they launched arrow after arrow, though without doing any execution. One of them fell before the rifle of Mrs. Coolidge. A second was brought to earth by the guide, who had by this time revived sufficiently to join in the fight. The third turned and galloped off towards his two companions, who were now hastening to the scene of conflict.

This gave our heroine and her associate in danger time to reload their rifles and to shield their horses behind the bank of the creek. Then, lying prostrate in the grass, they completely concealed themselves from sight. The three Indians, seeing them disappear behind the bank of the creek, and supposing that they had taken to flight again, rode unguardedly within range, and received shots which tumbled two of them from their saddles. The only remaining warrior gave up the contest and galloped away, leaving his comrades dead upon the field. One of the Indian mustangs supplied the place of the guide's horse, which was wind-broken, and the two now pursued their journey at a moderate pace, reaching Fort Leavenworth without encountering any more dangers.

Mrs. Coolidge (under her pseudonym of James Brown), after delivering her despatches, was promoted to the rank of sergeant, and was, at her own request, detached from the New Mexican division of the army and ordered to Matamoras, where she did garrison duty without any suspicion being awakened as to her sex. She afterwards entered active service, and accompanied the army on the march to the city of

Mexico. She took part in the storming of Chepultepec, and never flinched in that severe affair, covering herself with honor, and proving what brave deeds a woman can do in the severest test to which a soldier can be put.

During the recent war between the North and the South woman's position on the frontier was similar to that which she occupied in the war of 1812. The greater part of the army of the United States, which, in time of peace, was stationed along the vast border line from the Red River of the North to the Rio Grande, had been withdrawn. The outposts, by means of which the blood-thirsty Sioux, the savage Comanches, the remorseless Apaches, and numerous other fierce and war-like tribes had been kept in check, were either abandoned, or so poorly garrisoned that the settlements upon the border were left almost entirely unprotected from the treacherous savage, the lawless Mexican bandit, and the American outlaw and desperado.

What made their position still more unguarded and dangerous was the absence of their fathers, husbands, and brothers, as volunteers in the armies. The war fever raged in both the North and the South, and nowhere more hotly than among the pioneers from Minnesota to Texas. This brave and hardy class of men, accustomed as they were to the presence of danger, obeyed the call to arms with alacrity, and the women appear to have acquiesced in the enlistment of their natural protectors, trusting to God and their own arms to guard the household during the absence of the men of the family.

The women were thus left alone to face their human

foes, and the thousand other perils which beset them. They were, to all intents and purposes, soldiers. They belonged to the home army, upon which the frontier would have mainly to rely for security. Ceaseless vigilance by night and day, and a steady courage in the presence of danger, had to be constantly exercised.

Sometimes the savage foe came in overwhelming numbers, and in such cases the only safety lay in flight, during which all woman's address and fortitude was called into requisition, either to devise means of successfully eluding her pursuers, or to endure the toils and hardships of a rapid march. Sometimes she stood with loaded gun in her household garrison, and faced the enemy, either repelling them, or dying at her post, or, what was worse than death, seeing her loved ones butchered before her eyes, and their being led into a cruel captivity.

On the Texas border, in 1862, one of these home-warriors, during the absence of her husband in the Southern army, was left alone not far from the Rio Grande, and ten miles from the house of any American settler. Three Mexican horse thieves came to the house and demanded the key of the stable, in which two valuable horses were kept, threatening, in case of refusal, to burn her house over her head. She stood at her open door, with loaded revolver, and told them that not only would she not surrender the property, but that the first one that dared to lay violent hands upon her should be shot down. Cowed by her intrepid manner, the bandits slunk away.

On another occasion she was attacked by two American outlaws, while riding on the river bank. One of them seized the bridle of the horse, and the other

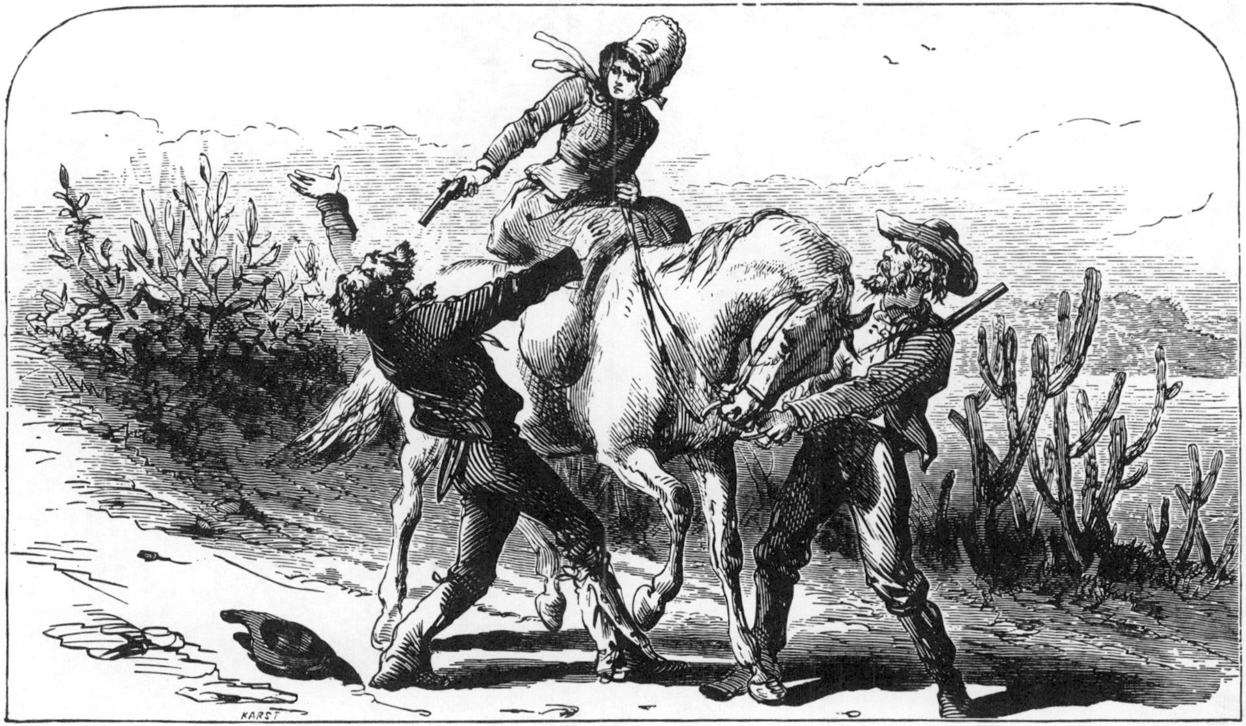

MASTERING BANDITS. Page 416.

attempted to drag her from the saddle. Turning upon the latter, she shot him dead, and the other, from sheer amazement at her daring, lost his self-possession and begged for mercy. After compelling him to give up his arms, she allowed him to depart unmolested, as there was no tribunal of justice near by where he could be punished for his villainy. These exploits gained for the borderer's wife a wide reputation throughout the region, and either through fear of her courage, or through an admiring respect for such heroism, when displayed by a lone woman, she was never again troubled by marauders.

The Sioux war in Minnesota, in 1862, was remarkable for the sufferings endured and the bravery displayed by women whose husbands had left them to join the army.

A notable instance of this description was that of two married sisters who lived in one house on the Minnesota River, some eighty miles above Mankato. One morning in the spring of that year their house was surrounded by Sioux Indians, but was so bravely defended that the savages withdrew without doing much damage. Two weeks of perfect peace passed away, and the two sisters renewed their outdoor work as fearlessly as ever, as their secluded situation prevented them from hearing of the ravages of the Indians in the eastern settlements.

Late one afternoon, while both the women were sitting in a small grove, not far from the house, they heard the war-whoop, and, stealing through the bushes, saw ten savages, who had dragged the three children from the house and cut their throats, and, after scalping them, were dancing about their mangled

27

corpses. They then set fire to the house and barns, and, butchering the cow, proceeded to prepare a great feast.

Not knowing how long the monsters would remain, and having no food nor means to procure any, the hapless women set out for the nearest house, which was situated ten miles to the east. They succeeded in reaching the spot at ten o'clock that night, but found nothing but a heap of ashes and two mangled bodies of a woman and her child.

Grief, fear, and fatigue kept them from obtaining that rest they so much needed, and before daylight they resumed their march towards the next house, eight miles farther east. This had also been destroyed. The younger sister, who was the mother of the three children who had been butchered, now gave up in grief and despair, and declared that she would die there. But she was at length induced to proceed by the urgent persuasions of the older and stronger woman.

The borders of the river at this point were covered with woods rendered impervious to the rays of the sun by the herbs, and shrubs that crept up the trunks, and twined around the branches of the trees. They resumed their melancholy journey; but observing that following the course of the river considerably lengthened their route, they entered into the wood, and in a few days lost their way. Though now nearly famished, oppressed with thirst, and their feet sorely wounded with briars and thorns, they continued to push forward through immeasurable wilds and gloomy forests, drawing refreshment from the berries and wild fruits they were able to collect.

At length, exhausted by hunger and fatigue, their strength failed them, and they sunk down helpless and forlorn. Here they waited impatiently for death to relieve them from their misery. In four days the younger sister expired, and the elder continued stretched beside her sister's corpse for forty-eight hours, deprived of the use of all her faculties. At last Providence gave her strength and courage to quit the melancholy scene, and attempt to pursue her journey. She was now without stockings, barefooted, and almost naked; two cloaks, which had been torn to rags by the briars, afforded her but a scanty covering. Having cut off the soles of her sister's shoes, she fastened them to her feet, and went on her lonely way. The second day of her journey she found water; and the day following, some wild fruit and green eggs; but so much was her throat contracted by the privation of nutriment, that she could hardly swallow such a sufficiency of the sustenance which chance presented to her as would support her emaciated frame.

That evening she was found by a party of volunteers who had been in pursuit of the Indians, and she was brought into the nearest settlement in a condition of body and mind to which even death would have been preferable.

Notwithstanding the dangers and distractions of this quasi-military life led by wives and mothers on the frontier, they did not neglect their other home duties.

When the scarred and swarthy veterans returned to their homes on the border there were no marks of neglect to be erased, no evidences of dilapidation and decay. "They found their farms in as good a condition as when they enlisted. Enhanced prices had balanced diminished production. Crops had been planted, tended, and gathered, by hands that before had been all unused to the hoe and the rake. The sadness lasted only in those households—alas! too numerous—where no disbanding of armies could restore the soldier to the loving arms and the blessed industries of home."

These women of the frontier during the late war may be called the irregular forces of the army, soldiers in all respects except in being enrolled and placed under officers. They fought and marched, stood on guard and were taken prisoners. They viewed the horrors of war and were under fire although they did not wear the army uniform nor walk in files and platoons. All these things they did in addition to their work as housewives, farmers, and mothers.

Many others took naturally to the rough life of a soldier, and enlisting under soldiers' guise followed the drum on foot or in the saddle, and encamped on the bare ground with a knapsack for a pillow and no covering from the cold and rain but a brown army blanket.

One of these heroines was Miss Louisa Wellman of Iowa. Born and nurtured on the border, habituated from childhood to an outdoor life, a fine rider, as well as a good shot with both a rifle and a pistol, it was quite natural that she should have felt a martial ardor when the war commenced, and having donned her brother's clothes, should have enlisted as she did in one of the Iowa regiments. Her most serious annoyance was the rough language and profanity of the soldiers. While in camp she managed to associate with the sober and pious soldiers, of whom there were several in the company. This was afterwards known as "the praying squad;" but she did not in consequence of her reluctance to associate with the others lose her popularity, owing to her unvarying cheerfulness, her generosity and her disposition to oblige often at the greatest inconvenience to herself. If a comrade was taken sick she was the first to tender her services as watcher and nurse, and in this way came to be known as "Doctor Ned."

She took part in the storming of Fort Donelson where she was slightly wounded in the wrist. Afterwards she served often in the picket line and distinguished herself by her courage, vigilance, and shrewdness. The boldness with which she exposed herself on every occasion, led to such a catastrophe as might have been expected. The battle of Pittsburgh Landing was an affair in which she figured with a cool bravery that kept her company steady in spite of the terrible fire which was decimating the ranks of the Federal Army. The pressure, however, was at last too great. Slowly driven towards the river, and fighting every inch of ground, the regiment in which she served seemed likely to be annihilated. They had just reached the shelter of the gun-boats when a stray shell exploded directly in the faces of the front rank, and Miss Wellman was struck and thrown violently to the earth, but instantly sprang to her feet and was able to walk to the temporary hospital which had been established near the river bank.

Like Deborah Samson, her sex was discovered by the surgeon who dressed her wound. The wound was in the collar bone and was made by a fragment of shell. Although not a dangerous one it required immediate attention. When the surgeon desired her to remove her army jacket she demurred, and not being able to assign any good reason for her refusal, the surgeon coupling this with the modest blush which suffused her features when he made his requisition for the removal of her outside garment, immediately guessed the truth. With chivalrous delicacy he immediately dispatched her with a note to the wife of one of the Captains who was in the camp at the time, recommending the maiden soldier to her care, and begging that she would dress the wound in accordance with a prescription which he sent. Although Miss Wellman begged that her secret might not be disclosed and that she might be permitted to continue to serve in the ranks, it was judged best to communicate the fact to the commanding officer, who, though he admired the bravery and resolution of the maiden, judged best that she should serve in another capacity if at all, and having notified her parents and obtained their consent she was allowed to do service in the ambulance department.

She was furnished with a horse, side-saddle, saddle-bags, etc., and whenever a battle took place she would ride fearlessly to the front to assist the wounded. Many a poor wounded soldier was assisted off the field by her, and sometimes she would dismount from her horse, and, aiding the wounded man to climb into the saddle, would convey him to the hospital. She carried bandages and stimulants in her saddle-bags, and did all she was able to relieve the sufferings of such as were too badly wounded to be removed.

During this service she was often exposed to the enemy's fire. She was with Grant in the Vicksburg campaign, and on one occasion, being attracted by a tremendous firing, rode rapidly forward, and missing her way found herself within one hundred yards of a battalion of the enemy, whose gray jackets could be seen through the smoke of their rapid firing. Wheeling her horse she galloped out of range, fortunately escaping the storm of bullets which flew about her.

She shared the hardships as well as the perils of the soldiers, and in the bivouac wrapped herself in her blanket and lay on the bare ground, with no other shelter but the sky, rising at the sound of reveille to partake with her comrades of the plain camp fare. All this she did cheerfully and with her whole heart. Her sympathy was not bounded by the wants and sufferings of the soldiers of the federal army, but embraced in its boundless outpouring those of her countrymen who were then ranged against her as foes. Many a sick and suffering Southerner had cause to bless the kindness and devotion of this noble girl. Herein she showed herself a Christian woman and a practical example of the teachings of Him who said,—" Love your enemies." Such deeds as her's shine amid the terrible passions and carnage of war with a heavenly radiance which time can never dim.

Either in the army or in close connection with it, woman's affectionate devotion was illustrated in all those relations of life in which she stands beside man. As a mother, as a wife,- and as a sister, she brightly displayed this quality. The following instance of wifely devotion is related of a woman who came from the Red River of Louisiana with her husband, who was a Southern officer.

In the fall of 1863, during the bombardment of

·Charleston by the federal batteries, this young woman, being tenderly attached to her husband, who was in one of the forts, begged the military authorities to allow her to join her husband and share the fearful dangers and hardships to which he was daily and nightly exposed.   All representations of the difficulties, privations, and perils she would encounter failed to daunt her in her purpose.   The importunities of the loving wife prevailed over military rules and even over the expostulations of her husband, and she was allowed to take her post beside the one whom she regarded with an affection amounting to idolatry. Sending her two children to the care of a maiden aunt some miles from the city, she was conveyed to her husband's battery, a large earth-work outside of the city.

Here she remained for sixty days, during which the battery where she was, made one of the principal targets for the federal cannon.   For weeks together she lay down in her clothes in the midst of the soldiers.   The bursting of the shells and the sound of the federal hundred-pounders, with answering volleys from the fort, scarcely intermitted night or day. Sleep was for several days after her arrival out of the question.   But at length she became used to the cannonade and enjoyed intermittent slumbers, from which she was sometimes awakened by the explosion of a shell which had penetrated the roof of the fort and strewed the earth with dead and wounded.

Her only food was the wormy bread and half-cured pork which was served out to the soldiers, and her drink was brackish water from the ditch that surrounded the earth-work.   The cannonading during

the day was so furious that the fort was often almost
reduced to ruins, but in the night the destruction was
repaired. A fleet of gunboats joined the land batteries in bombarding the fort, and at last succeeded in
making it no longer tenable. Guns had been dismounted, the bomb-proof had been destroyed, and the
sides of the earth-work were full of breaches where
the huge ten-inch balls had ploughed their way.

During all these terrifying and dreadful scenes, our
heroine stayed at her post of love and duty beside
her husband. When the little garrison evacuated the
fort at night and retired to the city, she was carried
in an ambulance drawn by four of the soldiers in
honor of her courage and devotion.

One of the most singular and romantic stories of the
late war, is that of two young women who enlisted at
the same time, and were engaged in active service for
nearly a year without any discovery being made or
even a suspicion excited as to their true sex.

Sarah Stover and Maria Seelye, for these were the
names of these heroines of real life, being homeless
orphans, and finding it difficult to earn a subsistence
on a small farm in Western Missouri, where they lived,
determined to enlist as volunteers in the Federal
Army. Accordingly, having donned male attire and
proceeded to St. Louis early in 1863, they joined a
company which was soon after ordered to proceed to
the regiment, which was a part of the army of the
Potomac.

Within two weeks after their arrival at the scene of
conflict in the East, the battle of Chancellorsville was
fought, the two girls participating in it and seeing
something of the horrors of the war in which they

were engaged as soldiers. In one of the minor battles which occurred the following summer they were
separated in the confusion of the fight, and upon calling the muster, Miss Stover, known in the regiment as
Edward Malison, was found among the missing. Her
comrade, after searching for her among the killed and
wounded in vain, at last ascertained that she had been
taken prisoner and conveyed to Richmond.

Miss Seelye, although she was well aware of the
serious consequences which might follow, decided to
adopt a bold plan in order to reach her friend whom
she loved so devotedly, and who was now suffering
captivity and perhaps wounds or disease. Through
an old negress she obtained a woman's dress and bonnet, and disguising herself in these garments, deserted
at the first favorable opportunity. She reached Washington in safety and was successful in an application
for a pass to Fortress Monroe, from which place she
made her way after many difficulties to the lines of
the Southern Army. By artful representations she
overcame the scruples of the officers and passed on
her way to Richmond, where she soon arrived, and
overcoming by her address and perseverance all obstacles, obtained admission to Libby Prison, representing
that she was near of kin to one of the prisoners.

Her singular success in accomplishing her object
was due doubtless to her intelligence, fine manners,
and good looks, with great tact in using the opportunities within her reach.

She found her friend just recovering from a wound
in her arm. The secret of her sex was still undiscovered; and after her wound was entirely healed they
prepared to attempt an escape which they had already

planned. Miss Seelye contrived to smuggle into the prison a complete suit of female attire, in which, one night just as they were relieving the guard, she managed to slip past the cordon of sentries, and joining her friend at the place agreed upon, the two immediately set out for Raleigh, to which city Miss Seelye had obtained two passes, one for herself, the other for a lady friend. They traveled on foot, and after passing the lines struck boldly across the country in the direction of Norfolk. When morning. dawned they concealed themselves in a wood and at night resumed their march.

On one occasion, just as they were emerging from a wood in the evening, they were discovered by a cavalryman. Their appearance excited his suspicions that they were spies, and he told them that he should have to take them to headquarters. But their ladylike manners and straightforward answers persuaded him that he was wrong, and he allowed them to proceed. Another time they narrowly escaped capture by two soldiers who suddenly entered the cabin of an old negro where they were passing the day.

After a tedious journey of a week, they reached the Federal pickets, and finally were transported to Washington on the steamer. This was in the autumn of 1863; their term of service would expire in two months, but after great hesitation they resolved to report themselves to the headquarters of their regiment as just escaped from Richmond. Accordingly, procuring suits of men's attire, they again disguised their sex and proceeded to rejoin their regiment, which was encamped near Washington.

The desertion of Miss Seelye having been explained

in this manner, she escaped its serious penalty, and both the girls were soon after regularly discharged from service. As we have already remarked, no suspicion was excited as to their sex, each shielding the other from discovery, and it was only after their discharge that they themselves revealed the secret.

The stories of women who have served as soldiers often disclose motives which would have little influence in impelling the other sex to enter the army. Love and devotion are among the most prominent of the moving causes of female enlistment. Sometimes a maiden, like Helen Goodridge, followed her lover to the war; sometimes a mother enlisted in the hospital department in order to nurse a wounded or sick husband or son. It was often some species of devotion, either to individuals or to her country, that led gentle woman to march in the ranks and share the dangers and privations of army life. Such an instance as the following furnishes a singularly striking illustration of this unselfish love and devotion of which we are speaking.

While the hostile armies were fighting, in the summer of 1864, those desperate battles by which the issues of the war were ultimately decided, a small, slender soldier fighting in the ranks, in General Johnson's division, was struck by a shell which tore away the left arm and stretched the young hero lifeless on the ground. A comrade in pity twisted a handkerchief around the wounded limb as an impromptu tourniquet, and thus having staunched the flowing blood, placed the slender form of the unfortunate soldier under a tree and passed on. Here half an hour after he was found by the ambulance men and brought to the hospital, where the surgeon discovered that the heroic heart, still faintly beating, animated the delicate frame of a woman.

Powerful stimulants were administered, and as soon as strength was restored the stump of the wounded limb was amputated near the shoulder. For a week the patient hovered between life and death. But her vitality triumphed in the struggle, and in a few days, with careful nursing she was able to sit up and converse. One of those noble women, who emulated the example and the glory of Florence Nightingale in nursing and ministering to the sick and wounded in the army, won the maiden-soldier's confidence, and into her ear she breathed her story.

She and a brother aged eighteen had been left orphans two years before. They were in destitute circumstances and had no near relations. They both supported themselves by honest toil, and their lonely and friendless situation had drawn them together with a warmth of affection, that even between a brother and sister has been rarely felt. They were all in all to each other, and when, in the spring of 1864, her brother had been drafted into the army, she learned the name of the regiment to which he had been assigned, and unknown to him assumed male attire and joined the same regiment.

She sought out her brother, and in a private interview made herself known to him. Astonished and grieved at the step she had taken he begged her to withdraw from the army, which she could easily do by disclosing the fact of her true sex. She remained firm against all his affectionate entreaties, informing him that if he was wounded or taken sick she would be near to nurse him, and in case of such a disaster she would reveal her secret and get a discharge so that she could attend constantly upon him.   On the morning of the battle in which she had been wounded they had met for the last time, and, as they well knew the battle would be a bloody one, agreed that each one would notify the other of their respective safety in case they both survived.   A note had reached her just after the battle, that her brother was safe, and she on her part had sent a message to him that she was alive and well, believing that she would recover, and not wishing to alarm him by telling the truth. Since that time she had heard nothing from him, and begged with streaming eyes that the lady would inquire if he had been wounded in any of the recent severe battles.   The lady hastened to procure the much desired information.   After diligent inquiries she discovered that the brother had been shot dead in a battle which occurred the day following that in which his sister had been wounded.

The good lady, sadly afflicted by this intelligence, and fearing its effect upon the invalid, strove to assume a cheerful countenance as she approached the couch. A smile of almost painful sweetness shone on the face of the girl soldier when she first glanced at the serene face of the lady who kindly put her off in her penetrating inquiries, but could not avoid showing a trace of grief and anxiety over the sad message with which she was burdened.

The smile slowly faded from the girl's face, her voice grew tremulous, her questions more searching and direct.   The lady tried to commence to break the sad truth gently to her, but already the unfortunate maiden had comprehended the fact. Her face grew a shade paler, then flushed; she breathed with difficulty, they raised her up, a crimson stream gushed from her lips, and an instant after the strong heart of the true and loving sister was still for ever.

———◆◆◆———

CHAPTER XIX.

ACROSS THE ROCKY MOUNTAINS.

THE frontier of to-day is on the plains and in the mountains. In that immense territory bounded by the Pacific on the west, and on the east by a line running irregularly from the sources of the Red River of the North to the Platte, one hundred miles from Omaha, and thence to the mouth of the Brazos in Texas, wherever a settlement is isolated, there is the frontier.

Life in these remote regions is affected, of course, by external surroundings. The same is true of the passage of the pioneer battalions from the eastern settlements through the country westward. The mountain-frontier presents, both to the settler who makes her abode there, and to her who passes through its wild pathways, a distinct set of difficulties and dangers besides those which are incident to every family which settles far from the more populous districts.

The enormous extent of the mountain region can be measured in linear and square miles; it can be bounded roughly by the Pacific Ocean and the fountains of the great rivers which course through the Mississippi valley; it can be placed before the eye in an astronomical position between such and such latitudes and longitudes, but such descriptions convey to the mind only an idea which is quite vague and general. When we say that one hundred and fifty states like Connecticut, or twenty states like New York or Illinois, spread over that infinitude of peaks and ranges, would scarcely cover them, we gain a somewhat more adequate idea of their extent. But it is only by actually traversing this wilderness of hills and mountains, east and west, north and south, that we can more fully comprehend its extent and the difficulties to be encountered by the emigrant who crosses it.

A straight line from Cheyenne on the east, to Placer at the foot of the Sierra Nevada in California, is eight hundred and fifty miles; by the shortest traveled route between these points it is upward of one thousand miles. A straight line from the same point in the east to Oregon City, among the Cascade Mountains in Oregon, measures nine hundred and fifty miles; by the traveled routes it is more than twelve hundred.

Thirty years ago, when railroads were unknown west of Buffalo, the journey by ox-teams across the continent, from the Atlantic to the Pacific, was more than three thousand miles, and might occupy from one year to eighteen months, according to circumstances.

After leaving the regions where roads and settlements made their march comparatively comfortable and secure, they struck boldly across the plains, fording rivers, hewing their way through forests, toiling across wide tracks of desert, destitute of food, herbage, and water, until they reached the Rocky Mountains. The region they were now to pass through had been penetrated by scarcely any but hunters, fur traders, soldiers, and missionaries. It was to the peaceful settler who was seeking a home, a *terra incognita*, an unknown land. Those mountain peaks were veiled in clouds, those devious labyrinthine valleys were the abode of darkness. The awful majesty of nature's works, the Titanic wonder-shapes which God hath wrought, are calculated to burden the imagination and subdue the aspiring soul of man by their vastness. Those mountain heights, seen from which the files of travelers passing through the profound defiles, look like insects; the relentless sway of nature's great forces—the storm roaring through the gorges, the flood plunging from the precipice and wearing trenches a thousand feet deep in the flinty rock; the walls which rear themselves into giant ramparts which human power can never scale; the wide circles of desolation, where hunger and thirst have their domain; such spectacles must indeed have thrilled the hearts, awed the minds, and filled the imaginations of the early pioneers with forebodings of difficulty and danger.

And yet the actual difficulties encountered by the emigrants, the actual toils, dangers, and hardships endured then in conquering a passage through and over the Rocky Mountains and their kindred ranges, must have surpassed the anticipations of the shrewdest forethought, and the bodings of the gloomiest imagination. Tongue cannot tell, nor pen describe, nor hath it entered into the heart of the eastern home-dweller

28

to conceive of the forlorn and terrible stories of those early mountain passages. We may wonder whether the fortunate traveler of these days, who is whirled up and down those perilous slopes by a forty-ton locomotive, often looks back to the time when those rickety wagons and lean oxen jogged along, drearily, eight or ten miles a day through those terrible fastnesses, or reverting to such a scene, expends upon it a merited sympathy. *Now* a seven days' journey from Manhattan to the Golden Gate, sitting in a palace car, well fed by day, well rested by night, scarcely more fatigued when one steps on the streets of San Francisco than by a day's journey on horseback in the olden time! *Then* a year's journey in the emigrant wagon, scantily fed, poorly nourished with sleep, foot-sore and haggard, the weary emigrant and his wife dragged themselves into the spot in the valley of the Sacramento, or the Columbia, where they were to commence anew their homely toils!

Who can sit down calmly, and, casting his eyes back to those heroes and heroines—the Rocky Mountain pioneers—and not feel his heart swell with pride and gratitude! Pride, in that, as an American, he can count such men and women among his countrymen; gratitude, in that he and the whole country are reaping fruits from their heroic courage, fortitude, and enterprise. Dangers met with an undaunted heart, hardships endured with unshrinking fortitude, trials and sufferings borne with cheerful patience, forgetfulness of self, devotion and sacrifice for others: such, in brief words, is the record of woman in those first journeys of the pioneers who crossed the continent for the pur-

pose of making homes, forming communities, and building states on the Pacific slope.

Among these histories, which illustrate most clearly
the virtues of the pioneer women, we count those
which display her battling with the difficulties of the
passage through the mountains, as proving that the
heroine of our own time may be matched with those
who have lived before her in any age or clime. One
of these histories runs as follows: In the corps of pioneers who, in 1844, were pushing the outposts of
civilization farther towards the setting sun, was a
young couple who left Illinois late in the summer of
that year, and, journeying with a white-tilted wagon,
drawn by four oxen, crossed the Missouri near the site
of old Fort Kearney, and moving in a bee line over
the prairie, early in November, encamped for the winter just beyond the forks of the Platte.

A low cabin, built of cotton-wood, banked up with
earth, and consisting of a single room, which contained
their furniture, farming utensils, and stores, sufficed as
a shelter against the severe winds which sweep over
those plains in the inclement season; their oxen, not
requiring to be housed, were allowed to roam at large
and browse upon the sweet grass which remains nourishing in that region throughout the winter.

At that period immense herds of bison roved through
that section, and in a few days after the arrival of Mr.
and Mrs. Hinman—for this was their name—they had
each shot, almost without stirring from their camp,
three fat buffalo cows, whose flesh was dried and added
to their winter's store. A supply of fresh meat was
thus near at hand, and for five weeks they fared
sumptuously on buffalo soup and ribs, tender-loin and

marrow bones, roasted with succulent tidbits from the hump, and tongue, which, with boiled Indian meal, formed the staple of their repasts.

Both Mr. Hinman and his wife were scions of that hardy stock which had, even before the Revolutionary War, set out from Connecticut, and, cutting their way through the forest, had crossed the Alleghany Mountains and river, and pitched their camp in the rich valley of the Muskingum, near the site of the present city of Marietta. Both had also grown up amid the surroundings of true frontier life, and were endowed with faculties, as well as fitted by experience, to engage in the bold enterprise wherein they were now embarked, namely, to cross the Rocky Mountains with a single ox-team and establish themselves in the fertile vale of the Willamette in Oregon.

The spare but well-knit frame, the swarthy skin, the prominent features, the deep-set eyes, the alert and yet composed manner, marked in them the true type of the born borderer. To these physical traits were united the qualities of mind and heart which are equally characteristic of the class to which they belonged; an apparent insensibility to fear, a capacity for endurance that exists in the moral nature rather than in the body, and a self-reliance that never faltered, formed a combination which fitted them to cope with the difficulties that environed their perilous project.

As early in the spring of 1845 as the ground would permit, they re-packed their goods and stores, hung out the white sails of their prairie schooner and pursued their journey up the north fork of the Platte, crossed the Red Buttes, went through Devil's Gate, skirted the banks of the Sweet Water River, and winding through the great South Pass, diverted their course to the north in the direction of the head-waters of Snake River, which would guide them by its current to the Columbia.

At this stage in their journey they consulted a rough map of the route on which two trails were laid down, either of which would lead to the stream they were seeking. With characteristic boldness they chose the shorter and more difficult trail.

Following its tortuous course in a northwesterly direction they reached a point where the path was barely wide enough for the wagon to pass, and was bounded on the one side by a wall of rock and on the other by a ragged precipice descending hundreds of feet into a dark ravine.

Here Mrs. Hinman dismounted from her seat in the wagon to assist in conducting the team past this dangerous point. Her husband stood between the oxen and the precipice when the hind wheel of the wagon slipped on a smooth stone, the vehicle tilted and being top-heavy upset and was precipitated into the abyss, dragging with it the oxen who, in their fall, carried down Mr. Hinman who stood beside the wheel yoke.

He gave a loud cry as he fell, and gazing horror-stricken over the brink Mrs. Hinman saw him bounding from rock to rock preceded by the wagon and oxen which rolled over and over till they disappeared from view.

In the awful stillness of that solitude the beating of her heart became audible as she rapidly reviewed her terrible situation, and taxed her mind to know what

she should do. Summoning up all her resolution she
ran swiftly along the edge of the precipice in search
of a place where she could descend, in the hope that by
some rare good fortune her husband might have survived his fall. Half a mile back of the spot where
the accident occurred she found a more gradual descent into the ravine, and here, by swinging herself
from bush to bush she managed at length with the utmost difficulty and danger to reach the bottom of the
ravine, but could find there no trace either of her husband or of the ox-team.

Scanning the face of the precipice she saw, at last,
one hundred feet above her the wreck of the wagon,
and the bodies of the oxen, which had landed upon a
projecting ledge.

At great risk of being dashed to pieces, she succeeded in climbing to the spot. The patient beasts
which had carried them so far upon their way were
crushed to a jelly; among the remains of the wagon
scarcely a vestige appeared of the furniture, utensils,
and stores with which it was laden. She marked the
track it had made in its descent, and digging her fingers and toes into the crevices of the rock, and drawing herself from point to point in a zigzag course, by
means of bushes and projecting stones, she slowly
scaled the declivity and reached a narrow ledge some
three hundred feet from the ravine, where she paused
to take breath.

A low moan directed her eyes to a clump of bushes
some fifty feet above her, and there she caught sight
of a limp arm hanging among the stunted foliage.
Climbing to the spot she found her husband breathing
but unconscious. He was shockingly bruised, and al-

though no bones had been broken, the purple current trickling slowly from his mouth showed that some internal organ had been injured. While there is life there is hope. If he could be placed in a comfortable position he might still revive and live. Feeling in his breast pocket she found a leather flask filled with whisky with which she bathed his face after pouring a large draught down his throat. In a few moments he revived sufficiently to comprehend his situation.

"Don't leave me, Jane," whispered the suffering man, "I shan't keep you long." It was unnecessary to prefer such a request to a woman who had gone through such perils to save one whom she loved dearer than life. "I'll bring you out safe and sound, Jack," returned she, "or die right here with you."

While racking her brain for means to remove him fifty feet lower to the ledge from which she had first spied him, a welcome sight met her eye. It was the axe and the coil of rope which had fallen from the wagon during its descent, and now lay within easy reach. Passing the rope several times around his body so as to form a sling she cut a stout bush, and trimming it, made a stake which she firmly fastened into a crevice, and with an exertion of strength, such as her loving and resolute heart could have alone inspired her to put forth, she extricated him from his position, and laying the ends of the rope over the stake gently lowered him to the ledge, and gathering moss made a pillow for his bleeding head. Then descending to the spot where the carcasses of the oxen lay she quickly flayed one, and cutting off a large piece of flesh she ransacked the wreck of the wagon and found a blanket and a pot. Returning to her husband she kindled a fire, and made broth with some water which she found in the hollow of a rock.

Gathering moss and lichens she made a comfortable couch upon the rock, and gently stretched her groaning patient upon it, covering him with the blanket for the mountain air was chill even in that August afternoon. The wounded man's breathing grew more regular, the bloody ooze no longer flowed from his white lips, but his frame was still racked by agonizing pains.

The hours sped away as the devoted wife bent over him ; the height of the mountains in that region materially shortens the day to such as are in the valleys, but though the sun sets early behind the western summits twilight lingers long after his departure. When the orb of day had disappeared, Mrs. H. still viewed with wonder, not unmixed with fear, the savage grandeur of the mountains which lifted their heads still glittering in the passing light; and gazing into the profound below she watched the shades as they deepened to blackness.

The ledge on which the forlorn pair lay was barely four feet wide and less than ten feet long. There, on the face of that precipice, one hundred miles from the nearest settlement, all through the lonely watches of the night, the strong-hearted wife, with tear-dimmed eyes, hung over the sufferer. Many a silent prayer in the weary hours of that moonless night did she send up to the Father of mercies. Many a plan for bringing succor or for alleviating pain on the morrow did she devise.

Will-power is the most potent factor in giving a satisfactory solution of the problem of vitality. Just as the gray light was shimmering in the eastern sky the wounded man moaned as if he wished to speak. His wife understood that language of pain and weakness, and placed her ear to his lips. " I *won't die*, Jane," he said scarcely above a whisper. "You shan't die, Jack," was the reply. A great hope dawned like a sun upon her as those four magic syllables were uttered.

He fell into a doze, and when he woke the sun was up. "Can you stay here all alone for a few hours," inquired Mrs. H———, after feeding her patient, "I am going to see if I can fetch some one to help us out of this." "Go," he answered. Placing the flask and broth within reach of her husband, and kissing him, she sprang up the acclivity as though she had wings, reached the trail and sped along it southward. Fifteen miles would bring her to the spot where the two trails met: here she hoped to meet some wayfaring train of emigrants, or some party of hunters coursing through the defiles of the mountains.

Sooner than she expected, after reaching the fork, her wish was gratified. In less than half an hour six hunters came up with her, and, hearing her story, three of them volunteered to go and bring her husband to their cabin, which stood half a mile away from the trail. A horse was furnished to Mrs. H———, and the three hunters and she rode rapidly to the scene of the disaster.

Skipping down the declivity like *chamois*, and helping their brave companion, who was now quite fatigued with her exertion, they reached the rocky shelf. The mountain air and the delicious consciousness that he would live, coupled with implicit confidence in the success of his wife's errand, had acted like a charm on the vigorous organization of the wounded man, and he begged that he might be immediately removed.

He was accordingly carried carefully to the trail, and placed astride of one of the horses in front of one of the hunters. After a slow march of four hours, he was safely stowed in the cabin of the hunters, where, in a few weeks, he entirely recovered from his injuries.

It might be readily supposed after such a grave experience of the dangers of mountain life, that our heroine and her husband would have been inclined to return to their old home on the sunny prairies of Illinois. On the contrary, they strongly desired to continue the prosecution of their Oregon enterprise, and were only prevented from carrying it out by the lack of a team and the necessary utensils, etc.

The hunters, learning their wishes, returned to the scene of the mishap, and scoured the side of the mountain in search of the articles which had been thrown from the wagon in its descent. They succeeded in recovering uninjured a large number of articles, including a few which still remained in the wrecked vehicle. Then clubbing together, they made up a purse and bought two pair of oxen and a wagon from a passing train of emigrants, who also generously contributed articles for the use and comfort of the resolute but unfortunate pair. Such deeds of charity are habitual with the men and women of the frontier, and the farther west one goes the more spontaneously and warmly does the heart bound to relieve the sufferings and supply the wants of the unfortunate, particularly of those who have been injured or reduced while battling with the hardships and dangers incident to a wild country. The more rugged the region on our western border, the more boundless becomes the sympathetic faculty of its inhabitants. Nowhere is a large and unselfish charity more lavishly exercised than among the Rocky Mountain men and women. Free as the breezes that sweep those towering summits, warm as the sun of midsummer, bright as the icy peaks which lift themselves into the sky, the spirit of loving-kindness for the unfortunate animates the bosoms of the sons and daughters of that mountain land.

After wintering with their hospitable friends, Mr. and Mrs. Hinman pursued their journey the following spring, and, after a toilsome march, attended by no further startling incidents, reached their destination in Oregon.

There in their new home, which Mrs. H———, by her industry and watchfulness, contributed so largely to make, they found ample scope for the exercise of those qualities which they had proved themselves to possess. It is men and women like these whom we must thank for building up our empire on that far off coast.

The old hunters and gold-seekers in that region are the faithful depositaries of the mountain legends respecting the adventures of the early emigrants, and the observers and annotators, as it were, of the passages made by the pioneers in later times. Around their camp-fires at night, when their repast is made and their pipes lighted, they beguile the lonely hours with tales of dreadful suffering, or of hair-breadth escapes from danger, or of heroism displayed by mountain wayfarers. This, as we have elsewhere remarked, is the hunters' pastime.

While a hunting party were once threading the defiles of the mountain, they espied below them in the valley certain suspicious signs. Approaching the spot, they discovered that a train of emigrants had been attacked by the savages, their wagons robbed, their oxen killed, a number of the party massacred and scalped, and the rest dispersed.

One of the hunters proceeds with the story from this point.

" Thirsting for a speedy revenge, the men at once divided. With Augur-eye as guide, I took command of the detachment who had to search the river bank; the old Sergeant commanded the scouting party told off to cross the ford and scour the timber on the right side of the river; whilst the third band was appropriated to the Doctor. The weather was cold, and the sky, thickly covered with fleecy clouds, foreboded a heavy fall of snow. The wind blew in fitful gusts, and seemed to chill one's blood with its icy breath, as, sweeping past, it went whistling and sighing up the glen. The rattle of the horses' hoofs, as the receding parties galloped over the turf, grew fainter and fainter, and, when our little band halted on a sandy reach, about a mile up the river, not a sound was audible, save the steady rhythm of the panting horses and the noisy rattle of the stream, as, tumbling over the craggy rocks, it rippled on its course. The 'Tracker' was again down; this time creeping along upon the sand on his hands and knees, and deliberately and carefully examining the marks left on its impressible surface, which, to his practiced eye, were in reality letters, nay, even readable words and sentences. As we watched this tardy progress in impatient silence, suddenly, as if stung by some poisonous reptile, the Indian sprang upon his legs, and, making eager signs for us to approach, pointing at the same time eagerly to something a short distance beyond where he stood. A near approach revealed a tiny hand and part of an arm pushed through the sand.

"At first we imagined the parent, whether male or female, had thus roughly buried the child—a consolatory assumption which Augur-eye soon destroyed. Scraping away the sand partially hiding the dead boy, he placed his finger on a deep cleft in the skull, which told at once its own miserable tale. This discovery clearly proved that the old guide was correct in his readings, that the savages were following up the trail of the survivors. A man who had escaped and just joined us, appeared so utterly terror-stricken at this discovery, that it was with difficulty he could be supported on his horse by the strong troopers who rode beside him. We tarried not for additional signs, but pushed on with all possible haste. The trail was rough, stony, and over a ledge of basaltic rocks, rendering progression not only tedious, but difficult and dangerous; a false step of the horse, and the result might have proved fatal to the rider. The guide spurs on his Indian mustang, that like a goat scrambles over the craggy track; for a moment or two he disappears, being hidden by a jutting rock; we hear him yell a sort of 'war-whoop,' awakening the echoes in the encircling hills; reckless of falling, we too spur on, dash round the splintered point, and slide rather than canter down a shelving bank, to reach a second

sand-beach, over which the guide is galloping and
shouting. We can see the fluttering garments of a
girl, who is running with all her might towards the
pine trees; she disappears amongst the thick foliage of
the underbrush ere the guide can come up to her, but
leaping from off his horse, he follows her closely, and
notes the spot wherein she has hidden herself amidst
a tangle of creeping vines and maple bushes. He
awaited our coming, and, motioning us to surround
the place of concealment quickly, remained still as a
statue whilst we arranged our little detachment so as
to preclude any chance of an escape. Then gliding
noiselessly as a reptile through the bushes, he was
soon hidden. It appeared a long time, although not
more than a few minutes had elapsed from our losing
sight of him, until a shrill cry told us something was
discovered. Dashing into the midst of the underbrush,
a strange scene presented itself. The hardy troopers
seemed spell-bound, neither was I the less astonished.

Huddled closely together, and partially covered with
branches, crouched two women and the little girl whose
flight had led to this unlooked-for discovery. In a
state barely removed from that of nudity, the unhappy trio strove to hide themselves from the many
staring eyes which were fixed upon them, not for the
purpose of gratifying an indecent curiosity, but simply
because no one had for the moment realized the condition in which the unfortunates were placed. Soon,
however, the fact was evident to the soldiers that the
women were nearly unclad, and all honor to their
rugged goodness, they stripped off their thick top-
coats, and throwing them to the trembling females,
turned every one away and receded into the bush. It

was enough that the faces of the men were white which
had presented themselves so unexpectedly. The destitute fugitives, assured that the savages had not again
discovered them, hastily wrapped themselves in the
coats of the soldiers, and, rushing out from their lair,
knelt down, and clasping their arms round my knees,
poured out thanks to the Almighty for their deliverance with a fervency and earnestness terrible to witness. I saw, on looking round me, streaming drops
trickling over the sunburnt faces of many of the men,
whose iron natures it was not easy to disturb under
ordinary circumstances.

" It was soon explained to the fugitives that they
were safe, and as every hour's delay was a dangerous
waste of time, the rescued women and child were as
carefully clad in the garments of the men as circumstances permitted, and placed on horses, with a hunter
riding on either side to support them. Thus reinforced,
the cavalcade, headed by Augur-eye, moved slowly
back to the place where we had left the pack-train
encamped, with all the necessary supplies. I lingered
behind to examine the place wherein the women had
concealed themselves. The 'boughs of the vine-maple,
together with other slender shrubs constituting the
underbrush, had been rudely woven together, forming,
at best, but a very inefficient shelter from the wind,
which swept in freezing currents through the valley.
Had it rained, they must soon have been drenched, or
if snow had fallen heavily, the ' wickey' house and its
occupants soon would have been buried. How had
they existed? This was a question I was somewhat
puzzled to answer.

" On looking round I observed a man's coat, pushed

away under some branches, and on the few smouldering embers by which the women had been sitting when
the child rushed in and told of our coming, was a small
tin pot with a cover on it, the only utensil visible.
Whilst occupied in making the discoveries I was sickened by a noisome stench, which proceeded from the
dead body of a man, carefully hidden by branches,
grass, and moss, a short distance from the little cage
of twisted boughs.   Gazing on the dead man a suspicion too revolting to mention suddenly flashed upon
me.   Turning away saddened and horror-stricken, I
returned to the cage and removed the cover from the
saucepan, the contents of which confirmed my worst
fears.   Hastily quitting the fearful scene, the like of
which I trust never to witness again, I mounted my
horse and galloped after the party, by this time some
distance ahead.

" Two men and the guide were desired to find the
spot where the scouting parties were to meet each
other, and to bring them with all speed to the mule
camp.   It was nearly dark when we reached our destination, the sky looked black and lowering, the wind
appeared to be increasing in force, and small particles
of half-frozen rain drove smartly against our faces,
telling in pretty plain language of the coming snow-
fall.   Warm tea, a good substantial meal, and suitable
clothes, which had been sent in case of need by the
officers' wives stationed at the 'Post,' worked won-
ders in the way of restoring bodily weakness; but the
shock to the mental system time alone could alleviate.
I cannot say I slept much during the night.   Anxiety
lest we might be snowed in, and a fate almost as terrible as that from which we had rescued the poor women,

should be the lot of all, sat upon me like a nightmare. More than this, the secret I had discovered seemed to pall every sense and sicken me to the heart, and throughout the silent hours of the dismal darkness I passed in review the ghostly pageant of the fight and all its horrors, the escape of the unhappy survivors, the finding of the murdered boy and starving women, and more than all—the secret I had rather even now draw a veil over, and leave to the imagination."

A fugitive woman in the wilds of the Rocky Mountains is indeed an object of pity ; but when she boldly faces the dangers that surround her in such a position, and succeeds by her courage, endurance, and ingenuity in holding her own, and finally extricating herself from the perils by which she is environed, she may fairly challenge our admiration. Such a woman was Miss Janette Riker, who proved how strong is the spirit of self-reliance which animates the daughters of the border under circumstances calculated to daunt and depress the stoutest heart.

The Riker family, consisting of Mr. Riker, his two sons, and his daughter Janette, passed through the Dacotah country in 1849, and late in September had penetrated to the heart of the mountains in the territory now known as Montana. Before pursuing their journey from this point to their destination in Oregon, they encamped for three days in a well-grassed valley for the purpose of resting their cattle, and adding to their stock of provisions a few buffalo-humps and tongues.

On the second day after their arrival at this spot, the father and his two sons set out on their buffalo hunt with the expectation of returning before night-

29

fall. But the sun set and darkness came without bringing them back to the lonely girl, who in sleepless anxiety awaited their return all night seated beneath the white top of the Conestoga wagon. At early dawn she started on their trail, which she followed for several miles to a deep gorge where she lost all trace of the wanderers, and was after a long and unavailing search compelled in the utmost grief and distraction of mind, to return to the camp.

For a week she spent her whole time in seeking to find some trace of her missing kinsmen, but without success. As the lonely maiden gazed at the mighty walls which frowned upon her and barred her egress east and west from her prison-house, hope died away in her heart, and she prayed for speedy death. This mood was but momentary; the love of life soon asserted its power, and she cast about her for some means whereby she could either extricate herself from her perilous situation, or at least prolong her existence.

To attempt to find her way over the mountains seemed to her impossible. Her only course was to provide a shelter against the winter, and stay where she was until discovered by some passing hunters, or by Indians, whom she feared less than an existence spent in such a solitude and surrounded by so many dangers.

Axes and spades among the farming implements in the wagon supplied her with the necessary tools, and by dint of assiduous labor, to which her frame had long been accustomed, she contrived to build, in a few weeks, a rude hut of poles and small logs. Stuffing the interstices with dried grass, and banking up the earth around it, she threw over it the wagon-top, which she fastened firmly to stakes driven in the ground, and thus provided a shelter tolerably rain-tight and weather-proof.

Thither she conveyed the stoves and other contents of the wagon. The oxen, straying through the valley, fattened themselves on the sweet grass until the snow fell; she then slaughtered and flayed the fattest one, and cutting up the carcase, packed it away for winter's use. Dry logs and limbs of trees, brought together and chopped up with infinite labor, sufficed to keep her in fuel. Although for nearly three months she was almost completely buried in the snow, she managed to keep alive and reasonably comfortable by making an orifice for the smoke to escape, and digging out fuel from the drift which covered her wood-pile. Her situation was truly forlorn, but still preferable to the risk of being devoured by wolves or mountain lions, which, attracted by the smell of the slaughtered ox, had begun to prowl around her shelter before the great snow fall, but were now unable to reach her beneath the snowy bulwarks. She suffered more, however, from the effect of the spring thaw which flooded her hut with water and forced her to shift her quarters to the wagon, which she covered with the cotton top, after removing thither her blankets and provisions. The valley was overflowed by the melting of the snows, and for two weeks she was unable to build a fire, subsisting on uncooked Indian meal and raw beef, which she had salted early in the winter.

Late in April, she was found in the last stages of exhaustion, by a party of Indians, who kindly relieved her wants and carried her across the mountains with her household goods, and left her at the Walla Walla station. This act on the part of the savages, who were a wild and hostile tribe, was due to their admiration for the hardihood of the "young white squaw," who had maintained herself through the rigors of the winter and early spring in that awful solitude—a feat which, they said, none of their own squaws would have dared perform. The fate of her father and brothers was never ascertained, though it was conjectured that they had either lost their way or had fallen from a precipice.

Miss Riker afterwards married, and, as a pioneer wife, found a sphere of usefulness for which her high qualities of character admirably fitted her.

Among the most authentic histories of these bands of early pioneers which undertook to make the passage of this region thirty years since, when it involved such difficulties and dangers, is the following :

In the year 1846, soon after the commencement of the Mexican War, a party of emigrants undertook to cross the Continent, with the intention of settling on the Pacific coast. The party consisted of J. F. Reed, wife, and four children; Jacob Donner, wife, and seven children; William Pike, wife, and two children; William Foster, wife, and one child; Lewis Kiesburg, wife, and one child; Mrs. Murphy, a widow woman, and five children; William McCutcheon, wife, and one child; W. H. Eddy, wife, and two children; W. Graves, wife, and eight children; Jay Fosdicks, and his wife; John Denton, Noah James, Patrick Dolan, Samuel Shoemaker, C. F. Stanton, Milton Elliot, —— Smith, Joseph Rianhard, Augustus Spized, John Baptiste, —— Antoine, —— Herring, —— Hallerin, Charles

Burger, and Baylie Williams, making a total of sixty-five souls, of whom ten were women, and thirty-one were children.

Having supplied themselves with wagons, horses, cattle, provisions, arms, ammunition, and other articles requisite for their enterprise, they set out on their journey from the Mississippi, and, after a toilsome march of many weeks across the prairies, they reached, late in the summer of that year, the foot-hills of the Rocky Mountains. Resting for a few days in a grassy valley, and, gazing with wistful eyes on the mighty peaks which towered beyond them, they girded up their loins for the novel toils and perils they were soon to encounter, and pushed on, expecting to follow the great military route which would conduct them, before the winter snows, to the sunny slopes which are fanned by the breezes of the peaceful ocean.

They reached the Sweet-Water River, on the eastern side of the mountains, late in August. While in camp there, they were induced, by the representations of one Lansford W. Hastings, to take a new route to the Pacific coast. Relying on the truth of these statements, and full of hope that they would thus shorten their journey, they left the beaten track and started onward through an unknown region. Long before they had reached the valley of the Great Salt Lake, they began to encounter the greatest difficulties. At one time they found themselves in a dense forest, and, seeing no outlet or passage, were forced to cut their way through, making only forty miles progress in thirty days.

In September, they were passing through the Utah Valley, since occupied by the Mormons. Here death

invaded their ranks, and removed Mr. Hallerin.   This
and an accident to one of the wagons, detained them
two days.

Pursuing their march, they were next forced to
travel across a desert tract without grass or water,
and lost many cattle.

At this point of the journey, the gloomiest forebodings seized the stoutest heart.   They were in a rugged
and desolate region, far from all hope of succor,
surrounded by hostile Indians, their cattle dying, and
their stock of provisions lessening rapidly, with the
sad conviction hourly forcing itself upon their minds,
that they had been betrayed by one of their own
countrymen.

Some of the families had already been completely
ruined by the loss of their cattle and by being forced
to abandon their goods and property.   They were in
complete darkness as to the character of the road
before them.   To retreat across the desert to Bridger,
was impossible.   There was no way left to them but
to advance; and this they now regarded as perilous
in the extreme.   The cattle that survived were exhausted and broken down; but to remain there was
to die.   Some of the men, broken by their toils and
sufferings, lay down and declared they might as well
die there as further on; others cursed the deception
of which they had been the victims; others uttered
silent prayers, and then sought to raise the drooping
spirits of their comrades, and encourage them to press
forward.   Of these last were the females of the party
—wives, who never faltered in these hours of trial,
but sustained their husbands in their dark moods; and

mothers, who fought the dreadful battle, thinking more of their children than of themselves.

Once more the party resumed their journey, but only to meet fresh disasters.

"Thirty-six head of working cattle were lost, and the oxen that survived were greatly injured. One of Mr. Reed's wagons was brought to camp; and two, with all they contained, were buried in the plain. George Donner lost one wagon. Kiesburg also lost a wagon. The atmosphere was so dry upon the plain, that the wood-work of all the wagons shrank to a degree that made it next to impossible to get any of them through.

Having yoked some loose cows, as a team for Mr. Reed, they broke up their camp, on the morning of September 16th, and resumed their toilsome journey, with feelings which can be appreciated by those only who have traveled the road under somewhat similar circumstances. On this day they traveled six miles, encountering a very severe snow storm. About three o'clock in the afternoon, they met Milton Elliot and William Graves, returning from a fruitless effort to find some cattle that had strayed away. They informed them that they were in the immediate vicinity of a spring."

This spring they succeeded in reaching, and there they encamped for the night. At the early dawn, on September 17th, they resumed their journey, and, at four o'clock A. M. of the 18th, they arrived at water and grass, some of their cattle having meanwhile perished, and the teams which survived being in a very enfeebled condition. Here the most of the little property which Mr. Reed still had was burned, or *cached*, together with that of others. Mr. Eddy now proposed putting his team on Mr. Reed's wagon, and letting Mr. Pike have his wagon so that the three families could be taken on. This was done. They remained in camp during the day of the 18th, to complete these arrangements, and to recruit their exhausted cattle.

The journey was continued with scarcely any interruption or accident, until the first of October, when some Indians stole a yoke of oxen from Mr. Graves. Other thefts followed, and it became evident that the party would suffer severely from the hostility of the Indians.

A large number of cattle were stolen or shot by the merciless marauders. The women were kept in a perpetual state of alarm by the proximity of the savages. Maternal love and anxiety for those thirty-one innocent children now exposed to captivity and death at the hands of the prowling redskins, made the lives of those unfortunate matrons one long, sad vigil. They could meet death locked in the fastnesses of the mountains, or in the desolate plain; they could even lay the remains of those dear to them, far from home, in the darkest cañon of those terrible mountains, but the thought of seeing their children torn from their embrace and borne into a barbarous captivity, was too much for their woman's natures. The camp was the scene of tears and mourning from an apprehension more dreadful even than real sufferings.

The fear of starvation, also, at this stage in their journey, began to be felt. An account was taken of their stock of provisions, and it was found that they would last only a few weeks longer, and that only by putting the party on allowances.

Here, again, the self-sacrificing spirit that woman always shows in hours of trial, shone out with surpassing brightness. Often did those devoted wives and mothers take from their own scanty portion to satisfy the cravings of their husbands and children.

For some weeks after the 19th of October, 1846, the forlorn band moved slowly on their course through those terrible mountains. Sometimes climbing steeps which the foot of white man had never before scaled, sometimes descending yawning cañons, where a single misstep would have plunged them into the abyss hundreds of feet below. The winter fairly commenced in October. The snow was piled up by the winds into drifts in some places forty feet deep, through which they had to burrow or dig their way. A sudden rise in the temperature converted the snow into slush, and forced them to wade waist deep through it, or lie drenched to the skin in their wretched camp.

One by one their cattle had given out, and their only supply of meat was from the chance game which crossed their track. At last their entire stock of provisions was exhausted, and they stood face to face with the grim specter of starvation. They had now encamped in the mountains, burrowing in the deep snow, or building rude cabins, which poorly sufficed to ward off the biting blast, and every day their condition was growing more pitiable.

On the 4th of January, 1847, Mr. Eddy, seeing that all would soon perish unless food were quickly obtained, resolved to take his gun and press forward alone. He informed the party of his purpose. They besought him not to leave them. But some of the women, recognizing the necessity of his expedition, and excited by the feeble wails of their perishing children, bade him God-speed. One of them, Mary Graves, who had shown an iron nerve and endurance all through their awful march, insisted that she would accompany him or perish. The two accordingly set forward. Mr. Eddy soon afterwards had the good fortune to shoot a deer, and the couple made a hearty meal on the entrails of the animal.

The next day several of the party came up with them, and feasted on the carcass of the deer. Their number during the preceding night had again been lessened by the death of Jay Fosdicks. The survivors, somewhat refreshed, returned to their camp on the following day.

The Indians Lewis and Salvadore, being threatened with death by the famished emigrants, had some days before stolen away. After the deer had been consumed, and while Mr. Eddy's party were returning to camp, they fell upon the tracks of these fugitives; Foster, who was at times insane through his sufferings, followed the trail and overtook and killed them both. He cut the flesh from their bones and dried it for future use. Mr. Eddy and a few of the party, in their wanderings, at length reached an Indian village, where their immediate sufferings were relieved.

The government of California being informed of the imminent peril of the emigrants in the mountain camp, took measures to send out relief, and a number of inhabitants contributed articles of clothing and provisions. Two expeditions, however, failed to cross the mountains in consequence of the depth of the snow.

At length, a party of seven men, headed by Aquilla Glover, and accompanied by Mr. Eddy, who, though weak, insisted on returning to ascertain the fate of his beloved wife and children, succeeded in crossing the mountains and reaching the camp.

The last rays of the setting sun were fading from the mountain-tops as the succoring party arrived at the camp of the wanderers. All was silent as the grave. The wasted forms of some of the wretched sufferers were reposing on beds of snow outside the miserable shelters which they had heaped up to protect them from the bitter nights. When they heard the shouts of the new comers, they feebly rose to a sitting posture and glared wildly at them. Women with faces that looked like death's heads were clasping to their hollow bosoms children which had wasted to skeletons.

Slowly the perception of the purpose for which their visitors had come, dawned upon their weakened intellects; they smiled, they gibbered, they stretched out their bony arms and hurrahed in hollow tones. Some began to stamp and rave, invoking the bitterest curses upon the mountains, the snow, and on the name of Lansford W. Hastings; others wept and bewailed their sad fate; the women alone showed firmness and self-possession; they fell down and prayed, thanking God for delivering them from a terrible fate, and imploring His blessing upon those who had come to their relief.

Upon going down into the cabins of this mountain camp, the party were presented with sights of woe and scenes of horror, the full tale of which never will and never should be told; sights which, although the emigrants had not yet commenced eating the dead, were so revolting that they were compelled to withdraw and make a fire where they would not be under the necessity of looking upon the painful spectacle.

Fourteen, nearly all men, had actually perished of hunger and cold. The remnant were in a condition beyond the power of language to describe, or even of the imagination to conceive. A spectacle more appalling was never presented in the annals of human suffering. For weeks many of the sufferers had been living on bullocks' hides, and even more loathsome food, and some, in the agonies of hunger, were about to dig up the bodies of their dead companions for the purpose of prolonging their own wretched existence.

The females showed that fertility of resource for which woman is so remarkable in trying crises. Mrs. Reed, who lived in Brinn's snow-cabin, had, during a considerable length of time, supported herself and four children by cracking and boiling again the bones from which Brinn's family had carefully scraped all the meat. These bones she had often taken and boiled again and again for the purpose of extracting the least remaining portion of nutriment. Mrs. Eddy and all but one of her children had perished.

The condition of the unfortunates drew tears from the eyes of their preservers. Their outward appearance was less painful and revolting, even, than the change which had taken place in their minds and moral natures.

"Many of them had in a great measure lost all self-respect. Untold sufferings had broken their spirits and prostrated everything like an honorable and commendable pride. Misfortune had dried up the fountains of the heart; and the dead, whom their weakness had made it impossible to carry out, were dragged from their cabins by means of ropes, with an apathy that afforded a faint indication of the change which a few weeks of dire suffering had produced in hearts that once sympathized with the distressed and mourned the departed. With many of them, all principle, too, had been swept away by this tremendous torrent of of accumulated and accumulating calamities. It became necessary to place a guard over the little store of provisions brought to their relief; and they stole and devoured the rawhide strings from the snowshoes of those who had come to deliver them. But some there were whom no temptation could seduce, no suffering move; who were

'Among the faithless faithful still.'

The brightest examples of these faithful few were to be found among the devoted women of that doomed band. In the midst of those terrible scenes when they seemed abandoned by God and man, the highest traits of the female character were constantly displayed. The true-hearted, affectionate wife, the loving, tender mother, the angel of mercy to her distressed comrades—in all these relations her woman's heart never failed her.

On the morning of February 20th John Rhodes, Daniel Tucker, and R. S. Mootrey, three of the party, went to the camp of George Donner, eight miles distant, taking with them a little beef. These sufferers were found with but one hide remaining. They had determined that, upon consuming this, they would dig up from the snow the bodies of those who had died

from starvation. Mr. Donner was helpless. Mrs.
Donner was weak, but in good health, and might have
come into the settlements with Mr. Glover's party,
yet she solemnly but calmly declared her determination to remain with her husband, and perform for him
the last sad offices of affection and humanity. And
this she did in full view of the fact that she must
necessarily perish by remaining behind."

The rescuing party, after consultation, decided that
their best course would be to carry the women and
children across the mountains, and then return for the
remnant of the sufferers. Accordingly, leaving in the
mountain-camp all the provisions that they could spare,
they commenced their return to the settlement with
twenty-three persons, principally women and children,
from whom, with a kind thoughtfulness, they concealed
the horrible story of the journey of Messrs. Eddy and
Foster.

A child of Mrs. Pike, and one of Mrs. Kiesburg,
were carried in the arms of two of the party. Hardly
had they marched two miles through the snow, when
two of Mrs. Reed's children became exhausted—one
of them a girl of eight, the other a little boy of four.

There were but two alternatives: either to return
with them to the mountain-camp, or abandon them to
death. When the mother was informed that it would
be necessary to take them back, a scene of the most
thrilling and painful interest ensued. She was a wife,
and her affection for her husband, who was then in the
settlement, dictated that she should go on; but she
was also a mother, and all-powerful maternal love
asserted its sway, and she determined to send forward

the two children who could walk, and return herself with the two youngest, and die with them.

No argument or persuasion on the part of Mr. Glover could shake her resolution. At last, in response to his solemn promises that, after reaching Bear River, he would return to the mountain-camp and bring back her children, after standing in silence for some moments, she turned from her darling babes and asked Mr. Eddy, "Are you a mason?" A reply being given in the affirmative, she said, "will you promise me, upon the word of a mason, that when you arrive at Bear River Valley, you will return and bring back my children if we do not meantime meet their father going for them?" "I do thus promise," Mr. Glover replied. "Then I will go on," said the mother, weeping bitterly as she pronounced the words. Patty, the little girl, then took her mother by the hand and said, "Well, mamma, kiss me good-bye! I shall never see you again. I am willing to go back to our mountain-camp and die, but I cannot consent to your going back. I shall die willingly if I can believe that you will see papa. Tell him good-bye for his poor little Patty."

The mother and the children lingered in a long embrace. As Patty turned from her mother to go back to the camp, she whispered to Mr. Glover and Mr. Mootrey, who were to take her, that she was willing to go back and take care of her little brother, but that she should never see her mother again.

Before reaching the settlement Mrs. Reed met her husband, who had been driven, for some cause, from the party several weeks before, and had succeeded in crossing the mountains in safety.

Messrs. Reed and McCutchen next headed a relief party, and crossed the mountains with supplies for the remainder of the emigrants. The Reed children were alive, but terribly wasted from their dreadful sufferings.

Hunger had driven the emigrants to revolting extremities. In some of the cabins were found parts of human bodies trussed and spitted for roasting, and traces of these horrid feasts were seen about the space in front of the doors where offal was thrown.

The persons taken under Mr. Reed's guidance on the return, were Patrick Brinn, wife and five children; Mrs. Graves, and four children; Mary and Isaac Donnor, children of Jacob Donner; Solomon Work, a step son of Jacob Donner, and two of his children. They reached the foot of the mountain without much difficulty; but they ascertained that their provisions would not last them more than a day and a half. Mr. Reed then sent three men forward with instructions to get supplies at a *cache* about fifteen miles from the camp. The party resumed its journey, crossed the Sierra Nevada, and after traveling about ten miles, encamped on a bleak point, on the north side of a little valley, near the head of the Yuba River. A storm set in, and continued for two days and three nights. On the morning of the third day, the clouds broke away and the weather became more intensely cold than it had been during the journey. The sufferings of the emigrants in their bleak camp were too dreadful to be described. There was the greatest difficulty in keeping up the fire, and during the night the women and children, who had on very thin clothing, were in great danger of freezing to death; when the storm passed away, the whole party were very weak, having passed two days without food. Leaving Patrick Brinn and his family and the rest of the party who were disabled, Mr. Reed, and his California friends, his two children, Solomon Hook and a Mr. Miller, pressed forward for supplies, and in five days they succeeded in reaching the settlement.

It was some weeks before a new relief party organized by Messrs. Eddy and Foster were successful in reaching the party which Reed had left. A shocking spectacle was presented to the eyes of the adventurers at the "Starved Camp" as they rightly named it. Patrick Brinn and his wife were sunning themselves with a look of vacuity upon their faces. They had eaten the two children of Jacob Donner: Mrs. Graves' body was lying near them with almost all the flesh cut from the arms and limbs. Her breasts, heart, and liver were then being boiled over the fire. Her child sat by the side of the mangled remains crying bitterly.

After being supplied with food they were left in charge of three men who undertook to conduct them to the settlement. Meanwhile Messrs. Eddy and Foster went on to the horrible mountain-camp only to be shocked and revolted by new scenes of horror. Strewed about the cabins and burrows, in the snow, were the fragments of human bodies from which the flesh had been stripped; among the *débris* of the hideous feasts sat the emaciated survivors looking more like cannibal-demons than human beings. Kiesburg had dug up the corpse of one of Mr. Eddy's children and devoured it, even when other food could be obtained, and the enfuriated father could with difficulty

30

be restrained from killing the monster on the spot. Of the five surviving children at the mountain-camp, three were those of Mr. and Mrs. Jacob Donner. When the time came for the party of unfortunates to start for the settlement under the guidance of their generous protectors, Mr. Donner's condition was so feeble that he was unable to accompany them, and though Mrs. Donner was capable of traveling, she utterly refused to leave her husband while he survived. In response to the solicitations of those who urged that her husband could live but a little longer, and that her presence would not add one moment to the remaining span of his life, she expressed her solemn and unalterable purpose which no hardship or danger could change, to remain and perform for him the last sad offices of duty and affection. At the same time she manifested the profoundest solicitude for her beloved children, and implored Mr. Eddy to save them, promising all that she possessed if he would convey them in safety to the settlement. He pledged himself to carry out her wishes without recompense, or perish in the attempt.

No provisions remained to supply the needs of these unhappy beings. At the end of two hours Mr. Eddy informed Mrs. Donner that a terrible necessity constrained him to depart. It was certain that Jacob Donner would never rise from the wretched couch on which he lay, worn out with toil and wasted by famine. It was almost equally certain that unless Mrs. Donner then abandoned her unfortunate partner and accompanied Mr. Eddy and his party to the settlement, she would die of wasting famine or perish violently at the hands of some lurking cannibal. By accompanying her children she could minister to their wants and perhaps be the means of saving their lives. The all-powerful maternal instinct combined with the love of life, urged her to fly with her children from the scene of so many horrors and dangers. Well might her reason have questioned her, "Why stay and meet inevitable death since you cannot save your husband from the grave which yawns to receive him? and when your presence, your converse and hands can only beguile the few remaining hours of his existence?" Time passed. By no entreaties could she enlarge the hour of departure which had now arrived. Nor did she seek to and thus endanger the lives of those who were hastening to depart. She must decide the dread question that moment.

Rarely in the long suffering record of woman, has she been placed in circumstances of such peculiar trial, but the love of life, the instinct of self preservation, and even maternal affection, could not triumph over her affection as a wife. Her husband begged her to save her life and leave him to die alone, assuring her that she could be of no service to him, as he could not probably survive under any circumstances until the next morning; with streaming eyes she bent over him, kissed his pale, emaciated, haggard, and even then, death-stricken cheek, and said:

"No! no! dear husband, I will remain with you, and here perish rather than leave you to die alone, with no one to soothe your dying sorrows, and close your eyes when dead. Entreat me not to leave you. Life, accompanied with the reflection that I had thus left you, would possess for me more than the bitterness of death; and death would be sweet with the thought in my last moments, that I had assuaged one pang of yours in your passage into eternity. No! no! no!" she repeated, sobbing convulsively.

The parting interview between the parents and the children is represented to have been one that can never be forgotten as long as reason remains or the memory performs its functions. In the dying father the fountain of tears was dried up; but the agony on his death-stricken face and the feeble pressure of his hand on the brow of each little one as it bade him adieu for ever, told the story of his last great sorrow. As Mrs. Donner clasped her children to her heart in a parting embrace, she turned to Mr. Eddy with streaming eyes and sobbed her last words, " O, save, save, my children!"

This closing scene in the sad and eventful careers of those unfortunate emigrants was the crowning act in a long and terrible drama which illustrated, under many conditions of toil, hardship, danger, despair, and death, the courage, fortitude, patience, love, and devotion of woman.

CHAPTER XX.

MIND-POWER and heart-power—these are the forces that move the moral universe. Which is the stronger, who shall say? If the former is within the province of the man, the latter is still more exclusively the prerogative of woman. With this she wins and rules her empire, with this she celebrates her noblest triumphs, and proves herself to be the God-delegated consoler and comforter of mankind. This is the power which moves the will to deeds of charity and mercy, which awakens the latent sympathies for suffering humanity, which establishes the law of kindness, soothes the irritated and perturbed spirit, and pours contentment and happiness into the soul.

If we could collect and concentrate into one great pulsating organ all the noble individual emotions that have stirred a million human hearts, what a prodigious agency would that be to act for good upon the world! And yet we may see something of the operation of just such an agency if we search the record of our time, watch the inner movements which control society and reflect that nearly every home contains a fractional portion of this beneficent agency, each fraction working in its way, and according to its measure, in harmony with all the others towards the same end.

Warm and fruitful as the sunshine, and subtle, too, as the ether which illumines the solar walk, we can

(469)

gauge the strength of this agency only by its results. Nor can we by the symbols of language fully compass and describe even these results.

The man of science can measure the great forces of physical nature; heat, electricity, and light can all be gauged by mechanisms constructed by his hand, but by no device can he measure the forces of our moral nature.

The poet, whose insight is deeper than others' into this great and mysterious potency, can only give glimpses of its source, and draw tears by painting, in words, the traits which it induces.

The historian and biographer can record and dwell with fondness upon the acts of men and women, which were prompted by this power of the soul.

The moralist can point to them as examples to follow, or as cheering evidence of the loftier impulses of humanity. But still, in its depth and height, in its fountain, and in its remotest outflow, this power cannot be fully measured or appreciated by any standards known to man. The comprehensive and conceptive faculty of the imagination is wearied in placing before itself the springs, the action, and the boundless beneficence of this grand force, which flourishes and lives in its highest efficiency in the breast of woman. "Thanks," cries the poet of nature and of God,

> " Thanks, to the human heart, by which we live,
> Thanks to its tenderness, its joys, its fears."

We have shown how in all the ages since the landing, woman has proved her title to the possession of the manly virtues. We have shown her as a heroine, battling with the hostile powers of man and nature,

and yet, even in those cases, if we were to analyze
the motives which prompted her heroic acts, we should
find them to spring at last from the source of power
whereof we are speaking.   It is out of her abounding
and forceful emotional nature that she becomes a
heroine.   It is to relieve, to succor, or to save her dear
ones, that she is brave, strong, enduring, patient, and
devoted.

Frontier life has called upon her for the exercise of
these qualities, and she has nobly responded to the
call.   She fought; she toiled; she was undaunted by
the apprehension of dangers and difficulties as well as
intrepid in facing them.   She bore without complaint
the privations and hardships incident to such a life,
and taxed every resource of body and mind in efforts
to secure for her successors a home which neither
peril nor trial should assail.

But this did not embrace the entire circle of her
acts and her influence.   To soothe, to comfort, to sustain in the trying time, to throw over the darkest hour
the brightness of her sunny presence and sweet voice—
by these influences she did more to establish and con-
firm that civilization which our race has been carrying
westward, than by even those exhibitions of manly
heroism of which we have spoken.

Nine generations of men and women, through a
period which a few years more will make three centuries, have been engaged in extending the frontier line,
or have lived surrounded by circumstances similar to
those which environ the remote border.   The aggregate number of these men and women cannot be any
more than estimated.   Doubtless it will amount to
many millions.   A million helpmeets and comforters

ın a million homes! Mothers, wives, daughters, sisters—all supporting and buoying up the well-nigh
broken spirits of the "stronger sex," and, by simple
words, encouraging and stimulating to repair their
desperate fortunes. Who can calculate the sum total
of such an influence as this?

Among the myriad instances of the solacing and
soul-inspiring power of a woman's voice in hours of
darkness on the lonely border, we select a few for
the purpose of showing her in this her appropriate
domain.

Nearly two centuries ago, in one of those heated
religious controversies which occurred in a river settlement in Massachusetts, a young man and his wife
felt themselves constrained, partly through a desire
for greater liberty of thought and action, and partly
from natural energy of disposition, to push away from
the fertile valley and establish their home on one of
those bleak hillsides which form the spurs of the
Green Mountain range. Here they set up their
household deities, and lit the lights of the fireside in
the darkness of the forest, and amid the wild loneliness of nature's hitherto untended domain.

In such situations as these, not merely from their
isolation, but from the sterility of the soil and the
inhospitable air of the region, the struggle for existence
is often a severe one. Perseverance and self-denial,
however, triumphed over all difficulties. Year after
year the trees bowed themselves before the axe, and
the soil surrendered its reluctant treasures in the fur-
row of the ploughshare.

Plenty smiled around the cabin. The light glowed

on the hearth, and the benighted traveler hailed its welcome rays as he fared towards the hospitable door.

Apart from the self-interest and happiness of its inmates, it was no small benefit to others that such a home was made in that rugged country. Such homes are the outposts of the army of pioneers: here they can pause and rest, gathering courage and confidence when they regard them as establishments in the same wilderness where they are seeking to plant themselves.

Five years after their arrival their house and barns were destroyed by fire. Their cattle, farming utensils, and household furniture were all fortunately saved, and before long the buildings were replaced, and in two years all the ravages of the devouring element had been repaired. Again a happy and plenteous abode rewarded the labors of the pair. Three years rolled away in the faithful discharge of every duty incumbent upon them, each toiling in their respective sphere to increase their store and rear their large family of children.

A series of severe rains had kept them within doors for nearly ten days. One afternoon as they were sitting before their fire they experienced a peculiar sensation as though the ground on which the house stood was moving. Running out doors, they saw that the rains had loosened the hill-side soil from the rock on which it lay, and that it was slowly moving into the ravine below. Hastily collecting their children, they had barely time to escape to a rock a short distance from their house, when the landslide carried the house and barns, with the ground on which they stood, into the ravine, burying them and their entire contents beneath twenty feet of earth.

Almost worn out with his unremitting toils continued through ten years, and seeing the fruits of that
toil swept away in an instant, looking around him in
vain for any shelter, and far away from any helping
hand, it was not surprising that the man should have
given way to despair. He wept, groaned, and tore
his hair, declaring that he would struggle no longer
with fates which proved so adverse. "Go," said he,
"Mary, to the nearest house with the children. I
will die here."

His wife was one of those fragile figures which it
seemed that a breath could blow away. Hers, however,
was an organization which belied its apparent weakness. A brave and loving spirit animated that frail
tenement. Long she strove to soothe her husband's
grief, but without avail.

Gathering a thick bed of leaves and sheltering her
children as well as she could from the chilly air, she
returned ever and anon to the spot where her husband
sat in the stupor of despair, and uttered words of
comfort and timely suggestions of possible means of
relief.

"We began with nothing, John, and we can begin
with nothing again. You are strong, and so am I.
Bethink yourself of those who pass by on their way to
the great river every year at this time. These folk are
good and neighborly, and will lend us willing hands
to dig out of the earth the gear that we have lost by
the landslip." Thus through the night, with these
and like expressions, she comforted and encouraged
the heart-broken man, and having at length kindled
hope, succeeded in rousing him to exertion.

For two days the whole family suffered greatly

while awaiting help, but that hope which the words of the wife had awakened, did not again depart. A party of passing emigrants, ascertaining the condition of the family, all turned to, and having the necessary tools, soon dug down to the house and barn, and succeeded in recovering most of the buried furniture, stores, and utensils. The unlucky couple succeeded finally in retrieving themselves, and years after, when the father was passing a prosperous old age in the valley of the Mohawk, to which section the family eventually moved, he was wont to tell how his wife had lifted him out of the depths of despair by those kind and thoughtful words, and put new life and hope into his heart during those dark days among the mountains of Massachusetts.

There is no section of our country where the presence of woman is so strong for good, and where her words of lofty cheer to the stricken and distressed are so potential as in the mountain republics on our extreme western border. There are in that section communities composed almost entirely of men who not only treat the few of the other sex who live among them, with a chivalrous respect, but who listen to their words as if they were heaven-sent messages. In one of the mining settlements of California, during the early years of that State, an epidemic fever broke out, and raged with great malignity among the miners. The settlement was more than two hundred miles from San Francisco, in a secluded mountain gorge, barren of all but the precious metal which had attracted thither a rough and motley multitude. There was no doctor within a hundred miles, and not a single female to nurse and watch the forlorn subjects of the pestilence.

Mrs. Maurice, a married lady who had recently come from the east to San Francisco with her husband, hearing of the distress which prevailed in that mountain district, immediately set out, in company with her husband, who heartily sympathized with her generous enterprise, and crossed the Sierra Nevada for the purpose of ministering to the wants of the sick. She carried a large supply of medicines and other necessaries, and after a toilsome journey over the rough foot-paths which were then the only avenues by which the place could be reached, arrived at the settlement. By some means the miners had become apprised of her approach, and she was met by a cavalcade of rough-bearded men, a score in number, mounted on mules, as a guard of honor to escort her to the scene of her noble labors. As she came in sight, riding down the mountain side, the escort party waved their huge hats in the air and hurrahed as if they were mad, while the tears streamed down their swarthy cheeks. With heads uncovered they ranged themselves on either side of the lady and her husband, and accompanied them to the place where the pestilence was raging. Some of the sick men rose from their beds and stood with pale, fever-wasted faces at the doors of their wretched cabins, and smiled feebly and tried to shout as the noble woman drew near. Their voices were hollow and sepulchral, and the ministering angel who had visited them witnessed this moving spectacle not without tears. For two months she passed her time night and day in watching over and ministering to those unfortunate men. Snatching a nap now and then, every other available moment was given to her patients. Many died, and after receiving their last messages to friends far away in the east, she closed their eyes and passed on in her errand of mercy.

One of her patients thus testified to the efficacy of her ministrations : " As I owe my recovery to her exertions, I rejoice to give my testimony to her un- tiring zeal, her self-sacrificing devotion, and her angelic kindness. She never seemed to me to be happy ex- cept when engaged in alleviating the sufferings of us who were sick, and she watched over us with all the tenderness and love of a mother. Many of the sick men called her by that endeared name, and we all seemed to be her children.

" Even in the gloomiest cabins and to the most dis- heartened of the fever-stricken, her presence seemed to bring sunshine. Her face always wore a smile so sweet that I forgot my pain when I gazed upon her. Her voice rings in my ears even now. It was pecu- liarly soft and musical, and I never heard her speak but I recalled those lines of the great dramatist, ' Her voice was ever low, an excellent thing in woman.' Every sufferer waited to hear her speak and seemed to hang upon her accents. Her words were few, but so kind that we all felt that with such a friend to help us we could not long be sick.

" She was entirely forgetful of herself, so much did the poor invalids dwell in her thoughts.

" The storms of autumn raged with frightful violence throughout that gorge, and yet I have known her, while the wind was howling and the rain pouring, to go round three times in one night to the bedsides of those whose lives were hanging by a thread. Once I rccollect after my recovery, going to see a young man who was very low and seemed to have life only while Mrs. Maurice bent over him. She had visited him early that evening, and had promised to come and see him again after making her rounds among her other patients. A fierce snow storm had come up and a strong man could barely maintain himself before the blast. I found the poor fellow very low. He was evidently sinking rapidly. He moved feebly and turned away his eyes, which were fixed upon me as I entered. It was already considerably past the hour when it was expected she would return, and as I bent to ask him how he was, he looked into my face with a bright eager gaze, and said in a whisper, "ask mother to come." I knew in an instant whom he meant and said I would go in search of her and conduct her thither through the storm.

I had only reached the door when she met me. I never shall forget her appearance as she entered out of the howling storm and stood in that dim light all radiant with kindness and sympathy, which beamed from her face and seemed to illumine the room. The sufferer's face brightened and his frame seemed to have a sudden life breathed into it when he saw her enter. It seemed to me as if she had a miraculous healing power, for that moment he began to mend, and in a few weeks was restored to his pristine health."

It was beyond doubt that her presence and gentle words were more potent in effecting cures than were the medicines which she administered. Those who recovered and walked out when they saw her approaching, even at a distance, were wont to remove their hats and stand as she went by gazing at her as if she was an angel of light.

The scene after the last patient was convalescent, and when she came to take her departure, was indescribable. All the miners quit work and gathered in the village; a party was appointed to escort her to the mountain and the rest formed a long line on each side and stood bareheaded and some of them weeping as she passed through.

The mounted men accompanied her and her husband and their guide to the top of the mountain. All of the escort had been her patients and some of them were still wasted and wan from the fever. When they bade her farewell there was not a dry eye among them, and long after she had left them they could have been seen gazing after the noble matron who had visited and comforted them in their grievous sickness and pain.

Life in the Rocky Mountains before the great transcontinental line was built was remarkable for concentrating in itself the extremest forms of almost every peril, hardship, and privation which is incident to the frontier. Even at the present day and with the increased facilities for reaching the Atlantic and Pacific coast by that single railroad, the greater part of the region far north and far south of that line of travel is still isolated from the world by vast distances and great natural obstacles to communication between the different points of settlement.

So much the more valuable and stronger therefore upon that field is the emotional force of good women. Such there were and are scattered through that rocky wilderness whose ministrations, in many a lonely cabin, and with many a wayfaring band, are like those of the angel who visited the prophet of old when he dwelt "in a desert apart."

An incident is told of a party of emigrants, who were journeying through Idaho that powerfully illustrates this idea.

There were five in the party, viz. James Peterson, an aged man, his two daughters, his son, and his son's wife.

While pursuing their toilsome and devious course through the gorges and up and down the steeps, a friendly Indian whom they met informed them that a few miles from the route they were following, a body of men were starving in an almost inaccessible ravine where they had been prospecting for gold. Mr. Peterson and his son, although they pitied the unfortunate gold hunters, were disinclined to turn from their course, judging that the difficulties of reaching them, and of conveying the necessary stores over the rocks and across the rapid torrents were such that they would render the attempt wholly impracticable.

The two daughters, as well as the wife of young Peterson, refused to listen to the cold dictates of prudence which controlled Mr. Peterson and his son: they saw in imagination only the wretched starving men, and and their hearts yearned to relieve them.

Turning a deaf ear to the arguments and persuasions of the elder and younger Peterson, they urged in eloquent and pleading tones that they might be allowed to follow the impulses of kindness and pity and visit the objects of their compassion. The father could stay with the team and the brother and husband could accompany them under the guidance of the Indian, on their errand of mercy.

Their prayers and persuasions at last prevailed over the objections which were offered. Selecting the most concentrated and nourishing food which their store of provisions embraced, young Peterson and the Indian loaded themselves with all that they could carry, the three women, who were strong and active, also bearing a portion of the supplies. The party, after a most difficult and toilsome march on foot, succeeded in reaching the top of the mountain, from which they could look down into the ravine upon the spot where the unfortunate men were encamped. They could see no sign of life, and feared they had come too late.

As they neared the place, picking their way down precipices where a single misstep would have been death, one of the women waved her handkerchief and the men shouted at the top of their voices. No response came back except the echoes which reverberated from the wall of the mountain opposite. The rays of the setting sun fell on seven human forms stretched on the ground. One of these forms at length raised itself to a sitting posture and gazed with a dazed look at the rescuers hastening towards them. The rest had given up all hope and lain down to die.

A spoonful of stimulant was immediately administered to each of the seven sufferers, and kindling a fire, the women quickly prepared broth with the dried meat which they had brought. The starving men were in a light-headed condition, induced by long fasting, and could scarcely comprehend that they were saved. "Who be those, Jim, walking round that fire; not women?" said one of the men. "No, Pete," was the reply, "them's angels; didn't you hear 'em sing to us a spell ago?" The kind words with which the three women had sought to recall the wretched way-farers to life and hope might well have been mistaken for an angel's song. One of the men afterwards said he dreamed he was in heaven, and when his eyes were opened by the sound of those sweet voices, and he saw those noble girls, he knew his dream had come true.

Another said that those voices brought him back to life and hope, more than all the food and stimulants.

For a week these angels of mercy nursed and fed the starving men, the Indian meanwhile having shot a mountain goat, which increased their supplies, and at the end of that period the men were sufficiently recruited to start, in company with their preservers, for the camp, where Mr. Peterson was awaiting the return of his daughters, of whose safety he had been already informed by the Indian.

When the rescued men came to bid them farewell, they brought a bag containing a hundred pounds weight of gold dust, the price for which would have been their lives, but for those devoted women, and begged them to accept it, not as a reward, but as a token of their gratitude. The girls refused to take the gift, believing that the adventurous miners needed it, and that they had been amply rewarded by the reflection that they had saved seven lives.

The parting, on both sides, was tearful, the rough miners being more affected than even the women. Each party pursued its separate course, the one towards Oregon, the other towards Utah; but after the Peter-sons had reached the spot where they encamped that night, they discovered the bag of gold, which the miners had secretly deposited in the wagon. The treasure thus forced upon them was divided between the Miss Petersons and their sister-in-law. Bright and pure as that metal was, it was incomparably less lustrous than the deeds which it rewarded, and infinitely less pure than the motives which prompted them.

Finely has a poet of our own time celebrated the wondrous power of those words of cheer and comfort which woman utters so often to the unfortunate.

> O! ever when the happy laugh is dumb,
> All the joy gone, and all the sorrow come,
> When loss, despair, and soul-distracting pain,
> Wring the sad heart and rack the throbbing brain,
> The only hope—the only comfort heard—
> Comes in the music of a woman's word.
> Like beacon-bell on some wild island shore,
> Silverly ringing through the tempest's roar,
> Whose sound borne shipward through the ocean gloom
> Tells of the path and turns her from her doom.

Acting within their own homes, who can sum up the entire amount of good which the frontier wife, mother, sister, and daughter have accomplished in their capacities as emotional and sympathetic beings? How many fevered brows have they cooled, how many gloomy moods have they illumined, how many wavering hearts have they stayed and confirmed!

This service of the heart is rendered so freely and so often that it ceases to attract the attention it merits. Like the vital air and sunshine, it is so free and spontaneous that one rarely pauses to thank God for it. The outflow of sympathy, the kind word or act, and all the long sacrifice of woman's days pass too often without a thought, or a word, from those who perhaps might droop and die without them.

England has its Westminster Abbey, beneath whose clustered arches statesmen, philanthropists, warriors, and kings repose in a mausoleum, whither men repair to gaze at the monumental bust, the storied urn, and proud epitaph; but where is the mausoleum which preserves the names and virtues of those gentle, un-obtrusive women—the heroines and comforters of the frontier home?   In the East, the simple slabs of stone which record their names have crumbled into the dust of the churchyard.   In the far West, they sleep on the prairie and mountain slope, with scarcely a memorial to mark the spot.

Nowhere more strongly are the manifestations of heart-power shown than among the women of our remote border.   Speaking of them, one who long lived in that region says, "If you are sick, there is nothing which sympathy and care can devise or per-form, which is not done for you.   No sister ever hung over the throbbing brain, or fluttering pulse, of a brother with more tenderness and fidelity.   This is as true of the lady whose hand has only figured · her embroidery or swept her guitar, as of the cottage-girl, wringing from her laundry the foam of the mountain stream.   If I must be cast, in sickness or destitution, on the care of a stranger, let it be in California; but let it be before avarice has hardened the heart and made a god of gold."

What is said of the California wives, mothers, and sisters, may, with equal force, be applied to woman throughout the whole vast mountain region, including ten immense states and territories.   In the mining districts, on the wild cattle ranche, in the eyrie, perched, like an eagle's nest, on the crest of those sky-piercing summits, or on the secluded valley farm, wherever there is a home to be brightened, a sick bed to be tended, or a wounded spirit to be healed, there is woman seen as a minister of comfort, consolation, and joy.

The military posts on the frontier have long had reason to thank the wives of the soldiers and officers for their kindness, manifested in numberless ways.

One of these ladies was Mrs. R————, who accompanied her husband to his post on the Rio Grande, in 1856.

Here she remained with him for more than three years, till that grand mustering of all the powers of the Republic to the long contested battle-grounds along the Potomac. Their life on the Mexican frontier was full of interest, novelty, and adventure. The First Artillery was often engaged in repulsing the irregular and roving bands of Cortinas, who rode over the narrow boundary river in frequent raids and stealing expeditions into Texas. When in camp, Mrs. Ricketts greatly endeared herself to the men in her husband's company by constant acts of kindness to the sick, and by showing a cheerful and lively disposition amid all the hardships and annoyances of garrison life, at such a distance from home and from the comforts and refinements of our American civilization.

She was a spirit of mercy as well as good cheer; and many a poor fellow knew that, if he could but get her ear, his penance in the guard-house for some violation of the regulations, would be far less severe on account of her gentle and womanly plea.

She afterwards shared her husband's imprisonment

in Richmond. Captain R—— had been severely wounded and grew rapidly worse. The gloomiest forebodings pressed like lead upon the brave heart of the devoted wife. Again the surgeons consulted over his dreadfully swollen leg, and prescribed amputation; and again it was spared to the entreaties of his wife, who was certain that his now greatly enfeebled condition would not survive the shock. Much of the time he lay unconscious, and for weeks his life depended entirely on the untiring patience and skill with which his wife soothed down the rudeness of his prison-house, cheering him and other prisoners who were so fortunate as to be in the room with him, and alleviating the slow misery that was settling like a pall upon him.

As the pebble which stirs the lake in wider and ever wider circles, so the genial emotion which begins in the family extends to the neighborhood, and sometimes embraces the whole human race. Hence arises the philanthropic kindness of some, and the large-hearted charity that is willing to labor anywhere and in any manner to relieve the wants of all who are suffering pain or privation.

In all our wars from the Revolutionary contest to the present time, woman's work in the army hospitals, and even on the battle-field, as a nurse, has been a crown to womanhood and a blessing to our civilization and age. Many a life that had hitherto been marked only by the domestic virtues and the charities of home, became enlarged and ennobled in this wider sphere of duty.

Wrestling in grim patience with unceasing pain; to lie weak and helpless, thinking of the loved ones

on the far off hillside, or thirsty with unspeakable
longing for one draught of cold water from the spring
by the big rock at the old homestead; to yearn,
through long, hot nights, for one touch of the cool,
soft hand of a sister or a wife on the throbbing
temples, the wounded soldier saw with joy unspeakable the coming of these ministering angels. Then
the great gashes would be bathed with cooling washes,
or the grateful draught poured between the thin,
chalky lips, or the painful, inflamed stump would be
lifted and a pad of cool, soft lint, fitted under it.
These ministrations carried with them a moral cheer
and a soothing that was more salutary and healing
than medicines and creature comforts.

The poor wounded soldier was assured in tones, to
whose pleasant and homelike accents his ear had long
been a stranger, that his valor should not be forgotten,
that they too had a son, a brother, a father, or a
husband in the army. After a pallid face and bony
fingers were bathed, sometimes a chapter in the New
Testament or a paragraph from the newspapers would
be read in tones low but distinct, in grateful contrast
to the hoarse battle shouts that had been lingering in
his ear for weeks.

Then the good lady would act as amanuensis for
some poor fellow who had an armless sleeve, and write
down for loving eyes and heavy hearts in some distant
village the same old soldier's story, told a thousand
times by a thousand firesides, but always more charming than any story in the Arabian Nights,—how, on
that great day, he stood with his company on a
hillside, and saw the long line of the enemy come
rolling across the valley; how, when the cannon

opened on them, he could see the rough, ragged gaps opening in the line; how they closed up and moved on; how this friend fell on one side, and poor Jimmy ———— on the other; and then he felt a general crash, and a burning pain, and the musket dropped out of his hand; then the ambulance and the amputation, and what the surgeon said about his pluck; and then the weakness, and the pain, and the hunger; and how much better he was now; and how kind the ladies had been to him.

Such offices as these lift woman above the plane of earthly experience and place her a little lower than the angels. Only she *can* fill the measure of such duties, and only she *does* fill them.

Among the deities of the Eastern Pantheon, the god representing the destroyer is embodied under the form of a man, while the preserver is symbolized under the form of a woman. This is an adaptation in Polytheism of a great and true idea. Woman is a preserver. Her's is the conservative influence of society. It is from man that the destructive forces that shake the social organization emanate. He wars on his kind and the earth shakes under the tread of his armies. He organizes those mighty revolutionary movements which pull down the fabric of states. He is restless, aggressive, warlike. But it is woman's province to keep. Her mission is peace.

A party of soldiers passing through the western wilds, sees in the distance a body of horsemen approaching. Cocking their rifles and putting themselves in a defensive attitude, they prepare for battle. But when they see that there are women among the riders who are galloping towards them, they relax their line and restore their rifles to their shoulders. They know there will be no battle, for woman's presence means peace.

Woman is the guardian of our race. In the household she is saving; in the family she is protecting, and everywhere her influence is that which keeps.

It is this characteristic that makes her presence on the frontier so essential to a successful prosecution of true pioneer enterprises. The man's work is one of destruction and subjugation. He must level the forest, break the soil, and fight all the forces that oppose him in his progress. Woman guards the health and life of the household, hoards the stores of the family, and economizes the surplus strength of her husband, father, or son.

We are speaking now of the sex as it is seen in a new country and in remote settlements. In crowded cities, amid a superabundant wealth, and an idle and luxurious mode of life, we see too often the types of selfish, frivolous, and conventional females such as are hardly known on the border. But even in these populous districts the same spirit is not unfrequently shown, with important results, in respect to the accumulation of great fortunes.

Some forty years since, a capitalist who now counts his fortune by the tens of millions, informed his wife that if he was only in possession of five thousand dollars, he could derive great gains from a business into which he designed to enter. To his astonishment she immediately brought him a bank book showing a balance of five thousand dollars, the savings of many years, and told him to use it as he thought best.

Those hoardings judiciously invested laid the foundation of one of the largest properties owned by a single man upon this continent.

As a conserving agency, the spirit and influence of woman is of course most strongly exerted within the circle of her own family. Here she knits the ties that binds that circle together, and gathers and holds the material and moral resources which make the household what it is. When disaster comes, it is her study to prevent disintegration and keep the home uninjured and unbroken.

While a family were flying from a ferocious band of tories during the Revolution, in the confusion, one of the children was left behind. It was the eldest daughter who first discovered the fact, and only she dared to return and save her little brother from their blood-thirsty enemies. It was dark and rainy, and imminent danger would attend the effort to rescue the lad. But the brave girl hastened back; reached the house still in possession of the British; begged the sentinel to let her enter; and though repeatedly repulsed doubled the earnestness of her entreaties, and finally gained admittance. She found the child in his chamber, hastened down stairs and passing the sentry, fled with the shot whizzing past her head, and with the child soon joined the rest of the family.

When deprived of her natural protector and left the sole guardian of her children she becomes a prodigy of watchful care.

Some years since, one of the small islands on our coast was inhabited by a single poor family. The father was taken suddenly ill. There was no physician. The wife, on whom every labor for the household devolved, was sleepless in care and tenderness by the bedside of her suffering husband. Every remedy in her power to procure was administered, but the disease was acute, and he died.

Seven young children mourned around the lifeless corpse. They were the sole beings upon that desolate spot. Did the mother indulge the grief of her spirit, and sit down in despair? No! she entered upon the arduous and sacred duties of her station. She felt that there was no hand to assist her in burying her dead. Providing, as far as possible, for the comfort of her little ones, she put her babe into the arms of the oldest, and charged the two next in age to watch the corpse of their father. She unmoored her husband's fishing boat, which, but two days before, he had guided over the seas to obtain food for his family. She dared not yield to those tender recollections which might have unnerved her arm. The nearest island was at the distance of three miles. Strong winds lashed the waters to foam. Over the loud billows, that wearied and sorrowful woman rowed, and was preserved. She reached the next island, and obtained the necessary aid. With such energy did her duty to her desolate babes inspire her, that the voyage which depended upon her individual effort was performed in a shorter time than the returning one, when the oars were managed by two men, who went to assist in the last offices to the dead.

But female influence in the way of conservation, is not bounded by the narrow limits of home, family, and kindred. It is also seen on a wider field and in the preservation of other interests. The property, health, and life of strangers often become the object of woman's careful guardianship. Nearly thirty years since a heavily freighted vessel set sail from an English port bound for the Pacific coast. After a voyage of more than three months it reached the Sandwich Islands, and after remaining there a week, sailed in the direction of Oregon and British Columbia.

When two days out from Honolulu, the captain and mate were taken down with fever, which not only confined them to their berths, but by its delirium incapacitated them from giving instructions respecting the navigation of the vessel. The third officer, upon whom the command devolved, was shortly afterwards washed overboard and lost in a gale. The rest of the crew were of the most common and ignorant class of sailors, not even knowing how to read and write. The heavens, overspread with clouds which obscured both the sun and the stars, was a sealed book to the man at the wheel, and the good ship, at the mercy of the winds and waves, was drifting they knew not whither.

At this juncture the wife of the captain stepped to the front, and boldly assumed the command. She had been reared on Cape Cod, and was a woman of uncommon intelligence and strength of character. Her husband, in the early stages of his illness, had thoughtfully instructed her in the rudiments of navigation, and foreseeing that such knowledge might be the means of enabling her to steer the ship safely to port, she diligently employed every moment that she could spare from the necessary attendance on the sick men, in studying the manual of navigation. She soon learned how to calculate latitude and longitude. When the third officer was washed overboard she knew that all must then depend upon her, and at once put herself in communication with the steersman, and instructed him as to their true position. The men all recognized the value of her knowledge, and obeyed her as if she had been their chief from the outset. The correctness of her calculations was soon proved, and such was her firmness and kindness while in command, that the sailors came to regard her as a superior being who had been sent from heaven to help them out of their dangers. The clouds at length cleared away, the wind subsided, and after a voyage of twenty-five days, the ship made the mouth of the Columbia River. Meanwhile by diligent nursing she had also contributed to save the lives of her husband and his second officer. But for her knowledge and firmness it was acknowledged by all that the ship would have been lost; and a large salvage was allowed her by the owners as a reward for her energy and intelligence in saving the vessel and its valuable cargo.

Another of these guardians on the deep was Mrs. Spalding, of Georgia. She was one of those patriot women of the Revolution of whom we have already spoken. The part she bore in that struggle, and the anxieties to which she had been necessarily subjected, so impaired her health that some years after the termination of the war an ocean voyage and a European climate was prescribed for her restoration.

While crossing the Atlantic a large ship painted black, carrying twelve guns, was seen to windward running across their course. She was evidently either a privateer or a pirate. As there was no hope of outsailing her, it was judged best to boldly keep the ves-

sel on her course, trusting that its size and appearance
might deter the strange craft from attacking it.

Mr. Spalding, realizing the danger of their situation,
and not daring to trust himself with an interview till
the crisis was past, requested the captain to go below
and do what he could for the security of his family.

The captain on visiting the cabin, found that Mrs.
Spalding had placed her daughter-in-law and the other
inmates of the cabin, for safety, in the two state-rooms,
filling the berths with the cots and bedding from the
outer cabin.   She had then taken her station beside
the scuttle, which led from the outer cabin to the
magazine, with two buckets of water.   Having noticed
that the two cabin-boys were heedless, she had determined herself to keep watch over the magazine.
She did so till the danger was past.   The captain took
in his light sails, hoisted his boarding nettings, opened
his ports, and stood on upon his course.   The privateer
waited till the ship was within a mile, then fired a gun
to windward, and stood on her way.   This ruse preserved the ship.

America, like England, has had her Grace Darlings,
whose lives have been devoted to the rescue of drowning sailors.   Such a life was that of Kate Moore, who
some years since resided on a secluded island in the
Sound.   Disasters frequently occur to vessels which
are driven round Montauk Point, and sometimes in
the Sound when they are homeward bound; and at
such times she was always on the alert.   She had so
thoroughly cultivated the sense of hearing, that she
could distinguish amid the howling storm the shrieks
of the drowning mariners, and thus direct a boat,
which she had learned to manage most dexterously,

in the darkest night, to the spot where a fellow mortal was perishing. Though well educated and refined, she possessed none of the affected delicacy which characterizes too many town-bred misses, but, adapting herself to the peculiar exigencies of her father's humble yet honorable calling, she was ever ready to lend a helping hand, and shrank from no danger if duty pointed that way. In the gloom and terror of the stormy night, amid perils at all hours of the day and all seasons of the year, she launched her barque on the threatening waves, and assisted her aged and feeble father in saving the lives of twenty-one persons during the last fifteen years. Such conduct, like that of Grace Darling, to whom Kate Moore has been justly compared, needs no comment; it stamps its moral at once and indelibly upon the heart of every reader.

That great land ocean which stretches southwestward from Fort Leavenworth on the Missouri, to the fountains of the great rivers of Texas, has its perils to be guarded against as well as the stormy Atlantic. The voyagers over that expanse, as well as the mariners on the ocean, have not seldom owed their safety to the watchfulness of the prairie woman, who possesses, in common with her more cultivated and conventional sisters, a keen insight into character. This enables her to take early note of danger arising from the agency of bad men, and avoid it.

In 1858, a gentleman, accompanied by a Creek Indian as a guide, while escorting his sister to her husband, who was stationed at Fort Wayne, in the Indian Territory, near the southwest corner of Missouri, lost the trail, and the party found themselves, at nightfall, in an immense plain, which showed no signs of any habitation. Riding southward in the darkness, they saw, at last, a light twinkling in the distance, and, directing their course toward it, they discovered that it proceeded from the window of a lonely cabin. Knocking at the door, a man of singularly repulsive appearance responded to the summons—invited them in. Three rough-looking characters were sitting around the fire. The hospitalities of the cabin were bargained for, the horses and Indian being quartered in a shed, while the gentleman and his sister were provided with shakedowns in the two partitions of the loft. The only inmates of the house besides the four whom we have mentioned was a girl some fifteen years of age, the daughter of one of the men. The lady, who was very much fatigued, was waited upon by this girl, who moved about as if she was in a dream. She was very pale, and had a look as if she was repressing some great fear, or was burdened by some terrible secret.

When she accompanied the lady to her sleeping apartment, she whispered to her hurriedly that she wished to speak to her brother, but begged her to call him without making any noise, as their lives depended upon their preserving silence. The lady, though astonished and terrified at such a revelation at that hour and place, checked the exclamation which rose to her lips, and, lifting the partition of cotton cloth which hung between the apartments, in a low tone asked her brother to come and hear what the girl had to say.

Her information was of a terrible character. They were, she said, in a den of murderers. She knew not how they could escape, unless by a miracle. It was the intention of the assassins, she believed, to murder and rob the whole party: Then, telling them to keep awake and be on their guard, she glided down to the room below. The brother and sister, listening sharply for a few minutes, heard the girl say in a loud tone, as if she intended the guests should hear her, that she was going out to the shed to look for her ear-ring, which she believed she had dropped there. They surmised she was going to put the Indian on his guard.

The gentleman had a pair of revolvers, and resolved to sell his life dearly, should he be attacked. Peering down into the room below, he saw, by the dim light, the ruffians making preparations for bloody work. Axes, knives, pistols, and guns had been brought out, and, in low whispers, the miscreants were evidently discussing the plan of attack. Sometime after midnight two of the men stole out of the door, with the obvious intention of killing the Indian, as the first act in the bloody drama. For a few minutes after their disappearance all was still, and then the silence was broken by two pistols shots in quick succession, followed by a triumphant war-whoop, which served to tell the story. The Indian, who was also armed with a revolver, must have shot his two assailants. The gentleman fired down the hatchway of the loft, killing one of the villains as he was running out of the door. The other, after shouting loudly for his partners in murder, took to his heels and fled away.

It appeared that the Indian guide, having been notified of his danger by the girl, rose from his bed and ensconced himself behind the shed. When the two men came out to attack him, he shot them both dead, and then waited, expecting that the others

32

would have come out and furnished him with a new target.

The girl came out of her hiding place, whither she had run on hearing the shots, and looked sharply into the faces of the three dead ruffians, and finding that her father was not among them, expressed her joy that her unworthy parent had escaped the fate he richly deserved.

She told her story to the gentleman and lady while they were standing on guard and waiting for the morning to dawn. It appeared that she had been brought to the den a few days before by her father, and had become knowing to a murder which he and his companions had committed. Her mother, a pious woman, had instructed her daughter in the principles of Christianity, and had checked the evil propensities of her husband as long as she lived, but after her death, which had taken place shortly before the events we have been describing, all constraint had been removed from the evil propensities of the misguided man, and he joined the murderous gang who had just met their fate.

The natural goodness of the young girl's nature, fostered by the teachings of her guardian mother, thus exerted itself to save three lives from the assassin's stroke.

She gladly accompanied the lady on her route the following morning, and ever remained her attached *protegé.*

Montana is one of the newest and wildest of our territories. Its position so far to the north and the peculiarly rugged face of the country, make it the fitting abode for the genius of the storms. Gathering their battalions the tempests sweep the summits and whirling round the flanks of the mountains, roar through the deep, lonely gorges with a sound louder than the ocean surges in a hurricane. The snows fill the ravines in drifts one hundred feet in depth, and such are the rigors of winter that the women who live in the fur-trading posts on that section of our northern border, are often carried across the mountains into Oregon or Washington territory, to shield them from the severities of the inclement season.

Late in the fall of 1868, a party consisting of thirty soldiers, while faring on through the mountains of that territory, were overtaken by one of these fearful snowstorms. The wind blew from the north directly in their faces, and the snow was soon piled in drifts which put a thorough embargo upon their further progress. Selecting the fittest place that could be found they pitched their tents on the snow, but hardly had they fastened the tent ropes when a blast lifted the tents in a moment, and whirled them into the sky. After a night of great suffering they found in the morning that all their mules were missing. They had probably strayed or been driven by the fury of the blast into a deep ravine south of the camp, where they had been buried beneath the enormous drifts.

The storm raged and the snow fell nearly all day. The rations were all gone, and progress against the wind and through the drifts was impossible. Another night of such bitter cold and exposure would in all probability be their last.

They shouted in unison, but their shouts were drowned in the shrieks of the tempest. Towards night the storm lulled and again they shouted, but no sound came back but the sigh of the blast. Help! help! they cried. Unhappy men, could help come to them except from on high! What was left to them but to wind their martial cloaks around them and die like soldiers in the path of duty!

But what God-sent messenger is this coming through the drifts to meet them? Not a woman! Yes, a poor, weak woman has heard their despairing cry and has hastened to succor them. Drenched and shivering with the storm she told them to follow her, and conducted them to a recess in the crags, where beneath an overhanging ledge and between projecting cliffs, a spacious shelter was afforded them. They crowded in and warmed their numbed limbs before a great fire, while their preserver brought out her stores of food for the wayfarers.

But how could a woman be there in the heart of the mountains in the wintry weather, with only the storm to speak to her?

Her husband was a miner and she a brave and self-reliant woman. He had left her two weeks before to carry his treasure of gold dust to the nearest settlement. She was all *alone! Alone* in that rock-encompassed cabin in the realms of desolation, and still the heroine-guardian who had snatched thirty fellow beings from the jaws of death.

Solitude is the theatre where untold thousands of devoted women—the brave, the good, the loving—for ages past have acted their unviewed and unrecorded dramas in the great battle of frontier life. Warriors and statesmen have their meed of praise, and crowds surround them to throw the wreath of laurel or of bay upon their fainting brows, or to follow their plumed hearse to the mausoleum which a grateful people has raised to their memory.

> " Yet it may be a higher courage dwells
>   In one meek heart which braves an adverse fate,
> Than his whose ardent soul indignant swells.
>   Warmed by the fight or cheered through high debate,
> The soldier dies *surrounded :* could he live
> *Alone* to suffer and alone to strive ?"

———— ◆◆◆ ————

CHAPTER XXI.

WOMAN AS AN EDUCATOR ON THE FRONTIER.

" WITHIN the house, within the family the woman is all: she is the inspiring, moulding, embellishing, and controlling power." This terse description of woman's influence in the household applies with double force and significance to the position of the pioneer wife and mother. Her life in that position was one long battle, one long labor, one long trial, one long sorrow. Out of this varied, searching, continuous educational process came discipline of the body, of the mind, and of the whole moral nature. Adversity, her

> " Stern, rugged nurse, whose rigid lore,
>   With patience, many a year, she bore,"

taught her the practice of the heroic as well as of the gentler virtues; courage, labor, fortitude, plain living, charity, sobriety, pity. In that school these virtues became habitual to her mind, because their practice was enforced by the stress of circumstances. Daily and nightly, in those homes on the frontier, there is some danger to be faced, some work to be done, some suffering to be borne or some self-denial to be exercised, some sufferer to be relieved or some sympathy to be extended.

There is a two-fold result from this educational process: first, the transmission, by the law of hereditary descent, of marked traits of character to her children, who show, in a greater or less degree, their mother's nature as developed in this severe school; second, woman becomes fitted to mould the character and instruct the mind of her children in the light of her own experience and discipline. Woman is the great educator of the frontier.

Within the first half of the 18th century, in that narrow belt of thinly settled country which follows the indentation of the Atlantic ocean, in lonely cabins in the forest, or on the hill-slope, or by the unvisited sea, most of the representative men of our Revolutionary Era first saw the light, and were pillowed on the breasts of the frontier mothers.

The biographical records of our country are bright with the names of men—the brave, the wise, the good—who were born of pioneer women, and who inherited from them those traits which, in after life, made them great and illustrious in the learned professions, in the camp, and in the councils of their native country. Who can doubt that the daughters, too, of those strong women, and the sisters of those eminent men, inheriting similar traits, exercised in their sphere as potent though silent an influence as did their brothers in the high stations to which they were called.

As by a strain of blood, inherited traits come down to succeeding generations, and, as from the breast of the mother the first elements of bodily strength are received, so from her lips are obtained those first principles of good and incentives of greatness which the sterner features and blunter feelings of the father are rarely sufficient to inculcate.

On parent knees, or later, in intervals of work or play, the soldier who fought to make us a free republic, and the statesman who laid deep and wide the foundations of our constitution, acquired from their mothers' lips those lessons of virtue and duty which made their after careers so useful to their country and memorable in history.

We have said that woman was the great *educator* on the frontier. She was something more than an *educator*, as the term is usually applied. The teaching of the rudiments of school-learning was a fraction in the sum-total of her training and influence.

The means of moulding and guiding the minds of the young upon the border are very different from what they are in more settled states of society. Education in the older states of the Union is organized in the district and high school, in the academy and the college, and is maintained by large taxation of the town, city, or state. Here are wealth, aggregations of intelligence, and a surplus of the educated labor class. Commodious and often beautiful edifices shelter the bright tribes whom the morning bell calls together beneath the eye of cultured teachers. Stately halls and quaint chapels are the seats where the higher learning is inculcated; the paraphernalia of education is splendid, the appliances are adequate, and the whole machinery by which knowledge is diffused among the young, works with a smooth regularity that makes it almost automatic.

Contrast this system which prevails to-day, and in the more settled conditions of American society, with that which prevailed in earlier years in a thinly and newly-inhabited country, and which now obtains on our frontier line, and how striking is the difference!

Indeed, how could we look for any such organism where small settlements were separated from each other by long spaces and bad roads, and where single cabins were so completely isolated, as in the New England and the Middle and Southern States a century and a half ago, or as in the earlier settled States of the West seventy years ago, or as in the newly-settled States of the West within the present generation, or as on the frontier proper to-day? Under such conditions even the district school was impracticable or inaccessible. To supply its place, each household where there were children was a training school, of which the mother was the head.

The process, under her eyes and hand, of forming the mind and character, is very slow, but it is healthy and natural. It is conducted in the short interval of severe toil. She reverts to first principles, and teaches by objects rather than by lessons. It is the character that she forms more than the mind.

She has about her a band of silent but powerful co-adjutors. The sunshine and free air of the wilderness are poured around the little stranger, which soon grows into a handsome, largely-developed, vigorous nursling.

The air of the wilderness, too, is the native air of

freedom: this, and the ample space wherein the young plant flourishes, makes it large in frame and broad in mind and character.

Transplant a cypress from a garden in a populous community to the deep black mould of the west, and it grows to be a forest monarch. It is Hazlitt who says "the heart reposes in greater security on the immensity of nature's works, expatiates freely there and finds elbow room and breathing space."

In the log-cabin there is perhaps but a single room: there is a bed, a table, blocks of wood for chairs, and a few wretched cooking utensils. Thank God! The life of the pioneer woman is not "cribbed and confined" to this hovel. The forest, the prairie, the mountain-side are free to her as the vital air, and the canopy of heaven is her familiar covering. A life out doors is a necessary part of both the moral and the physical education of her children.

Riding through one of the prairies of the far West, some years since, we arrived just at dusk in front of a cabin where a mother was sitting with her four young children and teaching them lessons from the great book of nature. She had shown them the sun as it set in glory, and told them of its rising and of its going down; of the clouds and of the winds, and how God made the grass and trees, and the stars, which came trooping out before their eyes. She taught them, she said, little as yet from books. She had but a Bible, a catechism, an almanac. The Bible was the only Reader in her little school. Already she had whispered in their ears the story of Jesus' life and death, and charged their infant memories with the wise and beautiful teachings of the Sermon on the Mount.

What a practical training was that which children had in that outdoor knowledge which had been useful to their mother! The chemistry of common life learned from the processes wrought out by the air and sunshine; astronomy from the great luminaries which are the clocks of the wilderness, and the science of the weather from the phenomena of the sky. There was no " cramming " in that home-school; each item of knowledge was well absorbed and assimilated, for the mother's toils made the intervals long between the lessons. So much the better for the young heart and mind, which grows, swells, and gathers force unlaced and unfettered by scholastic pedantry and repression.

It is from the mother, too, that the boy or girl must take their first lessons in the tillage of the soil, which are most readily learned in the garden, for the women are the gardeners of the frontier. Gardening is a labor of patience and virtue, and is excellent discipline for the character. A child's true life is in the fields, and should be early familiarized with the forms of vegetable life. No small part of the education of a child may be carried on by the care and assiduous contemplation of plants and flowers. Observation, experience, reflection, and reasoning, would all come of it. A flower is a whole world, pure, innocent, peacemaking.

Woman's natural fitness for the work of an educator of the human plant is seen in the readiness and zeal with which she enters into this work of tending and training the plants in a vegetable or flower garden,

and the garden is one of the outdoor schools where
her little ones gain their most useful instruction. The
difference between plants, the variegation of colors,
their relations to the air, the sunshine, the dew, the
rain; the habits of plants, some erect, some creeping,
some climbing, the seasons of flowering, fruitage, and
seed, are impressed with ease upon the plastic mind
of childhood.

From the garden it is but one step to the meadow
and the forest. Here the boy and girl sees nature
unaided by man working out similar processes on a
grander scale. There is heroic force and valor in the
trees and grasses, and the child is early brought into
antagonism with these strong forms of wild nature,
and learns that he and his parents live by subjugating
or converting them to their use. This is the lesson of
contention in carrying through a useful purpose. The
native sward is to be overturned and a new growth
implanted; bushes are to be torn up root and branch
so that the cattle may have pasture; the trees must
be hewn down and cut into beams and boards.

Thus, too, is learned the great lesson of labor.
There is no rest for the mother. The stove, the broom,
the needle, the hoe, and the axe are ever the familiar
implements of her household husbandry. The cows
and poultry are her *protégés*. Her brown arms and
sunburned face are seen among the mowers and reap-
ers. Endowed with the practical faculty for small
things, she reaches into details which escape the
blunter senses of the stronger sex. The necessities
and contingencies of frontier life make her variously
accomplished in the useful arts. She becomes a " jack
at all trades," carding, spinning, weaving, cobbling

shoes, fitting moccasins, mending harness, dressing leather, making clothes, serving as cook, dairy-maid, laundress, gardener, and nurse. From example and from precept the children learn the lesson of labor from the mother.

The girls of course remain longer than their brothers under her tutelage. Theirs is a lofty destiny— lofty because as wives and mothers they are to carry the shrine of civilization into the wilderness, and build upon the desert and waste places the structure of a new civil and social state. Serving as a duty and a pleasure is woman's vocation. The great German poet and philosopher has finely amplified this idea :

> " Early let woman learn to serve, for that is her calling,
> For by serving alone she attains to ruling;
> To the well-deserved power which is hers in the household.
> The sister serves her brother while young; and serves her parents,
> And her life is still a continual going and coming,
> A carrying ever and bringing, a making and shaping for others.
> Well for her if she learns to think no road a foul one,
> To make the hours of the night the same as the hours of the day;
> To think no labor too trifling, and never too fine the needle ;
> To forget herself altogether, and live in others alone.
> And lastly, as mother, in truth, she will need every one of the virtues."

A French traveler in the course of his wanderings through the western wilds of our country, came to a single cabin in one of the remotest and most inaccessible of our mountain territories. The only inmates in that lonely home were a middle-aged woman and four girls, ranging from eight to fifteen. The father was a miner, who spent a large part of the time in digging or "prospecting" for precious ores, as yet with only moderate success. The matron did the work of both man and woman. The cabin was a museum of household mechanisms and implements. Independent of the clothier, the merchant, and the grocer, their dress was the furry covering of the mountain beasts; their tea was a decoction of herbs; their sugar was boiled from the sap of the maple; the necessaries of life were all of their own culture and manufacture. Yet, thanks to the unwearied toils of the good woman and her little help-meets, there was warmth, comfort, and abundance, for love and labor were inhabitants of those rocks.

The girls had already been taught all that their mother knew, and she had sent out to fight their own battle, three sons, strong, brave, and versed in border-lore.

It was my mother, said the matron, that taught me all that I know, forty years ago in the forests of Michigan, and I am trying to bring up my girls so that they shall know everything that their grandmother taught me. They could read, and write, and cypher. They were little farmers, and gardeners, and seam-stresses, and housewives. Nor had their religious and moral training been neglected. The good Book lay well thumbed and dogeared on the kitchen shelf. The sound of the "church-going bell" had never been heard by those children, but every Sunday the mother gathered them about her, and they read together from the New Testament. "It is ten years," said the matron, "since I have seen a church. I remember the last time I visited San Francisco, awaking Sunday morning and hearing the sound of the bell which called us to meeting. It was sweeter than heavenly music to my ears, and I burst into tears." What a suggestion was that, pointing to the unsatisfied craving of that lonely heart for the consolation of the promises uttered by consecrated lips! Right and fitting it is that woman, God-beloved in old Jerusalem, that she, the last at the cross and the first at the sepulcher, though far from the Sabbath that smiles upon eastern homes, should keep alive in the hearts of her children the remembrance of the Saviour and of the Lord's day.

Rove wherever they may, the sons and daughters of the wilderness will find amid the stormiest lives a safe anchorage in the holy keeping of the Christian Sabbath, and in the word of God, for these are the best and surest legacies of a pious mother's precepts. A civilization in which the early lispings of childhood are of God and Christ, cannot become altogether corrupt and degenerate, for woman here is the depository and transmitter of religious faith.

From the earliest times to a comparatively recent period, a large proportion of the distinguished men of our country have necessarily passed their first years in remote settlements, if not on the extreme border of civilization. The lives of those men who have risen to eminence as generals, statesmen, professional men, and authors, and date their success from the lessons received from woman's lips in the early homes of their childhood, would fill volumes. We pass by the first generations of these pupils, and come to the men of that period from which to-day we date the birth of the Republic.

The heroic age of American statesmanship commenced in 1776. Of all those illustrious men who signed the immortal Declaration, or framed the Constitution of the United States, a considerable number passed their childhood and youth in secluded and remote settlements. They were the sons of " Women on the American Frontier." They drew in with their mother's milk the intellectual and moral traits, and gathered from their mother's lips those lessons which prepared them in after years to guide the councils of their country in the most trying period of its history.

Let us commence the list with the deathless name of Washington. Born in a secluded and primitive farm-house at Bridge's Creek, Virginia, he was left by the death of his father to the care and guardianship of his mother. " She," says his biographer, " proved herself worthy of the trust. Endowed with plain, direct good sense, thorough conscientiousness, and prompt decision, she governed her family strictly, but kindly, exacting deference while she inspired affection. George, being her eldest son, was thought to be her favorite, yet she never gave him undue preference, and the implicit deference exacted from him in childhood continued to be habitually observed by him to the day of her death. He inherited from her a high temper and a spirit of command, but her early precepts and example taught him to restrain and govern that temper, and to square his conduct on the exact principles of equity and justice. Tradition gives an interesting picture of the widow, with her little flock gathered round her, as was her wont, reading to them lessons of religion and morality out of some standard work. Her favorite volume was Sir Mathew Hale's Contemplations, moral and divine. The admirable maxims therein contained, for outward action as well as self-government, sank deep into the mind of George, and doubtless had a great influence in forming his character. They certainly were exemplified in his conduct throughout life. His mother's manual, bearing his mother's name, Mary Washington, written with her own hand, was ever preserved by him with filial care, and may still be seen in the archives of Mount Vernon. A precious document! Let those who wish to know the moral foundation of his character, consult its pages."

Among the signers of the Declaration of Independence, Thomas Jefferson, the author of that immortal document; George Wythe, afterwards Chancellor of Virginia; Francis Hopkinson, the poet and patriot; Benjamin Franklin, Samuel Huntington, Edward Rutledge, and many others, have left upon record testimonials of their great obligations to their mother's care and teachings.

In the second era of American statesmanship, a large number of those most eminent for public services were also born and nurtured on the frontier. A cursory examination of the biographies of those distinguished men will show how largely they were indebted to the early training which they received from their mothers.

Incidents drawn from the early life of the seventh President of the United States, will prove with striking clearness the lasting influence of a mother's teachings.

During one of the darkest periods of the Revolution, and after the massacre at Warsaw by the bloodthirsty Tarleton, when the British prison-pens in South Carolina were crowded with wounded captive patriots, an elderly woman, with the strongly marked physiognomy which characterizes the Scotch-Irish race, could have

been seen moving among the hapless prisoners, relieving their wants and alleviating their sufferings.
She had come the great distance, alone and on foot,
through swamps and forests, and across rivers, from a
border settlement, on this errand of compassion.

After her work of charity and mercy had been finished, she set out alone and on foot, as before, upon
her journey home. She sped on, thinking doubtless
of her sons, and most of all of the youngest, a bright
and manly little fellow whom she had watched over
and trained with all of a mother's care and tenderness.
The way was long and difficult, the unbridged streams
were cold, the forest was dark and tangled. Wandering from her course, weary and worn with her labors
of love and pity, she sank down at last and died.

That woman who gave her life to her country and
humanity was the mother of Andrew Jackson, and
that youngest son, her especial pupil, was the seventh
president of the United States. He had lost his father
when an infant, and his early training devolved upon
that patriot mother, from whom he also inherited some
of those marked and high traits of character for which
he was afterwards so conspicuous. She was an earnest
and devoted Christian woman, and strove, like the
mother of Washington, to glorify God as much in the
rearing of her children as in the performance of any
other-duty. She taught Andrew the leading doctrines
of the Bible, in the form of question and answer, from
the Westminster catechism : and these lessons he never
forgot. In a conversation with him some years since,
says a writer, "General Jackson spoke of his mother
in a manner that convinced me that she never ceased
to exert a secret power over him, until his heart was

33

brought into reconciliation with God." Just before his death, which occurred in June, 1855, he said to a clergyman, "My lamp is nearly out, and the last glimmer is come, I am ready to depart when called. The Bible is true. Upon that sacred volume I rest my hopes of eternal salvation, through the merits and blood of our blessed Lord and Saviour, Jesus Christ."

If departed spirits, the saintly and ascended, are permitted to look from their high habitation, upon the scene of earth, with what holy transport must the mother of Andrew Jackson have beheld the death-bed triumph of her son. The lad whom she sent to an academy at the Warsaw meeting-house, hoping to fit him for the ministry, had become a man, had filled the highest elective office in the world, and was now an old man, able in his last earthly hour, *by the grace of God attending his early pious instruction*, to challenge death for his sting and to shout "victory" over his opening grave.

It is a faculty of the female mind to penetrate with singular facility into the true character of the young. Every intelligent mother quickly, and by intuition, discerns the native bent of her child and measures his endowments. Evidences of latent talent in any particular direction are scrutinized with maternal shrewdness, and encouraged by applause and caresses. The lonelier the cabin, the more secluded the settlement, the sharper seem to grow the mother's eyes, and the more profound this intuitive faculty. It is the mother who first discerns the native bent and endowments of her child, and she too is the quickest to encourage and draw them out. How many eminent and useful men whose childhood was passed in the outlying settlements have been able to trace their success to a mother's insight into their capabilities.

In one of the forest homes on the skirts of civilization in Pennsylvania, Benjamin West, the greatest historical painter of the last century, showed first to his mother's eyes the efforts of his infant genius. The picture of a smiling babe made on a summer's day, when the little painter was but a child of seven, caught his mother's delighted eyes, and she covered him with her kisses. Years after, when Benjamin West was the guest of kings and emperors, that immortal artist was wont to recall those electric caresses and say "my mother's kiss made me a painter."

Daniel Webster's childhood home was in a log-cabin on the banks of the Merrimac, in a sequestered portion of New Hampshire. Here he passed his boyhood and youth, and received from his admirable mother those lessons which formed his mind and character, and fitted him for that great part which he was to play in public life. She recognized the scope of his genius when she gave him the copy of the constitution on a pocket handkerchief. She pinched every household resource that he might go to Exeter Academy, and to Dartmouth College, as if she had had a prophetic vision that he would come to be called the defender of those institutions which his father fought to obtain. And when in after years he had grown gray in honors and usefulness, he was wont to refer with tears to the efforts and sacrifices of this mother who discerned his great capacity and was determined that he should enjoy the advantages of a college education.

It is the affectionate and noble ambition of many other pioneer mothers besides Mrs. Webster which has

secured to their sons the benefits of a thorough aca-
demical training.

The next step from the home-school is the district-
school. The cabin which shelters a single family is generally placed with shrewd eyes to its being the point around
which a settlement shall grow up. Wood and water
are contiguous : the soil is rich : not many seasons roll
away before other cabins send up their smoke hard
by : children multiply, for these matrons of the border
are fecund : out of the common want rises the school-
house, built of logs, with its rude benches : here the
school teacher is a woman—the grown-up daughter,
or the maiden sister of the pioneer.

How many of our greatest men have learned their
first rudiments from the lips of "school marms," in
their primitive school-houses on the frontier !

Population increases by production and accession.
There is soon a dearth of teachers ; all along the frontier the cry is sent up to the east, come and teach us !
Woman again comes to the front ; the schools of the
border settlements have been largely taught by the
faithful and devoted female, missionaries in the cause
of education from the east. These pioneer school
mistresses bore the discomforts of remote western life
patiently, and did their duties cheerfully. Most of
them afterwards became wives and mothers, and have
in both these relations done much towards building up
the settlements where they made their homes. Others have enrolled their names among the missionary
martyrs. The toils, hardships, and privations incident
to a newly settled country have often proved too
heavy for the delicate frames reared amid the comforts and luxuries of eastern homes, and they have

fallen victims to their noble ambition, giving their lives to the cause which they sought to promote.

One of these martyrs was Miss M. She was one of that band of lady-teachers, numbering several hundred who, nearly thirty years ago, went out to the then far west under the auspices of Governor Slade and Miss Catharine Beecher, to supply the crying need of teachers which then existed in that section of our country.

This, it should be remembered, was before railroads had brought that region within easy access from the east. That wild, primeval garden had been, as yet, redeemed from nature only in plots and patches. On the boundless prairies of Illinois the cabins of the settlers were like solitary vessels moored in a waste of waters, and between them rolled in green billows, under the wind, the tall, coarse grass. The settlers themselves were of the most adventurous and often of the roughest class. Society presented to the cultured eye a rude and almost barbarous aspect.

Man, while grappling, almost unaided, with untamed nature, and seeking to subdue her, seems to gravitate away from civilization and approach his primitive state. Everything is taken in the rough; the arts and the graces of a more settled condition of society are cultivated but little, because they are non-essentials. The physical qualities are prized more than mental culture, and the sentiments and sensibilities are in abeyance during the reign of the more robust emotions.

During the onset which the pioneer makes upon the wilderness he and his entire family bear the rugged impress which such a life stamps upon them. The wife, in the practice of the sterner virtues of courage, self-denial, and fortitude, may become hardened against the access of the quick sensibilities and tender emotions of her more delicately reared sisters. The children, bright-eyed, strong, and nimble, run like squirrels through the woods, and leap like fawns on the plain. The mother's tutelage has done much, but more remains to be done in the schooling to be had from books. After the first victory has been won over the forest and the soil, and the pioneer reposes for a season upon his laurels, in comparative ease, he discerns the needs of his flock, and craves the offices of one who can supply the place of the weary mother in schooling the children.

Out of the void that exists the appliances of education must be created; the nurslings of the plain must be brought together and taught to subject themselves to the regular discipline of the district school; and who but woman can best supply such a discipline!

Such was the condition of frontier society and education when Miss M. came to Illinois. Her immediate field of labor was a wide prairie, over which were thinly scattered the cabins of the pioneer families. There were no books, no school house, no antecedent knowledge of what was needed. But under the advice and suggestions of this intelligent young lady every want was, in a measure, supplied. A rough structure, with logs for seats, and planks for benches, was soon prepared, books provided, and the children gathered together into the comfortless room, where Miss M. made her first essay as a preceptor of the little pioneers.

The children were like wild things caught and confined in a cage. Their restlessness was a severe tax to the patience of the delicate girl. The long walk to and from the school room in all weathers, through the snows of winter, the mud of spring, and against the blast which sweeps those plains, formed no small part of her labor. Luxuries and even comforts were denied her. They gave her the best they had, but that was poor enough. Her chamber was an unplastered loft; her bed a shakedown of dried grass. The moonbeams showed her the crevices where the rain trickled in, and the snow fringed her coverlid. Her fare was of the coarsest, and her social intercourse, to her sensitive nature, was almost forbidding.

But she never swerved from the course she had marked out, nor shrank from the labors and duties incident to her mission. Her body, extremely fragile, was the tenement of an intellect of premature activity and grasp, a native delicacy, sensibility, and great moral force. She was a born missionary, and in the difficult and trying career which she had chosen, she showed courage, self-denial, tenacity of purpose, which, combined with a sweetness of disposition, soon made her beloved by her scholars and enabled her to soften their wildness, smooth their rudeness, and impress upon their minds the lessons of knowledge which it was her study to impart.

In sunshine or storm her presence was never wanting at her post of duty. On the dark mornings of winter she could have been seen convoying her little *protegés* through the driving sleet, or the snow, or slush, and those rough but not unkindly parents scarcely dreamed that her life was waning. The vivid carnation of her cheeks was not painted by the frosty air, nor by the scorching heat of the iron box which warmed her little charges as they gathered beneath the ethereal splendors of her eye in the school room. The destroyer had set his seal upon her, but her frail body was swayed and animated by the spirit whose energies even mortal disease could not subdue.

The discovery of the sacrifice was too late, though all that rude kindness and unlearned thoughtfulness could do was lavished upon her in those few days that remained to her. Months of exposure, hardship, solitude of the soul, and intense ambition in her noble mission had done their work, and before the light of the tenth day after she was driven to her couch, had faded, surrounded by a score of her pupils, she passed away, and was numbered in the army of missionary heroines and martyrs.

Those brave labors and that noble life was not for nought. The lessons taught those pupils, the high example set before them, and the life expended for their sake were not lost or forgotten. Some of those little scholars have grown to be good and useful men and women, and are now repeating, in other schools, farther towards the setting sun, the lessons and example of devotion which they learned from the teacher who gave her life that they might have knowledge.

The place which woman, as an educator, now fills, and so long has filled upon the frontier, is not bounded, however, by the home-school, nor by the district school, in both of which she is the teacher of the young. She is the educator of the man. She moulds and guides society.

The home where she rules is the center and focus from which wells out an influence as light wells out from the .sun. The glow of the fireside where the mother sits, is a beacon whose light stretches far out to guide and guard.

The word "home," as used among the old races of Northern Europe, contains in its true signification something mystic and religious. The female patriarch of the household was regarded with superstitious veneration. Her sayings were wise and good, and the warrior sat at her feet on the eve of battle and gathered from her as from an oracle, the confidence and courage which nerved him for the fight; and to-day the picture of an aged mother sitting· by the hearth, and the recollection of her counsels, is a source of comfort and strength to many a son who is far away fighting the battle of life. The home and mother is the polar-star of absent sons and daughters. She who sat by the cradled bed of childhood, "the first, the last, the faithfulest of friends," she, the guardian of infancy, is the loving and never to be forgotten guide of riper years. As far as thought can run upon this earthly sphere, or memory fondly send back its gaze, so far can the influence of a mother reach to cheer, to sustain, to elevate, and to keep the mind and heart from swerving away from the true and the right.

One who received his early training from a mother's lips in a frontier State, and afterward attained to wealth and influence in one of our mountain republics, lately told the writer that he kept the picture of his mother hanging up in his chamber, where it was the last object which his eyes lighted on before retiring, and the first upon rising; and whenever he was about to adopt any new course, or commence any new enterprise into which the question of right or wrong entered, he always asked himself, "what will my mother say if I do thus and thus?" That mother's influence was upon him though a thousand miles away from her, and the thought of her in the crises of his life was the load-star of his strong heart and mind.

We may well imagine those hardy sons who are now building up our empire in the Rocky Mountains, as finding in a mother's portrait a tie which binds them fast to the counsels and the love of their earliest guardian, and that as they gaze on the " counterfeit presentment " of those endeared features, they might long to hear again the faithful counsels which guided their youth, exclaiming with the poet,

> " O, that those lips had language! life has passed
> With me but roughly since I saw thee last."

We have elsewhere spoken of the refining and humanizing influence of woman, amid the rude and almost barbarous atmosphere of frontier life. The mother moulds and trains the child, the wife moulds and trains the husband, the sister moulds and trains the brother, the daughters mould and train the father. We speak now of moulding and of training in a broader sense than they are embraced in the curriculum of books. The influence exerted is subtle, but not the less potent. *Woman is the civilizer par excellence.* Society in its narrower meaning exists by her and through her. That state of man which is best ordered and safest, is only where woman's membership is most truly recognized.

Man *alone* gravitates naturally towards the savage state. Communities of men, such as exist in some of our most remote territories, are mere clubs of barbarians. They may be strong, energetic, and brave, but their very virtues are such as those which savages possess.

Into one of the loneliest valleys in the Rocky Mountains, some years since, fifty men, attracted by the golden sands which were rolled down by the torrents, built their huts and gave the settlement a name. There were cabins, a tavern, and a bar-room. There were men toiling and spending their gain in gambling and rioting. There was rugged strength and hardihood. There was food and shelter, and yet there was no basis for civil and social organism, as those terms are properly understood, because no wife, no mother, no home was there.

Those strong and hardy men clove the rock and sifted the soil, and chained the cataract, but their law was force and cunning, and the only tie they recognized was a partnership in gain. What civilization or true citizenship could there be in a society in which the family circle and its kindred outgrowth—the school and the church—were unknown! The denizens of that mountain camp slid, by an irresistible law of gravitation, away from civil order, from social beneficence, and from humanity. They gorged themselves, and swore, and wrangled, and fought, and like the "dragons of the prime," they tore each other in their selfish greed for that which was their only care.

Into this savage semi-pandemonium entered one day, two unwonted visitors—the wives of miners who had come to join their husbands. Polite, kind, gentle, intelligent, and pious, their very presence seemed to change the moral atmosphere of the place. All the dormant chivalry of man's nature was awakened. Their appearance in the midst of that turbulent band was a sedative which soon allayed the chronic turmoil in which the settlement was embroiled. The reign of order commenced again: manners became softened, morals purified: the law of kindness was re-established, and slowly out of social chaos arose the inchoate form of a well-ordered civil society.

This illustrates woman's influence in one of the peculiar conditions of our American frontier communities. But in all other phases of true pioneer life, her influence is as strongly, if not as strikingly displayed as a humanizing, refining, and civilizing agent.

We have said that woman is the cohesive force which holds society together. This thesis may be proved by facts which show that power in all those relations in which she stands to the other sex. In cultured circles she shapes and controls by the charms of beauty and manner. But in the lonely and rude cabin on the border her plastic power is far greater because her presence and offices are essentials without which development dwindles and progress is palsied. There, if anywhere, should be the vivified germ of the town and the state. There, if anywhere, should be the embryonic conditions which will ripen one day into a mighty civil growth. A wife's devotion, the purity of a sister's and a daughter's love, the smiles and tears and prayers of a mother—these make the sunshine which transforms the waste into a paradise, the wild into a garden, and expands the home by a law of organic growth into a well ordered community.

The basis of civil law and social order is the silent compact which binds the household into one sweet purpose of a common interest, a common happiness.

Woman is the unconscious legislator of the frontier. The gentle restraints of the home circle, its calm, its rest, its security form the unwritten code of which the statute book is the written exponent.

The cross is emblazoned on the rude entablature above the hearth-stone of the cabin, and where woman is, there is the holy rest of the blessed sabbath. She, who is the child's instructor in the truths of revealed religion, is also the father's guide and mentor in the same ways. Faith and hope in these doctrines as cherished by woman are the sheet anchors of our unknit civilizations.

Law is established because woman's presence renders more desirable, life, property, and the other objects for which laws are made.

Religion purifies and sanctifies the frontier home because she is the repository and early instructress in its Holy Creeds.

The influence that woman exerts on man is one that exalts: while she educates her child she elevates and ennobles the entire circle of the family.

If we cast our eyes back over the vast procession of actors and events which have composed the migrations of our race across the continent, from ocean to ocean, we are first struck by the bolder features of the march. We see the battles, the feats of courage and daring, the deeds of high enterprise in which woman is the heroine, standing shoulder to shoulder beside her hero-mate. Again we look and see the wife and mother worn with toils and hardships, and wasted with suffering which she endures with unshaken heart—a miracle of fortitude and patience. Then we behold her as the comforter and the guardian of the household amid a thousand trying scenes, soothing, strengthening, cheering, and preserving.

Grand and beautiful indeed are such spectacles as these. They rivet the eye, they swell the breast, they lift the soul of the gazer, because they are an exhibition of great virtues exercised on a wide field, in a noble cause—the subjugation of the wilderness, and the extension of the area of civilization. The hero who fights, the martyr who dies, the sufferer who bleeds, the spirit of kindness and sympathy which comforts and confirms are objects which call for our tears, our praise, our gratitude. But after all, these are incidents merely, glorious and soul-stirring indeed, yet scarcely more than superficial features and external agencies of the grand march, compared to the moral influence which emanates from the wife and mother in a million homes and through a million lives with a steadfastness and power and beneficence which can best be likened to the sunshine.

We praise it less because it is everywhere. We hardly see it, but we know that it is present, and that society—frontier society—could not long exist without that penetrating, shaping, elevating force. And so while we applaud the heroine we may not forget the patient and often unconscious educator.

When the philosophical historian of the future collects the myriad facts upon which he is to base those generalizations which show the progress of the race upon this continent, and how that progress was induced, he will draw from woman's record a noble array of names and virtues, and a vast multitude of good, kind, and brave deeds, but he will not forget to take note also of the silent agencies, and the unobtrusive but ever-present influence of woman which will be found to outweigh the potency of the stronger and more brilliant virtues with all the acts that they have wrought.

And so it is to-day. As we gaze fixedly on the great expanse which the record of our time unrolls, we see high up on the majestic scroll a thousand bright and speaking evidences of woman's silent agency in the building of a new empire upon our dark and distant borderland.